The Constitutional Dimension of Contract Law

Luca Siliquini-Cinelli • Andrew Hutchison
Editors

The Constitutional Dimension of Contract Law

A Comparative Perspective

Springer

Editors
Luca Siliquini-Cinelli
Department of Law
Liverpool Hope University
Liverpool, UK

Andrew Hutchison
Faculty of Law
University of Cape Town
Cape Town, South Africa

ISBN 978-3-319-49842-3 ISBN 978-3-319-49843-0 (eBook)
DOI 10.1007/978-3-319-49843-0

Library of Congress Control Number: 2017934473

Printed on acid-free paper

This Springer imprint is published by Springer Nature
The registered company is Springer International Publishing AG
The registered company address is: Gewerbestrasse 11, 6330 Cham, Switzerland

Acknowledgement

The Editors would like to thank our respective partners, Livashnee Naidoo and Julie-Anne Hutchison, for their support in this endeavour. We also wish to thank Anke Seyfried and Julia Bieler at Springer for their assistance throughout the editorial process, as well as our editorial assistants, Katherine Timoney and Grethe Carr, for help in finalising the text of this Volume.

Introduction

Theme(s) and Context(s)

One of the hallmarks of the present era is the discourse surrounding Fundamental rights and the necessity that the law takes cognisance of these. Various national and supranational Human rights instruments have been developed and implemented in order to transition society away from atrocity and callousness toward a more just and inclusive future. In some countries, this is done through the mechanism of a supreme Constitution, while in others international conventions or ordinary legislation holds sway. Contract law has increasingly been playing a pivotal role in this phenomenon. According to many, this has been done especially through the much-debated 'civilising mission' of contract,[1] a notion that itself constitutes the canon of the Western liberal principle of 'civilised economy'. The movement away from the belief in the absolute freedom of contract, which reached its zenith in the nineteenth century, to the principles of fairness and justice that underpin contract law today, is often deemed to be a testament to this civilising influence.

This first volume of a two-book collection offers contributions from leading Contract law scholars, as well as emerging researchers from various jurisdictions who were asked to discuss the role that Constitutional/Human rights law played in Contract law in their home jurisdiction. The constitutionalisation of Private law and the impact of Fundamental rights on its development are well-known topics.[2] Hence, it comes as no surprise that a great deal of compelling scholarship has analysed them both over the past decade.[3] However, the value of these studies notwithstanding, what sets the present work apart from comparable literature on the subject is that we, the editors, did not simply want another collection of essays dealing with the impact of a given (typically: European) Human rights regime on

[1] Critically, see Supiot (2007) and Kahn (2008). See also Siliquini-Cinelli's chapter in this book.

[2] Markesinis (1990).

[3] Among others, see Barkhuysen and Lindenbergh (2006), Mak (2008) and Grundmann (2008).

Private law. We wanted to see the law in action. Our motive in this regard was a concern to highlight legal culture and legal context.[4] Hence, this collection broadens the field of inquiry, both methodologically and contextually.

Gathered together, this volume of collected essays offers contrasting and innovative perspectives from around the world on specific topics related to contracting that include a constitutional dimension. Contributors were asked not merely to describe how Fundamental rights and constitutional values have been incorporated into their national law but also to pick a particular topic and to analyse how the treatment of this particular area of contracting has changed in the jurisdiction represented. Hence, what characterises this book is that it does not merely collect essays on a given abstract topic (e.g., formation of contracts, performance, termination, remedies, *etc.*) but that it provides readers with different tangible and relevant examples on the everydayness of the interplay between Human rights policies, Constitutional law and Contract law. The variety of the themes chosen by the authors is in line with that of the approaches they have opted for. Both reflect the unconventional essence and aims of the overall project. Throughout the book, the reader will indeed find a broad range of methodologies of inquiry, ranging from the empirical to the philosophical. At times, the authors have also decided to provide a comparative constitutional angle on their own topic as a way to add a broader perspective on the issue in focus.

The result is a collection of essays with different focal points but a common idea that Human rights and constitutional values are an important dimension of modern Contract law. Exactly how important, we shall argue below when presenting each chapter, is a question of legal culture and context. What clearly emerges from this comparative study is, indeed, that the role given to Fundamental rights and values in a contractual context will vary from jurisdiction to jurisdiction. While in some countries the entire legal system is subject to a supreme Constitution or Bill of Rights, in other countries this is not the case. While for some there is no separate Contract and Constitutional law, but rather just one form of law, namely law under the Constitution, for others Human Rights are protected in other ways in the law and practice of contracting, and the actual Bill of Rights text is more peripheral, if such a text even exists. As examples of different contextual perspectives on this question, compare the following legal arguments:

> I cannot accept this contention, which treats the common law as a body of law separate and distinct from the Constitution. There are not two systems of law, each dealing with the same subject-matter, each having similar requirements, each operating in its own field with its own highest Court. There is only one system of law. It is shaped by the Constitution which is the supreme law, and all law, including the common law, derives its force from the Constitution and is subject to constitutional control.[5] [South Africa]

---

[4]Berger and Luckmann (1967), Bhasker (1989), Stammers (1993), Stammers (1999) and Searle (1995).

[5]*Pharmaceutical Manufacturers Association of SA and Another: In re ex parte President of the Republic of South Africa and Others* 2000 (2) SA 674 (CC) at para 44.

> As everyone knows, the purpose of the Human Rights Act 1998 was to make the Human Rights and fundamental freedoms set out in the European Convention on Human Rights directly enforceable in this country as part of its domestic law. ...The Act prescribes two principal means whereby it 'brings Human Rights home' from Strasbourg: first, by making provision for the interpretation and amendment of legislation and, secondly, by making it unlawful for a public authority to act in a way incompatible with a Convention right.[6] [United Kingdom]

Our argument is that the manner in which Human rights and constitutional values are protected in a given jurisdiction is an important question of national or supranational consciousness. This means that while there is a large degree of commonality between the various Human rights texts worldwide, the implementation thereof is a uniquely jurisdiction-specific question. In jurisdictions with a history of Human rights abuses, such as Germany, Italy or South Africa, the necessity for a Constitution to entrench Human rights and transform society is of great importance, and will have a deep impact on the implementation of the Constitution in question. In other countries, such as Australia, where a Bill of Rights is lacking and the Constitution, in Gaudron J's words, 'until 1967 ... was blatantly discriminatory',[7] the spread of fundamental values and policies within the private law dimension takes place differently in such a way as to fill the void of weak equal treatment provisions at the federal level.

In the context of Contract law in particular, there is a potential for a Human-rights- and constitutional-values-based revision of the law to have an impact on core concepts such as freedom of contract, possibly through a greater emphasis on policies and mechanisms protecting weaker parties. There may also be a distinction here between strictly Commercial law, in which business-to-business contracting operates subject to only minimal regulation and judicial interference, and specific statutory regimes designed to address an inequality of bargaining power, such as those dealing with consumers, tenants and employees. This also explains why our contributors were not instructed to focus on consumer or commercial transactions specifically: it is informative to see whether the constitutionalisation of Contract law meant to our contributors protection of the weaker party, particularly in contracts involving natural persons, or a broader vision for Contract law as an entire construct. This question may involve an investigation of the manner in which public Human rights law has affected private Contract law in a given jurisdiction. This will be seen from the discussions of this type of topic by most of our contributors.

Unsurprisingly, this leads us back to the vexed issue as to whether Private, and in particular Contract law, should be understood as a closed system, or rather as something that should transcend the mere regulation of private interests and forms of interaction. This debate has shaped the very essence and development of contractual reasoning in modern times. To contextualise its trajectory here would

---

[6] *Wilson v Secretary of State for Trade and Industry* [2003] UKHL 40 at paras 10–12.

[7] *Kruger v Commonwealth (Stole Generation Case)* (1997) 190 CLR 1 at 112, while describing the former s 127 of the Constitution.

fall beyond the scope of this Introduction. It will suffice to say that while Hugo Grotius promoted a methodological approach that would sever (contractual) legal doctrine from practical reality, Rudolph von Jhering stressed the importance of law's purposive nature, and thus of an understanding of contracts as legal arrangements that should not contrast with common interests. Both positions are echoed today, particularly in the works of Ernst Weinrib,[8] who argues that Private law should not be concerned with distributive justice, and of Duncan Kennedy, who instead believes that the 'technicalities' of Contract law are ultimately political.[9]

Both arguments have to be appreciated against the broader theoretical questions as to whether there is a public/private divide at all and what its potential impact may be. Writing in 2001, Raymond Geuss contended that

> [t]here is no such thing as the public/private distinction, or, at any rate, it is a deep mistake to think that there is a single substantive distinction here that can be made to do any real philosophical or political work. When one begins to look at it carefully, the purported distinction between public and private begins to dissolve into a number of issues that have relatively little to do with one another. It is thus unlikely one could come up with an interesting, general, substantive theory of the public and the private.[10]

We agree. As is well known, the legitimacy and effectiveness of distinguishing between public and private spheres have been much discussed in modern and contemporary times from different perspectives and through a variety of approaches. By way of example, Max Weber was of the idea that the working logic of capitalism is underpinned by a fundamental separation between these two dimensions. For his own part, the later scholar Carl Schmitt criticised the Hobbesian conception of sovereignty for not being truly absolutist and instead drawing the distinction between 'outer' and 'inner', or public and private. To Schmitt, the fact that Hobbes left something outside sovereignty's reach (namely, religious freedom) renders the state not an omnipotent 'total man' that unifies the people in a political community but rather a mere technical device whose functioning is in line with the apolitical essence of liberalism and positivism. Hannah Arendt too long stressed the importance that the separation of the private from the public had in antiquity and up until the emergence of the category of the 'social', the latter to be understood as the apolitical confusion between bourgeois ideology, civil society's sphere of influence and the sovereign's political prerogatives.

In this sense, it is commonly accepted that the 'Public/Private law' dichotomy is the result of a modern conceptualisation ultimately aimed at endorsing liberal theories of democracy, legitimation and accountability. More precisely, liberalism has used this antithesis to promote what might be defined as the 'depoliticisation' of societal affairs, that is, the principle of political neutrality according to which '[t]he state should abstain from intervening in the affairs proper to civil society'.[11] Yet,

---

[8]Weinrib (1995).

[9]Kennedy (2001).

[10]Geuss (2001), p. 106.

[11]Cristi (1984), p. 532.

since the fall of classical Greece, the development of the Western tradition has always been characterised by the inclusion of public life into its private counterpart and vice versa—the only discontinuity being represented by the reasons why this phenomenon has occurred, as well as its extent, manifestations and repercussions through time. Although in diverse forms and through different patterns, the same applies to other traditions addressed by this book as well. Of course, the evolutionary trajectory of juridical practices and normative settings is not extraneous to this phenomenon either.

This raises a socio-political and socio-legal question of the first order, namely, how the 'public/private' interaction takes place in its concrete manifestations in various jurisdictions. answer to this type of interrogative will of course vary from system to system. In a collection of essays written from different comparative perspectives, it will not be possible to fully investigate the position in each country covered herein beyond certain broad trends. For us, this is again a question of context and culture, which will be covered briefly in discussing broad trends in the chapters below.

Yet before moving on to introducing the chapters that comprise this collection, a preliminary interrogative ought to be addressed: that is, whether—and, if so, why—there is even the need to address the constitutional dimension of Contract law in an age, such as ours, undoubtedly post-Westphalian, globalised and decentralised. Or, put bluntly, in a post-national dimension in which the authority of the modern state, and thus of constitutional charters, is constantly at stake? The list of factors to document the demise of the modern form of polity and its legal structure as we have come to know it could be drafted endlessly. For present purposes, one could point at the emergence of hybrid functional equivalents to law at the local level, as well as to the transformations of public law and its accountability schemes, and to how state functions are increasingly delegated to the private sector and spread among multiple orderings of society without legitimate authorisation and efficient supervision—not to mention how state foreign strategies and internal agendas are undemocratically determined by market forces and corporate interests. It would therefore be a mistake to try to codify this trend through socio-political and juridical lenses only without realising the role that the economic structure has in moulding the state's prerogatives and capacity for regulation.[12]

Legal scholars are, of course, familiar with this phenomenon. The founding of dedicated law journals and book series, as well as the launch of new undergraduate and postgraduate courses in transnational and global law worldwide, is testament to this subject's increasing relevance within legal discourse.[13] Yet, if anything, the

[12]Hardt and Negri (2009), pp. 1–21; Brown (2012). See also Siliquini-Cinelli's contribution to this book.

[13]For present purposes, and in addition to Gunther Teubner's scholarship on societal constitutionalism, see Jansen and Michaels (2008), Twining (2009), Kuo (2010), Handl et al. (2012), Dobner and Loughlin (2010), Walker (2012), Krisch (2010), Amhlaigh et al. (2013), Zumbansen (2013) and Helfand (2015). See also the (2008) 6(3)-(4) Special Issues of the International Journal of Constitutional Law on the Symposium: Constitutionalism in an Era of Globalization and

same reasons that, at first glance, appear to suggest that the analysis that this book proposes would be unnecessary on closer inspection instead reveal that there is an urgent need to inquire into the Constitutional/Contract law (and thus, public/private justice) dialectic as way to ascertain whether or not constitutions still matter in the current regulative landscape, and if so, why, how and to what extent. More particularly, the complexities of current pluralist regulative phenomena and settings on the macro, meso and micro levels require us, as lawyers, to revisit and reconsider the axiomatic findings and statements that characterise this subject, as well as the perspectives from and methodologies through which we have come to form our insights into it. This is further demonstrated by the fact that, in opposition to those who argue for the impoverishment of the state's role, guidance, legitimacy and authority, some commentators are instead of the idea that what the state is currently witnessing ought to be inscribed within modernity's inner pluralist structure and, as such, cannot be considered as a wholly new phenomenon in the strict sense of the term.[14] Of course, the existence of supranational legal regimes, as well as the extent to which there is legal pluralism in a given jurisdiction, is a question that is highly dependent on the geographical location and regional integration of a given jurisdiction. The position in the European Union may differ from the position in (for example) Canada, Australia or parts of Asia. Legal pluralism may also refer to parallel systems of aboriginal or indigenous forms of law, as is the case in South Africa. Again, this socio-political dimension of both Constitutional and Contract laws highlights the role of legal context and culture in this regard.

This, however, does not tell us much on whether the constitutionalisation of Contract law and the influence of Fundamental rights and values over its development should be welcomed or criticised. A specific reference (by way of example) to Jan Smits' scepticism on this matter would in this sense be profitable.[15] Indeed, while Smits recognises that the constitutionalisation of Private law is becoming more and more noticeable, he raises a series of important 'normative questions' on the 'adverse effect of this development' and, thus, its 'desirability'.[16] More specifically, Smits points at the limited impact that an inclusion of Fundamental rights reasoning within the private dimension might have. This is so, Smits maintains, because of the indirect, subsidiary role that these rights inevitably play in legal

Privatization, and the interview released by Canada's Prime Minister, Justin Trudeau, with the New York Times, in which Canada is defined as the 'first post-national state', http://www.nytimes.come/2015/12/13/magazine/trudeaus-canada-again.html?_r=0 (last visited: February 15, 2016). For a philosophical, comparative-oriented account, see Marramao (2009), pp. 109–130.

[14]Among others, see Roughan (2011), Roughan (2013), Fontanelli (2011) and Thornill (2012). See also Riles (2008), pp. 206–207, according to whom the model of global private law and governance does not pose a substantial threat to state law as it is wholly in line with the 'knowledge practises[,] bureaucratization and proceduralism' that inform the working logic of the modern state. Hence, in the post-national dimension, 'the state is not so much challenged as mirrored, reflected, and deflected in new technical forms' (ibid.).

[15]Smits (2006).

[16]Ibid., p. 2.

decision-making. In his words, '[p]rivate law can be interpreted in the light of Fundamental Rights, but can in the end not be absorbed by these rights: the private law rules remain decisive for deciding the case'.[17]

Secondly, Smits reflects on Fundamental rights' incapacity to offer enough guidance. This is due, according to Smits, to the inevitably broad purview of the term 'Fundamental Rights', which itself does not allow for an efficient application.[18] Finally, Smits makes the provocative, yet well-grounded, argument that private parties are not bound by Fundamental rights. In particular, Smits notes, drawing on Montesquieu and Locke, 'Fundamental Rights have the function of guarding against the public from meddling with private affairs: the State cannot always intervene when public interest requires so'.[19] This point serves, in turn, to endorse Weinrib's well-known account of what distinguishes distributive justice (properly of the political, and thus public, sphere), from its corrective counterpart (properly of the private sphere).

Smits' claims are, in fact, less radical than what it might appear at first glance as they build upon the above-mentioned liberal view that aims to keep what is of public concern apart from all those sets of relationships that allegedly remain confined within private settings (as the reference to Montesquieu and Locke makes clear). In this sense, while certainly sound, Smits' arguments fall short of offering a comprehensive view on the benefits and perils implied by the constitutionalisation of Private law and, thus, are (in our view) open to criticism. It could be doubted, indeed, that Smits' view may be successfully applied to gain insights on the working logic of either socialist forms of polities or legislation where the socialist thread plays a considerable role.[20] Hence, Smits, particularly when he elaborates on the subsidiary essence of Fundamental rights and constitutional values, in our view, underestimates the function that ideology plays in shaping the development of Contract law and the impact that these two elements have in it. More importantly, while Smits aptly uses Weinrib's distinction between distributive and corrective justice to support his claims, it is Weinrib himself who more recently highlighted the relevance of the 'institutional guarantees of public rights [in] transforming private law into a community of rights'.[21] Finally, Smits' account remains silent on why Weinrib's above-mentioned argument that Private law is concerned with corrective justice, while distributive justice remains the preserve of Public law is ultimately difficult to reconcile with more radically transformative notions of the constitutionalisation of Contract law as found in certain modern jurisdictions, such as South Africa.

From this it follows that a critique of the constitutionalisation of Private law would need to be promoted through different paths to those pursued by Smits. By

---

[17]Ibid., p. 15.

[18]Ibid., pp. 16–18.

[19]Ibid., p. 19.

[20]See Monateri's contribution to this book.

[21]Weinrib (2011), p. 211.

way of an example, and narrowing the field of analysis to the Contract law dimension, it could be noted that to assign an incisive and direct role to fundamental values (such as that of contractual fairness) might prejudice the parties' ability to understand what their obligations would be under the contract. In turn, this might cause an economic uncertainty in markets. Conversely, one might favour the inclusion of constitutional values and Fundamental rights in contractual reasoning because of their capacity to lead to the formation of a society based upon a specific moral conception of justice. The reader will find in the following chapters valuable insights on these and other matters that will cast new light on the development of Contract law in comparative perspective.

Arguments: Outline of Book Chapters

Francois du Bois sets out in his chapter to defend a view that the English Human Rights Act 1998 (HRA) has had very little impact thus far on the law of contract in that country. He demonstrates that this is true through an appraisal of the leading case law, as well as by pointing to the existing English scholarship in point. In his excursus, du Bois adapts the analytical framework of Leigh in order to discuss the horizontal impact of the HRA on contract under the headings of (1) Direct Statutory Horizontality, (2) Public Liability Horizontality, (3) Remedial and Procedural Horizontality and (4) Substantive Horizontality.

Under the first heading, du Bois examines key cases dealing with employment, residential lease and consumer credit statutes to identify the major factors shaping horizontality in this context. His key findings are that courts prefer to avoid a finding of statutory incompatibility with the HRA, and indeed in specialist areas like discrimination are often crowded out by more detailed legislation directly in point. Under the second heading, du Bois attempts a definition of the concept of a 'public authority' under the HRA. He notes that the courts typically link this concept to a body exercising a governmental function, either in contracting as an equal with private parties or when ensuring adherence to the HRA by private parties as an intermediary. He does, however, note the important role of 'hybrid' public authorities, namely private parties performing public acts. Despite the existence of hybrid public authorities, du Bois notes a strong public/private distinction in the implementation of the HRA under this heading. Under the third category, du Bois deals in particular with the discretionary remedies of specific performance and injunction. He notes that these could conflict with certain Fundamental rights such as the prohibition of forced labour, the right to privacy and the right to freedom of religion. In the view of the author, this potential conflict is managed by the long-established preference of the common law for the remedy of damages, which entrenches individual liberty and obviates reference to the HRA. Finally, under the fourth heading, du Bois deals with leading cases on the development of the substantive common law, taking illegal contracts, insurance contracts, litigation and arbitration agreements and private leases as his examples. Although noting important case law in these areas, he concludes that the existing common law already meets the demands of the HRA and the ECHR.

In sum then, du Bois's conclusion is that the HRA has had little impact on the English law of contract outside of the limitation of public authorities' actions by Article 8 ECHR (protection of privacy and family life). He notes that unlike Germany's normative constitutional right to dignity, for example, the HRA omits such value-laden tendencies. Hence, the existing common law device of public policy is able to do most of the work of regulating Contract law. Indeed, du Bois's primary conclusion is that the constitutionalisation of contract law is a technique of legal development rather than a normative phenomenon.

In a contribution that evaluates present and future European Union responses to the regulation of privacy among consumers, Joasia Luzak tackles the difficult issue of how to 'nudge' consumers towards healthy and sustainable lifestyles without infringing on their autonomy or their right to privacy. The protected Fundamental right in question is Article 8 of the European Convention on Human Rights, as given effect to at present by two directives: the Data Protection Directive and the ePrivacy Directive. Luzak discusses by way of example the food and clothing industries. She describes the ideals of healthy consumer eating, as well as sustainable choices in clothing purchases, which ensure corporate social responsibility in the production supply chain. With regard to food, Luzak suggests two options: more detailed and accurate labelling of products, possibly using smart labels or RFID (radio-frequency identification) tags, or regulating the food industry. On the consumer nudging side, better information may provide the necessary push towards healthy eating. Perhaps in a futuristic world, a smart fridge could link with an RFID tag reader. With clothing, Luzak notes that RFID tagging is already useful to retailers in order to track garments through the production supply chain and could also provide a far larger canvas for presenting detailed information on a clothing product to a purchaser. The downside of increased technological interfacing in both industries, however, is the potential for RFID tags and other electronic devices to be used to profile consumers and for surveillance, even after goods have left the store. Luzak notes that existing regulation of technology used in the consumer sphere does not adequately protect consumer privacy, which can lead to data collection and a resultant manipulation of consumer choice.

Luzak ends her contribution with a brief discussion of the so-called Internet of Things: a state of being where advanced technology allows computers to communicate with each other and with smart machines. This can assist in consumer lifestyle choices, such as the smart fridge example above; however, the resultant potential for consumer data collection poses a massive threat to privacy. Luzak discusses the work of the European Commission in 2015 with the creation of an 'Alliance for the Internet of Things', which co-operates with stakeholders to control the development and standardisation of technology. She concludes by asking whether consumer privacy and autonomy will be the victims of the war on unhealthy lifestyles, noting that the right to privacy has not been the first priority of the European Commission thus far.

Jean-Baptiste Seube's chapter starts with the intriguing contention that, in France, the concrete influence of Constitutional law over contracts' essence and development cannot be measured with any degree of certainty. This is due, according to Seube, to the strict divide between Public and Private laws in the French legal system, which in turn affects the competences and prerogatives of the *Conseil constitutionnel* (or Constitutional Council) on the rules and techniques proper of the Contract law dimension. However, Seube also shows that the Council's rulings have an important, indirect role in inviting the judge to resort to a control of proportionality. More specifically, the Council exerts a direct influence on the substance of the rule of law, as well as an indirect influence on the judiciary's contractual legal reasoning. With respect to the former, Seube analyses two areas of contracting on which the Council's efforts have been more focused. These are the formation and the execution of contracts. Seube's aim in this part of his discussion is to show that the Council moved from holding that no constitutional provisions guarantee the principle of the freedom of contract (cf. Article 1102 *Code civil*) to admitting that this principle can in fact be invoked as long as the violation of another substantive principle (such as proprietary right or entrepreneurial freedom) is also invoked in further enshrining its respect by hooking its legitimacy to Article 4 of Universal Declaration of Human Rights. In regard to contractual execution, the Council has instead taken a clear stance on making sure that the entering into force of a new law does not alter the parameters of parties' contractual relationship and, thus, their rights and obligations. However, it is the Council's indirect influence over contractual reasoning that provides more terrain for discussion. Indeed, through the so-called control of proportionality, the Council regularly checks whether a given rule is justified by a legitimate interest, as well as whether its use may be considered to be proportionate in light of such an interest. Importantly, Seube also notes that while the control of proportionality has been implemented by the European and administrative jurisdictions, it has long been unrecognised by the ordinary judge. In addition, Seube explains why, notwithstanding the criticism on the subject, this proportionality mechanism is on the rise and is likely to become the key to litigation as regards the violation of Fundamental rights by contractual provisions. This, however, raises the question as to *how* the judiciary will concretely implement the control of proportionality in contractual relationships. The comparison between the rulings that have implemented the control of proportionality and those that have vertically and horizontally applied the European Convention on Human Rights (ECHR) serves Seube to show the practical implications of proportionality controls. The analysis then concludes with the discussion of an important case study on freedom of religion on the grounds of Article 9 ECHR and Article 9 of the Civil code.

Annekatrien Lenaerts sets out a detailed analysis of the role that the Private law doctrine of the prohibition of abuse of rights plays in the enforcement of Human rights in contractual relationships in Belgium. Lenaerts explains that this doctrine (in a contractual context) provides a means for policing the exercise of a subjective right by a contracting party on grounds of good faith, fairness and justice, where the true spirit in which that right was conferred has not been adhered to. Lenaerts's central claim is that there is a large degree of equivalence between the policing of conduct for non-compliance with fundamental Human rights in public law and the policing of conduct by private parties in a contractual setting using the abuse of rights doctrine. She argues that the doctrine of abuse of rights, essentially the limitative/negative aspect of the good faith doctrine, has been used as an appropriate existing Private law mechanism through which to channel a supervening public law concern for the protection of Human rights. In this way, Lenaerts shows that Human Rights are horizontally applicable in Belgian Contract law but that these operate indirectly through the prohibition of the abuse of rights. Specifically, she demonstrates that the public law criteria of legality, legitimacy and proportionality, used to review exercises of power by the State, are equally at home when evaluating private (contractual) conduct. She points out in this regard that the protection of weaker parties is as much the concern of Private law as it is of public law. However, this concern for inequality of power has to be balanced in a contractual context, she argues, against the important competing value of freedom of contract, such as (for example) the freedom not to enter into a contract. This theory is then concretised by Lenaerts in the latter half of her chapter through the use of examples from the Belgian case law. She demonstrates how abuses of contractual rights have been policed in order to protect Human rights such as non-discrimination, privacy, property, freedom of expression and freedom of religion. She demonstrates in this way how contractual power can be limited through the abuse of rights doctrine to protect weaker parties, such as students, employees and tenants. She concludes by arguing that there is a role for the doctrine of prohibition of abuse of rights in Private law to achieve a proportional balancing of conflicting constitutional rights, which thereby achieves a working synthesis between Public and Private laws.

In his chapter, Pier Giuseppe Monateri embarks upon an unconventional journey within the Italian Contract law dimension to unfold the liberal and socialist ideologies of contract and pose the basis for a social ontology of contract. More specifically, Monateri shows how the modern and contemporary development of Italian Contract law is characterised by the presence of inherent, ontological ambiguities that cannot be dismissed. Italy is, then, an exemplary case study to analyse the inconsistencies of Contract law discourse and values as emerged both before and after the entering into force of the Italian Constitution in 1948. This particularly emerges through a comparison with the French and German scenarios. To support his claim, Monateri uses ontology against itself and speaks of 'crystal' and 'mud' contracts. While the first label refers to the liberal conception according to which contract are a mere private ordering associated with a more or less strong judicial protection of the weaker party, the latter applies to the socialist approach to contracting. According to this model, contracts are 'social acts' instrumentally used to achieve a spontaneous order, with more or less limited but not absolute power of construction by the courts. Monateri is prompt in recognising that both models entail social risks and costs and different moral conception of justice. Against this framework, Monateri shows how both ideologies are but socio-political constructs that never work according to the logic they officially promote. The conception and use of the cause requirement in the French and Italian liberal traditions, for instance, shows that contracts are, in fact, neither 'crystal' nor free acts. Rather, they are always subject to a high degree of political control through judicial interventionism. The Nazi and fascist experiences, Monateri tells us, have to be analysed within this perspective of inquiry as well: while the values changed, these were promoted through the same technical (i.e., ontological) elements used by the liberal doctrine of contract. Finally, Monateri argues that the entering into force, in 1948, of the first Italian Constitution has pushed this phenomenon even further. Not only the limitations on property and freedom of contract introduced by the Civil code of 1942 have been preserved and further expanded in the 1948 Constitution, but also the whole legislation had (and still has) to be interpreted and applied through constitutional lenses. Hence, as it happened with the transition from the liberal to the fascist-socialist epoch, rather than being substituted, old norms have started being interpreted and used in light of new conceptual framework. The ontological constitutionalisation of Private, and in particular, Contract law, is therefore made evident by the Italian legal system's tendency to form a social conception of private interests. This is due, Monateri further maintains, to the Constitution's strong focus on the value of the 'Person'. The contextualisation of what is the nature of values in the legal, and in particular, contractual field serves Monateri to support his call for a social ontology of contract.

Rather than a conventional account of the constitutional dimension of Contract law in South Africa, Andrew Hutchison tackles this issue indirectly, by examining one of the key underlying themes here, namely the transformation of South African law and society. Under the politically relevant catchword of 'decolonisation', Hutchison examines the question as to how to incorporate a greater element of Afropolitanism in the South African law of contract to better reflect the culture and context of the majority of that country's population. This links to the constitutionalisation of Contract law through statements capturing the transformation ideal by the Constitutional Court in a contractual context and by its use of the African philosophical concept of 'ubuntu' (essentially a concept entailing communitarian values and solidarity). Hutchison examines the role of historiography of South African Contract law, noting the exclusion of the African in many older accounts. This is then applied through an examination of the concept of good faith, which the author argues is the equivalent concept to ubuntu in the South African common law. Historically, good faith in South Africa has been traced to Roman and Roman-Dutch laws, with no element of African values. Hutchison argues that a synthesis is possible here between good faith and the African concept of ubuntu, to allow for an Africanised concept of underlying contractual values and possibly even contract policing along these lines.

This begs the question, however, as to what exactly this new concept of good faith/ubuntu would entail. Hutchison answers this by examining the traditional African customary law of contracts, much of which reflects a pre-commercial sense of community through mutual interdependence and trust. Hutchison argues that a narrower concept of ubuntu is needed if this is going to be employed in a broader commercial context. He suggests that 'contractual ubuntu' should be the new governing value in the common law of contracts but that courts should clearly articulate what this concept entails to avoid uncertainty. A model for this could be foreign definitions of a duty of good faith in contracts, as is starting to emerge in the Common law world and has long been found in Civil law systems, such as Germany. In sum, the future of South Africa's system of uncodified Roman-Dutch law is facing a new struggle for political legitimacy and must now seduce a new cohort of black South African legal practitioners and judges if this system is to survive. A synthesis with African values and concepts is likely and also appropriate.

The purpose of Philip Clarke's chapter is to draw a comparison between the Australian and UK abuse of dominant position and unfair contract terms regimes as disciplined by the Australian Consumer law (set out in Schedule 2 of the Competition and Consumer Act 2010) and the Australian Securities and Investments Commission Act 2001, on the one hand, and the (UK) Consumer Rights Act 2015 and the Unfair Contract Terms Act 1977, on the other. To this, Clarke compellingly adds a comparison with the inspiring source of both regimes, namely the Council Directive 93/13/EEC of 5 April 1993 on unfair terms in consumer contracts. Such an analysis is all the more important for our theme on the constitutionalisation of Contract law as in neither country is there a constitutional restriction on the power of the legislature to intervene in this sense. Consequently, as Clarke himself notes at the very beginning of his contribution, 'although the doctrines of freedom and sanctity of contract have exerted a restraining influence in this respect, in both countries Parliament has been able to intrude into contractual relationships in the pursuit of securing just and fair outcomes'.

As it may be easily imagined, to address such a topic requires an engagement with the above-mentioned movement from the belief in the absolute freedom of contract, which characterised legal thought in the eighteen century, to the principles of fairness and justice, which underpin the law of contract today. And indeed, Clarke's account starts from the delicate relationship between the doctrine of contractual freedom and the limitation of the abuse of dominant position. The discussion reveals to be particularly productive as according to Anglo-Australian law, it is lawful to occupy a dominant position, as well as to seek to acquire such a position via competitive means. This conception notwithstanding, the recognition of collateral interests, as well as of anti-discriminatory values and principles of procedural fairness, has led to the introduction of important legislative and judicial limitations to the doctrine of contractual freedom. However, as Clarke shows, while these new measures turned out to be effective to a certain extent, dominant parties have retained considerable opportunity to abuse their dominant positions by dictating terms that are unfair to the weaker parties with whom they contract. Both the UK and Australian unfair contract term regimes are aimed to address this situation directly. Clarke's analysis therefore proceeds by outlining in detail the rationale for the new legislation in both legal systems, its scope and test of unfairness. Before discussing the consequences arising out of a term being found to be unfair, Clarke's investigation takes into account what he deems to be the most controversial aspects of the new regimes, namely, the subject matter and price exclusions—two delicate themes on which both the UK and Australia have followed the European Directive.

Finally, in his conclusive remarks, Clarke suggests that businesses will respond positively to the new regimes. However, he also identifies a number of areas in which one jurisdiction may benefit by following the lead of the other.

In her contribution, Béatrice Schütte elaborates on the constitutional dimension of Contract law in Germany, through a discussion of three pivotal topics, namely, good faith, control of contract terms, and limited party autonomy in labour law. Schütte's chapter makes it clear that, in Germany, constitutional values, and in particular Fundamental rights, exert an important theoretical and practical influence on Contract law. Schütte also notes that while in the past there has been a dogmatic discussion as to whether the influence was a direct or an indirect one, there is now a strong consensus that the effect is, in fact, an indirect one (*Drittwirkung der Grundrechte*). Yet a few exceptions apply, particularly regarding Article 9 III *Grundgesetz*, the German Basic Law, where the direct horizontal effect is implied. To understand the essence, aims, benefits and flaws of the German indirect approach to the constitutionalisation of Contract law, Schütte notes, attention ought to be paid to Günther Dürig's intention to safeguard private autonomy and the independence of Private law. This aim also explains why Fundamental rights exert their influence over Private law through the so-called comprehensive clauses, that is to say, through the performativity of legal provisions that are formulated with a wide scope so that they have to be substantiated in court practice. The best-known examples, Schütte argues, are good faith as codified in § 242 and *bonos mores* according to § 138 of the *Bürgerliches Gesetzbuch* (the German Civil code, usually known as BGB), both of which are discussed at length later in the chapter. Most importantly, this indirect, comprehensive approach has been welcomed by the German Constitutional Court starting with the well-known 1958 *Lüth* case. In a few words, according the Constitutional Court, Fundamental rights exert their influence mainly through those provisions that are to be considered as part of the *ordre public*, i.e. those principles that bind the parties to a contract by reason of public interest. As noted by Smits in his sceptical account of the constitutionalisation of Private law, discussed in the previous section of this Introduction, this socio-legal and socio-political approach does not prejudice, per se, the decisive role of Private law provisions in the resolution of contractual conflicts. Rather, Schütte contends, it merely requires that constitutional values are endorsed and promoted through contracts. The so-called *Schutzpflichtentheorie*, or theory of the state's duty of protection, is also analysed by Schütte when setting out the German landscape. In addition to this, Schütte thoroughly elaborates on the 'constitutional' function of such provisions as § 134 BGB concerning statutory prohibition, § 133 BGB concerning the interpretation of a declaration of intent, § 157 BGB concerning the interpretation of contracts, § 307 BGB on the control of standard contract terms. Particular attention is also paid to the above-mentioned Article 9 III *Grundgesetz* in regard to the right to form coalitions (*Koalitionsfreiheit*) and associations to safeguard and improve working and economic conditions.

In her contribution, Elsa Dias Oliveira discusses the question of the impact of constitutional rights and values on the existing Portuguese law dealing with agreements controlling personality rights. Oliveira defines personality rights as protecting aspects of the person, such as life, physical and psychological integrity, good name, privacy and the use of one's image or voice. The chapter begins with a brief account of the impact of the Portuguese Constitution on the Private law realm of contract. She also delves into the overlapping legal regimes governing personality rights in Portugal, including the Constitution, the Civil code and specific statutes. She underlines the fact that the interplay between these various instruments is far from clear and that there are conflicting viewpoints on this issue. In this process, she tackles the important constitutional question as to whether this instrument applies directly or indirectly to personality agreements and whether it may be horizontally invoked or is only applicable in disputes involving the state. She also argues for a role for the general clauses of the Portuguese Civil code in policing agreements regulating personality rights, such as the clauses dealing with public policy and good morals. A key feature of Oliveira's discussion of agreements controlling personality rights is whether these rights may be revoked once conferred, particularly in a commercial context. She explains that the standard position is that such rights are freely revocable, subject to two points: firstly, there may be a duty to compensate for losses caused to the grantee by such revocation under the Civil code, and, secondly, there may be a complicating factor from a constitutional point of view, where the right of the grantor to revoke may conflict with the legitimate right to economic enterprise of the opposing party. An example would be where the grantee is a professional photographer or artist who has depicted the grantor's image or used a recording of her voice.

Oliveira illustrates her arguments with depictions of the industry, which has grown up around popular culture figures, such as celebrities, models, actors and professional sportspersons, particularly footballers. She describes the industry norms in these contexts, including footballer's collective agreements and specific statute law governing this lucrative Portuguese showpiece. Particularly important for Oliveira is the view that personality interests last a lifetime and the personal viewpoints of models, celebrities and sportspersons may change as they mature, so that images or other depictions from an era of youth may later come back to haunt them with the experience of old age. For Oliveira, this implicates fundamental constitutional rights, such as human dignity, or even (potentially) religion. Finally, on the question of privacy, Oliveira draws once again on celebrity culture, noting that this Fundamental right may be limited where this is in the public interest, or perhaps where it has been waived, such as by partaking in a reality television show. Oliveira's central message is that constitutional rights have a role to play in personality agreements, but may be subject to limitation, and that sometimes protection of personality interests may be better achieved indirectly, through the use of existing Private law means.

Engaging with the pluralism that characterises the Canadian legal system, Nicholas Lambert's chapter delves into the constitutional aspect of Canadian Contract law through the lenses of the Constitution Act, 1867, and the Canadian Charter or Rights and Freedoms, which forms part of the Constitution Act, 1982. According to Lambert, the need to pursue such a roadmap is due to the fact that these two documents were drafted in vastly differing times and could represent different approaches to social and economic regulation. However, at the time of writing, it is not so clear as to what extent contract rights have received an updated constitutional consideration. Before embarking upon this comparative analysis, however, Lambert's efforts focus on whether there is such thing as *ius commune* of contracts in Canada. To answer this interrogative is all the more relevant for the correct understanding of the impact that constitutional values and HR policies have on Contract law in Canada. Indeed, at first glance, Lambert argues, the answer would be a clear-cut 'no'. Section 92(13) of the Constitution Act, 1867, confers indeed jurisdiction over 'property and civil rights' to provincial legislatures. However, Lambert further notes that the degree of fragmentism that one may see in the United States does not figure in Canadian law, the reason being that Canada, Quebec included, does not have an independent and final system of 'provincial courts' wielding jurisdiction over Private law: the rulings of the Supreme Court, the highest court in the judicial hierarchy, apply throughout the country. Having clarified this, Lambert embarks upon the above-mentioned comparative analysis between the Constitution Act, 1867, and the Canadian Charter of Rights and Freedoms. In so doing, Lambert pays particular attention not only to the forms of legislative control over contracts but also to the peculiarities of the judicial (including administrative) jurisdiction over contractual disputes, as well as to the Fundamental right of contractual freedom. The discussion of the last topic turns out to be particularly relevant for the purposes of this study as in the late 1980s the Supreme Court ruled that the parties to a contract are free to exclude all liabilities arising from a breach of their obligations. As Lambert tellingly notes, this approach to contractual freedom not only raises the question as to how individuals can exclude judicial jurisdiction when the legislature itself cannot do so but also requires a thorough engagement with the Canadian conception of what a contract is. Ultimately, what emerges from Lambert's investigation is that in Canada, contrarily to what may initially be thought, it is not the Constitution that informs the development of the law of contract. Rather, and bearing in mind that the Common law acts as a filter for the interpretation of constitutional provisions, it is the form of contractualism depicted by Canadian courts that has played a pivotal role at the public level.

Taking a lateral step from the positivistic focus of previous chapters, Luca Siliquini-Cinelli opts for a theoretical-philosophical method of investigation that compares the condition of the *pactum* at the public and private spheres. In particular, Siliquini-Cinelli compares the behaviouralisation of human existence and relations that informs the Hobbesian project to the recent emphasis on contractual good faith within the Common law tradition as epitomised by the Canadian and Irish cases of *Bhasin v. Hrynew* and *Flynn v. Breccia*, as well as by other important judgments in England, New Zealand, Australia and Scotland (a mixed legal jurisdiction). Siliquini-Cinelli's aim is to show that the movement toward the conceptualisation of good faith as an organising principle and implied term in the Common law dimension is due to the need to counterbalance our inhuman condition as made manifest by the illusory character of the modern constitutional project.

To understand this phenomenon fully, Siliquini-Cinelli contends, we ought to delve into the nature of the *pactum* as both substantial and functional bond, as well as mythical canon of any contractual-constituting initiative on the public and private spheres. This requires not only the unfolding of the notion of contractualism as depicted by such scholars as Alain Supiot and Roger Cotterrell, but also an unconventional engagement with a series of important philosophical, political and juridical accounts of modern secularism. A comparison between Martin Loughlin's, Hannah Arendt's and Giorgio Agamben's scholarship on Hobbes and sovereignty may represent an important starting point for such a discussion.

However, Siliquini-Cinelli also argues that this is not sufficient. What is also needed is a thorough contextualisation of the 'experience-knowledge' and 'action-behaviour' dichotomies in Constitutional and Contract law discourse. Importantly, Siliquini-Cinelli notes that some commentators would deem the aim of his contribution to be pretentious, or at least inappropriate, from a purely Comparative law perspective. This would be a conservative reaction to the fact that, over the last two decades, Comparative law has branched out in new directions, galvanising legal theorists and practitioners; sparking novel socio-political, legal and business models; and attracting worldwide attention. Such criticism, Siliquini-Cinelli contends, would fall short in recognising the increasing relevance of Comparative law's methodological pluralism. Yet Siliquini-Cinelli also notes that the variety of accounts on Comparative's law essence and method(s) has inevitably displaced the anthropological and philosophical, rather than legal, difference between self-dissolving 'behaviour' and 'knowledge' and self-defining 'action' and 'experience'. The re-discovery of this antithesis may shed new light on the paradoxical condition of the *pactum* in the Public and Private law dimensions.

Luca Siliquini-Cinelli
Andrew Hutchison

References

Berger P, Luckmann T (1967) The social construction of reality. Penguin Books, London

Brown W ([2009] 2012) We are all democrats now . . . . In: Democracy in what state? Columbia University Press, New York, pp 44–57

Cristi R (1984) Hayek and Schmitt on the rule of law. CJPS 17(3):521–535

Dobner P, Loughlin M (eds) (2010) The twilight of constitutionalism? OUP, Oxford

Fontanelli F (2011) Santi Romano and L'Ordinamento Giuridico: the televance of a forgotten masterpiece for contemporary international, transnational and global legal relations. TLT 2 (1):67–117

Geuss R (2001) Private goods, public goods. Princeton University Press, Princeton

Grundmann S (2008) Constitutional values and European contract law. Kluwer Law International, Alphaen aan den Rijn

Handl G, Zekoll J, Zumbansen P (eds) (2012) Beyond territoriality. Transnantional legal theory in an age of globalization. Brill, Leiden

Hardt M, Negri A (2009) Commonwealth. Belknap Press/Harvard University Press, Cambridge

Helfand MA (ed) (2015) Negotiating state and non-state law: the challenge of global and local legal pluralism. CUP, Cambridge
Jansen N, Michaels R (2008) Beyond the state: rethinking private law. Mohr Siebeck, Tübingen
Kahn PW ([2005] 2008) Putting liberalism in its place. Princeton University Press, Princeton
Kennedy D (2001) The political stakes in 'merely technical' issues of contract law. ERPL 1:7–28
Krisch N (2010) Beyond constitutionalism. The pluralist structure of postnational law. OUP, Oxford
Kuo M-S (2010) The end of constitutionalism as we know it? Boundaries and the state of global constitutional (dis)ordering. TLT 1(3):329–369
Mac Amhlaigh C, Michelon C, Neil W (eds) (2013) After public law. OUP, Oxford
Mak C (2008) Fundamental rights in European contract law. Kluwer Law International, Alphaen aan den Rijn
Markesinis B (1990) Comparative law – a subject in search of an audience. MLR 53(1):1–21
Marramao G (2009) Passaggio a Occidente. Filosofia e globalizzazione. Bollati Boringhieri, Turin
Michelman F (2012) Constitutions and the public/private divide. In: Rosenfield M, Sajo A (eds) The Oxford handbook of comparative constitutional law. OUP, Oxford, pp 298–317
Riles A (2008) The anti-network. Private global governance, legal knowledge and the legitimacy of the state. In: Jansen N, Michaels R (eds) Beyond the state. Rethinking private law. Mohr Siebeck, Tübingen, pp 183–207
Roughan N (2011) The relative authority of law: a contribution to 'pluralist jurisprudence'. In: Del Mar M (ed) New waves in philosophy of law. Palgrave Macmillan, New York, pp 254–277
Roughan N (2013) Authorities. Conflicts, cooperation, and transnational legal theory. OUP, Oxford
Searle JR (1995) The construction of social reality. Free Press, New York
Smits J (2006) Private law and fundamental rights: a sceptical view. In: Barkhuysen T, Lindenbergh SD (eds) Constitutionalisation of private law. Brill, Leiden, pp 9–22
Stammers N (1993) Human rights and power. PS 41(1):70–82
Stammers N (1999) Social movements and the social construction of human rights. HRQ 21:980–1008
Supiot A ([2005] 2007) Homo juridicus. On the anthropological function of the law, Saksia Brown trans. Verso, New York
Thornhill C (2012) National sovereignty and the constitution of transnational law: a sociological approach. TLT 3(4):393–460
Twining W (2009) General jurisprudence. Understanding law from a global perspective. CUP, Cambridge
Walker N (2012) Postnational constitutionalism and postnational public law: a tale of two neologisms. TLT 3(1):61–85
Weinrib EJ (2011) Private law and public right. UTLJ 61:191–211
Weinrib EJ (1995) The idea of private law. Harvard University Press, Cambridge
Zumbansen P (2013) Why global law is transnational. TLT 4(4):463–475

Contents

List of Contributors

François du Bois Professor, Leicester Law School, Leicester, UK

Philip H. Clarke Emeritus Professor of Law, Deakin University, Geelong, VIC, Australia

Adjunct Professor, Australian Catholic University, Banyo, QLD, Australia

Professor of Law, Swinburne University of Technology, Hawthorn, VIC, Australia

Andrew Hutchison Associate Professor, Department of Commercial Law, University of Cape Town, Capetown, South Africa

Nicolas Lambert Professor of Administrative Law, Comparative Law, and Contract Law, Université de Moncton, Moncton, NB, Canada

Annekatrien Lenaerts Référendaire at the Belgian Court of Cassation, Leuven, Belgium

Affiliated Senior Researcher, Institute for Law of Obligations, KU Leuven, Leuven, Belgium

Joasia Luzak Associate Professor, University of Exeter Law School, Exeter, UK

Pier Giuseppe Monateri Professor of Comparative Law and Law and Literature, University of Turin, Turin, Italy

Professor of Advanced Comparative Law, Sciences-Po, Paris, France

Elsa Dias Oliveira Assistant Professor, Faculty of Law, University of Lisbon, Lisbon, Spain

Béatrice Schütte PhD, Department of Law, Business and Social Sciences, Aarhus University, Aarhus, Denmark

Jean-Baptiste Seube Honorary Dean of the Faculty of Law of the Reunion Island, Saint-Denis, France

Luca Siliquini-Cinelli Department of Law, Liverpool Hope University, Liverpool, UK

The Impact of Human Rights on English Contract Law

François du Bois

Abstract This chapter examines the influence of fundamental rights on English Contract law since the enactment of the Human Rights Act 1998. Its aims are twofold—to provide a first comprehensive analysis of this phenomenon in English law and to tease out the factors that have shaped its contours. The chapter accordingly explores each of the various routes by which fundamental rights may touch on English Contract law: direct statutory horizontality, public liability horizontality, remedial horizontality and substantive horizontality. It is shown that although all permutations of horizontality have featured in contract litigation before English courts, the actual influence of fundamental rights on Contract law has been slight. Indeed, the gap between Contract law and fundamental rights is so wide that the contractual origin of a right frequently features as a reason for not finding a rights violation. The causes uncovered are complex and impossible to reduce to a single factor. The analysis nevertheless opens up a fresh perspective on the constitutionalisation of Contract law: it is not so much a normative phenomenon universally furthering specific values as a particular legal technique the impact and value of which are decisively moulded by the local environment in which it operates.

1 Introduction

Ever since the Human Rights Act 1998 (HRA) 'brought rights home' to the legal systems of the United Kingdom, English Contract law has been exposed to the influence of fundamental rights.[1] Section 6 of the HRA renders it unlawful for courts and tribunals to act in a way that is incompatible with the European

[1] For background on the Human Rights Act, see Klug (2000). There is scope for debate about when rights are 'fundamental'. I take this to be whenever they are meant to have an impact (whatever that might be) throughout a legal system and on all forms of law. This includes the Human Rights Act 1988 but excludes the Employment Rights Act 1996.

F. du Bois (✉)
Leicester Law School, University of Leicester, Leicester, UK
e-mail: francois.dubois@le.ac.uk

L. Siliquini-Cinelli, A. Hutchison (eds.), *The Constitutional Dimension of Contract Law*, DOI 10.1007/978-3-319-49843-0_1

Convention on Human Rights (ECHR),[2] and there is broad agreement that this includes the adjudication of disputes among private persons.[3] Yet little trace of such influence is to be found in the law reports.[4] Why? Several of the chapters in this book recount the influence of fundamental rights on Contract law in jurisdictions where the law does not appear to compel this any more forcefully than the HRA. What lies behind the English divergence from this trend? What does this tell us about the role of fundamental rights in relation to contracts and about English contract?

The burgeoning literature in England on the horizontal application of fundamental rights has surprisingly little to say about these questions. Authors typically concern themselves with how horizontal application should be treated as a matter of legal doctrine or legal theory, or with demonstrating its impact (or otherwise) in a particular jurisdiction or area of law, often arguing either for or against this phenomenon.[5] Scant effort has been expended on trying to identify the factors determining whether horizontal application flounders or rises to prominence.[6] In the field of English Contract law, the rarity of cases exhibiting fundamental rights influence is matched by the scarcity of writing on the topic. Although it is covered in the leading practitioners' manual, *Chitty on Contracts*,[7] books aimed primarily at an academic and student readership ignore the topic altogether,[8] restrict themselves to scattered references[9] or contain rather limited discussion.[10] There is not much more than a handful of book chapters or journal articles, and these mostly cover Contract law briefly as part of wider concerns.[11]

Against this background, the present chapter commences with a systematic mapping of the terrain, employing a framework adapted from Ian Leigh's helpful typology of horizontal effect.[12] The chapter accordingly explores each of the various routes by which fundamental rights may touch on English Contract law:

---

[2] More precisely, with Convention rights, which are those set out in Articles 2–12 and 14 of the Convention, Articles 1–3 of the First Protocol to the Convention, and Article 1 of the Thirteenth Protocol, as read with Articles 16–18 of the Convention, and subject to any designated derogation or reservation by the United Kingdom—see s 1 HRA.

[3] Young (2011), p. 16.

[4] References to the small number of reported cases are provided in the following sections of this chapter.

[5] See the contributions in Friedmann and Barak-Erez (2001); Ziegler (2007); Oliver and Fedtke (2007); Hoffman (2011). There is also a large volume of journal articles.

[6] A notable exception is Giliker (2015).

[7] Beale (2015), Ch 1.

[8] Andrews (2015).

[9] Beatson et al. (2016); Peel (2015).

[10] McKendrick (2013), pp. 11–13; Collins (2008), pp. 44–45, 100, 104.

[11] Beale and Pittam (2001), p. 131; Brownsword (2001), p. 181; Duffy (1997), Ch. 23; Cherednychenko (2007), Ch. 3; Mak (2008), Ch. 2; Rose (2011), p. 300; Davey and Richards (2015); Collins (2011); Collins (2013); Collins (2014).

[12] Leigh (1999), pp. 74–85.

direct statutory horizontality, public liability horizontality, remedial horizontality and substantive horizontality.[13] The purpose of doing so is twofold—to provide a first comprehensive analysis of this phenomenon in English law and to tease out the factors that have shaped its contours. This investigation concentrates on the impact of Convention rights via the HRA, leaving to one side a more recent addition to the fundamental rights landscape, the European Union Charter of Fundamental Rights.[14] The Charter is not only too recent to have produced much relevant effect but is also affected by the 'Brexit' referendum result. The chapter concludes with a closer focus on the factors so identified, tracing their impact to the intersection of an ambivalent reception of the Convention rights with a strong tradition of a comparatively dynamic and open Contract law already engaged in an overt balancing of interests. This conclusion opens up a fresh perspective on the 'constitutionalisation of Contract law': it is not so much a normative phenomenon universally furthering values such as 'protection of the weaker party',[15] social justice,[16] autonomy[17] or a reconceptualisation of contractual freedom,[18] as a particular legal technique the impact and value of which are decisively moulded by the local environment in which it operates.

2 Direct Statutory Horizontality

Direct statutory horizontality occurs where a legislative provision regulating rights and duties among private persons is affected by Convention rights. This can be due to s 3(1) of the HRA, which requires that primary and secondary legislation should, 'so far as it is possible to do so', 'be read and given effect in a way which is compatible with Convention rights'. This duty has been held to apply 'to the same degree in legislation applying between private parties as it does in legislation which applies between public authorities and individuals'.[19] Its effect is thus to impose indirectly an obligation to comply with Convention rights on private parties.[20] Statutory horizontality can also involve s 4 HRA, which empowers a court to issue a 'declaration of incompatibility' when a legislative provision is found to be

---

[13]The final category combines what Leigh refers to as indirect horizontality and full or direct horizontality.

[14]For discussion, see Leczykiewicz (2013a, b), p. 171.

[15]See Mak (2008), p. 323; Colombi Ciacchi (2014), p. 126.

[16]Meli (2006).

[17]Collins (2014), pp. 57–60.

[18]Brownsword (2001).

[19]*X v Y*, [2004] EWCA Civ 662, [2004] IRLR 625 (Court of Appeal (Civil Division)), para 66; See also *Pirabakaran v Patel & Anor*, [2006] EWCA Civ 685, [2006] 1 WLR 3112 (Court of Appeal (Civil Division)), para 45.

[20]Amos (2014), p. 55.

incompatible with a Convention right. Such a declaration does not affect the validity of a statute but requires Parliament to consider what, if anything at all, to do about it.

This form of horizontality is found where contracts deal with subject matter that has been subjected to considerable and detailed statutory regulation: especially employment contracts, consumer contracts and residential leases. For example, in *X v Y*, the Court of Appeal, in the words of Mummery LJ, 'blended' unfair dismissal legislation with Article 8 ECHR 'by a process of interpretation ... but without creating new private law causes of action against private sector employers'.[21] A charitable body working with young offenders had dismissed the applicant when it discovered that he had received a caution for gross indecency following a consensual sexual act with another man in a public toilet. The applicant argued that his dismissal was unfair as it infringed his right to private life under Article 8 ECHR, and the Court of Appeal went on to hold that employment tribunals must read and give effect to the unfair dismissal legislation so as to be compatible with Article 8. In *Wilson v First County Trust Ltd (No. 2)*,[22] the House of Lords considered whether a creditor's inability under the Consumer Credit Act 1974 to enforce a consumer credit agreement against a debtor where the documentation failed to contain all the prescribed contract terms was compatible with the rights guaranteed by Article 6 ECHR and Article 1 of its First Protocol (A1P1). And in *Ghaidan v Godin-Mendoza*,[23] the House of Lords held that, in light of the Article 14 Convention right not to be discriminated against on the ground of sexual orientation in the enjoyment of Article 8, a provision in the Rent Act 1977 obliging a landlord to grant a statutory tenancy to someone 'living with the original tenant as his or her wife or husband' had to be interpreted to protect also the same-sex partner of a deceased tenant. Each of these cases highlights a distinctive aspect of the courts' approach to statutory horizontality.

The most noteworthy feature of *X v Y* is the discussion by Mummery LJ of whether there should be any distinction in the law of unfair dismissal between public sector and private sector employers.[24] In his view, there would normally be no sensible ground for making such a distinction, especially against the background of widespread outsourcing by public authorities to private contractors. He thought it 'unlikely that the HRA was intended to produce different results' depending on whether the employer was in the private sector but (as in this case) working closely with a public authority or was itself a public authority. However, because s 3 HRA, the provision that empowers an intervention such as this, is restricted to the interpretation of statutes, it is not always open to the courts to pursue the equal treatment of private and public contracting parties in this way. Thus, in *Lee v Leeds*

---

[21] See *X v Y*, [2004] EWCA Civ 662, para 59.

[22] *Wilson v First County Trust Ltd (No. 2)* [2003] UKHL 40, [2004] 1 AC 816 (House of Lords).

[23] *Ghaidan v Godin-Mendoza*, [2004] UKHL 30, [2004] 2 AC 557 (House of Lords).

[24] *X v Y*, [2004] EWCA Civ 662, para 59.

City Council,[25] the Court of Appeal rejected the argument that the obligation imposed on every landlord by s 11(1)(a) of the Landlord and Tenant Act 1985 'to keep in repair the structure' of a dwelling house must, in view of Article 8 ECHR, be read as imposing an obligation to put and keep the structure in good habitable repair. Because this provision had a settled meaning established by earlier Court of Appeal decisions, such a reading was no longer considered possible.[26] Nevertheless, proceeding on the basis that a local authority landlord providing public housing was, by virtue of s 6 HRA,[27] required to comply with its tenants' rights to respect of their private and family life under Article 8, the Court did feel able to hold that such a *public* landlord owed the claimed obligation.[28] Likewise, in *McDonald v McDonald*, the Supreme Court refused to employ s 3 HRA to subject a private landlord's power to evict a tenant to the same Article 8 restrictions as a local authority because this 'would not "go with the grain of the legislation" but positively contradict it'.[29]

In *Wilson v First County Trust Ltd (No. 2)*, four members of the House of Lords considered that the Court of Appeal had erred in concluding that s 127(3) of the Consumer Credit Act 1974 was incompatible with Article 6(1) ECHR, which safeguards the right to a fair trial in the determination of civil rights and obligations and the protection of possessions in Article 1 of ECHR Protocol 1 (A1P1).[30] Article 6(1) was held only to target procedural bars on bringing claims to court and 'does not itself guarantee any particular content for civil rights and obligations in the substantive law of the contracting states'.[31] It did not apply to these facts because s 127(3) restricted the scope of the creditor's contractual right rather than bar access to a court for determining whether the case was covered by this restriction. The most important aspect of their lordships' opinions concerns their views regarding the applicability of A1P1. For Lord Nicholls, '"possessions" in Article 1 is apt to embrace contractual rights', which 'may be more valuable and enduring than proprietary rights'.[32] Hence, on his reading, s 127(3) would engage A1P1: 'The lender's rights were extinguished in favour of the borrower by legislation for which the state is responsible.'[33] Lord Hobhouse expressly rejected 'the proposition that a statutory provision which prevents a transaction from having the quality of legal

[25] *Lee v Leeds City Council*, [2002] EWCA Civ 6, [2002] 1 WLR 1488 (Court of Appeal (Civil Division)).

[26] Ibid., paras 56–58.

[27] Explored in the next section.

[28] *Lee*, [2002] EWCA Civ 6, para 59.

[29] *McDonald v McDonald*, [2016] UKSC 28, [2016] 3 WLR 45 (Supreme Court (UK)), para 69.

[30] *Wilson* [2003] UKHL 40. This was obiter as their lordships held that the CA had been wrong to apply sects. 3 and 4 of the 1998 Act retroactively. Lord Rodger expressed no views on these hypothetical issues: para 220. Section 127(3) of the 1974 Act was subsequently repealed by the Consumer Credit Act 2006 s 15.

[31] Ibid., para 33.

[32] Ibid., para 39.

[33] Ibid., para 44.

enforceability can be regarded as an interference for article 1 purposes with the possessions of the party who would have benefited if the transaction had had that quality'.[34] Instead, he emphasised that on the facts of this case, s 127(3) would deprive a creditor of its special title to possession of the security for the loan under a contract of pledge.[35] Lords Hope and Scott concurred in this rejection of Lord Nicholls' reasoning, concluding, however, that A1P1 would not be engaged on the facts before them.[36] Lord Hope insisted: 'One must ... distinguish carefully between cases where the effect of the relevant law is to deprive a person of something that he already owns and those where its effect is to subject his right from the outset to the reservation or qualification which is now being enforced against him.'[37] In this case, 'the agreement which was entered into ... was from the outset an agreement which was improperly executed' and thus 'was always subject to the restrictions on its execution'.[38] Nevertheless, all four were in agreement that there had been no breach of either Convention right since s 127(3) was a 'legitimate exercise in consumer protection'.[39] Parliament's response to the circumstances of vulnerable borrowers who do not bargain on an equal footing with lenders could not be said to have been disproportionate to the policy underlying the statute.[40]

There is a clear divergence of approach between Lord Nicholls on the one hand and Lords Hope and Scott on the other. On Lord Nicholls' approach, 'it is the parties' agreement (possibly as recognised by the common law) which forms the source of their contractual rights, which are then eligible for protection under art.1'.[41] In his view, the characterisation of the nature and effect of the relevant provisions of the Consumer Credit Act had to be considered as a matter of substance rather than form.[42] Lords Hope and Scott, however, regarded the statute as co-determining when the agreement will give rise to rights: it delimits creditors' rights from the moment of their creation as it prevents these from ever being enforceable. This divergence has wide-ranging potential implications that reach beyond statutory horizontality to touch also on substantive horizontality and the common law. This is explored in Sect. 5 below. Here it should be noted that both of these approaches to the distinction between the delimitation and the deprivation of rights have been applied in subsequent English cases.[43] However, Lord Nicholls'

[34]Ibid., para 137.

[35]Ibid., para 136.

[36]Ibid., paras 108 and 168.

[37]Ibid., para 106.

[38]Ibid., para 107.

[39]Ibid., para 138.

[40]Ibid., para 74.

[41]Beale (2015), p. 1-067.

[42]*Wilson*, [2003] UKHL 40, para 44.

[43]Lord Nicholls's approach is endorsed in *Shaws (EAL) Ltd. v Pennycook*, [2004] EWCA Civ 100, [2004] Ch 296 (Court of Appeal (Civil Division)), paras 34–35, but that of Lords Hope Hobhouse and Scott in *Soteriou v Ultrachem Ltd*, [2004] EWHC 983 (QB), [2004] IRLR

approach arguably provides the better fit with the subsequent ECHR decision in *Stretch v UK*,[44] holding that A1P1 was engaged where a lessee's option to renew a lease was rendered void as ultra vires the powers of a public authority lessor. The Court here rejected the UK government's argument that there was no 'possession' of which the tenant could be deprived as the option had been a nullity from the start.[45] This led Neuberger J to accord 'a wide ambit' to this term.[46] According to *Chitty*, the approach of Lord Nicholls is to be preferred '[f]or the overall function of art.1 is to prevent states from depriving persons of their possessions illegitimately and for this purpose legislation which denies a right which would otherwise arise (i.e. under the general law) can be seen to have such a depriving effect'.[47]

Two cases illustrate the limitations of statutory horizontality. The first limitation is that it only reaches instances where it is the legislation itself, rather than the contract, that has a depriving effect. In *Horsham Group Properties Ltd v Clark*, Briggs J held that A1P1 did not cover a mortgagee's right to appoint a receiver under s 101(1)(i) of the Law of Property Act 1925 because 'section 101 serves to implement rather than override the private bargain between mortgagor and mortgagee'.[48] The second limitation concerns the intensity of the impact of the legislative provision on the contractual right. In *K Ltd v National Westminster Bank Plc*,[49] the Court of Appeal doubted whether A1P1 covered the effect of certain sections in the Proceeds of Crime Act 2002 on a bank customer's contractual entitlement that a bank carry out its mandate, as the legislation merely deferred performance of the mandate by the bank while it investigated a suspicion of money laundering. There is intricate Strasbourg jurisprudence on what constitutes an interference with possessions.[50]

In *Ghaidan v Godin-Mendoza*,[51] the House of Lords endorsed a two-stage approach in the application of s 3, for which this decision remains the leading authority. The first stage involves the ordinary interpretation of the statute and

870 (England and Wales High Court (Queen's Bench)), para 89 and in *Salat v Barutis*, [2013] EWCA Civ 1499, [2013] CTLC 250 (Court of Appeal (Civil Division)), para 27.

[44] *Stretch v UK,* [2003] ECHR 320, (2004) 38 EHRR 12 (European Court of Human Rights).

[45] Ibid., para 32.

[46] *PW & Co Ltd v Milton Gate Investments Ltd*, [2003] EWHC 1994 (Ch), [2004] Ch 142 (England and Wales High Court (Chancery Division)), para 126. Noteworthy is the observation that here 'it is ultimately the common law, rather than Statute, which gives rise to the Article 1 infringement in the present case' (para 127) although the case was dealt with as one involving statutory construction under Article 3.

[47] Beale (2015), p. 1-068.

[48] *Horsham Group Properties Ltd v Clark,* [2008] EWHC 2327 (Ch), [2009] 1 WLR 1255 (England and Wales High Court (Chancery Division)), para 35.

[49] *K Ltd v National Westminster Bank Plc,* [2006] EWCA Civ 1039, [2007] 1 WLR 311 (Court of Appeal (Civil Division)).

[50] The starting point is *Sporrong and Lonnroth v Sweden*, (1983) 5 EHRR 35 (European Court of Human Rights).

[51] *Ghaidan,* [2004] UKHL 30.

requires consideration of whether the legislative provision would breach the Convention right. If it would, the second stage is triggered, which requires a new interpretation that renders the provision compatible with the right. This is subject to the requirement 'that a section 3 interpretation should not be inconsistent with a "fundamental feature" of the statute, and should not determine "issues calling for legislative deliberation"'.[52] This restricts the extent to which this Convention right could be used to extend the reach of legislation; it has been argued, for example, that attempts 'to read the Sex Discrimination Act, which is clearly based around a comparison between men and women, as covering sexual orientation, are unlikely to succeed'.[53] The recent Supreme Court decision in *McDonald v McDonald*[54] brings home the significance of these limitations on the potential to use s 3 HRA as a means for indirectly rendering private relations subject to Convention rights. It features repeated emphasis on the legislature's authority to decide for itself how best to balance competing rights and interests.[55]

Three points should be highlighted. The first is that *Ghaidan* illustrates the forceful impact of the HRA, as their lordships departed from their earlier decision in *Fitzpatrick v Sterling Housing Association Ltd.*[56] This had held, before the coming into force of the HRA, that, on an ordinary reading of the legislation, the survivor of a homosexual couple could not become a statutory tenant by succession. The second, however, is the unusualness of this case. Apart from *Ghaidan*, there are, according to Hazel Oliver, 'no leading private law cases in discrimination law that have grappled directly with the extent of the courts' powers of statutory interpretation under section 3'.[57] One reason is that Article 14 operates only in combination with another Convention right. The right to private life in Article 8, which was relied on in *Ghaidan*, does have a rather wide ambit, but it does not cover everything.[58] In Oliver's opinion, 'perhaps the most significant reason is the fact that the existing regime of discrimination legislation is so comprehensive and largely based on EU law'.[59]

The importance of such legislation is illustrated by *Bull and Bull v Hall and Preddy*,[60] where the UK Supreme Court held that the refusal on religious grounds by the owners of a private hotel to rent a double bedroom to a same-sex couple contravened the Equality Act (Sexual Orientation) Regulations 2007, which does directly address discrimination by private persons. Moreover, the Court concluded unanimously that, despite engaging Article 9 ECHR, the EASOR did not have to be

[52]Van Zyl Smit (2011), p. 85.

[53]Oliver (2011), p. 211.

[54]*McDonald* [2016] UKSC 28.

[55]Ibid., paras 40, 43, 45 and 69.

[56]*Fitzpatrick v Sterling Housing Association Ltd,* (2001) 1 AC 27 (House of Lords).

[57]Oliver (2011), p. 206.

[58]On Article 8, see Amos (2014), pp. 409–527.

[59]Oliver (2011), p. 207.

[60]*Bull and Bull v Hall and Preddy,* [2013] UKSC 73, [2013] 1 WLR 3741 (Supreme Court (UK)).

read down, as it constituted a justified and proportionate protection of the rights of others. Here, as Hugh Collins has observed, 'the normal liberty respected in private law, the freedom to choose a contractual partner, was curtailed in order to uphold the importance of the rights of the customers of the hotel to equal treatment and respect'.[61] However, this result was brought about by the application of subordinate legislation rather than through reliance on Convention rights.

A third point to stress is the state-focused nature of the ECHR: because it imposes obligations on states only, the conduct of private persons escapes its net if it cannot be connected to a rights infringement by the state. In this regard, Oliver points to a series of cases in which employees challenged potentially discriminatory workplace practices but the European Court of Human Rights held that it was not an infringement of the right to freedom of thought, conscience and religion in Article 9 to require compliance with employment contracts.[62] As is explained in the discussion of public liability horizontality immediately below, there are cases where the enforcement of an employer's demands does constitute an infringement of the Convention. Nevertheless, this resonates with the remarks in *Horsham Group Properties* noted above: a contractual context appears to render the finding of an infringement less likely.

This survey has revealed a number of factors that have shaped statutory horizontality in Contract law. Three stand out. The first of these is the impact of the nature of the powers granted to the courts by s 3 HRA. Because these are confined to engaging in Convention conforming interpretation and making declarations of incompatibility, courts are limited in their capacity to remould legislation in line with Convention rights. The second factor, which may be connected to this, is that the courts appear to be quick to adopt interpretations and lines of reasoning that avoid a finding of incompatibility. It is clear that they are concerned to avoid second-guessing and modifying legislative judgments about how to balance rights. Third, legislation may be drafted broadly enough already to cover the interest in question, rendering reliance on Convention rights unnecessary.[63] In relation to discrimination, for example, where the Convention could potentially significantly modify the established commitment to freedom of contract, Convention rights are crowded out by more extensive and more detailed legislation and regulations. This goes hand in hand with a fourth factor, which is the limited reach of the Convention rights themselves: there is much that they do not cover.

---

[61]Collins (2014), p. 52.

[62]Oliver (2011), p. 212.

[63]As Mummery LJ observed in relation to the Employment Rights Act: 'It is ... difficult to conceive of a case, in which the unjustified interference with respect for private life under Article 8 (by dismissal for eating cake) would not also be an unfair dismissal under s 98. Put another way, it would not normally be fair for a private sector employer to dismiss an employee for a reason, which was an unjustified interference with the employee's private life. If that is right, there would, in general, be no need for an applicant to invoke Article 8 in order to succeed on the unfair dismissal claim and there would be no question of incompatibility between s 98 of the ERA and Article 8 to attract the application of s 3 of the HRA.' (See *X v Y*, [2004] EWCA Civ 662, para 59).

3 Public Liability Horizontality

Public liability horizontality can arise in three ways. Firstly, because it is unlawful by virtue of s 6(1) HRA 'for a public authority to act in a way which is incompatible with a Convention right', such rights are pertinent in cases where a public authority interacts horizontally, as an equal, with private persons. A contractual relationship with a private person falls into this category. Secondly, public bodies may be obliged to protect Convention rights from infringement by private persons, which gives rise to the possibility of actions brought against public bodies as intermediaries and intended primarily to affect the relations among private persons.[64] Thirdly, s 6(3)(b) HRA defines 'public authority' to include 'any person certain of whose functions are functions of a public nature', although this is qualified by the stipulation in s 6(5) that, '[i]n relation to a particular act, a person is not a public authority by virtue only of subsection 3(b) if the nature of the act is private'. Thus, a private person, whether natural or artificial, is treated as a public authority when performing a public act provided that some of its functions are of a public nature.

The identification of such 'hybrid public authorities' has received considerable attention. Briefly put, the courts have shown themselves reluctant to saddle private persons with Convention rights, identifying hybrid bodies only in straightforward cases such as the exercise by a private organisation of statutory coercive powers[65] or where a private organisation is created and assisted by a public authority to take over the running of a particular public service.[66] This stems from a particular judicial understanding of the purpose of the HRA generally, and s 6 specifically, which surfaced in *Aston Cantlow and Wilmcote with Billesley Parochial Church Council v Wallbank*.[67] For the law lords deciding this case, the purpose of s 6(1) is to subject those bodies for whose acts the state is answerable before the European Court of Human Rights to a domestic law obligation not to act incompatibly with Convention rights.[68] Hence, 'public authority' in s 6(1) is 'essentially a reference to a body whose nature is governmental in the broad sense of the expression', and the factors to take account of include

[64]Leigh (1999) treats this as a distinct type of horizontality, 'intermediate horizontality'.

[65]*R (A) v Partnership in Care Ltd*, [2002] EWHC 529 (Admin), [2002] 1 WLR 2610 (England and Wales High Court (Administrative Division)).

[66]*Poplar Housing and Regeneration Community Association Ltd v Donoghue*, [2001] EWCA Civ 595, [2001] 3 WLR 183 (Court of Appeal (Civil Division)); *R (Beer) v Hampshire Farmer's Markets Ltd*, [2003] EWCA Civ 1056, [2004] 1 WLR 233 (Court of Appeal (Civil Division)).

[67]*Aston Cantlow and Wilmcote with Billesley Parochial Church Council v Wallbank*, [2003] UKHL 37, [2004] 1 AC 546 (House of Lords).

[68]Ibid., see paras 6–7 (Lord Nicholls), 52 (Lord Hope), 88 (Lord Hobhouse) and 171 (Lord Rodger).

> ... the extent to which in carrying out the relevant function the body is publicly funded, or is exercising statutory powers, or is taking the place of central government or local authorities, or is providing a public service.[69]

This approach has been followed in subsequent cases. In *R (West) v Lloyd's of London*,[70] the Court of Appeal held that decisions by Lloyd's of London under powers contained in its byelaws were not subject to challenge by way of judicial review under HRA s 6, as the relationship between Lloyd's and its members was entirely voluntary and contractual and their rights to participate in a syndicate were governed exclusively by the terms of their contracts with their managing agents.[71] The objectives of Lloyd's were 'wholly commercial' and 'not governmental even in the broad sense of that expression'.[72] The courts have also not been prepared to regard the delivery of privatised services[73] or the provision by a private organisation of public services under a contract with a public authority as, of itself, a public function. Affirming the approach adopted by the Court of Appeal in *R (Heather) v Leonard Cheshire Foundation*,[74] a majority in the House of Lords held in *YL v Birmingham City Council*[75] that a private company providing residential and nursing care to the claimant in terms of a contract between them did not fall within s 6(3)(b) HRA, even though this arrangement had been entered into within the framework of a contract that the company had concluded with a local authority in furtherance of the latter's statutory duties to provide residential accommodation. Key considerations for the majority were the commercial character of the undertaking (the 'private, profit earning' nature of the company), the fact that the care recipient was seeking to enforce 'a Private law contract', as well as the fear that the HRA would otherwise bind any commercial company that carried on an operation similar in nature to one carried on by a local authority under statutory powers.[76] Interestingly, Lords Mance and Neuberger took the view that a resident staying privately under a contract with the company and one staying under an arrangement between the company and a local authority should equally be unable to rely on Convention rights against the company as there was no relevant moral distinction

[69]Ibid., para 12 (Lord Nicholls).

[70]*R (West) v Lloyd's of London*, [2004] EWCA Civ 506, [2004] 3 All ER 251 (Court of Appeal (Civil Division)).

[71]Ibid., paras 8–9.

[72]Ibid., para 38, per Brooke LJ.

[73]*Cameron v Network Rail Infrastructure Ltd*, [2006] EWHC 1133 (QB), [2007] 1 WLR 163 (England and Wales High Court (Queen's Bench)); *James v London Electricity Plc*, [2004] EWHC 3226 (QB) (England and Wales High Court (Queen's Bench)).

[74]*R (Heather) v Leonard Cheshire Foundation*, [2002] EWCA Civ 366, [2002] 2 All ER 936 (Court of Appeal (Civil Division)).

[75]*YL v Birmingham City Council*, [2007] UKHL 27, [2007] 3 WLR 112 (House of Lords).

[76]Ibid., paras 30 and 82: Lord Mance raised the position of private contractors cleaning the windows of premises let to council tenants.

between them.[77] The upshot is that the HRA has not served to turn contracts into effective means for protecting vulnerable persons.[78]

The specific effect of these two decisions has been reversed by Parliament,[79] and this line of decisions has attracted much criticism, not least from Paul Craig, who argues that

> . . . the nature of the function does not change if the task is contracted out to a body that is nominally private. It cannot be correct as a matter of principle for the availability of Convention rights to be dependent upon the fortuitous incidence as to how the core public authority chooses to discharge its functions.[80]

However, once it is recognised as a hybrid authority, it is not so easy for a private body to escape the application of Convention rights. Thus, in *R (Weaver) v London and Quadrant Housing Trust*,[81] the Court of Appeal held that the termination of a tenancy by a registered social landlord did not constitute a 'private act' within the meaning of s 6(5) HRA. Especially notable are the following remarks by Elias LJ (with whom Lord Collins of Mapesbury agreed):

> [I]f an act were necessarily a private act because it involved the exercise of rights conferred by private law [including contract], that would significantly undermine the protection which Parliament intended to afford to potential victims of hybrid authorities.

A number of cases involving 'pure' or 'core' public authorities illustrate the reach of Convention rights to encompass contractual relationships between public authorities and private persons.[82] Both the refusal to enter into a contract and the conclusion and content of a contract can be affected.[83] The European Court of Human Rights held in *Stretch v UK* that A1P1 was engaged where a tenant's option to renew a lease was subsequently found to be void as ultra vires the lessor public authority's powers.[84] Several cases involving local authority landlords have applied Article 8 ECHR to the implementation of contracts. *In Lee v Leeds City Council*,[85]

---

[77]Ibid., paras 117–118 and 151.

[78]Choudhry (2013).

[79]Under s 145 of the Health and Social Care Act 2008, the delivery of residential care services in such circumstances amounts to a public function under s 6(3)(b) of the HRA.

[80]Craig (2012), p. 20-024.

[81]*R (Weaver) v London and Quadrant Housing Trust,* [2009] EWCA Civ 587, [2010] 1 WLR 363 (Court of Appeal (Civil Division)).

[82]In addition, actions by public authorities which deprive private persons of contractual rights against other, are also covered as deprivations of possessions under A1P1: *Breyer Group Plc & Ors v Department of Energy and Climate Change,* [2014] EWHC 2257(England and Wales High Court); *James v UK,* [1986] ECHR 2, (1986) 8 EHRR 123 (European Court of Human Rights). This falls outside the scope of this paper.

[83]Beale (2015), pp. 1-076–1-079.

[84]*Stretch,* [2003] ECHR 320. The Court held that: '[A]ccording to the established case law of the Convention organs, "possessions" can be "existing possessions" or assets, including claims, in respect of which the applicant can argue that he has at least a 'legitimate expectation' of obtaining effect enjoyment of a property right."

[85]*Lee,* [2002] EWCA Civ 6.

the Court of Appeal held that, as a public authority, a local government body was under a duty to take steps to ensure that the condition of the houses that they provided did not infringe their tenants' rights to respect of their private and family life under Article 8 ECHR. The steps required to ensure compliance with Article 8 must, however, according to the Court, 'be determined, in each case, by having due regard to the needs and resources of the community and of individuals. . . . The allocation of resources to meet the needs of social housing is very much a matter for democratically determined priorities.'[86] This approach leaves little practical scope for successful reliance on Article 8 even where it applies.

In *Manchester City Council v Pinnock*[87] and in *Hounslow LBC v Powell, Leeds CC v Hall, Birmingham CC v Frisby*,[88] the Supreme Court applied ECHR case law regarding the Article 8 right to respect for one's home to claims for possession brought by public authority landlords upon the termination of leases. In the first of these, the ECtHR's 'unambiguous and consistent approach' led the Supreme Court to abandon the contrary approach endorsed in three previous decisions and to hold that in possession proceedings courts must consider whether the local authority landlord had taken account of its tenant's Article 8 rights. In the second, the Supreme Court held that in all cases where a local authority seeks possession in respect of a property that constitutes a person's home for the purposes of Article 8, the court must have the power to consider whether the order is necessary in a democratic society, meaning that it must be proportionate to a legitimate aim that the local authority is seeking to achieve.

This has been within strict confines, however. The Supreme Court held in *Sims v Dacorum BC* that full respect was accorded to the claimant's Article 8 rights by the facts that his tenancy had been 'determined in accordance with its contractual terms to which . . . he had agreed', he was considered for rehousing, and he could be evicted lawfully only by a court order and with the opportunity to argue that the eviction was disproportionate.[89] The tenancy had been held jointly, and in such cases the common law rule is that, subject to the contract, the tenancy will be terminated by service on the landlord of a notice to quit by only one of the joint tenants. Here the tenancy agreement contained an express term to the same effect, and the necessary notice was served on the local authority landlord by the claimant's joint tenant, his estranged wife. The Court also rejected an attack based on A1P1, adopting counsel's statement that 'the loss of [Mr Sims's] property right is the result of a bargain that he himself made'.[90] The Court did consider whether the contractual term was 'irrational or at least so unreasonable as to offend the right to enjoy the property concerned' but did so assuming (without deciding) that such

---

[86]Ibid., para 49.

[87]*Manchester City Council v Pinnock*, [2010] UKSC 45, [2011] 2 AC 104 (Supreme Court (UK)).

[88]*Hounslow LBC v Powell, Leeds CC v Hall, Birmingham CC v Frisby*, [2011] UKSC 8, [2011] 2 AC 186 (Supreme Court (UK)).

[89]*Sims v Dacorum BC*, [2014] UKSC 63, [2014] 3 WLR 1600 (Supreme Court (UK)), para 23.

[90]Ibid., para 15.

arguments are available in relation to an A1P1 claim.[91] However, because the term 'is consistent with a common law principle which is not now attacked' and 'is not an unreasonable provision, in that someone's interest has to suffer when one of two joint periodic tenants serves a notice to quit',[92] this did not change the outcome.

The second mode of public liability horizontality, which arises from the duties that public bodies may owe to protect Convention rights against infringement by private persons, has had an impact in the employment context. In *Eweida and Others v the United Kingdom*,[93] the ECtHR ruled that the UK had not sufficiently protected the rights of an employee under Article 9 ECHR to manifest her beliefs when it gave effect to the prohibition in her (private) employer's uniform code on the wearing of symbolic religious jewellery. The Court concluded that a fair balance had not been struck between, on the one hand, her desire to manifest her religious belief and to be able to communicate that belief to others by wearing a Christian cross and, on the other hand, her employer's wish to project a certain corporate image (no matter how legitimate that aim might be). However, in the case of a nurse subjected to the same restriction, the Court held in the same proceedings that protection of health and safety on a hospital ward was inherently of much greater importance and that the prohibition had not been disproportionate. In cases such as these, a contracting party is in effect required to explain and justify its choices to the other party, and may find that its liberty of action is limited by the other party's fundamental rights. As this case illustrates, the doctrine of positive obligations exposes the state to liability not only for its statutory rules but also for the operation of its common law rules. The doctrine's radical potential is evident from *Pla and Puncernau v Andorra*, where the ECtHR stated that it would not

> remain passive where a national court's interpretation of a legal act, be it a testamentary disposition, a private contract, a public document, a statutory provision or an administrative practice, appears unreasonable, arbitrary or, as in the present case, blatantly inconsistent with the prohibition of discrimination established by article 14 and more broadly with the principles underlying the Convention.[94]

This holds obvious significance for the largely common-law-based law of contract, not least because under s 6 HRA the courts are obliged to comply with such obligations.[95] The Supreme Court decision in *McDonald* indicates, however, that there is little practical scope for employing this means of horizontality where

---

[91]Ibid., para 16.

[92]Ibid., para 17.

[93]*Eweida and Others v the United Kingdom,* [2013] ECHR 37, [2013] IRLR 231 (European Court of Human Rights).

[94]*Pla and Puncernau v Andorra,* [2004] ECHR 334, (2006) 42 EHRR 25 (European Court of Human Rights).

[95]In *Mustafa and Tarzibachi v Sweden,* (2008) 52 EHRR 24 the European Court of Human Rights held that a court ruling upholding the termination of a lease violated had violated a Convention right in the circumstances of the case.

there is legislation in place that seeks to balance the parties' conflicting interests.[96] The following sections explore this dimension of horizontality further in relation to the common law.

Drawing all this together, the key factors shaping public authority horizontality are the wording of the HRA, especially s 6, and the formulation of the Convention rights. In combination, these have fashioned a judicial understanding of the reach of these documents that attaches strong significance to the private/public distinction, notwithstanding the HRA's recognition of hybrid authorities and widespread privatisation and contracting out of public services. Importantly, the existence of a 'Private law contract' and of a practice of providing the relevant services on commercial terms under contract has been taken to militate against an expansive approach to the opportunities provided by s 6 HRA for public liability horizontality. The enforcement of contractual rights and duties can nevertheless be profoundly affected by the duties of public bodies, including the courts, to protect Convention rights from being infringed by private persons—provided that a pertinent right can be identified.

4 Remedial and Procedural Horizontality

Because s 6(3)(a) HRA expressly includes courts and tribunals in the category of public authorities, the powers of courts to grant remedies and issue orders in disputes among private persons must, in accordance with s 6(1) HRA, be exercised compatibly with Convention rights, at least if they involve the exercise of a discretion.[97] This is clearly pertinent in cases where a court is asked to issue an order, such as an injunction, aimed at preventing an individual from breaching the Convention rights of another individual, but they are not limited to such cases: it also means that the exercise of judicial remedial discretions should not in themselves contravene Convention rights. It has been held that 'when asked to grant injunctive

[96]*McDonald,* [2016] UKSC 28, see especially paras 40 and 45.

[97]Beale (2015), pp. 1-082–1-083. Where it lacks discretion, as Lord Millett explained in *Harrow London Borough Council v Qazi* [2003] UKHL 43, [2004] 1 AC 983 (House of Lords), paras 108–109, the court is 'merely the forum for the determination of the civil right in dispute between the parties' and 'once it concludes that the [claimant] is entitled to an order . . . there is nothing further to investigate'. Where a court gives effect to a mandatory rule the issue falls to be dealt with under s 3 HRA if it is statutory rule (see Lord Nicholls in *Wilson,* [2003] UKHL 40, para 25), and, if a common law rule, raises questions of substantive horizontality (discussed in the next section) if the state is under a pertinent positive obligation.

relief ... the court must consider whether, on the facts of the case, such relief is proportionate in the Convention sense, and grant relief only if it judges it to be so'.[98]

This is of particular importance in the context of Contract law, where some of the most significant remedies, such as the equitable remedies of specific performance and injunction, are discretionary rather than available as of right.[99] As a rule, the courts only exercise that discretion in favour of ordering specific performance if damages would not be an adequate remedy in the circumstances of the case.[100] There are also statutory remedial discretions, such as the power to award damages in lieu of rescission for misrepresentation or the determination of the 'just sum' for the purposes of relief on frustration.[101]

A number of Convention rights are potentially relevant, especially to specific performance. The Article 4 prohibition on forced or compulsory labour could be engaged by an order of specific performance of an employment contract, for example. The Article 6 right to a fair trial, which covers the determination of civil rights and obligations, is also potentially relevant but has been held to cover only procedural matters.[102] The right in Article 8 to respect for a person's private and family life, home and correspondence could be relevant in an appropriate case, especially when a contract is concerned with residential premises, as could the Article 9 right to freedom of conscience and religion, especially in the context of employment contracts, and the rights to freedom of expression in Article 10 and freedom of association and assembly in Article 11. In *Ashworth v The Royal National Theatre*,[103] Cranston J applied Article 10 in deciding whether to grant an interim injunction until trial to claimants who were disputing the termination of their employment as musicians by the defendant theatre. The injunction was refused, as it would interfere with the National Theatre's right of artistic freedom without justification—the claimants could exercise *their* rights under Article 10 by playing their instruments elsewhere, while their contractual rights could be adequately protected by an award of damages.[104]

The most significant case so far has been *McDonald v McDonald*, where all three judicial levels refused to subject a private landlord's claim for possession against a residential occupier upon termination of a tenancy agreement to a proportionality analysis in eviction proceedings in the light of s 6 HRA and Art 8 HRA. Although this case concerns the enforcement of property rights and was decided within the

---

[98] *South Buckinghamshire District Council v Porter*, [2003] UKHL 26, [2003] 2 AC 558 (House of Lords). This was a planning control case, brought under the Town and Country Planning Act 1990.

[99] Beale (2015), pp. 27-034 f. and 27-065 ff.

[100] Beale (2015), pp. 27-005 ff.

[101] Misrepresentation Act 1967 s 2(2); Law Reform (Frustrated Contracts) Act 1943 s 1(3).

[102] See above text to n 31 and below text to n 148.

[103] *Ashworth v The Royal National Theatre*, [2014] EWHC 1176 (QB), [2014] 4 All ER 238 (England and Wales High Court (Queen's Bench)).

[104] Ibid., paras 27 and 31–33.

particular statutory context of the Housing Act 1988,[105] the Supreme Court's reasoning is relevant also to contractual litigation between private parties. One important aspect of this is their lordships' fear that '[t]o hold otherwise would involve the Convention effectively being directly enforceable as between private citizens so as to alter their contractual rights and obligations, whereas the purpose of the Convention is, as we have mentioned, to protect citizens from having their rights infringed by the state'.[106] In their view, applying a proportionality analysis to the enforcement of the landlord's rights 'would also mean that the Convention could be invoked to interfere with the A1P1 rights of the landlord, and in a way which was unpredictable'.[107] More generally, their lordships were concerned that, because Article 8 could only be invoked in cases where a private person 'was either required by law, or voluntarily chose, to enforce its rights through the court, as opposed to taking the law into its own hands—e.g. by changing the locks when the residential occupier was absent'—a 'perverse incentive' might be created for pursuing self-help 'rather than the more civilised course of seeking possession through the courts'.[108] These remarks reveal little judicial appetite for human rights constraints to the granting of judicial remedies, an attitude which is likely to be reinforced in the contractual context where self-help remedies, such as termination, are frequently available. Strikingly, the Court found a 'sharp contrast' between disputes resulting 'from contractual arrangements made between two private parties' and those arising 'from tortious or quasi-tortious relationships, where the legislature has expressly, impliedly or through inaction, left it to the courts to carry out the balancing exercise'.[109]

Generally, the fact that only monetary remedies such as damages are available as of right, coupled with long-established practices in the exercise of the discretion concerning the equitable remedies, leaves no meaningful practical space for the application of Convention rights. The discretionary nature of their remedial powers enables the courts to carefully consider the circumstances of each case,[110] while the very fact of the secondary role of specific performance reflects an assiduous concern for individual liberty, reflected, for example, in the standard refusal to order specific performance of employment contracts.[111] Moreover, the courts have

[105] *McDonald*, [2016] UKSC 28, para 44. The Supreme Court saw this as a case where the court is merely the forum for the determination of the civil rights of the parties with nothing further to investigate once it has determined these.

[106] Ibid., para 41.

[107] Ibid.

[108] Ibid., para 42.

[109] Ibid., para 46.

[110] How much flexibility there is, is a complex matter, and depends on how the choice between damages and specific performance is described. The orthodox test of inadequacy of damages appears less flexible than the test of appropriateness of specific performance found in *Tito v Waddell (No.2)*, [1977] Ch. 106 (Court of Appeal), 322. See Peel (2015), 1106.

[111] See Beale (2015), p. 27-05; also the reasoning of Lord Hoffmann in *Co-operative Insurance Society Ltd v Argyll Stores (Holding) Ltd*, [1998] AC 1 (House of Lords).

long exercised their remedial discretion in a manner that takes account of the interests now protected by Convention rights. For example, specific performance was ordered in respect of an agreement to lease premises to a political organisation for a public meeting because of this advanced freedom of political speech and assembly.[112] On the other hand, although specific performance of contracts to sell land is (by way of exception to the general rule) normally granted, such an order is refused where granting it would cause particular hardship to a person by depriving them of their home.[113]

Article 1 of Protocol 1 has the greatest potential relevance to judicial remedies for breach. If, as the courts have held, a contractual claim is a possession,[114] does it not deprive the creditor of his possession if he is unable to obtain the promised performance as such but is confined to a money claim?[115] This does not appear yet to have been argued before a court, and the prospects for the success of such an argument are very slim indeed. It is, firstly, doubtful that there is in such circumstances a deprivation of a contractual claim. Following Lord Hope's approach in *Wilson*,[116] this is so because contractual rights are from their inception subject to this remedial state of affairs: they do not limit any existing rights but determine the contours with which they come into existence. In any event, whereas in *Wilson* 'the lender's rights were extinguished', in the words of Lord Nicholls,[117] the right to performance remains very much in force as it underwrites the entitlement to damages. As Lord Hoffmann made clear, the primacy of damages is also not arbitrary but based on a coherent set of reasons.[118] It therefore fulfils a legitimate purpose of some weight and falls within the public interest exception to the right. As importantly, specific performance is not excluded altogether but remains available if there is a particular need on the facts of a given case for such an order. Overall, the approach of English law therefore appears to strike a reasonable balance between the interests of the perpetrator and the victim of a breach of contract, leaving no meaningful scope for horizontal application of Convention rights.

---

[112] *Verrall v Great Yarmouth Borough Council,* [1981] QB 202 (CA) (Court of Appeal) (specific performance granted where the defendant council had agreed to let a public hall for two days to the National Front but refused to go ahead with it after an election resulted in a change of political control).

[113] *Patel v Ali,* [1984] Ch 283(High Court) (specific performance refused when sought by buyer of a house 4 years after sale; by then, seller had become very ill). See also Beale and Pittam (2001), p. 157.

[114] *Wilson,* [2003] UKHL 40, para 39; *Breyer Group Plc & Ors v Department of Energy and Climate Change,* [2014] EWHC 2257 (England and Wales High Court), para 45: 'the existence of a concluded contract is capable of constituting a possession for the purposes of A1P1'.

[115] See e.g. the critique by Shiffrin (2006–2007), pp. 722–724.

[116] *Wilson,* [2003] UKHL 40, para 107.

[117] Ibid., para 44.

[118] Beale (2015), p. 16. See also *Lamare v Dixon,* (1873) LR 6 HL 414 (House of Lords), p. 423; *Holliday v Lockwood,* [1917] 2 Ch 56 (High Court (Chancery Division)), p. 57.

5 Substantive Horizontality

Substantive horizontality refers to the effect of Convention rights on the substantive rights and duties that private persons have against each other irrespective of legislation. It is especially pertinent to Contract law, which is largely a product of judicial development of the common law and equity.[119] There appears to be broad agreement that, in the words of Lord Rodger, enforcing these rights 'may require a court to modify the common law'[120] and in that event 'a court must balance the interests of both parties'.[121] This effect can, however, vary along a spectrum ranging from 'weak indirect horizontal effect', which imposes 'an obligation on courts to develop the common law so as to reflect the values underpinning the Convention rights',[122] through strong indirect horizontal effect requiring development of the common law 'to ensure its compatibility with Convention rights themselves',[123] to direct horizontality when courts are 'required to create appropriate rights and remedies by revising the common law to protect Convention rights'.[124]

Which of these fits best with the HRA against the background of UK constitutional and legal traditions, and which has received judicial endorsement, has been hotly debated by a wide range of eminent authors.[125] Given the aims of this chapter, there is no need here to take sides. The very existence of this debate is nevertheless highly relevant to the quest for understanding the factors shaping fundamental rights horizontality in English Contract law. The debate itself generates part of the environment within which that process takes place and reflects deep features of both the HRA itself and its interaction with the legal landscape in which it has been placed.

Although the evidence is sparse, there appears to be even less judicial inclination towards direct horizontality in contract cases than elsewhere in English Private law.[126] Thus, in *Horsham Group Properties Ltd v Clark*,[127] it was Briggs J's conclusion that a mortgagor 'lost her equity of redemption by virtue of the exercise of powers conferred purely by contract',[128] rather than as a result of the statutory power to appoint a receiver, that led him to hold that A1P1 was not infringed. On his reasoning, the contractual nature of the power precluded the application of the

---

[119]Ibbetson (1999), Chs. 11–13.

[120]*Wilson,* [2003] UKHL 40, para 180.

[121]Ibid., para 181.

[122]Young (2011), p. 40.

[123]Ibid., pp. 40–41.

[124]Leigh (1999), p. 86.

[125]See the literature cited in Young (2011), p. 16 f. 1; Beale (2015), p. 1-084 f. 622.

[126]Compare, for example, the emergence and elaboration of a privacy tort. See Phillipson (2011).

[127]*Horsham Group Properties Ltd,* [2008] EWHC 2327 (Ch) (England and Wales High Court (Chancery Division)).

[128]Ibid., para 33.

Convention: although a mortgagor's equity of redemption did amount to a 'possession' for the purposes A1P1, the latter was not infringed by its loss because the statutory provision 'serves to implement rather than override the private bargain between mortgagor and mortgagee'.[129] The reach of A1P1 was of course crucial in shaping this outcome,[130] but it is noteworthy that Briggs J's reasoning also reflects the broader presupposition that Convention rights do not apply directly to private contracts.

This follows the path taken by the European Commission for Human Rights in two admissibility decisions concerning cases brought against the United Kingdom. *Di Palma v UK*[131] arose from the exercise of a forfeiture clause in a private lease of a flat. Most leases in England contain such a clause, which provides for termination by the landlord upon non-payment of rent or breach of another term of the lease. Because of the potentially draconian consequences, especially where a long lease still has a substantial period left, statute provides for relief against forfeiture. Due to bad statutory drafting (since rectified), the 99-year lease in question fell outside the relevant provisions so that no English court could grant relief to the tenant when it was forfeited by the landlord for non-payment of £299 in service charges just a few years after being granted. The tenant's application to Strasbourg, which was based on Articles 6, 8, 13 and 14 and on A1P1, was rejected by the Commission as manifestly ill-founded since the UK's Convention responsibilities were not engaged by an 'exclusively private law relationship between the parties'.[132] In the Commission's view, it made no difference that a domestic court had made the orders granting forfeiture and refusing relief, as the court 'merely provided a forum for the determination of the civil right in dispute between the parties'.[133] The state would be implicated only if it was 'under a positive obligation to protect the ... rights of an individual in the context of their dispute with another individual'.[134] In *Wood v United Kingdom*,[135] similar reasoning led to the conclusion that a mortgagor had no Article 8 complaint if a private sector mortgagee obtained repossession of a home after non-payment of instalments due under a mortgage that gave the mortgagee the right to seek repossession. The Commission found that repossession was in accordance with domestic law and 'necessary for the protection of the rights and freedoms of others, namely the lender', as well as 'in the public interest ... in ensuring payment of contractual debts'.

Regardless of where on the spectrum of horizontal effect the influence of the HRA is located, the fact that English Contract law is a creature of judge-made

[129] Ibid., para 35.

[130] He emphasises that 'Miss Beech lost her equity of redemption without any State intervention at all' (para 33).

[131] *Di Palma v UK*, (1988) 10 EHRR 149 (European Court of Human Rights).

[132] Ibid., p. 154.

[133] Ibid., p. 155.

[134] Ibid., p. 210.

[135] *Wood v United Kingdom*, (1997) 24 EHRR 69 (European Court of Human Rights).

common law (and equity) rather than statute, at least as far as its general principles are concerned, means that substantive horizontality has the potential to reach much further into Contract law than the other types discussed so far. Significantly, it also appears to be the one to which the courts have been least amenable. The courts' lack of enthusiasm for substantive horizontality is especially evident from the judicial reaction to two Convention-based attacks on long-established common law doctrines. The first concerns contracts that are illegal; the second, the treatment of fraudulent claims under contracts of insurance. It is also visible in how the courts respond when agreements relating to litigation and arbitration are challenged on Convention grounds and to attempts to extend the application of Convention rights to public sector leases to private rental agreements. These four groups of cases deserve closer examination.

5.1 *Illegal Contracts*

The classic statement of the principle governing illegal contracts is by Lord Mansfield CJ in *Holman v Johnson*[136]:

> No court will lend its aid to a man who founds his cause of action upon an immoral or an illegal act. If, from the plaintiff's own stating or otherwise, the cause of action appears to arise ex turpi causa, or the transgression of a positive law of this country, there the court says he has no right to be assisted.

In accordance with this, the courts have long refused to award any remedy at all—not only can such a contract not be enforced, but a party who has conferred a benefit on another party to such a contract is also not permitted to recover that benefit by way of an unjust enrichment claim.

The Supreme Court has now adopted a more flexible approach, assessing the policy underlying the prohibition, other relevant policies, and the proportionality of denying a remedy.[137] Prior to this change, the compatibility of the second aspect of the principle with the HRA/ECHR was considered by the Court of Appeal in *Al-Kishtaini v Shanshal*.[138] Here the claimant sought to recover a sum of money paid to the defendant as part of a transaction that contravened regulations implementing United Nations sanctions against Iraq. It was argued that the trial court's dismissal of the claim by reason of the illegality of the transaction was incompatible with A1P1 as a deprivation of the claimant's right to possession of the money claimed. It is not altogether surprising that this aspect of the principle should have been challenged, for it has long been recognised, in the words of Lord Goff in *Tinsley v Milligan*, that 'the principle is not a principle of justice; it is a principle of

[136]*Holman v Johnson*, (1775) 1 Cowp 341 (King's Bench).

[137]*Patel v Mirza*, [2016] UKSC 42, [2016] 3 WLR 399 (Supreme Court (UK)), para 120 (Lord Toulson).

[138]*Al-Kishtaini v Shanshal*, [2001] EWCA Civ 264 (Court of Appeal (Civil Division)).

policy, whose application is indiscriminate and so can lead to unfair consequences as between parties to litigation'.[139]

The claim was nevertheless dismissed by a unanimous Court of Appeal. All three judges held that the illegality defence to an unjust enrichment claim clearly falls within the public interest exception to A1P1 as pursuing a legitimate aim through proportionate means. In coming to this conclusion, Mummery LJ stated that the requirement of proportionality was satisfied in this case because of 'the very high public interest originating in the resolutions of the Security Council of the United Nations in an international emergency' and because the plaintiff could have avoided the prohibition by obtaining advance clearance from the Treasury.[140] Interestingly, Rix LJ observed that, in light of Lord Goff's critical remarks on the principle noted above:

> It may therefore be insufficient merely to say that the rule is founded in the public interest. It may be necessary to justify the rule's application in the instant case as representing that "fair balance", between the demands of the general interest and the requirements of the protection of an individual's fundamental rights.[141]

On the basis of essentially the same considerations as those cited by Mummery LJ, he concluded that this justificatory burden was easily met on the facts of the case.[142]

This leaves open the possibility that the refusal to allow a restitutionary claim might be held to be disproportionate in a case where the public interest in the illegality is less strong.[143] It is therefore also important to emphasise that the Court expressly refrained from deciding that the claimant could invoke A1P1, going no further than assuming that he could do so. Rix LJ questioned whether there was any deprivation of possessions in a case such as this, 'for ... the claimant's cause of action is itself only acquired by reason of the claimant's illegal and prohibited act'.[144] He also did not endorse 'the claimant's submission that he is entitled to invoke Convention rights in respect of private claims'.[145]

In *Soteriou v Ultrachem Ltd*,[146] the claimant attacked the other aspect of this principle, that a remedy will not be granted to enforce an illegal contract. This, too, was unsuccessful. The High Court rejected a challenge based on Article 6 ECHR mainly on the ground that the principle is 'part and parcel of the substantive law of contract'[147] and thus not 'a procedural bar so as to engage Article 6'.[148] A challenge

[139] *Tinsley v Milligan*, [1994] 1 AC 340, p. 335 (House of Lords).

[140] *Al-Kishtaini*, [2001] EWCA Civ 264, paras 58–59.

[141] Ibid., para 96.

[142] Ibid., paras 97–98.

[143] McKendrick (2013), p. 14.

[144] *Al-Kishtaini*, [2001] EWCA Civ 264, para 95.

[145] Ibid.

[146] *Soteriou*, [2004] EWHC 983 (QB).

[147] Ibid., para 73.

[148] Ibid., paras 72 and 75.

founded on A1P1 was likewise rejected because 'the unenforceability of the contract results in there being no possession in the shape of a claim of which the claimant has been deprived of by the court'.[149] Here the High Court echoed the approach to these articles adopted by the majority of the law lords in *Wilson* in respect of statutory grounds of unenforceability.[150] Regarding A1P1, the judge added:

> Whilst it may be that the claim for breach of contract can be regarded as a "possession", . . . the claimant has not been "deprived" of it. On the contrary, he commenced his claim and that part of it that involved examination of the enforceability of the contract in the event of illegality was fully litigated.[151]

The court also examined, for the purposes of both articles, the justifiability and proportionality of the principle and concluded that it passed muster: the law as to illegality fulfils a legitimate purpose of considerable importance,[152] and, at least on the facts of this case, unenforceability of the claim was a proportionate response.

It is not obvious that the *Wilson* approach to A1P1 is also apt for common law restrictions on enforceability. The reason for such doubt lies in the difference between the courts' powers in respect of statutory provisions and common law principles. Whereas the courts do not have the power to modify the former, but are restricted to making a declaration of incompatibility and Convention-conforming interpretation,[153] they are able to change the common law. Thus, while any statutory restriction must, once properly interpreted, be treated as fixed, a common law restriction of a right remains open to modification and judicial development. The possibility of doing so in response to A1P1 should not be dismissed from the outset. Just as the right is from its inception subject to the common law principle, which may render it unenforceable, so too, one might argue, is that principle inherently subject to the courts' power to modify the common law.

Soteriou nevertheless does not appear to leave any scope for applying either of these two general Convention rights to substantive common law contractual principles applicable between private persons. Article 6 does not cover them because they are not procedural, and A1P1 lacks bite even if the objection raised in the previous paragraph is accepted because the claim can still be litigated before a court and the impact of the common law principle on the contract examined.

Interestingly, these two decisions diverge from earlier observations by the Law Commission. Its 1999 Consultation Paper on *Reform of the Law relating to Illegality of Contracts and Trusts* concluded that 'there is a . . . risk of successful challenge under the present common law illegality rules, which provide no

[149]Ibid., para 96. Also para 90: 'Where there is no "contractual bite", as Miss Eady put it, the claimant does not have possession of contractual rights that are eligible for protection.'

[150]*Wilson,* [2016] UKSC 28, paras 106–108, 136–137 and 168.

[151]*Soteriou,* [2004] EWHC 983 (QB), para 96.

[152]This was found to be deterrence, punishment, and respect for the court and the preservation of the rule of law. *Soteriou,* [2004] EWHC 983 (QB), para 76.

[153]See the discussion of statutory horizontality above.

opportunity to assess the proportionality of allowing an illegality defence to defeat the plaintiff's claim to his or her usual rights and remedies and do not apply any test based on the public interest'.[154] In its eventual Report, the Commission nevertheless decided not to recommend new legislation but believed that 'the illegality defence should be left to developments in the common law'.[155] It is significant that the Supreme Court has recently adopted such a more flexible approach, as mentioned above[156]—notably, however, without relying on human rights considerations.

5.2 *Insurance Contracts*

A1P1 was again invoked before the Court of Appeal in *Versloot Dredging BV & Anor v HDI Gerling Industrie Versicherung AG, The DC Merwestone*[157] to support a challenge to a well-established common law doctrine in the field of insurance law. According to this doctrine, an insured who employs a 'fraudulent device' by embellishing his claim under an insurance policy with a lie forfeits the whole claim even if it would otherwise have been recoverable in full.[158] Here it was 'common ground between the parties that the Court should, so far as possible, develop the common law in a way that gives effect to the ECHR or, as it has been put, to "*weave the Convention rights into the principles of the common law and of equity*"', and the Court accepted that it was incumbent upon it to consider A1P1.[159] In contrast to *Soteriou*, neither the parties nor the Court doubted that the contractual claim in question was a 'possession' for the purpose of A1P1.[160] The Court's reasoning accordingly focused on whether this doctrine pursued a legitimate aim by proportionate means.

There was no doubt that the fraudulent device doctrine pursues a legitimate public policy aim: it plainly seeks to deter fraud in the making of claims.[161] Whether it is a proportionate means of securing that aim was contentious, however,

[154]The Law Commission (1999) Illegal transactions: The effect of illegality on contracts and trusts. Consultation Paper No. 154.

[155]The Law Commission (2010) The Illegality Defence. Consultation Paper No. 189, para 1.8.

[156]*Patel*, [2016] UKSC 42, para 120.

[157]*Versloot Dredging BV & Anor v HDI Gerling Industrie Versicherung AG, The DC Merwestone*, [2014] EWCA Civ 1349, [2015] QB 608 (Court of Appeal (Civil Division)).

[158]*Agapitos v Agnew, The Aegean* [2002] EWCA Civ 247, [2003] QB 556 (Court of Appeal (Civil Division)).

[159]*The DC Merwestone*, [2014] EWCA Civ 1349, paras 141, 142.

[160]The Underwriters, who were relying on the common law principle, accepted 'that an amount payable under an insurance contract – a right which accrues at the time of loss – is a "possession" within the meaning of the Article and that forfeiture of an insurance claim is an interference that engages Article 1'—*The DC Merwestone*, [2014] EWCA Civ 1349, para 141.

[161]Ibid., para 145.

principally because its consequences are harsh and ignore the gravity or culpability of the device:

> The same consequence applies . . . to the man who claims a large sum for a totally fictitious loss as it does to someone who has a house and contents claim worth £ 500,000 including the real loss of a computer, who provides an invoice for a similar one which he has not lost because he cannot be bothered to find the right one.[162]

Notwithstanding its severity, the Court upheld the doctrine on the basis that the employment of 'a bright line rule' was proportionate. It only applies in a case of 'fraud, which crosses a moral red line, and has . . . "a fundamental impact upon the parties' relationships", and may be difficult to detect'.[163] Moreover, a case-by-case determination of the extent of forfeiture that would be just and proportionate would give rise to unpredictability, litigation and dilemmas of incommensurability, as well as dilute the deterrent effect.[164]

This line of reasoning brings to light something of the values that shape the way in which the courts approach the potential impact of Convention rights. As revealing and significant is the court's reliance on the ECtHR's observation in *Pye v UK*[165] that a margin of appreciation was particularly essential in commercial matters as providing 'an indication that in this field the range within which a measure may be treated as proportionate is greater than in others'.[166] Thus, the Court attaches special significance to the fact that those who challenged the fraudulent device rule 'invoke the Convention not in respect of some legislative or administrative act but in relation to the operation of a common law doctrine which is an incident of a commercial relationship of a special character'.[167] This chimes with the courts' deeply entrenched concern for the needs of commerce, as does the assertion by Clarke LJ:

> [T]he court should, in my view, be reluctant now to characterise as disproportionate a common law doctrine of general application, which, so far as fraudulent claims is concerned, is of long standing, and which has operated in the insurance field for over 150 years. The fraudulent claims doctrine arises, as Lord Mance put it, "from a perception of appropriate policy and jurisprudence on the part of our 19th century predecessors, which time has done nothing to alter". The need to deter fraud which underlies the fraudulent claims doctrine applies also to fraudulent devices and, although the rule in relation to the latter was most clearly expounded only 12 years ago in *The Aegeon*, it has been applied both before and since.[168]

Moreover, although the Court of Appeal was willing in this case to scrutinise the compatibility of a horizontal common law rule with Convention rights, it was not

[162]Ibid., para 147.

[163]Ibid., para 155.

[164]Ibid., paras 157–8.

[165]*Pye v UK,* (2008) 46 EHRR 1083 (European Court of Human Rights).

[166]*The DC Merwestone,* [2014] EWCA Civ 1349, para 160.

[167]Ibid.

[168]Ibid., para 162.

prepared to apply such rights directly to resolve the conflict between the parties.[169] This focus on the proportionality of the rule rather than the proportionality of the deprivation in the individual case has been criticised as inconsistent with recent decisions of the Supreme Court.[170] However, these cases concerned statutory provisions, where, as was noted above, the courts are not able to develop the rule itself. Where a common law principle is at issue, the courts do have such power and thus have both the responsibility to reflect on the rule itself and the means to mould the rule to Convention requirements. There is no reason to assume in advance that those requirements can only be met by a common law rule that requires a case-by-case proportionality assessment. As the survey in this chapter shows, the focus on the implications of Convention rights for the rule rather than on private persons is also in keeping with the approach adopted in other cases involving substantive horizontality.

When *The DC Merwestone* reached the Supreme Court, the human rights arguments fell by the wayside. A majority of 4 to 1 reversed the Court of Appeal, holding that the fraudulent device rule did not cover collateral lies. For the majority, the questions regarding A1P1 therefore did not arise.[171] Lord Mance nevertheless briefly expressed his agreement with the reasoning of the Court of Appeal.[172]

5.3 *Litigation and Arbitration Agreements*

The question whether an agreement is rendered unenforceable by virtue of itself contravening a Convention right has received attention in the context of agreements to waive Article 6 rights. In light of the decision by the ECtHR that 'neither the letter nor the spirit of [Article 6(1)] prevents a person from waiving of his own free will, either expressly or tacitly, the entitlement to have his case heard in public',[173] the Court of Appeal has upheld a contractual undertaking by a litigant that he will not proceed to trial upon a dispute unless he has issued proceedings by a particular date,[174] as well as a clause requiring arbitration under the Arbitration Act 1996 of

[169]Ibid., paras 143, 154, 158 and 164.

[170]Davey and Richards (2015), pp. 322–323, referring to *Axa General Insurance Ltd v The Lord Advocate,* [2011] UKSC 46 [2012] 1 AC 868 (Supreme Court (UK)), para 128 and *Barnes v The Eastenders Group* [2014] UKSC 26, [2015] AC 1 (Supreme Court (UK)) para 94. The authors also deny that the case-by-case assessment of proportionality would dramatically increase insurance litigation.

[171]*The DC Merwestone,* [2014] EWCA Civ 1349, para 37.

[172]Ibid., para 132.

[173]*Hakansson v Sweden,* (1991) 13 EHRR 1 (European Court of Human Rights), para 66.

[174]*Di Placito v Slater,* [2003] EWCA Civ 1863, [2004] 1 WLR 1605 (Court of Appeal (Civil Division)).

disputes between the parties,[175] and an agreement not to appeal an arbitration award under s 69 of this Act.[176] In these cases, the Court concluded that English law met the requirement under Article 6 that its waiver must take place without compulsion or constraint.

A striking feature of the reasoning in these cases is the Court's finding that this requirement is met in English law by the principles of duress, undue influence and mistake, as well as the restrictive approach, articulated in *Interfoto Library Ltd v Stiletto Ltd*,[177] to the incorporation of an onerous or unusual clause into a contract.[178] In *Sumukan Ltd v The Commonwealth Secretariat*, the Court of Appeal considered whether the application of Article 6 would alter the conclusion that an agreement to waive the right to appeal an arbitration award was not an unusual or onerous clause to which the *Interfoto* principle would ordinarily be applied.[179] The Court concluded that it would not.[180]

This recognition that it is by virtue of the existing principles of Contract law that English law is compatible with the Convention highlights the role of the present state of the law as a factor in shaping substantive horizontality. Little if any room is left for this type of influence if the common law principles are already Convention compatible.

5.4 *Private Leases*

The application of Article 8 ECHR to the termination of leases has also been pressed outside the context of public sector housing discussed above,[181] but without success. Observations in *Harrow LBC v Qazi*[182] suggested that the positions of private and public landlords are distinct.[183] Lord Hope tied this to the ambit of Article 8, observing that, according to the Strasbourg jurisprudence, 'the object of Article 8 is to protect the individual against arbitrary interference *by the public authorities* with his right to privacy and that it is not concerned, as such, with the

175 *Stretford, v The Football Association Ltd* [2007] EWCA Civ 238, [2007] 2 Lloyd's Rep 31 (Court of Appeal (Civil Division)).

176 *Sumukan Ltd v The Commonwealth Secretariat,* [2007] EWCA Civ 243, [2007] 2 Lloyd's Rep. 87 (Court of Appeal (Civil Division)), paras 53–62.

177 *Interfoto Library Ltd v Stiletto Ltd,* [1989] 1QB 433 (Court of Appeal (Civil Division)).

178 See *Stretford,* [2007] EWCA Civ 238 and *Sumukan,* [2007] EWCA Civ 243, paras 53–62.

179 *Sumukan,* [2007] EWCA Civ 243, para 60.

180 Ibid., para 61.

181 See discussion on Public Authority Horizontality discussed in Sect. 2 above.

182 *Qazi,* [2003] UKHL 43.

183 Ibid., para 23 (Lord Bingham); para 26 concurring (Lord Steyn) (both expressly refraining from commenting on whether a private landlord is bound) and paras 52–53 (Lord Hope).

protection of his right to own or to occupy property'.[184] In *Pinnock*, the leading decision on public landlords, the Supreme Court subsequently noted that '[c]onflicting views have been expressed both domestically and in Strasbourg' on this issue and insisted that nothing said in this case was 'intended to bear on cases where the person seeking the order for possession is a private landowner'.[185] In *Sims v Dacorum BC*, a unanimous Supreme Court stated that '[n]o judgment of the Strasbourg court begins to justify . . . [the] proposition' that a notice to quite by a joint tenant infringed another joint tenant's Article 8 right to a home.[186] In *McDonald v McDonald*, the Court has now ruled definitively that in possession proceedings instituted by private landlords under s 21 of the Housing Act 1988, courts are not obliged to engage in an Article 8 proportionality exercise so as to balance the parties' rights.[187]

Crucial to this outcome was the distinction between private and public status. While 'public authorities are obliged to use their powers lawfully in accordance with the general principles of public law', their lordships stated, 'a private landlord . . . is entitled to recover possession of his property in accordance with the law for whatever reason he likes'.[188] Thus, 'a private landlord . . . is not obliged to act compatibly with the Convention rights' by s 6(1) HRA[189] but does enjoy A1P1 rights, which would have to be balanced against a tenant's rights.[190] While recognising the potential impact of positive public duties to protect private rights, the Court adopted a strict approach that leaves only limited opportunity for achieving horizontal effect via this route. It rejected an argument relying on *Mustafa and Tarzibachi v Sweden*,[191] where the ECtHR had held that the applicants' Article 10 rights had been violated when they were evicted by a court order at the suit of their private landlord, who had terminated their tenancy for installing a satellite dish in breach of contract. The Supreme Court took this to mean only that, in the absence of legislation, the applicant's rights would be infringed 'unless the [Swedish] court had power to give effect to such rights *despite* the terms of the relevant contract'.[192] It therefore did 'not consider that this decision involved holding that article 10 could be invoked to vary the contractual rights as agreed between two private persons, in a case such as the present, where there is no suggestion that the

[184]Ibid., para 53. Emphasis added.

[185]*Pinnock,* [2010] UKSC 45, para 50.

[186]*Sims,* [2014] UKSC 63, para 22. Similarly it was held in *Austin Hall Building v Buckland Securities* [2001] EWHC 434 (TCC) [2001] BLR 272 that the HRA does not apply to adjudication under construction contracts because the adjudicator is not a public authority for the purposes of the HRA.

[187]*McDonald,* [2016] UKSC 28, para 69.

[188]Ibid., para 64.

[189]Ibid., para 66.

[190]Ibid., para 39.

[191]*Tarzibachi v Sweden,* [2008] 52 EHRR 24 (European Court of Human Rights).

[192]*McDonald,* [2016] UKSC 28, para 57.

legislature has failed to protect the relevant Convention rights'.[193] Nor did the Court think that there was any scope for applying *Pla and Puncernau v Andorra*[194]: this case concerned matters that were 'a long way from what this case is about'.[195]

5.5 Factors Shaping Substantive Horizontality

A common thread running through the cases surveyed in this section is that the legitimacy of horizontal application was typically assumed by the courts rather than decided. Moreover, the courts have invariably found that the existing law passes muster as pursuing a legitimate public aim through proportionate means.[196] As in the case of statutory horizontality, judicial reasoning tends to favour an analysis that treats restrictions as inherent limitations rather than subsequent deprivations, and to emphasise the limits of the Convention rights.[197] In addition, a number of normative commitments have served to inhibit substantive horizontality: predictability, minimising litigation and commercial needs.[198]

Underlying this are two mutually reinforcing features of the human rights norms applicable under the HRA, both flowing from the character of the ECHR as an international treaty that imposes obligations on states. The first is that, as the Commission recognised in *Di Palma*, state responsibility must be engaged for a Convention right to have any bite.[199] Although this can occur, as the Commission noted, where the state is under a positive obligation to protect an individual's rights, a second feature of the Convention restricts access to this route to horizontality: Convention rights and duties were drafted with state interferences with private individuals in mind and thus do not necessarily cover the conflicts of interest that might arise among individuals.

The impact of these two factors is evident, particularly in *The DC Merwestone*[200] and *McDonald v McDonald*.[201] These judgments reveal how this leads to a focus on the state of the law rather than on the position of the parties in their concrete circumstances. This directs attention to whether the pertinent common law principle satisfies Convention requirements such as the pursuit of a legitimate purpose

---

193 Ibid.

194 *Sims*, [2014] UKSC 63, para 16.

195 Ibid.

196 *Al-Kishtaini*, [2001] EWCA Civ 264, paras 58–59 and 97–98; *Soteriou*, [2004] EWHC 983 (QB), para 76; *The DC Merwestone*, [2014] EWCA Civ 1349, paras 145, 155 and 162. See also *Sims*, [2014] UKSC 63, para 17.

197 *Al-Kishtaini*, [2001] EWCA Civ 264, para 95; *Soteriou*, [2004] EWHC 983 (QB), para 96.

198 *The DC Merwestone*, [2014] EWCA Civ 1349, paras 145, 160 and 162.

199 *Di Palma* [1988] 10 EHRR 149, p. 154.

200 *DC Merwestone*, [2014] EWCA Civ 1349.

201 *McDonald*, [2016] UKSC 28.

and proportionality. As these are very broad requirements, it is surely unsurprising that they were held to be satisfied by the common law in all the cases surveyed in this section: it is hardly likely that principles gradually fashioned by the courts in the process of resolving private conflicts would fall foul of requirements of this kind.[202]

The quick and decisive dispatch of *Mustafa* and *Pla* in *McDonald* is especially noteworthy, as these decisions seem to signal a departure by the ECtHR from the depiction in *Di Palma* of a (domestic) court as providing no more than a forum for the determination of rights in private disputes.[203] Although in *Mustafa* the ECtHR still maintains that it 'is not in theory required to settle disputes of a purely private nature', these decisions manifest a marked willingness nevertheless to apply the Convention to court decisions in private disputes and to assess the domestic law that 'made lawful the treatment of which the applicants complained'.[204] The reference in *Pla* to a judicial interpretation of a private contract that 'appears unreasonable' or 'blatantly inconsistent ... with the principles underlying the Convention'[205] is particularly suggestive as this is, along with the implication of terms, a well-established, and judicially preferred, mechanism for balancing contracting parties' rights and controlling their conduct towards one another.[206] *McDonald* strikes a decidedly more cautious note about the impact of Convention rights on private contracts, with *Di Palma* continuing to exert a powerful influence.[207]

6 Conclusion: Rethinking Horizontality

The preceding analysis shows that all permutations of horizontality have featured in contract litigation before English courts. But it also highlights that the actual influence of fundamental rights on English Contract law has been slight. The only situation in which it has reshaped contractual rights and obligations is where one of the parties is a 'core' public authority whose exercise of contractual rights threatens to compromise the other party's Convention rights. Indeed, the gap between Contract law and fundamental rights is so wide that the contractual origin of a right frequently features as a reason for not finding a rights violation.

The forces at work are complex and impossible to reduce to a single factor. The most direct cause appears to lie in the route by which fundamental rights have

[202]See also the doubts expressed Beale and Pittam (2001), pp. 158–159 that the forfeiture of deposits or part performance generally permitted by English contract law is liable to fall foul of A1P1.

[203]*Di Palma* [1988] 10 EHRR 149, p. 155.

[204]*Mustafa* [2008] 52 EHRR 24, paras 33 and 34.

[205]*Pla* [2004] ECHR 334.

[206]Beale (2015), pp. 1-087–1-088.

[207]See *McDonald,* [2016] UKSC 28, paras 44 and 48.

entered English law: neither the HRA nor the ECHR is well-suited to horizontality. The HRA may be 'a statute of peculiar significance which either represents in its enactment, or has the potential to bring about, change in the order of a cultural transformation'.[208] But it is also, as its long title indicates, no more than an 'Act to give *further* effect to rights and freedoms guaranteed under the European Convention on Human Rights'. As this suggests, its transformational reach is rather modest. In the words of Lord Bingham of Cornhill:

> [T]he purpose of the Human Rights Act 1998 was not to enlarge the rights or remedies of those in the United Kingdom whose Convention rights have been violated but to enable those rights and remedies to be asserted and enforced by the domestic courts of this country and not only by recourse to Strasbourg.[209]

This is a far cry from the foundational, often transformational, aspiration of constitutional charters of fundamental rights in several other jurisdictions surveyed in this book.

The comparatively modest aspiration of the HRA is reinforced by the character of the ECHR, at least as it is understood in England. Despite the evolution of the European Court of Human Rights into a court of compulsory jurisdiction to which individuals have a right of recourse, and notwithstanding the court's ambitious extension of the ambit of Convention rights, as Lord Bingham explains, 'the focus of the Convention is still on securing observance by member states of minimum standards in the protection of the human rights specified in the Convention'.[210] One result, observed throughout this chapter, is that in the contractual context recourse can successfully be had to only a limited number of rights,[211] which have a limited reach and are easily satisfied by common law principles and statutory provisions. Compared to, for example, the German Constitution with its rights to dignity and to the free development of personality,[212] the ECHR offers meagre normative resources to support horizontal application. Another consequence, which is of particular significance when it comes to Private law, is that the Convention imposes obligations on states, not individuals, and that these may be complied with in different ways. As Lord Hoffmann observed in *Campbell v MGN Ltd*:

> Although the Convention, as an international instrument, may impose upon the United Kingdom an obligation to take some steps (whether by statute or otherwise) to protect rights

---

[208]Hunt (1999), p. 87.

[209]*R (Begum) v Governors of Denbigh High School* [2006] UKHL 15, [2007] 1 AC 100 (House of Lords), para 29. To the same effect are *R (Quark Fishing Ltd) v Secretary of State for Foreign and Commonwealth Affairs* [2005] UKHL 57, [2006] 1 AC 529 (House of Lords), para 34 (Lord Nicholls); and *R (Ullah) v Special Adjudicator* [2004] UKHL 26, [2004] 2 AC 323 (House of Lords), para 20 (Lord Bingham).

[210]*R (Greenfield) v Secretary of State for the Home Department,* [2005] UKHL 14, [2005] 1 WLR 673 (House of Lords), para 4.

[211]A point also emphasised by Beale and Pittam (2001), p. 156. The UK has not ratified Protocols 4, 7 and 12, which extend the list of rights, and has not made these part of the HRA regime.

[212]These featured in such leading cases as *Handelsvertreter,* [1990] BVerfGE 81, 242 and *Bürgschaft*, [1994] BVerfGE 89, 214.

. . . against invasion by private individuals, it does not follow that such an obligation would have any counterpart in domestic law.[213]

Previous sections have thrown up several examples of how this shapes the courts' understanding of the ambit of ECHR rights so as to restrict the potential for their horizontal application. In particular, it narrows the scope for substantive horizontality, which under this scheme can only be achieved via the indirect route of identifying an appropriate positive obligation on the state (including its courts) to protect the rights of one private individual against their invasion by another. In a jurisdiction where both the legislature and the courts are reasonably active in balancing conflicting individual interests, the prospects for success via this route are, as the cases show, slim indeed.

Lord Hoffmann's perception of the ECHR as a source of rights that remains external to the English legal system even as they are connected via the HRA is also detectable in the Supreme Court's emphasis on the common law as a distinct source of fundamental rights in a series of recent decisions.[214] This is typically accompanied by a manifest commitment to the primacy of common law fundamental rights[215] and a concern that European human rights law may extend too far.[216] The lack of enthusiasm among (some) senior judges for the ECHR is unmistakeable in Lord Toulson's criticism of what he has called 'a baleful and unnecessary tendency to overlook the common law', accompanied by his insistence that 'it was not the purpose of the Human Rights Act that the common law should become an ossuary'.[217]

This '(re)turn to the common law'[218] shows, in the words of Mark Elliott, that '[t]he reception and application of the HRA have not been dry matters of textual analysis': they have been shaped by 'prior and underlying conceptions of the judicial function and of the proper relationship between the courts and the political

[213] *Campbell v MGN Ltd*, [2004] UKHL 22 [2004] 2 AC 457 (House of Lords), para 49.

[214] See especially *AXA General Insurance Company Ltd*, [2011] UKSC 46, para 128; *R (Osborn) v Parole Board*, [2013] UKSC 61, [2014] AC 1115 (Supreme Court (UK)); *Kennedy v The Charity Commission*, [2014] UKSC 20, [2014] 2 WLR 808 (Supreme Court (UK)); *R (HS2 Action Alliance Ltd) v Secretary of State for Transport*, [2014] UKSC 3, [2014] 1 WLR 324 (Supreme Court (UK)); *A v BBC*, [2014] UKSC 25, [2014] 2 WLR 1243 (Supreme Court (UK)); and *R (Evans) v Attorney-General*, [2015] UKSC 21, [2015] AC 1787 (Supreme Court (UK)). For discussion of this trend, see Elliott (2015), Masterman and Wheatle (2015) and Clayton (2015).

[215] E.g.: '[O]ur own legal principles rather than the judgments of the international court' should be the starting point in fundamental rights cases should be (Lord Reed in *R (Osborn)*, [2013] UKSC 61, para 62) 'the natural starting point in any dispute is to start with domestic law, and it is certainly not to focus exclusively on the Convention rights, without surveying the wider common law scene'. (Lord Mance in *Kennedy*, [2014] UKSC 20, para 46).

[216] In his 2013 Hamlyn lecture on 'The Common Law and Europe', Laws LJ reminded his audience that the historic role of human rights law has been to protect what are 'properly regarded as fundamental values' and not 'to make marginal choices about issues on which reasonable, humane and informed people my disagree'. Laws (2014) Lecture III, para 36.

[217] See *Kennedy*, [2014] UKSC 20, para 133.

[218] O'Neill (2015).

branches'.[219] Such legal 'cryptotypes', to use the term imported from modern linguistics by the great comparative lawyer Rodolfo Sacco, shape the outcomes of cases in all legal systems.[220] They are implicit patterns of reasoning that 'insider' jurists take to be obvious and hence frequently do not perceive or articulate and 'are ... passed on from one generation of jurists to another just as the legal rules of the society without a written alphabet are preserved and handed down'.[221] Against the background of this broader response to the HRA, it is patent from the cases surveyed in this chapter how powerfully the encounter between English Contract law and fundamental rights has been shaped by such 'cryptotypes' as a vision of the common law as the bedrock of the English legal system,[222] an orientation towards servicing of commercial needs,[223] parliamentary sovereignty[224] and a commitment to incremental legal development through case-by-case reasoning.[225]

These factors are reinforced by the content and character of English Contract law. This appears to be at least as important in restricting the influence of Convention rights. Take for example the long-established common law position that both a money lending contract imposing quasi-servile obligations on a borrower[226] and a contract by which a trade journal promises not to comment on the affairs of a company are illegal.[227] There is simply no need to rely in such cases on either Article 4 (prohibition of slavery or forced labour) or Article 10 (freedom of expression) to achieve these outcomes. The principle that contracts contrary to public policy are illegal is inherently flexible, enabling the courts to modernise the law. In this way, ordinary Contract law protects the interests secured by Convention rights and has been doing so since well before the enactment of the HRA.[228]

---

[219]See especially *AXA General Insurance Company Ltd,* [2011] UKSC 46, para 128; *R (Osborn),* [2013] UKSC 61; *Kennedy,* [2014] UKSC 20; *R (HS2 Action Alliance Ltd),* [2014] UKSC 3; *A,* [2014] UKSC 25; and *R (Evans),* [2015] UKSC 21. For discussion of this trend, see Elliott (2015), Masterman and Wheatle (2015) and Clayton (2015).

[220]Sacco (1991), pp. 1–34 and 343–401.

[221]Ibid., pp. 386–387.

[222]See especially *Sims,* [2014] UKSC 63, para 17; *The DC Merwestone,* [2014] EWCA Civ 1349, para 162. Morgan (2013) dismisses the HRA as one of a number of impractical 'grand regulatory designs'. For a strong articulation of the general position, see Allan (2014), particularly pp. 81 and 83 and Allan (2006), p. 31. This is not a universal sentiment, however—see Gearty (2015), pp. 2–3.

[223]*R (West) v Lloyd's of London,* [2004] EWCA Civ 506; *YL v Birmingham City Council,* [2007] UKHL 27; *The DC Merwestone,* [2014] EWCA Civ 1349, para 160.

[224]*McDonald,* [2016] UKSC 28, para 69.

[225]See the value attached to stability and predictability in *McDonald,* [2016] UKSC 28, para 41; *The DC Merwestone,* [2014] EWCA Civ 1349, paras 157–158.

[226]*Horwood v Millar's Timber & Trading Co,* [1917] 1 KB 305 (King's Bench Division).

[227]*Neville v Dominion of Canada News Ltd,* [1915] 3 KB 556 (King's Bench Division). The rationale is that such an agreement may prevent the exposure of frauds by the company.

[228]See also *Stretford,* [2007] EWCA Civ 238 and *Sumukan,* [2007] EWCA Civ 243, paras 53–62.

An important instantiation of this is the well-developed law on contractual undertakings that prevent or regulate business competition ('restraints of trade'). In contrast with their counterparts in Germany, where the *Handelsvertreter* decision is one of the prime examples of the horizontal effect of constitutional rights in Contract law,[229] English courts have not had to turn to fundamental rights in order to avoid a contractual term restricting an agent from working for a competitor after the expiry of the agency contract.[230] An equally prominent example of the resourcefulness of English Contract law is the courts' ability to develop the principle of undue influence into a sophisticated response to the problems arising when vulnerable family members stand surety for bank loans. Here, German law again had recourse to constitutional rights,[231] whereas the English judiciary managed perfectly well with ordinary Private law principles.[232] There is therefore no special connection between the constitutionalisation of Contract law and the pursuit of objectives such as 'protection of the weaker party'[233] or 'reconsideration of the requirements of positive freedom in the light of modern values'.[234] It does not inject any values that Contract law should not already adhere to.[235]

These examples epitomise a deeper feature of contemporary English Contract law: its responsiveness to social change and readiness to balance conflicting interests. One additional illustration must suffice: the judicial insertion into employment contracts of a duty of mutual trust and confidence. The evolution of this duty, which requires that 'a balance ... be struck between an employer's interest in managing his business as he sees fit and the employee's interest in not being unfairly and improperly exploited',[236] is a palpable demonstration of the common law's inherent capacity to respond to social change. Lord Hoffmann's account of its emergence is illuminating:

> At common law the contract of employment was regarded by the courts as a contract like any other. The parties were free to negotiate whatever terms they liked and no terms would be implied unless they satisfied the strict test of necessity applied to a commercial contract. Freedom of contract meant that the stronger party, usually the employer, was free to impose his terms upon the weaker. But over the last 30 years or so, the nature of the contract of employment has been transformed. It has been recognised that a person's employment is usually one of the most important things in his or her life. It gives not only a livelihood but an occupation, an identity and a sense of self-esteem. The law has changed to recognise this

---

[229] *Handelsvertreter,* [1990] BVerfGE 81, 242.

[230] 'The doctrine of restraint of trade is probably one of the oldest applications of the doctrine of public policy; cases go back to the second half of the sixteenth century.' Beale (2015), p. 16-085.

[231] *Bürgschaft*, [1994] BVerfGE 89, 214.

[232] *Barclays Bank v O'Brien,* [1993] UKHL 6, [1994] 1 AC 180 (House of Lords); *Royal Bank of Scotland v Etridge (No. 2)* [2001] UKHL 44, [2002] 2 AC 773 (House of Lords).

[233] See Mak (2008), p. 323; Colombi Ciacchi (2014), p. 126; Meli (2006).

[234] Collins (2014), p. 60.

[235] See also Gutmann (2013), pp. 49–51.

[236] *Malik v Bank of Credit; Mahmud v Bank of Credit,* [1997] UKHL 23, [1998] AC 20 (House of Lords), para 46 (Lord Steyn).

> social reality. Most of the changes have been made by Parliament. The Employment Rights Act 1996 consolidates numerous statutes which have conferred rights upon employees. European law has made a substantial contribution. And the common law has adapted itself to the new attitudes, proceeding sometimes by analogy with statutory rights.[237]

There is a further reason why this is important in the present context. The frequency with which the existence of a contract has been taken to militate against finding that Convention rights have been violated might give rise to the suspicion that a Private law purism committed to warding off public law influences is at work in English law. However, as can be gleaned from Lord Hoffmann's reference to the Employment Rights Act, there is no innate hostility to developing the common law in line with new rights introduced via statute. This resonates with the importation into Contract law of the famous *Wednesbury*[238] test—tellingly another common law creation—from administrative law to control the exercise of contractual discretions,[239] as well as the recent employment of the public law concept of proportionality to reconcile contracting parties' conflicting interests.[240] What *is* revealing of the factors at work is that—again—these developments took place without any reference to fundamental rights.

For these reasons, the paucity of horizontal effect uncovered in this paper is best explained by the confluence of an ambivalent reception of the HRA/ECHR catalogue of rights with a comparatively strong tradition of a dynamic Contract law already open to (re-)balancing interests in a changing social context. This conclusion sheds light not only on this facet of English Contract law but also, more broadly and fundamentally, on the claims made by both proponents and detractors of the so-called constitutionalisation of Private law. It suggests that no general claims will withstand scrutiny—the scope for and the effect of the horizontal application of fundamental rights are too deeply enmeshed with the specific legal environment in which it comes into play. This holds a profound lesson: contrary to the prevailing approach,[241] the horizontal application of fundamental rights is better understood as a local legal technique, usefully employed in *some* systems, than as a normative phenomenon advancing certain values universally.

---

[237] *Johnson v Unisys Ltd,* [2001] UKHL 13, [2003] AC 518 (House of Lords), para 35.

[238] *Associated Provincial Picture Houses Ltd v Wednesbury Corporation,* [1948] 1 KB 223 (King's Bench Division).

[239] See particularly *Braganza v BP Shipping Ltd,* [2015] UKSC 17, [2015] 1 WLR 1661 (Supreme Court (UK)). Lord Hodges confined this to employment contracts but not so Lady Hale (see para 18). See also *IBM UK Holdings Ltd & Anr v Dalgleish & Ors,* [2014] EWHC 980 (Ch) (England and Wales High Court (Chancery Division)).

[240] *Cavendish Square Holding BV v Talal El Makdessi; ParkingEye Limited v Beavis,* [2015] UKSC 67, [2015] 3 WLR 1373 (Supreme Court (UK)); *Patel,* [2016] UKSC 42, para 120 (Lord Toulson).

[241] See Mak (2008), p. 323; Colombi Ciacchi (2014), p. 126; Meli (2006); Collins (2014), pp. 57–60; Brownsword (2001); Grundmann (2008); Brüggemeier et al. (2010) particularly vol 2, pp. 426–431.

Acknowledgements I am grateful to my Leicester Law School colleagues Ed Bates, Reza Beheshti and Haward Soper for very helpful suggestions and corrections.

References

Allan T (2006) Parliament's will and the justice of the Common law: The Human Rights Act in constitutional perspective. Curr Leg Probl 59:27–50

Allan TRS (2014) The rule of law as the rule of Private law. In: Austin LM, Klimchuk D (eds) Private law and the rule of law. OUP, Oxford, pp 41–66

Amos M (2014) Human rights law, 2nd edn. Hart, Oxford

Andrews N (2015) Contract law, 2nd edn. CUP, Cambridge

Beale H (ed) (2015) Chitty on contracts, 32nd edn. Sweet & Maxwell, London

Beale H, Pittam N (2001) The impact of the Human Rights Act 1998 on English tort and contract law. In: Friedmann D, Barak-Erez D (eds) Human rights in private law. Hart, Oxford, pp 131–159

Beatson J, Burrows A, Cartwright J (2016) Anson's law of contract, 30th edn. CUP, Cambridge

Bernitz U, Groussot X, Schulyok F (eds) (2013) General principles of EU law and European private law. Kluwer Law International, Alphen aan den Rijn

Brownsword R (2001) Freedom of contract, Human rights and Human dignity. In: Friedmann D, Barak-Erez D (eds) Human rights in private law. Hart, Oxford, pp 181–199

Brüggemeier G, Colombi Ciacchi A, Comandé G (eds) (2010) Fundamental rights and private law in the European Union, vol 1 and 2. CUP, Cambridge

Cherednychenko P (2007) Fundamental rights, contract law and the protection of the weaker party. Sellier, Munich

Choudhry S (2013) Children in 'care' after YL - the ineffectiveness of contract as a means of protecting the vulnerable. Public Law:519–537

Clayton R (2015) The Empire strikes back: Common law rights and the Human Rights Act. Public Law:3–13

Collins H (2008) The law of contract, 4th edn. CUP, Cambridge

Collins H (2011) The impact of Human rights law on contract law in Europe. Eur Bus Law Rev 22:425–435

Collins H (2013) The vanishing freedom to choose a contractual partner. Law Contemp Probl 76:71–88

Collins H (2014) On the (in)compatability of Human rights discourse and private law. In: Micklitz H (ed) Constitutionalization of European private law. OUP, Oxford, pp 26–58

Colombi Ciacchi A (2014) European fundamental rights, private law, and judicial governance. In: Micklitz H (ed) Constitutionalization of European private law. OUP, Oxford, pp 102–135

Craig P (2012) Administrative law, 7th edn. Sweet & Maxwell, London

Cranston R (ed) (1997) Making commercial law: essays in honour of Roy Goode. OUP, Oxford

Davey J, Richards K (2015) Deterrence, human rights and illegality: the forfeiture rule in insurance contract law. Lloyd's Maritime Commerc Law Q:315–345

Duffy P (1997) The protection of commercial interests under the European Convention on Human Rights. In: Cranston R (ed) Making Commercial law: essays in honour of Roy Goode. OUP, Oxford, pp 525–542 ch 23

Elliott M (2015) Beyond the European Convention: human rights and the common law. Curr Leg Probl 68:85–117

Friedmann D, Barak-Erez D (eds) (2001) Human rights in private law. Hart, Oxford

Gearty C (2015) On fantasy island: British politics, English judges and the European Convention on Human Rights. Eur Hum Rights Law Rev 1:1–6

Giliker P (2015) The influence of EU and European Human rights law on English private law. Int Comp Law Q 64:237–265
Grundmann S (ed) (2008) Constitutional values and European contract law. Wolters Kluwer, Alphen aan den Rijn
Gutmann T (2013) Some preliminary remarks on a liberal theory of contract. Law Contemp Probl 76:39–55
Hoffman D (ed) (2011) The impact of the Human Rights Act on private law. CUP, Cambridge
Hunt M (1999) The Human Rights Act and legal culture: the judiciary and the legal profession. J Law Soc 26:86–102
Ibbetson D (1999) A historical introduction to the law of obligations. OUP, Oxford
Klug F (2000) Values for a godless age: the story of the UK's new Bill of Rights. Penguin, London
Laws J (2014) The Common law constitution. CUP, Cambridge
Leczykiewicz D (2013a) Horizontal application of the Charter of Fundamental Rights. Eur Law Rev:479–497
Leczykiewicz D (2013b) Horizontal effect of fundamental rights: in search of social justice or private autonomy in EU law? In: Bernitz U, Groussot X, Schulyok F (eds) General principles of EU law and European private law. Kluwer Law International, Alphen aan den Rijn, pp 171–186
Leigh I (1999) Horizontal rights, the Human Rights Act and privacy: lessons from the Commonwealth? Int Comp Law Q 48:57–87
Mak C (2008) Fundamental rights in European contract law. A comparison of the impact of fundamental rights on contractual relationships in Germany, the Netherlands, Italy and England. Wolters Kluwer, Alphen aan den Rijn
Masterman R, Wheatle S (2015) A common law resurgence in rights protection? Eur Hum Rights Law Rev 1:57–65
McKendrick E (2013) Contract law. Palgrave Macmillan, Basingstoke
Meli M (2006) Social justice, constitutional principles and protection of the weaker contractual party. Eur Rev Contract Law 2:159–166
Micklitz H (ed) (2014) Constitutionalization of European private law. OUP, Oxford
Morgan J (2013) Contract law minimalism: a formalist restatement of commercial contract law. CUP, Cambridge
O'Neill A (2015) Not waving, but drowning?: EU Law, common law fundamental rights and the UK Supreme Court. In: UK Supreme Court Blog. Available at: http://ukscblog.com/not-waving-but-drowning-eu-law-common-law-fundamental-rights-and-the-uk-supreme-court/. Accessed 31 Aug 2016
Oliver H (2011) Discrimination law. In: Hoffman D (ed) The impact of the Human Rights Act on private law. CUP, Cambridge, pp 206–222
Oliver D, Fedtke J (eds) (2007) Human rights in the private sphere. A comparative study. Routledge Cavendish, London
Peel E (2015) Treitel on the law of contract, 14th edn. Sweet & Maxwell, London
Phillipson G (2011) Privacy: the development of breach of confidence – the clearest case of horizontal effect? In: Hoffman D (ed) The impact of the Human Rights Act on private law. CUP, Cambridge, pp 136–164
Rose F (2011) Commercial law. In: Hoffman D (ed) The impact of the Human Rights Act on private law. CUP, Cambridge, pp 300–320
Sacco R (1991) Legal formants: a dynamic approach to comparative law. Am J Comp Law 39:1–34
Shiffrin SV (2006–2007) The divergence of contract and promise. Harv Law Rev 120:708–753
Van Zyl Smit J (2011) Statute law: interpretation and declarations of incompatibility. In: Hoffman D (ed) The impact of the Human Rights Act on private law. CUP, Cambridge, pp 66–90
Young A (2011) Mapping horizontal effect. In: Hoffman D (ed) The impact of the Human Rights Act on private law. Cambridge University Press, Cambridge, pp 16–47
Ziegler KS (ed) (2007) Human rights and private law. Privacy as autonomy. Hart, Oxford

Is All Fair in War Against Unhealthy and Unsustainable Lifestyles? The Right to Privacy vs. Modern Technology in Consumer Contracts

Joasia Luzak

Abstract In their quest to curb unhealthy and unsustainable consumer lifestyles, policymakers may be tempted to use modern technology to nudge consumers to conclude only the 'right' contracts. However, this would create a tension between individual consumers' autonomy and their Fundamental rights, and public interests in safeguarding consumer welfare and environment. Rather than discussing restrictions of autonomy that may occur as a result of nudging, this chapter focuses on dangers to the protection of Fundamental rights in the regulation of consumer contracts in the food and textile industry sector. It considers to what extent the (European) legislators guarantee European consumers' constitutional right to privacy in light of technological developments that could be used to nudge consumers to choose healthy and sustainable lifestyles. The right to privacy may become a victim of the fight for better consumer lifestyles, when policymakers and traders support the use of modern technology, without introducing a well-thought-out regulation thereof. This chapter argues that since modern technologies are constantly developing, policymakers should keep a close vigil over them and not be afraid to introduce rules that would ensure consumer data safety and security.

1 Introduction

Overweight and obesity concern about 67% of men, 57% of women and more than 25% of children in the UK[1] and cause a serious public health problem in Europe.[2] Policymakers often perceive the modern lifestyle as the cause of the growing number of overweight and obese people; with sedentary work environment and

[1]Boseley (2014) and Knapton (2016).

[2]European Commission (Eurostat) (2016c).

J. Luzak (✉)
Centre for European Legal Studies, University of Exeter Law School, Exeter, UK

Centre for the Study of European Contract Law, University of Amsterdam, Amsterdam, the Netherlands
e-mail: J.Luzak@exeter.ac.uk

L. Siliquini-Cinelli, A. Hutchison (eds.), *The Constitutional Dimension of Contract Law*, DOI 10.1007/978-3-319-49843-0_2

cheap and easily available processed food, consumers receive more energy intake while spending less thereof.[3] Modern lifestyles demand also that consumers follow fashion choices and consume more clothing than is necessary due to their wear and tear. Increased consumption and demand for textile products dictate a more efficient and faster production line, which may negatively impact the supply chain of fashion companies, as well as working conditions within it.[4] The food and textile industries provide, therefore, examples of consumer products' sectors, which policymakers may want to regulate, among other things, in order to ensure that consumers receive healthy and sustainable products. The difference between these sectors is that to reach this goal, food and health policies, in principle, would focus on the well-being of consumers themselves, while policies in the textile industry would mostly concern the well-being of workers in the industry, as well as the protection of the environment. The commonality of these two sectors is that policymakers attempt to influence consumer behaviour in them through contract law measures. To curb unhealthy and unsustainable consumer lifestyles, European and national policymakers thus invest more in research and public policy campaigns, to find out what impacts consumer decision-making and how to influence it,[5] that is to say, how to nudge consumers to conclude only the 'right' contracts.[6]

Scholars have been debating the validity and the effectiveness of nudges, concerned with the need to preserve the main principle of contract law: parties' autonomy.[7] Nudging, e.g., through choice architecture, could obstruct consumers' free will as to what contracts, and on what conditions, they conclude.[8] The policymakers' intervention could, furthermore, not only negate contractual principles but also infringe consumers' constitutional rights, such as the right to privacy. There is clearly a tension between individual consumers' autonomy and their Fundamental rights, and public interests in safeguarding consumer welfare, environment, sustainable working conditions, etc. While the goal of policymakers to help consumers help themselves seems laudable,[9] it raises a question whether this goal should be achieved by employing any (technological) means, especially, if these could infringe on consumers' constitutional rights, like the right to privacy. Rather than discussing restrictions of autonomy that may occur as a result of nudging, this chapter focuses, therefore, on dangers to the protection of Fundamental rights in the regulation of consumer contracts. This chapter considers to what extent the (European) legislators guarantee European consumers' constitutional right to privacy in light of technological developments that could be used to nudge consumers to choose healthy and sustainable lifestyles.

[3]EHLA (European Healthy Lifestyle Alliance).

[4]Danyliak (2015) and European Parliament (2014).

[5]See specific examples thereof discussed further in this chapter.

[6]On increased consumer awareness of corporate social responsibility issues see Niemtzow (2013) and European Commission (2013). On various awareness campaigns to encourage healthier food habits see EATWELL (2013), pp. 24–29; Oliver and Ubel (2014), p. 333.

[7]Alemanno and Sibony (2015).

[8]Carolan and Spina (2015), pp. 161–178.

[9]Even though nudging as a form of soft paternalism has its staunch critics. See Waldron (2014).

Sections 2 and 3 set the scene for this research, outlining the battlefield. That is to say, they illustrate the friction between the use of technology to nudge consumers towards the 'right' choices and consumers' rights to privacy. Section 2 presents what strategic policy objectives policymakers may have in encouraging healthy and sustainable consumption, while Sect. 3 illustrates how these objectives may clash with constitutional and contractual rights and principles, specifically the right to privacy and consumer autonomy. Section 2 emphasises the importance given by policymakers to changing unhealthy and unsustainable consumer habits. It shows that policymakers may be tempted to allow the use of modern technological developments without much regulatory oversight, if empirical research could prove that their use would be effective and efficient. Two types of policy interventions distinguish themselves in this respect and will be discussed: measures supporting informed consumer choice and measures aiming to change the market environment. Regrettably, policy measures that are effective in combating unhealthy consumer choices may, nonetheless, simultaneously, infringe consumer autonomy and privacy. To determine whether this may indeed be the case, Sect. 3 clarifies existing European protection of consumer privacy, functioning on the basis of Data Protection Directive[10] and ePrivacy Directive,[11] which introduced a ban on collecting data that could identify consumers. The question arises whether modern technology that allows traders to gather more consumer data still protects the anonymity thereof and whether the increased risk of identifying individual consumers, growing with each additional data collected by a trader, is accounted for by policymakers. Considering that the newly adopted data protection rules uphold the same level of protection, we may question their suitability to guarantee consumer privacy in the beginning era of the Internet of Things.[12] Section 3 also illustrates what infringements of consumer privacy in (pre)contractual relationships could occur on the basis of collected data, through surveillance, targeted actions and profiling.

The right to privacy may become a victim of the fight for better consumer lifestyles, when policymakers and traders support the use of modern technology, without introducing a strict regulation thereof. Therefore, Sects. 4 and 5 discuss two modern technological developments that, when applied to consumer contracts without the introduction of additional safeguards, may indeed weaken protection of consumer privacy. Modern technology allows retailers to label their products electronically using so-called RFID (radio-frequency identification) tags. That is to

[10]Directive 95/46/EC of the European Parliament and of the Council of 24 October 1995 on the protection of individuals with regard to the processing of personal data and on the free movement of such data ("Data Protection Directive") [1995] OJ L281/31.

[11]Directive 2002/58/EC of the European Parliament and of the Council of 12 July 2002 concerning the processing of personal data and the protection of privacy in the electronic communications sector ("ePrivacy Directive") [2002] OJ L201/37.

[12]Regulation 2016/679 of the European Parliament and of the Council of 27 April 2016 on the protection of natural persons with regard to the processing of personal data and on the free movement of such data ("General Data Protection Regulation") [2016] OJ L119/89.

say, consumer products contain a smart chip that allows traders to track them.[13] On the one hand, this technology allows traders to improve their stock management and theft prevention. On the other hand, these smart chips, if not deactivated upon purchase, may track consumers' behaviour.[14] The double-edged sword character of RFID tags is a known concern. In past years, the EU legislators commissioned data protection impact assessments to ensure sufficient consumer protection when traders use the RFID.[15] Section 4 considers in more details the advantages and risks involved with allowing the use of RFID tags without strict oversight. The other example, presented in Sect. 5, refers the issue of privacy to the purchase of consumer goods within the so-called 'Internet of Things', which to an extent also relies on the use of RFID tags.[16] For instance, when a consumer buys a smart fridge that can communicate with her oven, a smartphone and a car, she may not realise the impact these goods may have on her privacy. Section 5 addresses the issue whether current data protection rules could still protect consumer's data and privacy in the new, 'smart' world.

The analysis of specific modern technologies gives an insight into the ongoing developments of consumer products and services and allows predicting challenges that they will pose to the principle of consumer autonomy, as well as to the right to privacy. These challenges will be taken into consideration in the conclusions while assessing whether policymakers could use these technologies either to support informed consumer choice or to influence market environment to the benefit of consumers.

2 Strategic Policy Objectives: Healthy and Sustainable Consumption

According to the World Health Organization, worldwide obesity has more than doubled since 1980 and its main cause is energy imbalance, i.e., consumption of more calories than their expenditure.[17] While promotion of healthy eating habits and lifestyles has long been on the policymakers' agenda, this growing undesirable trend raised questions as to how far policymakers could or should intervene to protect consumers from themselves. The European Commission funded research (the 'EATWELL' research project) to analyse the effectiveness of past diet and health-related policy interventions, both on the national and the international levels.[18] On the one hand, the EATWELL research project identified policy

[13]Peslak (2005), pp. 327–328.

[14]Ibid.; Eschet (2005), pp. 302–304.

[15]European Commission (2011, 2014).

[16]Weber (2010), pp. 23–30.

[17]See World Health Organization (2016).

[18]EATWELL (2013), p. 6.

measures that support informed consumer choice, i.e., provide better information to consumers prior to their decision-making, in the hope that informed consumers act rationally and make the 'right' contractual choice. On the other hand, in case informed choice strategies were not effective, the report also listed policy measures that could change the market environment. Through the use of these more intrusive policy measures, consumers would be more actively pushed towards making the 'right' choice.[19]

Policymakers could thus try to influence consumer lifestyles by either ensuring that better information reaches consumers as to their options or obstructing, or even eliminating, some of consumer choices. The first type of strategy would call for policymakers to provide more consumer education and to improve, e.g., the readability of nutritional labels.[20] The second type requires policymakers to, e.g., introduce higher taxes for undesirable food products; provide tax allowances and subsidies for healthy, nutritional food products[21]; introduce targets for certain harmful ingredients, like salt, in food products.[22] Modern technology could be useful in implementing either of these policies. Therefore, even though the report has not yet considered its advantages, we could expect policymakers to pay close attention to the technological developments and to be motivated to employ them, if research proves the effectiveness and efficiency of these measures in nudging consumers.

For example, the use of electronic, smart labels could potentially allow more information to reach consumers, in a more readable, standardised manner.[23] Smart labels would not have the space limitation of traditional labels and could encourage producers' creativity in conveying information to consumers, e.g., by allowing for the use of various graphs or colourful displays. Furthermore, electronic labels could facilitate a display of more personalised information, e.g., advising the consumer on the suitability of a given food product, considering consumer's blood sugar levels.[24]

It could also be beneficial for consumer health if certain processed, harmful food products were taxed higher than healthy food products; if healthy food products were subsidised by the government to lower their prices; if producers of food products were challenged by the policymakers to lower the intake of such harmful substances, as salt. Also with regard to this second type of policies, modern technology could be useful in facilitating better control over the production, supply and distribution processes, as well as accounting for healthy food choices of consumers, and providing insights on how to nudge consumers to make such 'right' decisions. For instance, through RFID tags it could be easy to control the

---

[19]Ibid., pp. 15–53.

[20]Ibid., pp. 24–30.

[21]Ibid., pp. 33–42.

[22]Ibid., pp. 47–50.

[23]Sunstein (2012); On smart disclosure still failing to effectively inform consumers see, for example, Kustin (2015).

[24]Kavis (2015).

content of a 'smart' fridge and the consumer's intake of calories, salt, vitamins, etc. A far-going, intrusive measure would involve placing an automatic lockdown on a fridge, when consumers have reached the daily amounts that were set for them.

Similarly, policymakers could adopt the above-mentioned strategies in their quest to convince consumers to conclude more sustainable contracts. If we look at the textile industry, as an example, we may observe that producers of textile goods often have difficulties verifying the validity of corporate social responsibility (CSR) claims and controlling the application of their CSR policies in the supply chain.[25] Also in this respect, intensifying the amount of awareness-raising campaigns may nudge consumers to consider CSR issues more often and may influence them when they are choosing between textile products of various brands, drawing their attention to fair trade brands. Additionally, policymakers may also steer consumer behaviour by adopting specific tax policy or setting specific targets for the textile industry. One of the most commonly mentioned benefits of using smart labels, as well as RFID tags, is their ability to track the product throughout the supply chain, ensuring its visibility, and easy verification of any made CSR claims, which could ensure better enforcement of set targets.[26]

It is clearly possible to use the new technology to the benefit of consumers, either by improving information provided to them or by facilitating enforcement of consumer protection through the introduction of easy checkpoints of compliance with consumer policies. Policymakers could, therefore, consider prescribing the use of such technologies to traders, to an extent that this could help policymakers nudge consumers in making healthier and more sustainable contractual choices. However, this new technology could also be used to undermine consumer autonomy and to infringe consumer privacy, through surveillance, profiling and targeted action, as will be discussed in the following parts. This potential of an abuse should, at least, give policymakers a pause in considering how to regulate the use of such technologies and could discourage them from attempting to employ these technologies in their own strategies.

3 Chokepoint: The Right to Privacy and Consumer Autonomy

The right to privacy is a well-established constitutional right in most Member States, one of the Fundamental rights of European citizens, protected under Article 8 of the European Convention on Human Rights.[27] This right to respect for private

[25]European Commission (2013).

[26]Peslak (2005), p. 334.

[27]Council of Europe, *European Convention for the Protection of Human Rights and Fundamental Freedoms, as amended by Protocols Nos. 11 and 14*, 4 November 1950, ETS 5. Available at: http://www.refworld.org/docid/3ae6b3b04.html. Accessed 4 August 2016.

and family life, home and correspondence encompasses also a right to protection against the collection and use of personal data by the State and its bodies.[28] In certain Member States, national courts have also given this provision direct horizontal effect, allowing parties to invoke it in a private dispute.[29] However, even if this right would not be directly effective, consumers should be able to invoke it against a Member State, which introduced a policy leading to the infringement of their right to privacy. This could occur if, e.g., policymakers prescribed the use of certain technological means to traders, without introducing sufficient safeguards, which allowed for an invasive collection of consumers' personal data.

European consumers are additionally protected against undue collection and use of their data through the Data Protection Directive and ePrivacy Directive, recently updated by the new General Data Protection Regulation, which will start applying as of May 2018. Since modern technology increasingly facilitates traders' collection, storage and processing of consumers' data, it is progressively more difficult for policymakers to create a system of protection that would effectively block infringements of consumer privacy,[30] especially, considering that policymakers are heavily lobbied by the business sector not to stand in the way of technological advances. Policymakers could, therefore, be inclined to leave it to the industry to decide how the modern technologies should guarantee consumer's personal data safety. Considering the feasible lack of standardisation and low effectiveness of self-regulation in this respect, due to its non-binding effect,[31] policymakers need to consider more carefully the impact of the lack of regulatory safeguards on consumers' constitutional and contract rights.

Many consumers, if aware of the occurrence of their data collection and processing, would likely consider their privacy invaded.[32] Conversely, consumers often seem rather at ease with 'selling' their privacy for various contractual benefits.[33] Some scholars suggest that this may signify the weakening of importance of the right to privacy as a Fundamental right in modern times.[34] In case this assumption held, policymakers would not need to account for protection of privacy when considering their recommendations. However, I question this assumption since consumer surveys seem to indicate consumers' lack of hope to be able to maintain their privacy in the face of advanced technological measures applied by traders and public authorities, rather than an alleviation of consumers' privacy

[28]European Court of Human Rights (2016); *Copland* vs *The United Kingdom*, judgment of 3 April 2007, No. 62617/00 (European Court of Human Rights) para 42.

[29]See for the Netherlands, in particular, judgment of the Dutch Supreme Court of 9.01.1987 (*Edamse bijstandsmoeder*) NJ 1987/181.

[30]It took over 4 years of negotiations to adopt the new General Data Protection Regulation.

[31]Hildner (2006), pp. 146–148.

[32]Hildebrandt and Koops (2010), p. 436.

[33]De George (2002), pp. 269–270.

[34]Ibid., p. 270; McArthur (2001), pp. 126–127; Van Wel and Royakkers (2004), p. 136.

concerns.[35] Alternatively, this could be seen as an example of a systemic erosion of privacy by information technology that allowed for data to be collected at a mass scale, instantaneously, pervasively and often without consumers' awareness thereof.[36] These online practices conflict with the status of the right to privacy as a Fundamental right in Europe, but enforcement thereof is neglected by the national regulators and authorities.[37] Despite inefficient enforcement, the right to privacy remains a Fundamental right and we may expect policymakers to give proper consideration to the status and observance thereof, when drafting new rules.[38]

Infringements of the consumers' constitutional right to privacy may affect the consumers' freedom of choice as to what contracts to conclude, and on what terms, consequently eroding party autonomy, one of the main principles governing Contract law.[39] If traders collect consumers' data and their preferences, they may use these to manipulate consumers into making choices in line with their, rather than with consumers', interests.[40] Currently, data protection laws in the EU aim at protecting consumers from such practices that would allow for the identification of a particular consumer on the basis of the collected data.[41] Any practices that would fully anonymise the data would be exempt from restrictions set by these laws.[42] Some scholars have argued that no data may be considered fully anonymised, that through connecting various anonymised data a specific consumer could be identified and this data used against her.[43] Still, policymakers allow generic aggregation of data to occur, through the use of anonymisation techniques, even if they are aware that these are imperfect, and that with a certain effort de-anonymisation could succeed.[44] Generally, modern technologies referred to in this chapter collect such aggregate, anonymised data, but the question remains how deep this anonymisation goes and how well do they protect personal data of consumers.

Various available modern technologies allow traders to collect a multitude of consumer data online. As a result, despite anonymisation of consumer data, traders have previously been able to, e.g., identify websites that women visit when they are expecting or products they start purchasing at the beginning of their pregnancy. Consequently, consumers assigned to this group could receive targeted advertising

[35] 43 per cent of European consumers worry that the information will be used without their knowledge, as well as that it will be shared with third parties without their consent. See European Parliament (2011), p. 77.

[36] Hildebrandt and Koops (2010), p. 443.

[37] On the need to improve enforcement of the right to privacy through the adoption of the General Data Protection Regulation see European Commission (2015).

[38] European Commission (2016b), p. 10.

[39] Eidenmüller (2009), pp. 116–117.

[40] Hildebrandt and Koops (2010), p. 436.

[41] Recital 26 and Article 6 para 1 lit. 2 Data Protection Directive; Recital 9, Articles 6 and 9 ePrivacy Directive.

[42] For the continuation of this policy see also Recital 26 of the General Data Protection Regulation.

[43] Malin et al. (2003).

[44] Article 29 Data Protection Working Party (2014).

recommending pregnancy supplements. Even if the name of a particular consumer is not revealed to traders, they obtain in this case personal data on consumer's health and know how to reach this consumer. The targeted advertising that is likely to follow may be in line with disclosed preferences of consumers, urging them to make already planned purchases in specific online shops.[45] This could be seen as a relatively minimally invasive measure. Alternatively, traders could try to change consumer preferences either by showing them advertisements for options they have not yet considered or by enabling easier pursuit of some options over others, drawing more consumer attention to them. These targeted actions could not only hinder consumer autonomy by changing the market environment but also infringe consumer privacy.[46] If policymakers prescribe the use of technologies that would allow for such practices to continue, we could wonder whether they should be liable for any breach to consumer privacy that would result from the application of such technologies.

Aside from targeted actions, the other infringement to consumer privacy and consumer autonomy through the use of modern technology could occur through profiling. Policymakers could potentially start cooperating with search engines such as Google and ensure that, whenever a consumer online is identified as a pregnant woman, search results popping up first on the consumer's screen would be related to healthy lifestyle choices for pregnant women. Since consumers are more likely to read only through first search results,[47] they would be nudged towards making the 'choice' policymakers foresee for them. A combination of profiling and targeted action techniques could, therefore, lead to a change in the market environment. Moreover, such manipulation of search results may infringe not only consumer privacy but also their right to equal treatment, as search engines could be set to not reveal certain options to consumers qualified by algorithms as, e.g., not being able to afford them or, contrarily, could show different prices for the same products or services to different consumers, varied accordingly to the data collected about a particular consumer.[48]

Finally, surveillance is the most commonly considered breach of consumer privacy.[49] If the collected online data allows, with the use of resources, to identify a particular consumer, it is imaginable that she could be traced both in the online and offline environment. Through following consumer's steps, traders could gather more information on her and then use profiling and targeted actions to personalise information provided to this consumer, as well as, potentially, adjust the market environment surrounding this consumer to better meet her needs.

---

[45]Or in some drastic cases even notifying consumers' families that they are pregnant. See Hill (2012).

[46]It is, however, beyond the scope of this chapter to consider the scope of targeted actions that would lead to the infringement of consumer privacy and consumer autonomy.

[47]75 per cent of internet users never read past the first page of search results. See Slu (2012).

[48]Hildebrandt and Koops (2010), p. 437.

[49]See further on this in the following part.

This section elaborated further on the infringements to consumer privacy that could be likely to occur with the introduction of modern technologies. Policymakers should keep in mind the need to protect this Fundamental right, when considering the need for adoption of a regulation applicable to such technologies, as well as when using them either to influence consumer information or to change the market environment. The following sections will look more closely into specific new technological developments that could be of service to policymakers in the pursuit of their goals but at the same time may endanger the protection of consumer privacy.

4 Trojan Horse: RFID

The European legislators are currently considering further regulation of the RFID, which could even require mandatory application thereof by producers of textile products.[50] This is under consideration, as RFID's assets in the enforcement of CSR policies seem plentiful. With a little investment, it could assist producers and suppliers in achieving better control over the production and supply chain, which could lower production costs and, therefore, also cut consumer prices.[51] Moreover, it could confirm producers' CSR claims, providing consumers with an insight into the sustainability of the production and supply chain of the textile industry. Therefore, it seems unquestionable that the RFID's use could increase contractual efficiency and, as such, could also be of interest to policymakers. Additionally, some of its features that are further discussed in this section could enable policymakers to nudge consumers to make specific choices. Unfortunately, so far, reports on the functioning and the security of the RFID technology show that it does not sufficiently guarantee consumer privacy.[52] Indeed, if policymakers are tempted to prescribe its use, they may cause significant damage to this Fundamental right and its enforcement.

The use of the RFID, even though spreading, often remains a mystery to consumers, who may be unaware of either its operation or the risk it may pose to their privacy.[53] There is currently no legal obligation for products with an embedded RFID tag to communicate this on the packaging or on a label. Furthermore, an addition of an RFID tag may not signify to consumers that their data could be collected and processed through this chip. They may trust in the assurances of traders and producers of products with RFID tags that they only use these tags to improve their inventory management or the supply chain, etc. However, privacy advocates notice that currently no guarantees can be made or are being made that

[50]See note 15 above.

[51]Weiss (2003), p. 25.

[52]Ibid.; Peslak (2005), pp. 333–334.

[53]Eschet (2005), p. 311; Hildner (2006), p. 160.

traders will switch these chips off at the moment of consumer purchase. This means that consumers purchasing a pair of trousers labelled with an RFID tag, showing, e.g., that these were made in fair trade conditions could potentially be followed home, through the use of the same chip.[54] Since RFID tags do not require a direct line of sight to be read, unlike barcodes, the data stored on them could be collected by an RFID reader nearby the product. Obviously, in order to systematically track the consumer's location, a whole infrastructure of RFID readers would need to be installed and operated, but random checkpoints could suffice to collect some personal data of a given consumer.[55] This could occur without consumers ever consenting to their data being collected and processed and even with them remaining unaware that such a practice occurs.[56] RFID tags could, therefore, quite easily be used for surveillance and, as such, endanger protection of consumer privacy.

Unfortunately, surveillance is just one of the potential privacy infringements that could materialise through the use of RFID tags. As mentioned in the previous chapter, traders could also use it for profiling and targeted actions.[57] For instance, a reader of RFID tags installed in a warehouse could identify products already placed in a consumer's shopping cart and show her personalised, virtual advertisements of products that the database would estimate could be of interest for this particular consumer, when she is moving throughout the store.[58]

We may distinguish the risk associated with the use of the RFID from general consumer fears of privacy infringements since information collected through RFID tags would be in the hands of private parties and traders and not of publicly regulated bodies.[59] Already the use of cookies by online traders and advertisers caused a lot of consumer concerns and raised issues of potential privacy infringements,[60] but the RFID has a potential to become more invasive as it would track consumers offline as well. For these reasons, privacy advocates suggest that the industry should introduce certain safeguards whenever they use RFID tags.

One such security measure is a 'kill switch' that could be installed on all RFID tags. Through the use of this switch, it would be possible to disable RFID tags at the moment of the consumer's purchase, or, at the latest, when consumers leave the store with the product.[61] Policymakers could, therefore, consider regulating only such RFID tags that would become passive with the consumer's purchase of the

---

[54]Weiss (2003), p. 28. For example, in Texas RFID tags are used to track the movement of school children, creating a record of them entering and exiting school buses and providing an early warning system in case of a kidnapping. See Richtel (2004), pp. 1–3.

[55]Weiss (2003), p. 29.

[56]Hildner (2006), p. 140.

[57]Ibid., p. 141.

[58]On similar practices through the use of eye-tracking technology, see Lewinski et al. (2016).

[59]Hildner (2006), p. 139.

[60]Luzak (2013), pp. 221–245.

[61]Privacy Rights Clearinghouse (2003); Hildner (2006), p. 148.

goods and prohibiting the use of the RFID without these safeguards. This may, however, not be that easy to either apply in practice or enforce. Moreover, policymakers have already had experience with the issues of privacy by design. For the privacy protection to be effective, policymakers would need to categorically prohibit the use of RFID tags outside the production, supply and distribution chain, regardless of the consumer's choice in this respect. That is to say, traders could not expect consumers to 'opt-out' from the RFID tag's activity, whether it would be by asking consumers to activate this switch or through the consumer's notification duty that the trader should disable the tag.

Another option leaves the choice entirely to consumers whether to deactivate the RFID tag by providing them with so-called blocker tags.[62] There are various ways in which this technology could operate, but generally it would be at the consumers' discretion to switch the RFID tag on and off. This solution could be beneficial to consumers if the RFID tag would provide them with some information that could be useful also in post-contractual situations and they had an option to access it through their own readers. However, it also brings with it the risk of consumers forgetting to deactivate the RFID tag after the use, not to mention that either policymakers through regulation or traders in practice would decide on the default setting for the RFID tag, that is to say, whether consumers would leave the store with a product with an embedded RFID tag switched on or off. Due to various consumer biases that may discourage consumers from changing the status quo,[63] in order to better protect consumer privacy this solution should come with a default passive setting for the RFID tag.

Traders have an incentive to implement RFID tags since these could increase the efficiency of their production and supply chain.[64] Considering the above-mentioned risks to privacy protection, the question arises whether the objectives of policymakers to encourage healthy and sustainable lifestyles compensate the risk involved, if they were to recommend the RFID's use to traders.

The benefits of the use of RFID tags for policymakers could be manifold. For instance, through the use of RFID, traders could simplify product labelling and thus, probably, better support informed consumer choice. They could place auxiliary information on the RFID tags instead of on the product's label, which could benefit consumer understanding of labels by limiting the amount of directly disclosed information. Simultaneously, through the RFID tags traders could give consumers an access to more information than a traditional label would allow for, due to its size limitations. This information could also be made more visible, since there would not be a need to limit the font's size, and attractive, through the use of, e.g.,

[62]Juels et al. (2003), pp. 103–111; Hildner (2006), pp. 147–148.

[63]Baron and Ritov (1994), pp. 478–479; Schweitzer (1994), p. 459; Gilovich et al. (1995), p. 189.

[64]Still, even traders are concerned about consumer perception of the RFID tags. For example, shortly upon announcing a trial use of 'smart shelves', on which RFID-tagged Gillette razors would be displayed, Wal-Mart withdrew its campaign. The official reason was a change to its operational strategy, but it seems clear that the change in strategy was motivated by privacy concerns. See Weiss (2003), pp. 27–28.

colourful graphs and diagrams.[65] This means that if only consumers were aware of the RFID tag and how to use it, had access to RFID tags' readers, they could potentially be better informed on nutrition, CSR-related claims, etc. It would require empirical research to assess whether consumers would make an effort to access the information stored on the chip since currently they seem to be mostly passive in their reception of contractual information.[66] Further research could also inquire whether traders would indeed be inclined to optimise the readability of information on the RFID tags and whether it would be easier to comprehend for consumers, as well as whether placing auxiliary information thereon instead of on the label would improve readership and understanding of labels. Conditional on the outcome of this research, policymakers could consider recommending the use of RFID tags to traders, and addressing privacy concerns related thereto, if through the use of the RFID consumers would be better informed, and, as a result, they would be more likely to make healthier and more sustainable choices.

Alternatively, RFID tags could be used to change the market environment or, at least, to ensure the suitability of the market environment. The RFID enables tracking the product through the distribution process, allowing both traders and consumers to confirm whether this product was produced in a sustainable, fair trade manner. This would facilitate policymakers in their enforcement of consumer protection against misleading commercial practices, as well as ensure that there is no confusion among consumers, which contractual choices are contributing to sustainable environment. If the policymakers would recognise the use of RFID tags as a method to promote better consumer lifestyles, they would, however, need to carefully consider what rules would need to be adopted to protect individual consumers' interests and how these could be enforced.

To further analyse potential benefits of the use of RFID tags, it is important to consider their role in the Internet of Things, which follows in the next section.

5 Divide and Conquer: Internet of Things

The Internet of Things describes a world in which advanced technology allows various machines and computers to communicate with each other, allowing people to connect and interact with the digital environment.[67] The data communicated between the machines often concerns consumers, their lifestyles and various behaviours, which could enable these machines to personalise services to a given consumer. Consequently, in order for the Internet of Things to function properly,

---

[65]For instance, in a Prada store in New York City changing rooms track RFID tags on a product selected by the consumer, and it will show her accessories that go with it. See Hildner (2006), p. 136.

[66]Luzak (2015), pp. 79–87; Milne and Culnan (2004), pp. 17, 19, 23–25.

[67]Sarma and Girão (2009), p. 359.

both technology and legal provisions need to allow machines to collect and process consumers' personal data, enabling them to establish consumer identity, even if it is just their virtual identity.[68] As a result of the data exchange between the machines, consumers could expect that their needs would be more easily and better met by their environment.

For instance, consumers going for a run while wearing a smartwatch that measures their speed, their heart rhythm and the amount of burned calories could expect this smartwatch to communicate to the fridge how many calories they have burned during this activity. The fridge, having received this communication, could message the consumer's smartphone with the list of groceries necessary to replenish these calories, considering what products may be missing from it, as well as the consumer's food preferences. Possibly, the fridge would receive a message from a computer in the doctor's office, which the consumer visits, confirming products the consumer is allergic to or should avoid for dietary concerns, which would influence the grocery list as well. The improvement of the control over consumer health data is definitely one expected beneficial effect of the Internet of Things.[69] Such improved communication between various machines would not only allow to better inform consumers but would also lead to the creation of a different market environment, in the above-mentioned example in the health sector, specifically.

Another advantage of the Internet of Things would be providing consumers with more control over the environment they inhabit. The most commonly used example in the literature concerns energy savings. We may imagine a consumer's computer screen communicating with the computer, ensuring automatic switch off of the screen if the consumer forgot to do this when shutting down the computer. Lights, heating and air conditioning in the consumer's apartment could all be notified by the consumer's car or a smartphone about the consumer's time of arrival and turn on at the appropriate, convenient time for the consumer.[70] With regard to the above-used example of the textile industry, we could again imagine a consumer's smartphone communicating with the consumer's digitalised wardrobe, informing the consumer whether a certain T-shirt she spotted in the store would match with the skirt in her wardrobe. Again, more personalised and detailed information could facilitate consumers in making better contractual decisions.

The above-mentioned examples illustrate just some, selected aspects of further developing the Internet of Things. Consumers may very well be attracted to the futuristic lifestyle, but the use of the Internet of Things holds a lot of potential also for traders and policymakers. Having a better insight into the supply chain, shop managers could have more control over the stocked products, which could, e.g., curb the waste of food products and contribute to more sustainable economy.[71] More real-time information on the transportation of goods would allow freight

[68] Ibid.

[69] Atzori et al. (2010), p. 2794.

[70] Ibid., p. 2795.

[71] Ibid., p. 2794.

companies to optimise their deliveries and lead to additional energy savings.[72] Policymakers could optimise healthcare, e.g., by using better health sensors to easily identify patients with allergies or by introducing automatic adjusting of doses of prescribed medications, according to patients' health stats, without the need for in-person doctor or nurse consultations.[73] The Internet of Things could, therefore, easily allow changing the market environment. Policymakers should be interested in retaining some control over this process since they could use these technologies themselves to increase their influence over consumers and their decision-making. Also in this case, however, policymakers should conduct a careful check of potential benefits and risks involved with the further-reaching introduction of the Internet of Things.

Many consumers will perceive the above-described Internet of Things as what they always imagined the twenty-first century to look like, having watched movies like 'The Fifth Element', 'The Terminator' or even 'Avatar', but they should also keep in mind 'Minority Report' and 'The Matrix', clearly illustrating additional privacy concerns. The Internet of Things is a broad term that may apply to any combination of goods and services, which facilitate the above-mentioned communication between machines. Some of the machines would be able to interface with others due to a presence of an RFID tag, but other technologies are likely to be employed as well.[74] Regardless of the particular technology used, the machines' objective is to collect consumer data and share it with other machines. We may, therefore, clearly identify a risk to consumer privacy involved with the use of the Internet of Things.

With various machines being able to collect consumer data, there is a need to ensure that these machines observe privacy policies individually, but also together, when the data is aggregated. Unfortunately, through the introduction of various points of data collection, remaining possibly under control of different market players, with no specified rules that apply in this situation, it is hard to foresee how consumer data could be held secured. Many questions arise in connection with the possible division of responsibility for privacy protection between producers or data controllers of different components of the Internet of Things.

The first inquiry could be as to whether within the Internet of Things one machine should be identified as the core centre of data collection and exchange, which could make its producer a data controller, responsible for ensuring privacy protection of all data flowing between the interconnected machines. Alternative strategy would be to continue to hold responsible for privacy protection only this data controller who has collected, processed and then shared consumer data, within his part of the Internet of Things network. In this last case scenario, since the

---

[72]Ibid.

[73]Ibid., p. 2795.

[74]Ibid., pp. 2787–2789; Weber (2010), p. 23. Technologies are constantly developing, but we could expect Near Field Communications (NFC) and Wireless Sensor and Actuator Networks (WSAN) to work together with RFID tags.

purpose of the Internet of Things is to facilitate data flow between various machines, we need to ask who then bears this burden during the transmission of data between the machines. Moreover, if the responsibility for privacy protection is shared, it may be difficult to establish at what moment that responsibility passes from one data controller to another, considering constant data flow. To look at this practically, we may ask whether a producer of a smart fridge could be able to control privacy protection settings on a smartphone that the fridge is communicating with. The Internet of Things not only enables data flow between the machines but also may infer some conclusions from the aggregated data. Who would bear the responsibility for the data that was aggregated from individual inputs, that is to say, collected separately by each machine?

Since the Internet of Things would require an involvement of complex technology, we may foresee that consumers would not be familiar with its functioning and processes, which could also leave them unaware of potential privacy infringements. Policymakers should consider introducing information duties about data collection through the machines of the Internet of Things, letting consumers know when, by whom and for what purposes their data is gathered. Ideally, consumers would also be granted some control over this process, but up-to-date experiences with online privacy protection do not leave much optimism that this could be achieved, with traders setting the defaults in a way that grants them consumers' consent to the collection and the use of their data, or restricting access to online content, if consumers do not provide their consent.[75]

Again, the potential for breach of privacy protection seems to outweigh the benefits of facilitating more healthy and sustainable consumer lives. However, the European legislators remain optimistic that proper regulation could be found, and with it, the investment in further development of the Internet of Things could yield good results. Currently, there are no specific rules applying to the Internet of Things. The European Commission started to place more emphasis on the regulation of the digital single market, but the so-far proposed regulations do not venture into the area of the Internet of Things, except for encouraging better interoperability between consumer technologies.[76] There are, however, ongoing research projects and collaboration of the European legislators and relevant stakeholders into the possibility of further development of the Internet of Things and its regulation.

For instance, in March 2015 the European Commission created the Alliance for Internet of Things Innovation (AIOTI), within which it aims to closely cooperate with relevant stakeholders, encouraging further technological developments and standardisation policies.[77] This follows earlier adoption of non-binding measures, in which attention was mostly given to the consumers' need to be able to disconnect from the digital environment at any time and to be able to disable the RFID tags.[78]

[75]Luzak (2013), pp. 221–245.

[76]European Commission (2016a).

[77]Van Der Klauw (2016).

[78]European Commission (2009).

In 2016, the European Commission published also a staff working document on how to advance the Internet of Things in Europe.[79] One of the risks mentioned in this document concerns the risk of the Internet of Things developing independently the already established principles of data protection, privacy and security, which could force consumers to share their data against their will. The European legislator, therefore, makes it clear that any further development in this sector would need to comply with the Fundamental rights, such as the right to privacy and data protection.[80] However, no specific measures have until now been adopted or even agreed on.

6 Conclusion

This chapter's analysis of the impact that the modern technology may have on consumer lifestyles and their privacy clearly shows a great potential of these new measures, not only when traders use them but also as to what policymakers could achieve, if they employed them. The fight against unhealthy and unsustainable consumer lifestyles has so far not showed major breakthroughs. Consumers remain uninformed or unmotivated to change their habits or underestimate the risks involved with continuing on their merry, but destructive, life paths. New, more efficient and effective tools for nudging consumers to making the 'right' contractual choices could tip the scales, bringing policymakers closer to reaching their objectives.

From this perspective, policymakers may consider using the modern technology either for improving consumer information or to influence the market environment. In the first case, the level of invasiveness into consumer lifestyles and their privacy is lower since policymakers would still leave the contractual choice to the consumer to make and only facilitate informed decision-making. In the second scenario, policymakers would be more active in nudging consumers, likely hiding certain, considered less healthy and less sustainable, contractual options from them and pushing them onto the socially desired path. The choice between these measures would, therefore, likely make a difference as to whether consumers could keep their contractual autonomy. In either case, however, to employ these measures, policymakers and traders would first need to gather extensive information on the consumer and her preferences, endangering consumer privacy.

Each war has its victims, and it is feasible that the protection of the right to privacy and the principle of consumer autonomy could be the victim of the fight against unhealthy and unsustainable lifestyles. So far, the European legislator does not seem to be ready to depose privacy and data protection of their status as Fundamental rights.[81] However, protection of privacy is not mentioned as the

---

[79]European Commission (2016b).

[80]Ibid., p. 10.

[81]Ibid.

first or even one of the most major concerns, when the European Commission considers further development of the Internet of Things. Instead, technological and financial issues related to this progress seem to be the frontrunners on the list of issues that need to be tackled prior to the implementation of the Internet of Things. This may not bode well for the future of the right to privacy. This data suggests that the answer to the research question posed in this chapter is that the policymakers only marginally, if at all, consider the need for protection of consumer privacy when regulating the use of modern technology, and this answer would likely not change when it concerned the use of this technology to nudge consumers towards healthy and sustainable contracts.

Since modern technologies are constantly developing, policymakers should keep a close vigil over them and not be afraid to introduce rules that would ensure consumer data safety and security. In any case, policymakers should conduct a careful check of benefits and risks involved and continue to invest in research, gathering of empirical evidence on the functioning and the impact of these modern technologies on contractual and constitutional principles and rights.

Acknowledgements The author would like to thank C. Mak and R. Edwards for their valuable comments regarding an earlier version of this paper.

References

Alemanno A, Sibony AL (2015) Nudge and the law: a European perspective. Hart Publishing, Oxford

Article 29 Data Protection Working Party (2014) Opinion 05/2014 on Anonymisation Techniques. 10 Apr 2014, 0829/14/EN/WP216. Available at: http://ec.europa.eu/justice/data-protection/article-29/documentation/opinion-recommendation/files/2014/wp216_en.pdf. Accessed 30 June 2016

Atzori L, Iera A, Morabito G (2010) The internet of things: a survey. Comput Netw 54:2787–2805

Baron J, Ritov I (1994) Reference points and omission bias. Organ Behav Hum Decis Process 59:475–498

Boseley S (2014) UK among worst in Western Europe for level of overweight and obese people. In: The Guardian 29 May 2014. Available at: https://www.theguardian.com/society/2014/may/29/uk-western-europe-obesity-study. Accessed 30 June 2016

Carolan E, Spina A (2015) Behavioural science and EU data protection law: challenges and opportunities. In: Alemanno A, Sibony AL (eds) Nudge and the law: a European perspective. Hart Publishing, Oxford, pp 161–178

Danyliak A (2015) Who's a real fashion victim?. In: European Year for Development, 11 Dec 2015. Available at: https://europa.eu/eyd2015/en/international-young-naturefriends/posts/fashion-and-sustainability. Accessed 30 June 2016

De George RT (2002) Business ethics and the information age. Bus Soc Rev 104:261–278

EATWELL (2013) Effectiveness of Policy interventions to Promote Healthy Eating and Recommendations for Future Action: Evidence from the EATWELL Project. Available at: http://eatwellproject.eu/en/upload/Reports/Deliverable%205_1.pdf. Accessed 30 June 2016

EHLA (European Healthy Lifestyle Alliance). Available at: http://www.ehla-europe.eu/risk-factors-and-prevention/. Accessed 30 June 2016
Eidenmüller H (2009) Party autonomy, distributive justice and the conclusion of contracts in the DCFR. ERCL 5:109–131
Eschet G (2005) FIPs and PETs for RFID: protecting privacy in the web of radio frequency identification. Jurimetrics 45:301–332
European Commission (2009) Internet of Things – An action plan for Europe. In: Communication from the Commission to the European Parliament, the Council, The European Economic and Social Committee and the Committee of the Regions, COM (2009) 278 final, 18 Jun 2009. Available at: http://eur-lex.europa.eu/LexUriServ/LexUriServ.do?uri=COM:2009:0278:FIN:EN:PDF. Accessed 30 June 2016
European Commission (2011) The Privacy and Data Protection Impact Assessment Framework for RFID Applications: a defining moment in the modern epic of co-regulation in ICT. In: Digital Single Market blog, 8 Apr 2011. Available at: https://ec.europa.eu/digital-single-market/en/blog/the-privacy-and-data-protection-impact-assessment-framework-for-rfid-applications-a-defining-moment-in-the-modern-epic-of-co-regulation-in-ict. Accessed 30 June 2016
European Commission (2013) Sustainability of textiles. In: Retail Forum for Sustainability Issue Paper No 11, Aug 2013. Available at: http://ec.europa.eu/environment/industry/retail/pdf/issue_paper_textiles.pdf. Accessed 30 June 2016
European Commission (2014) Digital privacy: EU-wide logo and "data protection impact assessments" aim to boost the use of RFID systems. In: Press release, 30 Jul 2014. Available at: http://europa.eu/rapid/press-release_IP-14-889_en.htm. Accessed 30 June 2016
European Commission (2015) Questions and Answers – Data protection reform. In: Press release, 21 Dec 2015. Available at: http://europa.eu/rapid/press-release_MEMO-15-6385_en.htm. Accessed 30 June 2016
European Commission (2016a) Advancing the Internet of Things in Europe. In: Commission Staff Working Document SWD (2016) 110/2. Available at: https://ec.europa.eu/digital-single-market/en/news/staff-working-document-advancing-internet-things-europe. Accessed 30 June 2016
European Commission (2016b) Commission proposes new e-commerce rules to help consumers and companies reap full benefit of Single Market. In: Press release, 25 May 2016. Available at: http://europa.eu/rapid/press-release_IP-16-1887_en.htm. Accessed 30 June 2016
European Commission (2016c) Overweight and obesity – BMI statistics. In: Eurostat. Available at: http://ec.europa.eu/eurostat/statistics-explained/index.php/Overweight_and_obesity_-_BMI_statistics. Accessed 30 June 2016
European Court of Human Rights (2016) Personal Data Protection. In: Documents, Apr 2016. Available at: http://www.echr.coe.int/Documents/FS_Data_ENG.pdf. Accessed 30 June 2016
European Parliament (2011) Consumer behaviour in a digital environment. Study. In: IMCO (Committee on the Internal Market and Consumer Protection of the European Parliament), Aug 2011. Available at: http://www.europarl.europa.eu/committees/en/studiesdownload.html?languageDocument=EN&file=42591. Accessed 30 June 2016
European Parliament (2014) Workers' conditions in the textile and clothing sector: just an Asian affair? Issues at stake after the Rana Plaza tragedy. In: European Parliament Briefing, Aug 2014. Available at: http://www.europarl.europa.eu/EPRS/140841REV1-Workers-conditions-in-the-textile-and-clothing-sector-just-an-Asian-affair-FINAL.pdf. Accessed 30 June 2016
Gilovich T, Husted Medvec V, Chen S (1995) Commission, omission and dissonance reduction: coping with regret in the "Monty Hall" problem. Personal Soc Psychol Bull 21:182–190
Hildebrandt M, Koops BJ (2010) The challenges of ambient law and legal protection in the profiling era. MLR 73:428–460
Hildner L (2006) Defusing the threat of RFID: protecting consumer privacy through technology-specific legislation at the state level. Harv Civil Rights Civil Liberties Law Rev 41:133–176

Hill K (2012) How target figured out a teen girl was pregnant before her father did. In: Forbes, 16 Feb 2012. Available at: http://www.forbes.com/sites/kashmirhill/2012/02/16/how-target-figured-out-a-teen-girl-was-pregnant-before-her-father-did/#7f5fdc6234c6. Accessed 30 June 2016

Juels A, Rivest RL, Szydlo M (2003) The blocker tag: selective blocking of RFID tags for consumer privacy. In: Proceedings of the 10th ACM conference on computer and communications security. Available at: http://dl.acm.org/citation.cfm?id=948126. Accessed 30 June 2016

Kavis M (2015) The smart labels that will power the internet of things. In: Forbes, 17 Feb 2015. Available at: http://www.forbes.com/sites/mikekavis/2015/02/17/the-smart-labels-that-will-power-the-internet-of-things/2/#4cc19fcc75e8. Accessed 30 June 2016

Knapton S (2016) British people will be fattest in Europe by 2025. In: Telegraph, 31 Mar 2016. Available at: http://www.telegraph.co.uk/science/2016/03/31/british-people-will-be-fattest-in-europe-by-2025/. Accessed 30 June 2016

Kustin ME (2015) 10 reasons why GMO smart label Isn't 'Smart' at all. In: EcoWatch, 16 Dec 2015. Available at: http://ecowatch.com/2015/12/16/gmo-smart-label/. Accessed 30 June 2016

Lewinski P, Trzaskowski J, Luzak J (2016) Face and emotion recognition on commercial property under EU data protection law. Psychol Mark 33:729-746

Luzak J (2013) Much ado about cookies: the European debate on the new provisions of the eprivacy directive regarding cookies. ERPL 21:221–245

Luzak J (2015) Online disclosure rules of the consumer rights directive: protecting passive or active consumers? J Eur Consum Mark Law 3:79–87

Malin B, Sweeney L, Newton E (2003) Trail re-identification: learning who you are from where you have been. In: Carnegie Mellon University, Mar 2003. Available at: http://dataprivacylab.org/dataprivacy/projects/trails/paper3.pdf. Accessed 30 June 2016

McArthur RL (2001) Reasonable expectations of privacy. Ethics Inf Technol 3:123–128

Milne GR, Culnan MJ (2004) Strategies for reducing online privacy risks: why consumers read (or don't read) online privacy notices. J Interact Mark 18:15–29

Niemtzow E (2013) Are consumers done with fast fashion. In: BSR blog, 4 Jun 2013. Available at: http://www.bsr.org/en/our-insights/blog-view/are-consumers-done-with-fast-fashion. Accessed 30 June 2016

Oliver A, Ubel P (2014) Nudging the obese: a UK-US consideration. Health Econ Policy Law 9:329–342

Peslak AR (2005) An ethical exploration of privacy and radio frequency identification. J Bus Ethics 59:327–345

Privacy Rights Clearinghouse (2003) RFID Position Statement of Consumer Privacy and Civil Liberties Organizations. 20 Nov 2003. Available at: https://www.privacyrights.org/ar/RFIDposition.htm. Accessed 30 June 2016

Richtel M (2004) In Texas, 28,000 Students Test an Electronic Eye. The New York Times, 17 Nov 2004

Sarma AC, Girão J (2009) Identities in the future internet of things. Wirel Pers Commun 49:353–363

Schweitzer M (1994) Disentangling status quo and omission effects: an experimental analysis. Organ Behav Hum Decis Process 58:457–476

Slu E (2012) 24 eye-popping SEO statistics. In: Search Engine Journal, 19 Apr 2012. Available at: https://www.searchenginejournal.com/24-eye-popping-seo-statistics/42665/. Accessed 30 June 2016

Sunstein C (2012) Informing consumers through smart disclosure. In: The White House blog, 30 Mar 2012. Available at: https://www.whitehouse.gov/blog/2012/03/30/informing-consumers-through-smart-disclosure. Accessed 30 June 2016

Van Der Klauw K (2016) Why there is more to the Internet of Things than just technology – the role of AIOTI. In: European Commission's Digital Single Market blog, 29 Jan 2016. Available at: https://ec.europa.eu/digital-single-market/en/blog/why-there-more-internet-things-just-technology-role-aioti. Accessed 30 June 2016

Van Wel L, Royakkers L (2004) Ethical issues in web data mining. Ethics Inf Technol 6:129–140

Waldron J (2014) It's all for your own good. In: The New York Review of Books, 9 Oct 2014. Available at: http://www.nybooks.com/articles/2014/10/09/cass-sunstein-its-all-your-own-good/. Accessed 30 June 2016

Weber RH (2010) Internet of things – new security and privacy challenges. Comput Law Secur Rev 26:23–30

Weiss A (2003) Me and My shadow. ACM netWorker 7(3):24–30

World Health Organization (2016) Available at: http://www.who.int/mediacentre/factsheets/fs311/en/. Accessed 30 June 2016

The Influence of Constitutional Law on French Contract Law: The Development of the Control of Proportionality in Case of an Infringement of a Fundamental Right by Contract

Jean-Baptiste Seube

Abstract On account of the French legal system's structure, it is rather difficult to measure the concrete influence of Constitutional law over contracts. After recalling the procedure before the Constitutional Council, the article shows that the Constitutional Council has little influence on the rules of law applicable to contracts. However, it considerably influences the judicial reasoning by inviting the judge to resort to a control of proportionality. Unknown by the judicial practice, this control is expected to become the key to litigation as regards the violation of Fundamental rights by contract (Sect. 2). After this overview, a case study will illustrate how the judicial judge still hesitates to implement this control of proportionality (Sect. 3).

1 Introduction

In French law, there is a *summa divisio*, which does not exist in common law. Indeed, one opposes Public law (relations between the state and the citizens) and Private law (relations between private individuals).[1] This results in a sort of intellectual and disciplinary compartmentalisation that extends itself to teaching. Despite the fact that it affects the unity of law, one is either a publicist or a privatist. This distinction is ill-suited to some subjects that tend to transcend it (the distinction). This applies to Fundamental rights and freedoms.

For a long time, Fundamental rights and freedoms were confined to Public law. Most often, a citizen would blame the state for violating one of its public freedoms: violation of the freedom of movement, his freedom of conscience, freedom of demonstration, freedom of religion ... privatists showed little interest for these

[1]Cabrillac (2015) n°62 *et seq.*; Cornu (2007), n°27; Malaurie and Morvan (2012), n°62 *et seq.*; Terré (2012), n°77 *et seq.*

J.-B. Seube (✉)
Faculty of Law, University of Reunion Island, Saint-Denis, France
e-mail: jean-baptiste.seube@univ-reunion.fr

L. Siliquini-Cinelli, A. Hutchison (eds.), *The Constitutional Dimension of Contract Law*, DOI 10.1007/978-3-319-49843-0_3

questions. However, Fundamental rights and freedoms quickly overstepped their initial framework and overran relations between private persons: Family law, human rights, property ownership rights that have been little by little colonised by Fundamental rights. Although the Civil code contains articles relating to Fundamental rights (Article 544 of the Civil code on property rights, Article 9 of the Civil code on private life), their implementation sidestepped their dimension of 'Fundamental right'. The situation changed when contractors asserted the fundamental nature of rights in order to give their arguments a greater weight and, even in some cases, make them produce new effects. This phenomenon is noticeable in Contract law.

In fact, it has become common that a contractor blames his partner for violating, by the means of a contract, one of his Fundamental rights. In order to describe this important movement, authors refer to various expressions, among which are 'contractualisation of Fundamental Rights' or 'fundamentalism of the law of the Contract'. This evolution, which began 30 years ago, led to a great upheavel in the French legal counsel's reasoning. Whereas the French legal reasoning traditionally relied on legal syllogism, nowadays it most often adopts new means of reasoning that allow the conciliation of the litigant's Fundamental rights.

The traditional reasoning is syllogism. This relies on three steps: first of all, the judge determines the rule of law, which is abstract and general (syllogism's major), then he applies it to the present case (syllogism's minor), then the judge infers a conclusion. According to this conception, the judge is presented as 'the mouth of law' to use Montesquieu's expression.[2] It implies that the judge only applies the law without being able to amend its severity accordingly. However important it might be, the resort to the syllogism does not form the basis of the entire legal reasoning: it admits its limitations when facts are imprecise and the rule of law is unclear.

This is especially the case with texts that stipulate Fundamental rights and freedoms without giving the judge the possibility to conciliate them. Take for instance a landlord who intended to do some work in a rented flat: the tenant will be able to object to it by underlining that this work constitutes a violation of his private life, whereas the landlord will be able to justify it by the protection of his proprietary rights. As regards both rights, the texts are written in a general and absolute manner. So how can both Fundamental rights be reconciled?

To do so, the Court of Cassation more and more frequently resorts to the control of proportionality, inspired by the European Convention on Human Rights' (ECHR) case law, the Constitutional Council and the Council of State. However, the recourse to such a control raises numerous difficulties since it obliges the Court of Cassation, judge of the law, to deal with substantial issues. Some authors fear that it might lose its role of judge of the correct application of the rule of law, only

[2]De Secondat de Montesquieu (1748), "*Les juges de la nation ne sont que la bouche qui prononce les paroles de la loi, des êtres inanimés, qui n'en peuvent modérer ni la force ni la rigueur*".

to become a jurisdiction that settles disputes in facts and in law.[3] A deep reflection is currently being held within the Court of Cassation as regards the control of proportionality.[4]

De facto, the development of the control of proportionality in the event of the violation of a Fundamental right by contract is a wonderful example since it allows one to study the influence of Constitutional law over Contract law, however difficult it might be to identify this influence given the French judicial organisation and the division between Public/Private law. However, despite these difficulties, one can believe that in itself, the Constitutional Council does not exert a major substantial influence over decisions rendered by the Court of Cassation. By contrast, it shows the fact that the Council exerts an important influence by encouraging judicial judges to adopt the control of proportionality. Therefore, it is in the field of the means of reasoning that the main evolutions are located.

In order to assert this idea, it is necessary to present in a general manner the influence of Constitutional law on Contract law (Sect. 2). After this presentation, a practical case study will illustrate the main difficulties raised by the implementation of the control of constitutionality (Sect. 3).

2 General Presentation of the Influence of Constitutional Law on Private Contract Law

Unlike many states, France does not have a Supreme Court. As a result, Contract law is apprehended by the top judicial jurisdiction (the Court of Cassation) and the top administrative jurisdiction (Council of State) and, in a lesser extent, by the Constitutional Council. Each of these institutions addresses Contract law through the mission entrusted to it: for the Court of Cassation, it implies ensuring that the lower courts have correctly applied the rule of law to the case brought before them; for the Council of State, it implies settling disputes between two public persons or between a private and a public person; for the Constitutional Council, it implies ensuring that the law complies with the Constitution. The level of intervention of these institutions is not the same; therefore, it makes it difficult to identify the actual influence of Constitutional law on Contract law. However, in order to identify it, it is undoubtedly necessary to recall the different hypothesis of the Constitutional Council's intervention.

First of all, the Constitutional Council does not settle disputes between litigants. Its sole purpose is to ensure that laws comply with the Constitution. It can intervene at two levels. The Constitutional Council can first be seized by the members of Parliament prior to the promulgation of the law if they consider that some

[3]Concerning the Court of cassation's originality, see Cabrillac (2015), n°238 *et sec.*; Malaurie and Morvan (2012), n°62 *et sec.*; Terré (2012), n°139 et seq.

[4]Louvel (2015a), p. 1326; Louvel (2015b); Jeuland (2016), p. 20.

provisions are contrary to the Constitution. Therefore, the control of the law is done a priori. As a part of this control, the Council has rendered a few rulings that are relevant to Contract law, in particular its decision concerning the law on the Civil Solidarity Pact.[5] The Constitutional Council can also be seized once the law has entered into force. It can be seized by a litigant who considers that the law on which his opponent based his claim is contrary to the Constitution. This is an ex post review named QPC (Question Prioritaire de Constitutionnalité). As part of this control, the Council does not resolve the dispute opposing the litigants but decides whether the law invoked by one of them is or is not in keeping with the Constitution.

Therefore, the Constitutional Council intervenes on a vastly different level than that of the judicial and administrative jurisdictions: the first one is treated in an abstract and theoretical manner, whether the bill does or does not comply with the Constitution; the second ones rule on actual cases and analyse each case with reference to the applicable law and its factual application in order to decide which claim will be successful. In such conditions, it seems rather difficult to identify the actual influence of the Constitutional Council on Contract law. One could have the feeling that the Constitutional Council and the jurisdictions live in two parallel universes: they both talk about the contract without real possibility to identify any mutual influences. This observation inspired P.-Y. Gahdoum, who wrote: 'when the Constitutional Council 'talks' about contracts, considering the role as a judge of the law, he never does it in direct hold, he isn't a judge of the contract, he is, in some respects, a judge of the law of the Contracts, that is to say of the legislation concerning contracts'.[6]

Imposed by the organisation of the French State, this observation can be considered as disappointing. However, it must be nuanced: it is indeed possible to identify direct influences, which relate to the substance of the rule of law (Sect. 2.1), and also indirect influences, which relate to ways of thinking (Sect. 2.2).

2.1 *The Influence Over the Substance of the Rule of Law*

Under the reserves set out above, Constitutional case law has often reinforced principles that irrigate Contract law. It has taken an interest in the formation (Sect. 2.1.1) and the execution (Sect. 2.1.2) of the contract.

---

[5]Cons. const., 9th of November, 1999, n°99-419 DC (Constitutional Council). On contribution of this ruling in contract law, see Blachèr and Seube (2000), p. 203; Molfessis (2000), I, 210; Raymond (2000), chron. 14.

[6]Gahdoum (2011), n°31.

2.1.1 The Formation of the Contract

The Constitutional Council rendered numerous rulings concerning contractual freedom. However fundamental it might be, this freedom has never been absolute and has always been subject to a rather imposing legislative framework. Invited to rule on the conformity of these laws to the Constitution, the Council has developed its case law.

Initially, the Constitutional Council considered that no provision of the Constitution guarantees the principle of contractual freedom.[7] The Council refused to control the rules of law that framed the formation of contracts. This approach was questionable since the absence of constitutional foundation is not a sufficient ground. Despite being absent from the main constitutional texts, there are numerous principles that still relate to it. De facto, if the Declaration of 1789 does not contain the word 'contractual freedom', Article 4 of the Declaration, which enshrines the principle of freedom in general terms, could serve as a legal basis to contractual freedom in a modernised reading of the bicentennial text.

In a second phase, the Council has reconsidered its statement by admitting that contractual freedom can be invoked, provided that the violation of another substantive principle such as proprietary right or entrepreneurial freedom[8] was also being invoked. This legal precedent resulted in making contractual freedom a principle of secondary importance or a 'sentinel principle',[9] which would only be the guarantor of another constitutional rule of law.

Third, the Council has enshrined the principle of contractual freedom as such by judging that 'contractual freedom derives from Article 4 of the human rights declaration',[10] then raising it to the same rank as entrepreneurial freedom by judging that 'it is open to the legislator to allow limitations to entrepreneurial freedom and contractual freedom which follow from Article 4 of the HRD, limitations which would be related to constitutional requirements or justified by public interest, provided it does not result in disproportionate infringements in the light of the objective pursued'.[11] As a consequence, when the legislator wants to regulate the conditions of access to a contract, he must do so while respecting the freedom of

[7]Cons. const., 3rd of August, 1994, n° 94-348 DC (Conseil constitutionnel); Adde, Prétot X (1996), Rec. Dalloz, p. 45; Melin-Soucramanien F (1995), Rec. Dalloz, p. 344; Gaïa P (1995), Rec. Dalloz, p. 351; Mestre J (1996), RTD. civ., p. 151.

[8]Cons. const., 20th of March, 1997, n° 97-388 DC (Conseil constitutionnel). Adde Fabre-Magnan M (1997), JCP, I, 4039, n°1; Verpeaux and Mathieu (1997), JCP, I, 4066, n°16; Melin-Soucramanien (1999), Rec. Dalloz, p. 236; Favoreu (1999), Rec. Dalloz, p. 234; Molfessis (1997), RTD civ. p. 787; Mestre (1998), RTD. civ. p. 99.

[9]Mathieu (1997), Les Petites Affiches, n° 125, p. 13.

[10]Cons. const., 19th of December, 2000, n° 2000-437 DC (Conseil constitutionnel). Adde, Ribes D (2001), Rec. Dalloz, p. 1766; Molfessis N (2001), RTD civ., p. 229.

[11]Cons. const., 13th of June, 2013 (Conseil constitutionnel). Adde, Ghestin J (2013), JCP éd. G, 929; Mekki M (2013), JCP éd. G, 974, n°1; Pérès C 2013), Rev. des contrats, p. 1285; Barbier H (2013), RTD. civ., p. 832.

conventions. The legislator must also minimise the impediments made necessary by the public interest or the protection of public order.

Therefore, it can be noted that the Council has established a principle that, although being a pillar of Contract law, is only mentioned in the Civil code by the course of Article 6.[12] The same phenomenon occurred as regards the execution of the contract.

2.1.2 The Execution of the Contract

Concerning the execution of the contract, the Council has raised the question as to whether a new law could violate contracts in force. It is an issue that directly affects the principles of predictability of the contract and the parties' legitimate expectations.

First, the Council considered that the 'fact that such changes have consequences on contracts in force is not in itself likely to lead to unconstitutionality'.[13] It is therefore a way of recognising that the legislator could modify laws regardless of the ongoing contractual situations at the time of the enactment of the new law.

Then, by a decision rendered on 10 June 1998, the Council noted that 'the legislator cannot prejudice the general framework of conventions and contracts legally concluded, so as to lead to an infringement of the freedom which arises from Article 4 of the Declaration'.[14] This principle was reaffirmed several times.[15]

Consequently, this implies that the contract benefits from a certain protection against possible infringements by the legislator. The legislator must frame the principle of the law's immediate implementation in contractual matters in order to avoid breaching the parties' forecasts. If the impact of the Constitutional Council

[12]*Code civil*, Article 6: "One may not by private agreement derogate from laws that concern public order and good morals."

[13]Cons. const. 4th of July, 1989, n° 89-254 DC (Conseil constitutionnel). Cons. const., 9th of April, 1996, n° 96-375 DC (Conseil constitutionnel). Adde, Schrameck O (1996), AJDA, p. 369; Gaïa P (1998), Rec. Dalloz, p. 150.

[14]Cons. const., 10th of June, 1998, n° 98-401 DC (Conseil constitutionnel). Adde, Schoettl JE (1998), AJDA, p. 495; Favoreu L (2000), Rec. Dalloz, p. 60; Molfessis N (1998), RTD civ., p. 796; Mestre J (1999), RTD. civ., p. 78; Verpeaux M, Mathieu B (1998), JCP éd. G, I, 179, n°14.

[15]Cons. const., 23 juillet, 1999, n° 99-416 DC (Conseil constitutionnel): Schoettl JE (1999), AJDA, p. 700; Gay L (2000), Rec. Dalloz, p. 422; Marino L (2000), Rec. Dalloz, p. 265; Fatin-Rouge M (2000), Rec. Dalloz, p. 423; Molfessis N (1999), RTD civ., p. 724; Cons. const., 13 janvier, 2000, n° 99-423 DC (Conseil constitutionnel): Bernaud V (2001), Rec. Dalloz, p. 1837; Cons. const., 7 décembre, 2000, n° 2000-436 DC (Conseil constitutionnel): Schoettl JE (2001), AJDA, p. 18; Favoreu L (2001), Rec. Dalloz, p. 1840; Fatin-Rouge M (2001), Rec. Dalloz, p. 1841; Cons. Cons. const., 27 novembre, 2001, n° 2001-451 DC (Conseil constitutionnel): Ribes D (2002), Rec. Dalloz, p. 1950; Cons. const., 12 janvier, 2002, n° 2001-455 DC (Conseil constitutionnel): Reneaud F (2002), AJDA, p. 1163; Gay L (2003), Rec. Dalloz, p. 1129; Mathieu B (2002), Rec. Dalloz, p. 1439, chron. B. Mathieu.

on the rule of law in itself appears to be, all in all, fairly small, the same cannot be said about the impact of the Constitutional Council on ways of thinking.

2.2 *The Influence Over the Way of Thinking*

The Constitutional Council has been referring to the notion of proportionality for quite some time when assessing the constitutionality of legislation.[16] In other words, the Council estimates whether the rule being controlled is justified by a legitimate interest and proportionate to this interest. This control of proportionality was also implemented by the European and administrative jurisdictions[17] ... to the point of becoming a veritable technique that guarantees the protection of Fundamental rights and liberties. However, it remained sovereignly unrecognised by the judicial judge.

Under the influence of these jurisdictions, the Court of Cassation increasingly resorts to the control of proportionality to assess whether the contract jeopardises any Fundamental rights of a contractual partner.[18] We can mention the various hypotheses as to how the judicial judge resorts to the control of proportionality (Sect. 2.2.1) before venturing to appreciate the legal reasoning's metamorphosis (Sect. 2.2.2).

2.2.1 Hypotheses of the Recourse to the Control of Proportionality by the Judicial Judge

The main difficulty relates to the domain in which the judicial judge is going to implement the control of proportionality. Fundamental rights and liberties being expressed both in international instruments (in particular the ECHR) and national instruments (Property law: Civil code, Article 544; privacy: Civil code, Article 9; etc.), the use of the control of proportionality is polymorphic. One can, by confining itself to the application of the ECHR by the judicial judge, distinguish two specific cases, that is to say, whether the application of the text is horizontal or vertical.

The application of the ECHR is vertical when the judicial judge is seized to determine whether a French law, which is voted by Parliament, is in accordance with the ECHR. In this type of litigation, the judge tends to neutralise the law.[19] In this type of control, the European Court of Human Rights has its own case law: it considers that infringements resulting from national legislation must be justified by

[16]Philippe (1990); Xynopoulos (1995); Duclerq (2015); Goesel-Le Bihan (2012), n°7.

[17]Muzny (2005); Eissen (1999), p. 65 *et sec.*

[18]Seube (2009), p. 86.

[19]ECHR, *Handyside/RU*, 7th of September, 1976, série A, n°24 and *Sunday Times/RU*, 26th of April, 1979, série A, n°30.

the defence of a compelling and social need and then be proportionate to the aim pursued. In strict logic and in order to avoid being disavowed, the Court of Cassation would have a direct interest in adopting the same type of control: it should first focus on justifying the violation (control of legitimacy or necessity) and then on the proportionate or disproportionate nature of this violation regarding the objective pursued. This is far from being the case. In this respect, we are struggling to discover a real case law trend. Most often, the control of proportionality is merely skipped. The Court of Cassation satisfies itself in asserting peremptorily the conformity of the national measure with the provisions of the Convention without caring about a control of necessity or a control of proportionality.[20] Such is the case of the litigation as regards the conformity of commercial lease statutes with the ECHR.[21]

The application of the ECHR is horizontal when the Court of Cassation applies the text between private parties.[22] Should the Court of Cassation then conduct a control of proportionality so as to know whether the infringement of a contractual partner's Fundamental right is proportionate? It is very tempting to reason by analogy with the control that exists in the vertical application ... but this is not the same thing at all: the ECHR required a control of proportionality in order to limit the state's interference; the sole issue here concerns private interests.[23] Despite being useful, the control of proportionality is not imposed by the ECHR. In order to distinguish it from the previous hypothesis, one talks about a 'privatized control of proportionality'. This question raises some confusion. The rulings that have implemented the control of proportionality have been criticised since they

---

[20]Debet (2002), n°246: '*la Haute juridiction préfère s'en tenir à un raisonnement traditionnel et rigide, fondé sur la compatibilité de la norme interne et de la norme européenne et sur la hié rarchie des normes*'.

[21]This example is interesting as it confirms that the courts guide the control: rather than assessing if an article alone infringes the fundamental rights, the courts most often examine the text as a whole (Dijon, 31st of May, 1989: Rozès L (1990), Rec. Dalloz, p. 256, obs. L. Rozès; Deruppé J (1990), Rev. dr. Immobilier, p. 126). The control of proportionality is consequently a symbolic once since it is obvious than each law aims at conciliating the interests involved.

[22]Moutel (2006), n°8 *et sec.*

[23]Debet (2002), n°251:

> on peut s'interroger, s'agissant de l'atteinte portée par un individu à un droit garanti par la Convention, sur la réelle nécessité de faire appel au contrôle de proportionnalité européen;

J.-P. Marguénaud et J. Mouly, note in D. 1999, p. 645:

> Lorsqu'il s'agit d'étendre les droits relatifs consacrés par la Convention aux relations de particuliers à particuliers, la proportionnalité inhérente à la mise en place des restrictions admises par les paragraphes seconds des articles 8 à 11 n'a plus cours... Dans ces conditions, la proportionnalité ne signifie plus grand chose; en tout cas, elle ne peut plus signifier la même chose puisque, par hypothèse, l'ingérence litigieuse a été commise par un autre particulier au nom d'un intérêt, certes légitime, mais qui reste un intérêt privé.

gave the feeling of being confused with the control of proportionality imposed by the vertical application of the ECHR.[24]

They have nothing to do with each other: one aims at authorising breaches from the state, based on public interest, whereas the other has for aim to combine two private rights. The decisions that have refused to implement the control of proportionality have been criticised because they exposed themselves, light-heartedly to retain coarse solutions. Human rights are to be handled with caution, and the control of proportionality can limit the excess that they might lead to.

2.2.2 Comment

Despite criticism, the control of proportionality is continuously conquering new lands and is expected to become a general method of resolution of litigation when a contract infringes a Fundamental right.

Criticisms directed at the control of proportionality relate to both the form and the substance. On the substance, the danger of a control of proportionality is linked to the imprecision of the notion.[25] Erecting proportionality into a rule of judgment amounts to forgetting the rule of law so as to judge only through the prism of balancing competing interests.[26] This results in two perils: first, to lead to a real casuistic approach, as each ruling would be a one-off decision, justified by the facts of the case. Second, we would gradually abandon the idea of a pre-established legal solution in order to resort, in all circumstances, to the judge's arbitration. Behind the control of proportionality would be hiding legal uncertainty and the unpredictability of law. Beautiful praetorian constructions would be over: we

---

[24]Cass. soc., 12th of January, 1999 (Cour de cassation (Chambre sociale)): Marguenaud JP, Mouly J (1999), Rec. Dalloz, p. 645; Ray JE (1999), Dr. social, p. 287; Garaud E (1999), RJPF mai 1999, p. 8; Hauser J (1999), RTD civ. p. 358; Mestre J (1999) RTD. civ., p. p. 395. Cass. civ. 3ème, 19th of March 2003 (Cour de cassation (3e Chambre civile)): Marguénaud JP (2003), RTD civ. p. 710:

> ayant relevé qu'il n'apparaissait pas anormal qu'un bailleur constitue des sûretés de nature à garantir le paiement des loyers à proportion des risques de possibles difficultés en cas de défaillance des preneurs et qu'au regard du droit international, il est plus difficile pour un ressortissant d'un Etat de l'Union européenne de faire valoir ses droits à l'extérieur de l'Union, et retenu que M. X n'établissait pas que lui seul se serait vu réclamer une caution pour la seule raison de son appartenance à un groupe ethnique particulier, la Cour d'appel en a exactement déduit, sans violer les textes susvisés (L. 6 juillet 1989, Art. 1, C. Pénal, Art. 235-1, CEDH, Art. 8 et 14), que les garanties prises en la circonstance ne sauraient être qualifiées de discriminatoires.

[25]Moutel (2006), n°296 *et sec.*; Debet (2002), n°256 *et sec.*

[26]Philippe (1990), p. 447: '*son caractère souple et malléable rejette toute idée de détermination a priori des rapports juridiques*'.

would welcome legal relativism.[27] In this form, the generalisation of the control of proportionality would, without doubt, imply a new draft of judgments of the Court of Cassation: it would have to abandon its concise style in order to justify, more explicitly, the decisions it consecrates. It would also have to weigh, more explicitly, the competing interests, just as the European Court for Human Rights does. As a result, it would progressively evolve from a jurisdiction dealing with the law to a court dealing with the substance of the cases.

Despite these criticisms, some authors consider that the control of proportionality should be generalised.[28] Considering their perceived absolute value, Fundamental rights must be used with caution in relations between private parties. The control of proportionality does permit this. Thus, restrictions would only be made possible if they were justified or necessary: they would only be justified if they are proportionate to the end sought and if they do not alter the liberty's substantive content. Article 1102 of the French Contract law reform, which is currently under debate in France and which should enter into force in February 2016, invites the adoption of such a result. Article 1102 of the Civil code will provide that 'Everyone is free to contract or not to contract, to choose the person with whom to contract, and to determine the content and form of the contract, within the limits imposed by legislation. However, this contractual freedom does not allow the parties to derogate from rules which are an expression of public policy, nor to infringe Fundamental rights and freedoms recognised by a provision which applies to relationships between private parties except where such infringement is indispensable to the protection of legitimate interests and proportionate to the intended purpose.' This text provides a generalisation of the control of proportionality. In order to know if a contract infringes Fundamental rights and freedoms of a contracting party, we will have to ask ourselves if the breach is justified by a legitimate interest and if it is proportionate to the objective pursued. Tomorrow, the control that will be provided by the Court of Cassation is quite near to the control that is already implemented by the Constitutional Council. If the Council has not shattered the substance of the law applicable to the contract, it has considerably influenced the methods of reasoning applied by the judge.

[27]The French legal reasoning would thus be threatened. See for instance, Guinchard (1999), p. 155: '*Avec de telles méthodes d'interprétation, on est loin du raisonnement juridique traditionnel français qui ne se satisfait guère de pesées ! Nous sommes dans une autre logique, celles des concepts flous ou 'logique de gradation'*...'. This reasoning has however to be tempered as the syllogistical reasoning never had the perceived strictness (Perelman (1999), n°98: '*il arrive bien des fois que ce sont de considérations extra juridiques qui lui dicteront sa décision, la motivation, qui insère le jugement dans le système de droit en vigueur, ne survenant qu'après coup*'). Indeed, the judicial courts often use, without saying it, the control of proportionality.

[28]Raynaud (2011), p. 243; Rochfeld J (2003), Rev. des contrats, p. 17 *et sec.*

3 Practical Illustration

A contract is likely to hinder a contracting party's Fundamental rights and freedoms,[29] for instance, a lease contract that forbids the tenant to accommodate his relatives. Can this clause be annulled since it violates the tenant's right to family life?[30] What about an employment contract that forbids a worker to wear an Islamic veil? Can we neutralise this clause considering it violates the employee's right to freedom of religion?[31] Here again a lease contract that concerns a residential accommodation equipped with a digicode—can we consider that, by respect for Jews who cannot touch any electronic device during Shabbat, the landlord should be compelled to equip the door with a mechanical lock?[32] And now, a contract in which a model assigns her rights to an agency—can we, considering the assignment is not strictly defined, assert that the contract infringes the model's private life?[33]

These questions are increasingly frequent. They show to what extent a contract is likely to prejudice one of the contracting party's Fundamental rights. The increasing invocation by the litigants of Fundamental rights and freedoms accompanies a new 'vision' of the contract: considered for a long time as the meeting of free, equal and enlightened wills (liberal and classical vision of the contract), the contract has become a place of conflict where a 'strong' contracting party is likely to impose its will on a 'weak' contracting party. Therefore, the risk of domination justifies the use of Fundamental rights in order to ensure that they will not be disregarded by the contract. The Court of Cassation is still hesitant about seizing the control of proportionality in order to settle a dispute: it hesitates to ask itself whether the violation of a contracting party's Fundamental right by the contract is justified by a legitimate interest and whether the infringement is proportionate to the defence of this interest. By doing so, judicial jurisdictions hesitate to follow the method of the control of proportionality, which has been developed by the constitutional judge (see above).

---

[29]For in-depth studies, Raynaud (2011); Dijoux (2012).

[30]Cass. civ. 3ème, 6th of March, 1996 (Cour de cassation (3e Chambre civile)): Jamin Ch (1996), JCP éd. G, I, 3958; de Lamy B (1997), Rec. Dalloz, p. 167; Mestre J (1996), RTD civ. p. 897; Marguenaud JP (1997), RTD. civ., p. 1024; Cass. civ. 3ème, 22th of March 2006 (Cour de cassation (3e Chambre civile)): Damas N (2007) Rec. Dalloz, p. 908; Seube JB (2006), Revue des contrats, p. 1149; Marguenaud JP (2006), RTD. civ., p. 722; Cass. civ. 3ème, 10th of May, 2010 (Cour de cassation (3e Chambre civile)): Seube JB (2010), Revue des contrats, p. 913; Gautier PY (2010), RTD. civ. p. 343.

[31]Cass. Ass. Plén., 25th of June, 2014 (Cour de cassation (assemblée plénière): (2014), Rec. Dalloz, p. 1386.

[32]Cass. civ. 3ème, 18th of December, 2002 (Cour de cassation (3e Chambre civile)): Damas N (2004), Rec. Dalloz, p. 844; Mestre J, Fages B (2003), RTD. civ. p. 290; Marguénaud JP (2003) RTD civ., p. 383; Libchaber R (2003), RTD. civ., p. 575; Marais A (2003), Revue des contrats, p. 220; Rochfeld J (2004), Revue des contrats, p. 231; Lardeux G (2004), Revue des contrats, p. 348.

[33]Cass. civ. 1ère, 14th of January, 2009 (Cour de cassation (1ère Chambre civile)): Hauser J (2009), RTD civ., p. 298; Loiseau G (2009), JCP éd. G, II, 10025; Revet T (2009), RTD civ. p. 342.

We would like to mention in particular an interesting ruling. Here are the facts: a couple owns a flat in a condominium. On the occasion of the Jewish celebration 'Feast of tabernacles', they have built a structure made out of plants on their terrace. Invoking the respect of the chart of joint ownership, which has a contractual value, the general meeting of joint owners quickly voted a resolution authorising the syndic of joint ownership to introduce a summary proceeding to obtain an interim order to withdraw this construction. The couple assigned the syndic of joint ownership in annulment of this resolution. Dismissed by the Court of Appeal, the appellant challenged the case before the Court of Cassation, invoking freedom of religion on the grounds of Article 9 ECHR and Article 9 of the Civil code. They consider that 'clauses of a joint ownership regulation cannot deprive a joint owner of his right to exercise freedom of worship, in the absence of any nuisance for the co-proprietors. By refusing the right to exercise their worship by the construction of a precarious and temporary cabin on their balcony for a week, on the sole grounds that this construction would be contrary to the condominium's rules, the Court of Appeal has violated Articles 9 of the Civil code and Article 9 of the European Convention on Human Rights'. They thus blamed the Court of Appeal for the abrupt nature of its ruling and summoned the Court of Cassation to conduct a control of proportionality. The Court of Cassation dismissed the appeal and judged that 'whereas the Court had been right in holding that however fundamental it might be, freedom of religion could not have the effect to render lawful violations of provisions of a co-ownership agreement and noted that the cabin was prohibited by the co-ownership regulations and undermined the building's global harmony since it was visible from the street. The Court of Appeal was not required to proceed to an analysis which its observations made ineffective and has correctly inferred that the general assembly was entitled to mandate its syndic in order to act in a court of law so as to obtain the removal of these objects or constructions.'[34] In this ruling, by stating that the 'Court of Appeal did not need to run an analysis which its observations rendered ineffective', the Court of Cassation eliminates all research of proportionality.

The ruling has been criticised and some authors reproached the French judges' failure to implement a control of proportionality. It would have been necessary, from their perspective, for the Court of Cassation to analyse whether the violation of the freedom of religion was provided by law, whether this violation pursued a legitimate aim and if there existed a ratio of proportionality between the violation of the religion and the aim pursued. They consider that if such a control of proportionality had been done, the ruling would undoubtedly have been different. The cabin was only erected for seven days; it did not disseminate either noise or smell, so there were sufficient reasons to believe the inconvenience caused to the neigh-

---

[34]Cass. civ. 3ème, 8th of June, 2006 (Cour de cassation (3e Chambre civile)): Atias C (2006) Rec. Dalloz, p. 2887; Fenouillet D (2006), Les petites affiches, n°113, p. 9; Marguénaud JP (2006), RTD civ., p. 722.

bours was slight.[35] *De facto*, they consider that the refusal to operate the control of proportionality is justified by the technique of cassation and by the French judicial reasoning, which, by using the judicial syllogism, would be reluctant to resort to it. Professor Dominique Fenouillet wrote: 'the inconvenience of such a control of proportionality is well known: it results from the fact that the general rule of law dilutes itself in the solutions of particular cases which are always closer to circumstances of the case'.[36]

However, some authors showed that the implementation of the control of proportionality does not necessarily lead to a casuistry solely factual. Professor Christophe Jasmin, in an important article, compares the reasoning that was adopted by the Court of Cassation to the one followed by the Canadian Supreme Court in identical cases. He considers that the balance between competing interests does not rest on facts but on norms (in this case, the joint ownership regulation and the freedom of religion) and that they must be combined by adopting a more subtle approach to that followed by the Court of Cassation. He wrote: 'let's go back to our case: the joint ownership's regulation can serve multiple interests (the building's overall harmony, security, a peaceful neighbourhood) and relies on a principle which has a fundamental importance (the binding nature of contracts). As regards the freedom of religion, one must break it down: is the installation of cabins a recommendation or a requirement in the Jewish religion? What is the thrust of this recommendation/obligation? Etc. In doing so, we will have analysed the intrinsic scope of the conflicting norms. Then, one must assess their relative scope. Concerning the joint ownership's regulation, it is the building's harmony which is put forward in the case. Question: can this specific purpose impose itself on freedom of religion? And more specifically to its incarnation in the set-up of cabins? In this case, the answer relies on the intrinsic scope we confer on the installation: acting as a simple recommendation, one can imagine it might take precedence over the preservation of the building's harmony. However, it could be different if we consider that it is an absolute requirement. Furthermore, if it is no longer the building's harmony which is at stake, but the co-proprietor's safety, then we can imagine the solution would not have been identical even though we keep in mind the fact that the installations were an absolute requirement. In addition, in order to answer these questions, one must bring into the debate various considerations which are not per se legal but rather moral, political, religious or economic, but which become legal as soon as they are weighed, and they are always weighed in every single case.'[37] Therefore, he demonstrates that the reasoning adopted not only is factual but also combines factual and legal elements. It is most probably this combination that, as far as French jurists are concerned, is the most disturbing aspect because it leads to the collapsing of the distinction between facts and law, a distinction on which the technique of cassation relies. However, he considers that

[35] Marguénaud (2006).

[36] Fenouillet (2006).

[37] Jamin (2015), p. 263.

the judges of the Court of Cassation should be able to reconcile legal norms and abandon the binary distinction between principle and exception. This conciliation should allow the reaching of a compromise between conflicting norms by creating a new norm. This new norm would integrate, in this particular case, elements of the freedom of religion and some of the co-proprietors' prerogatives. It would take away some elements and keep others, allowing variations depending on the situation and the prerogatives at stake (for instance, the judge could reason differently whether the syndic invokes the building's harmony or its safety or whether the co-proprietors wish to install a cabin for a duration of a week or a year).

4 Conclusion

As a conclusion, we have the feeling that the syllogistic reasoning that the Court of Cassation resorts to is threatened by the sudden development of the control of proportionality.

The first president of the Court of Cassation made no mistake: he has set up a committee that has the intention of reflecting on the new controls exercised by the Court of Cassation. He wrote:

> This is the reason why our Court thinks about the conceptualization of this control, said to be "of conventionality", in order to determine its scope and its level. The outcome of this reflection could lead to three series of consequences: 1. It could have an effect on the grounds of our rulings which are still deeply inspired by the legalistic shortness; they should then be enriched with more developed considerations as regards the context, which is necessary to the assessment of proportionality. 2. It could lead to the preparation of rulings with a multi-disciplinary scope by a greater opening of the Court towards external institutions, be they public or private, towards whom the public prosecutor, pending its role's redefinition, destabilized by the Court of Strasbourg for the past ten years, could complete the essential mission of interface. 3. It could lead to the implementation of conditions concerning the appeal's admissibility, stricter than that of the non-admission which is in force and which has lost a part of its original efficiency over the past years. This should allow the Court of Cassation, in the event of a predictable influx of new appeals founded on the expected developments of the control of proportionality before the trial judge, to limit its interventions to actions in line with a unifying and legislative rôle which is its "raison d'être".[38]

Thus, one can measure that the control of proportionality is going to have profound procedural repercussions and is significantly going to modify the grounds of the Court of Cassation's rulings. Often criticised for their shortness and their (very) concise nature, these rulings should be more developed and include more factual considerations allowing to explain and justify the proportionality withheld or discarded. The Court of Cassation's ruling could, to some extent, get a step closer to the ECHR's rulings.

[38] Louvel (2015a), p. 1326.

One has the feeling that the control of proportionality is likely to become increasingly important. This control will only develop itself once the reform of the French Contract law will enter into force. In its implementation, the Court of Cassation will be able to inspire itself from the Constitutional Council and the ECHR, which have been handling this concept for quite a long time.

Acknowledgements The author gratefully acknowledges English translation from Miss Jessica Jade Betti, student of Master at the Faculty of Law, University of Reunion Island, and Me Laetitia Rigault, lawyer at the Reunion Bar.

References

Blachèr P, Seube JB (2000) PACS. Revue de droit public: 203–246
Cabrillac R (2015) Introduction générale au droit, 11è éd., Dalloz, n°62 *et sec.*
Cornu G (2007) Introduction au droit, 13è éd., Montchrestien, n°27
Debet A (2002) L'influence de la Convention européenne sur le droit privé. Dalloz, coll. 'Nouvelle collection des thèses'
De Secondat de Montesquieu CL (1748) L'esprit des lois
Dijoux R (2012) La contractualisation des droits fondamentaux. L'Harmattan, Paris
Duclerq JB (2015) Les mutations du contrôle de proportionnalité dans la jurisprudence du Conseil constitutionnel. Thèse Paris I
Eissen ME (1999) Le principe de proportionnalité dans la jurisprudence de la Cour européenne des droits de l'homme. In: Pettiti LE, Decaux E et Imbert PH, La Convention européenne des droits de l'homme, Commentaire article par article, Economica, Paris, p 65 *et sec.*
Gahdoum PY (2011) Le droit des biens et le droit des obligations. Cahiers du Conseil constitutionnel, no. 31
Goesel-Le Bihan V (2012) Le contrôle de proprotionnalité exercé par le Conseil constitutionnel: technique de protection des libertés publiques. Jus politicum, no. 7
Guinchard S (1999) Le procès équitable: garantie formelle ou droit substantiel? Mélanges Farjat, Nice, p 155
Jamin C (2015) Juger et motiver, Introduction comparative à la question du contrôle de proportionnalité en matière de droits fondamentaux. RTD. civ., p 263
Jeuland E (2016) Réforme de la Cour de cassation, une approche non utilitariste du contrôle de proportionnalité. JCP G, suppl. 1 et 2, p 20
Louvel B (2015a) Réflexions à la Cour de cassation. Rec. Dalloz, p 1326
Louvel B (2015b) Pour exercer pleinement son office de cour suprême, la Cour de cassation doit adapter ses modes de contrôle. JCP G, 1122
Malaurie Ph, Morvan P (2012), Introduction générale, 4ème éd., Defrénois, n°62 *et sec.*
Molfessis N (2000) Pacte civil de solidarité, La réécriture de la loi par le Conseil Constitutionnel. JCP, I, 210
Moutel B (2006) L'effet horizontal de la CEDH en droit privé français. Thèse Limoges
Muzny P (2005) La technique de la proportionnalité et le juge de la Convention européenne des droits de l'homme, Essai sur un instrument nécessaire dans une société démocratique. PUAM, Aix-en Provence
Perelman C (1999) Logique juridique nouvelle rhétorique. Dalloz, Paris
Philippe X (1990) Le contrôle de proportionnalité dans les jurisprudences constitutionnelle et administrative françaises. Economica, coll. 'Science et droit administratifs', Paris
Raymond G (2000) PACS et droit des contrats. Contrats, conc., consom., chron. 14
Raynaud J (2011) Les atteintes aux droits fondamentaux dans les actes juridiques. Thèse Limoges

Seube JB (2009) Le contrôle de proportionnalité opéré par le juge judiciaire. Les Petites Affiches, 5 mars, p 86
Terré F (2012) Introduction générale au droit, 9ème éd., Dalloz, n°77 *et sec.*
Xynopoulos G (1995) Le contrôle de proportionnalité dans le contentieux de la constitutionnalité et de la légalité en France, en Allemagne et en Angleterre. LGDJ, Bibl. dr. public, Paris

Other Sources

Adde, Prétot X (1996), Rec. Dalloz, p. 45.
Melin-Soucramanien F (1995), Rec. Dalloz, p. 344.
Gaïa P (1995), Rec. Dalloz, p. 351.
Mestre J (1996), RTD. civ., p. 151.
Adde Fabre-Magnan M (1997), JCP, I, 4039, n°1.
Verpeaux and Mathieu (1997), JCP, I, 4066, n°16.
Melin-Soucramanien (1999), Rec. Dalloz, p. 236.
Favoreu (1999), Rec. Dalloz, p. 234.
Molfessis (1997), RTD civ. p. 787.
Mestre (1998), RTD. civ. p. 99.
Mathieu (1997), Les Petites Affiches, n° 125, p. 13.
Adde, Ribes D (2001), Rec. Dalloz, p. 1766.
Molfessis N (2001), RTD civ., p. 229.
Adde, Ghestin J (2013), JCP éd. G, 929.
Mekki M (2013), JCP éd. G, 974, n°1.
Pérès C (2013), Rev. des contrats, p. 1285.
Barbier H (2013), RTD. civ., p. 832.
Adde, Schrameck O (1996), AJDA, p. 369.
Gaïa P (1998), Rec. Dalloz, p. 150.
Adde, Schoettl JE (1998), AJDA, p. 495.
Favoreu L (2000), Rec. Dalloz, p. 60.
Molfessis N (1998), RTD civ., p. 796.
Mestre J (1999), RTD. civ., p. 78.
Verpeaux M, Mathieu B (1998), JCP éd. G, I, 179, n°14.
Schoettl JE (1999), AJDA, p. 700.
Gay L (2000), Rec. Dalloz, p. 422.
Marino L (2000), Rec. Dalloz, p. 265.
Fatin-Rouge M (2000), Rec. Dalloz, p. 423.
Molfessis N (1999), RTD civ., p. 724.
Bernaud V (2001), Rec. Dalloz, p. 1837.
Schoettl JE (2001), AJDA, p. 18.
Favoreu L (2001), Rec. Dalloz, p. 1840.
Fatin-Rouge M (2001), Rec. Dalloz, p. 1841.
Ribes D (2002), Rec. Dalloz, p. 1950.
Reneaud F (2002), AJDA, p. 1163.
Gay L (2003), Rec. Dalloz, p. 1129.
Mathieu B (2002), Rec. Dalloz, p. 1439, chron. B. Mathieu…
(Dijon, 31th of May, 1989: Rozès L (1990), Rec. Dalloz, p. 256, obs. L. Rozès; Deruppé J (1990), Rev. dr. Immobilier, p. 126).
J.-P. Marguénaud et J. Mouly, note in D. 1999, p. 645.
Marguenaud JP, Mouly J (1999), Rec. Dalloz, p. 645.
Ray JE (1999), Dr. social, p. 287.

Garaud E (1999), RJPF mai 1999, p. 8.
Hauser J (1999), RTD civ. p. 358.
Mestre J (1999) RTD. civ., p. p. 395.
Marguénaud JP (2003), RTD civ. p. 710.
Rochfeld J (2003), Rev. des contrats, p. 17 *et sec.*
Jamin Ch (1996), JCP éd. G, I, 3958.
de Lamy B (1997), Rec. Dalloz, p. 167.
Mestre J (1996), RTD civ. p. 897.
Marguenaud JP (1997), RTD. civ., p. 1024.
Damas N (2007) Rec. Dalloz, p. 908.
Seube JB (2006), Revue des contrats, p. 1149.
Marguenaud JP (2006), RTD. civ., p. 722.
Seube JB (2010), Revue des contrats, p. 913; Gautier PY (2010), RTD. civ. p. 343.
[no author] (2014), Rec. Dalloz, p. 1386.
Damas N (2004), Rec. Dalloz, p. 844.
Mestre J, Fages B (2003), RTD. civ. p. 290.
Marguénaud JP (2003) RTD civ., p. 383.
Libchaber R (2003), RTD. civ., p. 575.
Marais A (2003), Revue des contrats, p. 220.
Rochfeld J (2004), Revue des contrats, p. 231.
Lardeux G (2004), Revue des contrats, p. 348.
Hauser J (2009), RTD civ., p. 298.
Loiseau G (2009), JCP éd. G, II, 10025.
Revet T (2009), RTD civ. p. 342.
Atias C (2006) Rec. Dalloz, p. 2887.
Fenouillet D (2006), Les petites affiches, n°113, p. 9.
Marguénaud JP (2006), RTD civ., p. 722.
ECHR, *Handyside/RU*, 7th of September, 1976, série A, n°24
and *Sunday Times/RU*, 26th of April, 1979, série A, n°30.

The Role of the General Principle of the Prohibition of Abuse of Rights in the Enforcement of Human Rights in Contract Law: A Belgian Law Perspective

Annekatrien Lenaerts

Abstract This chapter will determine and evaluate the role of the general principle prohibiting the abuse of rights in the enforcement of human rights in contractual relations, essentially from the angle of Belgian law. Whereas this principle has been created and developed in private law relations, the influence of international human rights has increased the importance of the discussed principle. It will be demonstrated on the basis of the Belgian case law that the criteria to find an abuse of rights constitute appropriate tools to enforce human rights in contractual relations (e.g., the right to non-discrimination, the right to human dignity or the right to privacy). As such, these criteria and the technique of judicial review, which are applied in private law relations, have been concretised or modulated in light of the proportionality test used in the protection of human rights in vertical relations.

1 Introduction

The general principle of the prohibition of abuse of rights aims to correct the exercise of a subjective right on the basis of standards such as good faith, fairness and justice if, despite formal observance of the conditions laid down in the rule granting that right, the true spirit of that rule has not been achieved. Hence, this principle will reduce the 'abusive' exercise of a subjective right to an adequate use.[1]

Traditionally, the principle prohibiting the abuse of rights has been developed in private law relations, not only in Belgian law but also in various legal orders of the Member States of the European Union. Therefore, in the first section, the emergence and the development of this principle will be analysed both in Belgian private law and from a comparative perspective (see Sect. 2 *infra*). As such, the legal basis

---

All opinions expressed are personal.

[1]Stijns (2005b), pp. 62–63; Van Ommeslaghe (2010), pp. 52–54; Wéry (2011), p. 126.

A. Lenaerts (✉)
Belgian Court of Cassation, KU Leuven, Institute for Law of Obligations,
Leuven, Belgium
e-mail: annekatrien.lenaerts@law.kuleuven.be

L. Siliquini-Cinelli, A. Hutchison (eds.), *The Constitutional Dimension of Contract Law*, DOI 10.1007/978-3-319-49843-0_4

(Sect. 2.1), the conditions of application (Sect. 2.2) and the legal effects of the principle (Sect. 2.3) will be discussed.

Yet in Belgian law, it is striking that progressively the application of the principle of the prohibition of abuse of rights has been influenced by evolutions in public law, which have granted the latter principle an increasing importance, in particular in the field of human rights. Indeed, repeatedly the Belgian judge has applied the principle prohibiting the abuse of rights in order to refuse the exercise of a contractual right in a manner that imposed disproportional restrictions on the human rights of the other party (e.g., the right to non-discrimination, the right to human dignity or the right to privacy). This evolution will be investigated in the second section (see Sect. 3 *infra*).

First, the influence of the fundamental rights, as proclaimed in the European Convention on Human Rights (hereafter ECHR) and the Belgian Constitution, will be generally determined in contractual relations (Sect. 3.1). Thereafter, it will be demonstrated that not only there exists a remarkable similarity between the proportionality test used in the balancing of human rights in vertical relations and the specific criteria of the abuse of rights in private law relations. Also, this proportionality test applied in vertical relations may offer further guidelines as to how these criteria of the abuse of rights must be concretised or modulated in view of the protection of human rights (Sect. 3.2). Also, there appears to be a significant congruence between the judicial restraint applied in the protection of human rights in vertical relations and the degree of judicial review used in finding an abuse of rights in private law relations. This will be analysed below (Sect. 3.3). Finally, the contribution will examine various applications in Belgian case law illustrating that the criteria of the abuse of rights may constitute appropriate tools in the enforcement of human rights in contract law relations (Sect. 3.4).

2 The Principle of the Prohibition of Abuse of Rights as Traditionally Developed in Private Law

2.1 *Concept and Legal Basis*

The concept of abuse of rights refers to situations in which the holder of a subjective right acts within the formal limits of his right but exercises the right in a manner that is contrary to what may be expected from a reasonable person placed in the same circumstances. In such situations, on the basis of the prohibition of abuse of rights, the judge may completely refuse the exercise of the subjective right or reduce it to what would be a reasonable and fair exercise in the given circumstances. In that way, the inadequate use of a right is reduced to the limits of an adequate exercise.[2]

[2]Stijns (2005b), pp. 62–63; Wéry (2011), p. 126.

Hence, the general principle prohibiting the abuse of rights functions as a corrective mechanism to the strict exercise of a right in accordance with the rules of written law.[3] In contractual matters, the reduction of the improper exercise of a contractual right to a normal exercise constitutes a far-reaching correction to the basic principle of the autonomy of the parties.[4]

The principle prohibiting the abuse of rights is strongly anchored in several European Civil law traditions.[5] In Belgium and France, historically this general principle has been created outside contract law, in the field of property law. It was built on the basis of delictual liability under Article 1382 Civil code.[6] Thereafter, the general principle of the prohibition of abuse of rights has been recognised in contractual matters on the basis of the duty of good faith in the performance of contracts under Article 1134 (3) Civil code, in its limitative function. In an important decision of 19 September 1983, the Belgian Court of Cassation has explicitly recognised the limitative function of good faith in contract law: this function imposes a duty of moderation on the contracting parties and prohibits them to exercise their rights in an abusive manner.[7]

In its subsequent decision of 17 May 1990, the Belgian Court of Cassation has clarified that the limitative function of good faith merely applies if one of the criteria for the prohibition of abuse is fulfilled. Thus, the limitative function of good faith is fully assimilated with the general principle of the prohibition of abuse of rights.[8] This decision makes clear that the limitative function of good faith is entirely concretised through the strict criteria for the general principle prohibiting the abuse of rights. As such, in Belgian contract law, the limitative function of good faith is not granted an autonomous role.[9] Likewise, in French case law[10] and legal doctrine,[11] it is recognised that the limitative function of good faith entirely coincides with the principle prohibiting the abuse of rights in contractual matters ('abuse-based legal orders').

---

[3]De Page (1962), p. 168; Stijns (2005b), pp. 63 and 66; Van Oevelen (1991), p. 142. See for France: Ghestin et al. (1994), p. 792.

[4]Stijns (2005b), p. 63.

[5]See for an overview: Fleischer (2003), pp. 865–868; Neville Braun (1994), pp. 513–515.

[6]See for Belgium: Van Gerven (1987), pp. 197–201; see for France: Ghestin et al. (1994), pp. 747–795.

[7]See for Belgium: Judgment of 19 Sept. 1983, [1984] 1 Pasicrisie 55 (*Cour de cassation*); Judgment of 16 Jan. 1986, [1986] 1 Pasicrisie 602 (*Cour de cassation*); Judgment of 18 Feb. 1988, [1988] 1 Pasicrisie 728 (*Cour de cassation*); Judgment of 8 Feb. 2001, [2001] 1 Pasicrisie 244 (*Cour de cassation*); Stijns (2005b), pp. 64–72; Van Gerven and Van Oevelen (2015), pp. 100–101. See for France: Stoffel-Munck (2000), pp. 66 *et seq*.

[8]Judgment of 17 May 1990, [1990] 1 Pasicrisie, 1061 (*Cour de cassation*); Judgment of 20 Feb. 1992, [1992] 1 Pasicrisie 549 (*Cour de cassation*).

[9]Stijns (2005b), pp. 65–66; Van Gerven and Lierman (2010), p. 426.

[10]Judgment of 29 Nov. 1994, [1995] Dalloz 122 (*Cour de cassation* (Chambre civile)); Judgment of 20 Jan. 1998, [1998] Dalloz 413 (*Cour de cassation* (Chambre commerciale)).

[11]Stoffel-Munck (2000), pp. 60 and 85 *et seq*. See also Fauvarque-Cosson and Mazeaud (2008), pp. 258–260.

As opposed to the Belgian and French legal orders, in other Civil law traditions—such as Germany and the Netherlands—the prohibition of abuse of rights is founded on the restrictive function of reasonableness and fairness (*Treu und Glauben*,[12] *redelijkheid en billijkheid*[13]). In these legal orders, the limitative function of good faith plays an autonomous role. It may also apply if the criteria for the existence of an abuse of rights are not fulfilled. Thus, the prohibition of abuse of rights is not the exclusive criterion for the limitative function of good faith but merely one of the possible applications of this function ('reasonableness and fairness-based legal orders').[14]

Yet the duty of reasonableness and fairness, on the one hand, and the principle of the prohibition of abuse of rights, on the other hand, seem to constitute two sides of the same medal: a positive side, namely the duty of good faith in the performance of contracts, and a negative side, namely the prohibition of abuse of rights. Consequently, similar results can be obtained on the basis of either of these sides: in both cases, an inadequate exercise of a subjective right will be reduced within the limits of a proper use of that right.[15]

2.2 *Criteria of the Abuse of Rights*

2.2.1 Generic Criterion and Restrained Judicial Review

In Belgian private law, since the general principle prohibiting the abuse of rights and the limitative function of good faith fully coincide, in both situations the same criteria and the same sanction apply. In its landmark case of 10 September 1971, the Belgian Court of Cassation formulated a generic criterion of the abuse of rights: an abuse exists 'if the limits of a normal exercise of a subjective right by a careful and cautious person placed in the same circumstances are manifestly exceeded'.[16] This generic criterion is also applied to establish an abuse of a contractual right.

The term 'manifestly' makes clear that the judge may only exercise a restrained role in determining whether an abuse exists. He may not substitute his personal

[12] § 242 German Civil code.

[13] Articles 6:2 (2) and 6:248 (2) Dutch Civil code.

[14] See for Germany: Heinrichs (2006) § 242, pp. 246–251; Larenz and Wolf (2004), pp. 284–290. See for the Netherlands: Hartkamp (2005), pp. 320–341. However, in the Netherlands, originally the limitative function of good faith was entirely assimilated with the principle of the prohibition of abuse of rights. See Meijers, explanatory works to the Dutch Civil code, Parlementaire geschiedenis, Invoering boek 3, p. 1040 and Parlementaire geschiedenis, Voorlopig antwoord op vraagpunt 21, Boek 6, pp. 43–44, discussed in Stijns (1994), p. 403: the restrictions imposed on the exercise of a right based on reasonableness and fairness on the one hand and on abuse on the other hand coincide. It follows that the criteria for the existence of an abuse of rights are useful to evaluate whether the exercise of a right is contrary to reasonableness and fairness.

[15] See for more details: Lenaerts (2010), pp. 1121 *et seq.*

[16] Judgment of 10 Sept. 1971, [1972] 1 Pasicrisie 28 (*Cour de cassation*).

judgment for that of the party whose behaviour he is evaluating (i.e., a full review). This reserved role is defined as *contrôle marginal*: only if the margins of reasonableness are manifestly exceeded may the judge reduce the exercise of a right. This is the case if the judge can establish that no holder of a similar subjective right, placed in the same circumstances, would have chosen that specific manner of exercising this right. Hence, the intervention of the judge could find support in the general legal conviction.[17] The rationale for this principle of judicial restraint lies in the margin of discretion to which every party is entitled in the exercise of their subjective rights.[18] Indeed, since a party acts within the formal limits of his right, his behaviour is presumed to be lawful.[19] Moreover, in contractual relations, this reserved role of the judge is in conformity with the principle of the autonomy of the parties, which grants the parties the freedom to determine their own legal position.

2.2.2 Specific Criteria

The Belgian Court of Cassation has specified that in establishing an abuse of rights, the judge must take into account all the specific facts and circumstances of the case.[20] He must precisely determine why a particular exercise of a right goes beyond the limits of an adequate exercise in the same circumstances. For this, specific criteria of abuse have been developed and serve as an important tool for the judge in establishing an abuse.

The oldest specific criteria, as developed in Belgian[21] and French laws,[22] are, firstly, the exercise of a right with an exclusive intention to harm or without reasonable and sufficient interest for oneself and, secondly, the choice between different means to exercise a right with equal usefulness, of the one that is the most harmful for the other or that undermines the general interest. In Belgian law, a more recent, third criterion is the exercise of a right in a manner that benefits the holder of that right but that causes disproportionate harm to the other (criterion of proportionality).[23]

The application of these criteria has been extended to contractual rights. In this field particularly, the criterion of proportionality plays an important role

[17]Ronse (1977), pp. 210–211; Stijns (1990), pp. 41 *et seq.*; Stijns (2005b), p. 67; Van Ommeslaghe (2010), p. 74.

[18]Stijns (2005b), p. 67.

[19]Stijns (1994), p. 429.

[20]Judgment of 30 Jan. 2003, [2003] 1 Pasicrisie 227 (*Cour de cassation*).

[21]See for an overview: Van Gerven (1987), pp. 184–191.

[22]See Mazeaud and Tunc (1965), pp. 653–655.

[23]See on these specific criteria: Baeck (2007), pp. 64–74; Stijns (1990), p. 40; Stijns (2005b), pp. 67–70; Van Gerven and Van Oevelen (2015), pp. 99–100; Van Ommeslaghe (2010), pp. 77–81; Wéry (2011), pp. 127–128.

in Belgian law.[24] Likewise, in German law, the criterion of proportionality (*Unverhältnismässigkeit*) is an essential condition of application of the limitative function of good faith.[25]

Finally, some Belgian legal scholars consider the betrayal of the legitimate expectations that one has raised in the other party to be a specific criterion of the abuse of rights.[26] For instance, if a creditor inadequately remains passive after having submitted a claim against the debtor, the latter may suffer with the length of the procedure, in particular, when the claimed amount has been increased in the meantime or has produced legal interest.[27] In such a case, the amount to be received of the creditor may be reduced to a proper amount, or the interest may be suspended during the procedure.[28]

2.3 *Sanction of the Abuse of Rights*

It is recognised in Belgian and French laws that the sanctioning of an abuse of rights must result in the abusive behaviour being entirely deprived of any legal effect. Indeed, a party may neither rely on the abusive exercise of a right nor take any advantage of this exercise. Consequently, the parties must be restored as far as possible to the situation that would have existed if the agreement were exercised in an adequate manner.[29] In this respect, the Belgian Court of Cassation has clarified that the sanction against an abuse is not a complete dissolution of the right but either a reduction of the exercise of a right to an adequate use (i.e., imposing a proper exercise or a reparation *in natura*) or a reparation of the damages caused by the abuse (i.e., a reparation by equivalent).[30] Thus, it is the task of the judge to impose

---

[24]See for a recent application: Judgment of 9 March 2009, [2009] Journal des tribunaux 392 (*Cour de cassation*); Foriers (1994), pp. 217 *et seq*. According to this author, the criterion of proportionality even contains all other specific criteria of abuse.

[25]Larenz and Wolf (2004), p. 287; Krüger (2007), pp. 168–169 and 209 *et seq*.

[26]Van Gerven (1987), p. 194; Van Gerven and Van Oevelen (2015), p. 102.

[27]Judgment of 17 Oct. 2008, [2008] 1 Pasicrisie 2278 (*Cour de cassation*).

[28]Judgment of 17 June 2002, [2003] Revue générale de droit civil belge 446 (Civil Court of Appeal of Liège); Judgment of 4 June 2002, [2003] Revue régionale de droit 455 (Civil Court of Appeal of Liège); Judgment of 6 June 2006, [2006] Journal des tribunaux du travail 373 (Labour Court of Appeal of Liège). See Marchandise (2007), p. 157.

[29]Stijns (1994), pp. 432–433; Stijns et al. (1996), p. 707; Wéry (2011), p. 427. See for France: Ghestin et al. (1994), pp. 793–794.

[30]Judgment of 16 Dec. 1982, [1983] 1 Pasicrisie 472 (*Cour de cassation*); Judgment of 18 Feb. 1988, [1988] 1 Pasicrisie 728 (*Cour de cassation*); Judgment of 11 June 1992, [1992] 1 Pasicrisie 898 (*Cour de cassation*).

an adapted sanction, which is modulated and adjusted according to the nature and the form of the abuse.[31]

For example, if a creditor abuses his right to opt between a forced performance or a termination of the contract in the case of non-performance by the debtor (Article 1184 Civil code), the reduction may consist of the imposition on the creditor of the opposite, unrequested, option (in particular a non-requested termination).[32] Moreover, if a creditor abuses a valid penalty clause, this clause will be reduced to a reasonable amount.[33]

In an important decision of 8 February 2001, the Belgian Court of Cassation has ruled that if the abusive exercise of contractual rights concerns the application of a contractual term (*in casu* a penalty clause), the sanction against the abuse may consist of the complete refusal of the right of the creditor to rely on that term. In certain circumstances, this is the only way of depriving the abusive conduct of any legal effect.[34] In more recent cases of 1 October 2010 and 6 January 2011, the court has reaffirmed this principle.[35] Also in French and German laws, it is recognised that the sanction of an abuse of rights may consist in a partial or entire refusal of the exercise of a right.[36]

However, the sanction of an abuse of rights does not lead to the dissolution of the right since it is not permanently annulled. The right itself still exists, and the term remains valid; it is only the *exercise* of the right that is completely refused in the particular circumstances since it is manifestly unreasonable.[37] But if a right can only be exercised once, the distinction between the dissolution of a right and the refusal to *exercise* a right is rather theoretical.[38] Yet this distinction remains important in all other cases where a right may be exercised several times. For example, if a creditor abuses, in specific circumstances, his right to unilaterally terminate a contract because of non-performance by the debtor on the basis of an express resolutive term, the judge may sanction this abuse by completely depriving the decision of the creditor of any effect. But in subsequent cases, the creditor may still rely in a non-abusive manner on the express resolutive term.[39]

---

[31] See conclusion of Prosecutor-General Ganshof van der Meersch under the judgment of 10 Sept. 1971, [1972] 1 Pasicrisie 28 (*Cour de cassation*), pp. 37–38; Foriers (1994), p. 206; Van Ommeslaghe (1987), p. 110.

[32] Judgment of 16 Jan. 1986, [1986] 1 Pasicrisie 602 (*Cour de cassation*).

[33] Judgment of 18 Feb. 1988, [1988] 1 Pasicrisie 728 (*Cour de cassation*).

[34] Judgment of 8 Feb. 2001, [2001] 1 Pasicrisie 244 (*Cour de cassation*). See Wéry (2002), p. 127.

[35] Judgment of 1 Oct. 2010, [2010] 1 Pasicrisie 2470 (*Cour de cassation*); Judgment of 6 Jan. 2011, [2011] 1 Pasicrisie 44 (*Cour de cassation*).

[36] See for France: Ghestin et al. (1994), pp. 793–794; Le Tourneau (2008), p. 1400, § 6872. See for Germany: Schulze (2005), p. 201; Westerman (2008), p. 848.

[37] Baeck (2007), p. 96; Stijns (2005a), p. 98; Stijns (2005b), p. 71; Van Gerven and Van Oevelen (2015), p. 101; Wéry (2011), p. 429.

[38] Van Oevelen (2001), pp. 780–781; Van Ommeslaghe (2010), pp. 82–83.

[39] See Baeck (2007), pp. 99–102; Stijns (2005a), pp. 98–100; Vanderschot (2005), p. 87.

3 The Principle of the Prohibition of Abuse of Rights as an Instrument to Sanction Disproportionate Restrictions of Human Rights in Contract Law

3.1 Indirect Horizontal Effect of Human Rights in Private Law Relations

3.1.1 Different Doctrinal Views: Direct vs. Indirect Horizontal Effect

As indicated, in Belgian law, progressively the principle prohibiting the abuse of rights has been attributed an important role in the enforcement of human rights between contracting parties. Human rights refer to the fundamental rights that are enshrined in the international human rights treaties. These rights mostly correspond to an equivalent fundamental right anchored in the Belgian Constitution.[40] It must first be analysed which influence human rights can have in contractual relations.

In Belgian law, traditionally human rights were considered to affect only relations between the government and citizens (vertical relations).[41] Only progressively, human rights have initiated to penetrate the horizontal relations between citizens[42] through the imported German concept of *Drittwirkung*.[43]

This concept has led to two opposing views among Belgian legal scholars. The first view advocates a direct horizontal effect (*direct Drittwirkung*) of human rights.[44] These rights may be invoked not only against the government but also in the relation between private parties. In this view, human rights are considered as meta-norms, which apply in a similar manner in public law and private law relations.[45]

However, the second view, shared by the majority of the Belgian doctrine, favours an indirect horizontal effect (*indirect Drittwirkung*) of human rights. These rights may not be invoked directly in the relationship between private parties but are applied through 'open concepts' of private law, such as *bonus pater familias*, public order, unlawful cause, good faith or the abuse of rights.[46] The

---

[40]Van Leuven (2006), p. 171.

[41]See on this evolution: Rimanque and Peeters (1982), p. 11; Velaers (2003), pp. 289–290.

[42]Renauld (2009), p. 19; Rimanque and Peeters (1982), p. 3; Van Drooghenbroeck (2005), pp. 355–356. Critical about the (direct and indirect) horizontal effect of human rights: De Vos (2010), pp. 277–285. In the same sense: Cherednychenko (2004), pp. 1–17; Cherednychenko (2007), p. 553.

[43]In favour of a direct horizontal effect ('*unmittelbare Drittwirkung*'): Nipperdey (1972), p. 751; Leisner (1960), p. 354. In favour of an indirect horizontal effect ('*mittelbare Drittwirkung*'): Dürig (1978), pp. 66–67; Ganten (2000), pp. 26–27. See also Spielmann (1995), p. 28.

[44]Dirix (1982), pp. 49–51: fundamental rights may have direct effect between citizens but not in the same way as in vertical relations.

[45]Rimanque and Peeters (1982), pp. 16–17.

[46]De Boeck (2003), p. 424; Gallez (2005), pp. 410–411; Rimanque and Peeters (1982), pp. 19–21; Samoy (2004), p. 92; Velaers (2007b), pp. 129–132.

importation of human rights through 'open concepts' enables their application in several areas of the law, such as contract law.[47]

An author supports a 'strengthened indirect horizontal effect' of human rights: the judge should not be restricted by the norms of private law since these basic principles must be interpreted in conformity with the human rights, and if necessary, their traditional meaning must be revised.[48] Another theory stresses the importance of power relations between the private parties: the relation between a stronger and a weaker contracting party can to a certain extent be assimilated to the vertical relation between the government and a citizen, so that fundamental rights must apply in a stricter manner.[49]

3.1.2 Added Value of an Indirect Horizontal Effect

In my opinion, the application of the theory of an indirect horizontal effect of human rights must be advocated. In the first place, an indirect horizontal effect respects the principles of individual freedom and the autonomy of the parties, on which Belgian contract law is built. As opposed to the government, private parties are in principle free to determine their own legal position as long as the legislator has not prohibited them from acting in a certain way.[50] In this respect, a direct horizontal application of human rights entails the risk that these rights would impose similar obligations on private individuals as on the government, which serves the general interest.[51] Yet the application of human rights through the filter of existing principles of private law reconciles the basic principle of the freedom of private persons with the respect for human rights.[52] Considered as fundamental values, human rights will shape particular guidelines of conduct for private persons, which can be enforced via the open norms of private law.[53]

Moreover, in the relation between private parties, conflicts may arise between different human rights. In particular, the private autonomy of the parties in the conclusion or the performance of a contract may conflict with the human rights of another party, e.g. the right to non-discrimination, the right to human dignity or the right to privacy, and may limit these rights (see Sect. 3.4 *infra*). Some authors consider the private autonomy of the parties as a fundamental right that may be deduced from the right to liberty of person (guaranteed by Articles 5 ECHR and

---

[47] Jansen (2011), p. 383.

[48] Van Leuven (2009), p. 290. This theory has been first developed by Barak (2003), pp. 29–31.

[49] See Dirix (1982), pp. 50–51.

[50] Ibid., p. 43.

[51] Barak (2003), p. 17; Velaers (2007b), p. 130.

[52] Van Leuven (2006), pp. 174–175. See also De Boeck (2003), p. 424; De Ly (1992), pp. 1144 and 1159; Van Oevelen (1995), p. 371.

[53] Van Leuven (2009), pp. 279–281; Van Oevelen (1982), pp. 103–104.

12 Belgian Constitution) or the right to respect for private life (enshrined in Articles 8 ECHR and 22 Belgian Constitution).[54] Another author perceives this principle as an aspect of the right to property (Articles 1 First Protocol to the ECHR and 16 Belgian Constitution).[55] In any event, the freedom to contract is recognised as a general principle of law, which is implicitly laid down in Article 1134 (1) Civil code.[56]

An indirect horizontal effect of human rights has the advantage that conflicts between human rights in private law relations are evaluated in accordance with the specific principles of private law. These principles provide an appropriate normative framework to strike a proper balance between conflicting human rights while considering the public interest.[57] This balancing of conflicting fundamental rights is reflected in the 'open concepts' of private law, which permit a certain flexibility in the operation of private law.[58] As such, the limitative function of good faith, which imposes a minimum level of appropriate conduct between private parties, and the principle prohibiting the abuse of rights constitute accurate instruments to weigh conflicting values and to evaluate restrictions of human rights in the relation between contracting parties.[59] This will be further analysed below (see Sects. 3.2–3.4 *infra*).

In addition, an indirect horizontal effect of human rights has an added value as to the consequences that private law may attribute to a violation of human rights. Indeed, if human rights are enforced through specific rules of private law, these rules will indicate the specific sanction that should apply in case of an unlawful restriction of fundamental rights.[60]

Finally, the indirect horizontal effect enables the state to fulfil its positive obligation to protect human rights in the relation between private individuals.[61] Indeed, according to the case law of the European Court of Human Rights, the legislative power and the judicial power have to prevent the fundamental rights of one citizen from being affected by another citizen.[62]

---

[54]Van Gerven and Van Oevelen (2015), p. 71. See also Coester-Waltjen (2001), p. 42.

[55]Stijns (2005b), p. 47.

[56]De Boeck (2003), p. 419; Van Oevelen (1991), p. 105. Article 1134 (1) Civil code provides that agreements that are legally concluded have the same value as a legal act in relation to the concluding parties.

[57]Barak (2003), p. 29. See also De Boeck (2003), p. 433; Dirix (2011), p. 812.

[58]Barak (2003), p. 33. See also Jansen (2012), p. 180.

[59]Barak (2003), pp. 33 and 41; Van Leuven (2012), pp. 458–459.

[60]Van Leuven (2008), p. 100.

[61]Spielmann (1995), p. 30.

[62]*Young, James and Webster v United Kingdom*, judgment of 13 Aug. 1981, [1981] Series A No. 44 (European Court of Human Rights), § 63; *Fuentes Bobo v Spain*, judgment of 27 Feb. 2000, [2001] Reports VI (European Court of Human Rights), § 38; *Verlière v Switzerland*, judgment of 28 June 2001, App. No. 41953/98 (European Court of Human Rights); *Christine Goodwin v United Kingdom*, judgment of 11 July 2002, [2002] Reports VI (European Court of Human Rights); *Van Kück v Germany*, judgment of 12 June 2003, App. No. 35968/97 (European Court of Human

In an important case, *Pla and Puncernau v Andorra*, the court has explicitly recognised that the judge has a positive obligation to protect human rights in the private and contractual sphere. The court ruled that, although it is not in theory required to settle disputes of a purely private nature, it cannot remain passive where a national court's interpretation of a legal act (be it a testamentary disposition or a private contract, a public document, a statutory provision or an administrative practice) appears unreasonable, arbitrary or blatantly inconsistent with the prohibition of discrimination established by Article 14 and more broadly with the principles underlying the Convention.[63]

Consequently, applied to human rights in the sphere of contract law, the judicial power is obliged to interpret the open norms of contract law in light of international human rights.[64] These norms must embody the requirements of human rights.[65] Moreover, if necessary, the legislative power must introduce laws that prevent improper limitations of fundamental rights.[66]

3.1.3 Confirmation of an Indirect Horizontal Effect in the Recent Jurisprudence of the Belgian Constitutional Court and the Belgian Court of Cassation

In view of these diverging opinions in legal doctrine, several recent cases of the Belgian supreme courts have brought clarity with regard to the influence of human Rights in contractual relations. As such, the ruling of the Constitutional Court of 12 February 2009 confirmed the indirect horizontal effect of the principle of non-discrimination.[67] Articles 10 and 11 of the Belgian Constitution proclaim the equality before the law and the enjoyment of rights and freedoms without discrimination. The non-discrimination principle is equally enshrined in Article 14 ECHR. In the case brought before the Constitutional Court, the claimants argued that it was discriminatory that only a limited list of discrimination grounds was incorporated in the new discrimination laws of 2007, as opposed to the open non-discrimination principle of the Constitution.

Rights); *Khurshid Mustafa and Tarzibachi v Sweden*, judgment of 16 Dec. 2008, App. No. 23883/06 (European Court of Human Rights). See De Schutter (2014), pp. 441 and 446–447; Van Leuven (2012), pp. 445–450; Velaers (2007b), p. 128. It has been stressed that the state has to protect the fundamental rights of citizens against abuses of law which are imputable to other citizens: Flauss (1992), p. 465.

[63] *Pla and Puncernau v Andorra*, judgment of 13 July 2004, App. No. 69498/01 (European Court of Human Rights), § 59.

[64] Jansen (2011), pp. 383–384; Velaers (2007b), pp. 136–137.

[65] Barak (2003), pp. 21–24; De Schutter (2014), p. 466.

[66] Velaers (2007b), p. 133.

[67] Judgment of 12 Feb. 2009, No. 17/2009 (Constitutional Court), B.13 *et seq*.

In its answer to this complaint, the court ruled that there might be specific legislation and a procedure for a closed list of protected grounds, such as race, gender or political views. However, this does not mean that the victims of types of discrimination that are not included in the limited list remain without protection. Persons in that situation can always have recourse to the rules of civil responsibility or claim the nullity of discriminating contractual clauses on the basis of Articles 6, 1131 and 1333 Civil code since they are contrary to the public order.[68] In that way, the Constitution Court accepted an indirect horizontal application of the principle of non-discrimination via the traditional 'open concepts' of private law, to the extent that the grounds of discrimination are not protected by special legislation. The court ruled that no discrimination is allowed between private persons according to the articles in the Belgian Constitution and the international human rights treaties. Thus, the court referred to the conform interpretation of the 'open norms' of private law in light of the fundamental principle of non-discrimination.[69]

In a subsequent case of 29 March 2010, the Belgian Court of Cassation confirmed that the principle of non-discrimination cannot be granted any direct horizontal effect. The court ruled that this principle, laid down in Articles 10 and 11 of the Belgian Constitution, is only addressed to the government in its public law relation to the citizens. According to the court, these articles do not bring about any *direct* obligations for the citizens between each other nor do they apply *directly* in the labour relation between a public institution and its employees.[70] This ruling seems to be complementary to the previous ruling of the Constitutional Court: the Court of Cassation prohibits citizens to invoke the principle of non-discrimination *directly* in the relation between each other. However, the Court of Cassation leaves room for an *indirect* horizontal effect of that principle through reliance on the rules of private law.

Besides the non-discrimination principle, the Court of Cassation has undoubtedly recognised a horizontal effect of the other fundamental rights. In some cases, the court seems to attribute a direct effect to fundamental rights as it immediately refers to human rights in the relation between citizens.[71] Conversely, in other cases

[68] Article 1131 Civil code concerns the cause; Article 1133 Civil code provides that a cause is unlawful when it is forbidden by law, contrary to the public order or public morality; Article 6 Civil code provides that contracts may not harm the laws of public order.

[69] Jansen (2011), p. 384; Stijns and Jansen (2013), p. 13.

[70] Judgment of 29 March 2010, [2010] 1 Pasicrisie 1048 (*Cour de cassation*).

[71] See for example: Judgment of 27 April 1981, [1981] 1 Pasicrisie 964 (*Cour de cassation*) (direct application of the right to association based on Article 27 Belgian Constitution); Judgment of 27 April 2006, [2006] 1 Pasicrisie 968 (*Cour de cassation*) (direct application of the right to property based on Article 16 Belgian Constitution and 1 First Protocol ECHR); see for a discussion of the case law: Van Leuven (2009), pp. 189–198.

the court seems to favour an indirect effect by only applying the human rights in connection with private law rules.[72]

However, in a recent case of 29 September 2008, the court clearly opted for an indirect horizontal effect of human rights. This case concerned an agreement of indeterminate duration concluded between a football player and the chairman of his future football club. The parties agreed that the football player would become the exclusive property of the chairman. Following the agreement, the football player must pay a considerable amount of damages to the chairman in order to obtain the freedom to join another club.

The football player argued before the Court of Cassation that this agreement unlawfully restricted his right to freely exercise a paid professional labour. This right is anchored in Articles 12 Belgian Constitution, which guarantees the right to freedom; 23, 1° Belgian Constitution guaranteeing the right to a free choice of labour; and 4.1 and 4.2 ECHR prohibiting slavery and forced labour. He asserted that, beyond the restrictions to these rights that were provided by the law, an agreement that results in the payment of damages in order to have the possibility to pursue a professional activity is contrary to the public order and public morality laid down in Articles 6, 1108, 1131 and 1133 Civil code.

The Court of Cassation ruled that the freedom to carry out a paid professional labour can only be restricted by the law. Beyond such legal limitations, an agreement that restricts the right to a free choice of labour has an unlawful cause and is therefore absolutely void.[73]

The solution of the court seems to be correct. Indeed, the freedom of association of the football player (anchored in Article 11 ECHR) would be excessively curtailed if following an agreement the player had to buy himself out in order to be able to change his club. The court reached that solution on the basis of an indirect effect of human rights: the open concepts of public order and public morality were applied and interpreted in function of the fundamental rights at issue.[74]

In view of the above case law, it must be concluded that the 'open norms' of civil law have a particular importance in order to guarantee the respect for human rights in private law relations. In this way, the 'open norm' of the prohibition of the abuse of rights plays a particular role in the protection of human rights between contracting parties. This role will be examined hereunder.

[72] See for example: Judgment of 29 Sept. 1967, [1968] 1 Pasicrisie 132 (*Cour de cassation*) (indirect application of the right to a fair trial based on Article 6 ECHR: the Court ruled that a contractual restriction of that right between private parties violated the public order).

[73] Judgment of 29 Sept. 2008, [2008] 1 Pasicrisie 2076 (*Cour de cassation*).

[74] See Van Leuven (2011), pp. 138–139; Van Leuven (2012), pp. 452–453.

3.2 *Impact of the Proportionality Test Used in the Balancing of Human Rights on the Specific Criteria of the Abuse of Rights in Private Law Relations*

3.2.1 Proportionality Test Used in the Balancing of Human Rights in Public Law Relations and Application to Private Law Relations

3.2.1.1 Public Law vs. Private Law Context

In Belgian law, the balancing test resolving conflicts between human Rights in contractual relations occurs via the general principle prohibiting the abuse of rights. The essential question is whether the limitation of a human right is proportionate to its objective while taking into account the principles of the individual freedom and the autonomy of the contracting parties.[75] In this respect, the proportionality test used to evaluate limitations of human rights in the relations between the government and the citizens (i.e., vertical relations) has an influence on the assessment of proportionality in the horizontal relations between citizens. Indeed, from the proportionality test applied in public law has been inferred a so-called 'privatized proportionality test',[76] which will be analysed hereunder.

It has been mentioned that human rights prescribe certain guidelines of conduct for private parties, which are similar but not identical to those imposed on the government (see Sect. 3.1.2 *supra*). Indeed, whereas the government must realise the general interest and is not free in its behaviour, private persons have in principle a freedom to act, which is only limited by a minimum respect for fundamental rights. Hence, the conditions imposed on the government in order to control restrictions of human rights in vertical relations, namely the conditions of legality, of legitimacy and of proportionality (see *infra*), can merely be applied by analogy to the contractual relations between private parties. This will be further detailed below.[77]

3.2.1.2 Condition of Legality

In the first place, in vertical relations the condition of legality requires that any interference with a human right is prescribed by law.[78] This means that the imposed restriction must be sufficiently accessible and foreseeable. The relevant legislation, on the basis of which the restriction is imposed, must specify in detail the precise

---

[75]De Boeck (2003), p. 433; Van Leuven (2008), p. 99. See also Hartlief and Stolp (2000), pp. 256–257.

[76]Van Leuven (2009), p. 439.

[77]Van Leuven (2009), p. 439; Velaers (2007a), p. 90; Verhey (1992), p. 161.

[78]See on this condition De Schutter (2014), pp. 344–359; Sudre (2012), pp. 221–226; Vande Lanotte and Haeck (2005), pp. 124–134; Van Leuven (2009), pp. 127–128.

circumstances in which interferences may be permitted.[79] Thus, a prescription by law must constitute a protection from arbitrariness. 'Law' in that sense is understood in a broad, material manner rather than in the formal sense. This term includes not only formal legislation but also acts of the executive or even established case law.[80]

Applied to private law relations, this condition requires in an analogous way that restrictions of the human rights of the other party are as foreseeable as possible.[81] It can be expected from a contracting party, who limits the human rights of the other party in the performance of a contract, that he acts as transparent as possible. This means that providing detailed information on a determined limitation of a human right will be seen as a positive element in the frame of the privatised proportionality test. In contrast, concealing important information on a foreseeable restriction of a human right will be evaluated as a negative element in this proportionality test.[82] For instance, if an employer demands the wearing of specific costumes from his employees in the frame of a labour contract, he must announce this in a foreseeable and transparent way. Indeed, such a requirement could constitute a restriction of the freedom of religion.[83]

3.2.1.3 Condition of Legitimacy

In addition, in vertical relations the condition of legitimacy requires that any interference by the government with a human right is justified by the pursuance of a legitimate aim.[84] In this respect, Articles 8 to 11 ECHR contain an enumeration of specific legitimate objectives, which are based on the particular competences of the government in guaranteeing the public interest. These objectives include national security, public safety, the economic well-being of the country, the

[79]See e.g. *Sunday Times v United Kingdom*, judgment of 26 April 1979, [1979] Series A No. 30 (-European Court of Human Rights), § 49; *Silver and others v United Kingdom*, judgment of 25 March 1983, [1983] Series A No. 61 (European Court of Human Rights), §§ 85–88; *Malone v United Kingdom*, judgment of 2 Aug 1984, [1984] Series A No. 82 (European Court of Human Rights), §§ 66–68; *Barthold v Germany*, judgment of 25 March 1985, [1985] Series A No. 90 (-European Court of Human Rights), § 45; *Copland v United Kingdom*, judgment of 3 April 2007, App. No. 62617/00 (European Court of Human Rights), §§ 45–46; *Baczkowski v Poland*, judgment of 3 May 2007, [2007] Journal des tribunaux—Droit européen 192 (European Court of Human Rights), §§ 69–71.

[80]See e.g. *Klass and others v Germany*, Judgment of 6 Sept. 1978, [1978] Series A No. 82 (-European Court of Human Rights), § 79; *Malone v United Kingdom*, Judgment of 2 Aug 1984, [1984] Series A No. 82 (European Court of Human Rights), § 67.

[81]Verhey (1992), pp. 160–161.

[82]Van Leuven (2009), p. 440.

[83]See judgment of 17 Oct. 2002, [2002] Journal du droit des jeunes 42 (Labour Court of Appeal of Brussels).

[84]See on this condition: De Schutter (2014), pp. 360–368; Sudre (2012), pp. 226–228; Vande Lanotte and Haeck (2005), pp. 134–138; Van Leuven (2009), p. 128.

prevention of disorder or crime, the protection of health or morals, or the protection of the rights and freedoms of others. Yet in the examination whether other provisions of the Convention have been violated, which do not enclose a list of specific legitimate objectives, the European Court of Human Rights will take into account the more abstract aim of the public interest.[85]

In the specific context of private law relations, the legitimate aims that a private person may pursue must be defined in a broad sense.[86] Indeed, as stressed before, a private person has no obligation to serve the public interest but is allowed to act in view of his individual interests. However, as a limit to that individual freedom, a private party may not impose restrictions on fundamental rights with an exclusive aim to harm another party or without any reasonable interest.[87]

3.2.1.4 Condition of Proportionality

Finally, in vertical relations the condition of proportionality[88] requires, firstly, that a restriction of human rights by the government is appropriate in pursuing the objective justifying the interference (criterion of 'appropriateness' or 'rational connection'). Secondly, the interference must be limited to what is necessary for the fulfilment of the legitimate aim. This means that it must not go beyond what is strictly required in order to effectively achieve that aim (criterion of 'necessity' or 'minimal impairment').[89]

In the frame of this second criterion, it is sometimes specified that the balance of the various interests must be respected (criterion of 'proportionality in the strict sense').[90] This is particularly important where the aim pursued by the restriction was the protection of another fundamental right, so that two values come into conflict.[91] According to the case law of the European Court of Human Rights, the notion of 'necessity' implies that the government must demonstrate a 'pressing

---

[85] *Karner v Austria*, judgment of 24 July 2003, [2003] Reports IX (European Court of Human Rights), §§ 40–41; *Niedzwiecki v Germany*, judgment of 25 Oct. 2005, App. No. 58453/00 (European Court of Human Rights), § 32.

[86] Van Leuven (2009), p. 440; Verhey (1992), pp. 166–167.

[87] Raynaud (2003), pp. 228–232; Van Gerven (1987), p. 92; Van Leuven (2009), pp. 440–441; Velaers (2007a), p. 92.

[88] See on this criterion De Schutter (2014), pp. 368–381; McBride (1999), pp. 23 *et seq.*; Eissen (1995), pp. 65 *et seq.*; Sudre (2012), pp. 228–241; Vande Lanotte and Haeck (2005), pp. 138–147; Van Leuven (2009), pp. 128 *et seq.* and 441.

[89] See for these criteria, e.g. *Sunday Times v United Kingdom*, judgment of 26 April 1979, [1979] Series A No. 30 (European Court of Human Rights), §§ 63–66.

[90] De Prins et al. (2005), p. 9; Sottiaux (2008), p. 240; Van Gerven and Lierman (2010), p. 546. See also Van Drooghenbroeck (2001), pp. 119–135: this author stresses that the European Court of Human Rights constantly pursues a balancing of interests, even if the protection of particular human rights seems to have an absolute character according to the text of the provisions (e.g. Arts. 3 or 7 ECHR).

[91] De Schutter (2014), p. 368.

social need' to pursue the legitimate aim and to interfere with a fundamental right of a person or group of persons to that purpose.[92] In particular, the interference must be proportionate to the legitimate aim pursued.[93]

In private law relations, according to the privatised proportionality test, it will be evaluated to what extent a limitation of the human rights of a party is proportionate to the objective pursued by the private party who limits these rights. This balancing of interests implies that the benefits that a party draws from the restriction of the human rights of another party are weighed against the disadvantages that that restriction has caused to the latter party.[94] In that frame, the principle of freedom of private parties is taken into consideration. Since private persons are allowed to pursue their individual interests, they are principally permitted to do so even if they interfere with the private interests of others.[95] However, if a restriction of the human rights of a party causes a disadvantage to that party that is without any reasonable measure in comparison to the pursued advantage, the principle of proportionality has been violated.[96]

3.2.1.5 Margin of National Discretion and Degree of Judicial Protection of Human Rights

In respect of the condition of proportionality, in vertical relations, the government is granted a certain margin of appreciation in the determination of what is 'necessary' in a democratic society. Indeed, the principle of subsidiarity confers a discretionary power to the Member States to evaluate the necessity of an interference with human rights and prescribes a judicial restraint of the European Court of Human Rights.[97] Hence, the intensity of the protection of the human rights and the degree of judicial review carried out by the court, on the one side, and the margin of appreciation granted to the Member States, on the other side, are intrinsically connected.[98]

---

[92] *Handyside v United Kingdom*, judgment of 7 Dec. 1976, [1976] Series A No. 24 (European Court of Human Rights), § 48; *Barthold v Germany*, judgment of 25 March 1985, [1985] Series A No. 90 (European Court of Human Rights), § 55; *Norris v Ireland*, judgment of 26 Oct. 1988, [1988] Series A No. 142 (European Court of Human Rights), § 48; *Sunday Times v United Kingdom*, judgment of 26 Nov. 1991, [1991] Series A No. 217 (European Court of Human Rights), § 50; *Keegan v United Kingdom*, judgment of 18 July 2006, App. No. 28867/03 (European Court of Human Rights), § 30.

[93] *Olsson v Sweden*, judgment of 24 March 1988, [1988] Series A No. 130 (European Court of Human Rights), § 67.

[94] Ost and Van Drooghenbroeck (2005), p. 37; Raynaud (2003), pp. 257 *et seq.*; Van Leuven (2009), p. 441; Velaers (2007a), p. 105; Verhey (1992), pp. 177–179.

[95] Van Leuven (2009), p. 442; Velaers (2007a), p. 105.

[96] Ibid.

[97] Sudre (2012), p. 231.

[98] Henrard (2008), p. 266; Van Gerven and Lierman (2010), p. 546.

Yet the level of discretion that is left to the government will depend on the concrete circumstances of the case.[99] Firstly, the nature of the restricted human right and the gravity of the interference play a role: in more sensitive matters, the state will have less room for appreciation and the European Court of Human Rights will carry out a more intensive protection of the fundamental right. As such, interferences with rights affecting the private sphere of individuals[100] or characterising a democratic society[101] are placed under a stricter judicial review.

It must be specified that in the frame of the protection of the principle of non-discrimination (Article 14 ECHR), particularly suspect grounds of differentiation (e.g., based on nationality, gender, race, religion, unlawful birth or sexual identity) will give rise to a closer judicial review. In such cases, the court requires that the Member States prove the existence of 'particularly compelling reasons' for such a differentiation.[102]

Secondly, the objective of the government in interfering with the fundamental rights is considered. If the aim followed by a restriction can be analysed from the angle of an 'objective' value (e.g., the protection of the judicial power against violations of their freedom of expression),[103] the government will have less flexibility to conduct an own appreciation. In that case, the court will pursue a more intensive protection of the fundamental right. In contrast, when the legitimate aim that is pursued by the government has a contingent character (e.g., the protection of morality),[104] the state will have more extensive room to carry out a discretionary appreciation.[105]

Thirdly, it is taken into account whether the government has significantly more insight in a particular matter. If the government is better placed than the international judge to evaluate a specific issue, it has a larger margin of discretion in determining the degree of interference with the human rights (e.g., in matters of a

---

[99]See for an analysis: Sudre (2012), pp. 234–241; Vande Lanotte and Haeck (2005), pp. 143 and 146–147; Van Leuven (2009), p. 441.

[100]E.g. *Dudgeon v United Kingdom*, judgment of 22 Oct. 1981, [1981] Series A No. 59 (European Court of Human Rights), § 52 (right to have homosexual relations); *Johansen v Norway*, judgment of 7 Aug. 1996, [1996] Reports III (European Court of Human Rights), § 64 (parental rights and right to access to child).

[101]E.g. *Castells v Spain*, judgment of 23 April 1992, [1992] Series A No. 236 (European Court of Human Rights), § 43 (freedom of press); *UCP of Turkey and others v Turkey*, judgment of 30 Jan. 1998, [1998] Reports I (European Court of Human Rights) (freedom of association of political parties).

[102]E.g. *Abdulaziz, Cabalez and Balkandali v United Kingdom*, judgment of 28 May 1985, [1985] Series A No. 94 (European Court of Human Rights), § 78. See Henrard (2008), pp. 266–267; Sottiaux (2008), p. 241; Van Gerven and Lierman (2010), p. 547.

[103]*Sunday Times v United Kingdom*, judgment of 26 Nov. 1991, [1991] Series A No. 217 (European Court of Human Rights), § 59.

[104]*Handyside v United Kingdom*, judgment of 7 Dec. 1976, [1976] Series A No. 24 (European Court of Human Rights), § 48.

[105]Sudre (2012), pp. 236–237.

complex social or technical nature[106] or in cases of a 'public emergency').[107] More in general, the degree of judicial scrutiny will be more restrained as public life in a democratic society requires an increasing degree of interference by the government.[108]

Finally, the presence of a consensus within the Council of Europe on a particular issue is relevant. If such a consensus exists, the state has less room to conduct an own appreciation. The court will strictly evaluate state interferences with human rights that diverge from the reached consensus.[109]

3.2.2 Similarity Between the Proportionality Test Used in the Balancing of Human Rights and the Specific Criteria of the Abuse of Rights in Private Law Relations

In view of the above analysis, an important congruence appears to exist between the general principle of the prohibition of abuse of rights or the limitative function of good faith in private law relations and the proportionality test used to protect human rights in vertical relations.[110] Indeed, there is a striking similarity between the specific criteria to find an abuse of rights on the part of the holder of a subjective right (see Sect. 2.2.2 *supra*) and the elements contained in the test to assess the proportionality of state interferences with human rights.[111] In other terms, the specific criteria of the abuse of rights perfectly fit in the 'privatized proportionality test', as described above.[112]

As such, the first criterion of the abuse of rights, which prohibits the exercise of a right with an exclusive intention to harm or without any reasonable interest for oneself, clearly corresponds to the obligation in public law to pursue a legitimate aim in restricting fundamental rights (i.e., the condition of legitimacy; see Sect. 3.2.1.3 *supra*).[113] In addition, to the extent that this first criterion of the abuse of rights prohibits the exercise of a right without any sufficient personal interest, it is comparable to the public law requirement that an interference with human rights

---

[106] *Powell and Rayner v United Kingdom*, judgment of 21 Feb. 1990, [1990] Series A No. 172 (-European Court of Human Rights), § 44; *Chapman v United Kingdom*, judgment of 18 Jan. 2001, [2001] Reports I (European Court of Human Rights), § 91.

[107] E.g. *Ireland v United Kingdom*, judgment of 18 Jan. 1978, Series A No. 25 (European Court of Human Rights), § 207; *Branningan and Mc Bride v United Kingdom*, judgment of 26 May 1993, [1993] Series A No. 258-B (European Court of Human Rights), § 43.

[108] Van Gerven and Lierman (2010), p. 547; Viout (1995), p. 192.

[109] E.g. *Christine Goodwin v United Kingdom*, judgment of 11 July 2002, [2002] Reports VI (European Court of Human Rights), §§ 73–75.

[110] Van Drooghenbroeck (2001), p. 32; Van Gerven (1982–83), p. 970; Van Leuven (2009), p. 442.

[111] Van Gerven (1995), pp. 14–15; Van Gerven (1992), p. 307; Van Gerven (2004), pp. 279–280; Van Gerven and Lierman (2010), p. 551.

[112] Van Leuven (2009), p. 442.

[113] Ibid., p. 443.

must be appropriate in achieving the legitimate objective (criterion of 'appropriateness'; see Sect. 3.2.1.4 *supra*).[114]

Moreover, the second criterion of the abuse of rights, which prohibits the choice between different equally useful means to exercise a right, of the one that causes more harm to another's right or legitimate interest, corresponds to the public law requirement that a restriction of human rights must be limited to what is necessary for the fulfilment of the legitimate aim (criterion of 'necessity'). Indeed, a means to exercise a right, which is chosen by the holder of that right, is not strictly necessary if there exist other equally useful means, which are less harmful for the other party.[115]

Finally, the third criterion of the abuse of rights, which prohibits the exercise of a subjective right in a manner that benefits the holder of that right but which causes disproportionate harm to the other party, is equivalent to the condition in public law that a limitation of human rights must be proportionate to the sought objective (criterion of 'proportionality in the strict sense').[116] This means, in the relation between private parties, that a private person may not limit the fundamental rights of another person in a disproportionate manner.

An author stresses that the only difference between the third criterion of the abuse of rights and the criterion of proportionality in public law is a difference of perspective: on the one side, the private law criterion of the abuse of rights refers to the subjective right of a party that is potentially abused. This right may not be exercised in a disproportionate way. On the other side, the public law proportionality test focuses on the human right of the other party that is restricted. This right may not be disproportionately limited.[117]

It must be underscored that the equivalence between the latter criteria demonstrates the importance of the principle of proportionality in Belgian law. This principle finds its origins in German public law[118] and was imported into Belgian private law through the general principle of the prohibition of abuse of rights. Yet this principle appears to be a general principle of adequate administration, which is indispensable both in public law and in private law.[119]

More importantly, given this identity between the criteria applied to find an abuse of rights in private law relations and the proportionality test used to assess interferences with human rights in public law relations, the specific criteria of the abuse of rights may be considered as appropriate tools for the judge to review restrictions of human rights in contract law matters.

---

[114]Van Gerven and Lierman (2010), p. 551.

[115]Ibid.

[116]Dirix (2007), p. 51; Hannequart (1995), p. 127; Rochette (1971), p. 234; Van Gerven (2004), p. 281; Van Gerven (1997), p. 193; Van Gerven and Lierman (2010), p. 551; Van Leuven (2009), p. 445.

[117]Van Leuven (2009), p. 445.

[118]See on these origins in German law: Schwarze (2005), p. 685.

[119]See Van Drooghenbroeck (2001), p. 32; Van Gerven (1992), p. 308; Van Gerven (1995), p. 15.

3.2.3 Further Concretisation of the Specific Criteria of the Abuse of Rights in Private Law Relations in Light of the Proportionality Test Used in the Balancing of Human Rights

Yet the criteria of the abuse of rights or of the application of the limitative function of good faith in private law relations must be further concretised in light of the proportionality test applied in public law relations.[120] Indeed, as stressed above, the judicial power has a positive obligation to interpret the open norms of private law in light of international human rights (see Sect. 3.1.2 *supra*). Thus, the condition of proportionality as applied in the frame of public human rights law may offer some guidelines as to the intensity of the protection of human rights in the frame of the performance of contracts.[121] These guidelines will influence the concrete balancing of human rights in contractual relations.

In this way, as explained above, firstly, the nature of the restricted human right and the gravity of the restriction determine the degree of protection of that human right (see Sect. 3.2.1.5 *supra*). For instance, if a party exercises a contractual right in a manner that restricts a fundamental right of the other party affecting his human dignity, the exercise of the party's right is more likely to be assessed as disproportionate (see Sects. 3.4.2 and 3.4.3 *infra*). The protection of fundamental rights touching on the intimate sphere of individuals will be granted more weight in the balancing of the different interests of the contracting parties.[122]

Secondly, the objective of the interference with the human rights of a party must be taken into account. This means that the restriction of the human rights of a contracting party must be balanced against the interests that the other party may have in restricting these rights. These other interests will likewise influence the degree of protection of the human rights. For example, the security or health of private persons constitute important objectives that justify more far-reaching limitations of fundamental rights.[123] Also, if the contracting party who restricts a fundamental right of the other party invokes himself a fundamental right to legitimate that restriction, these different fundamental rights must be weighed against each other.[124] For instance, in the intimate sphere a contracting party may justify a restriction of the human rights of another party on the basis of his own right to respect for a private life or family life.[125]

---

[120] See in this sense Spielmann (1995), p. 28: the concept of good faith receives a more concrete content through the intermediate of fundamental rights as defined by the Constitution or the international treaties.

[121] Van Leuven (2009), p. 449.

[122] Ibid., p. 450.

[123] Ibid., p. 451.

[124] Van Gerven (1991), pp. 84–85; Theunis (1997), p. 178.

[125] E.g. *K.A. and A.D. v Belgium*, judgment of 17 February 2005, App. No. 42758/98 and 45558/99 (European Court of Human Rights), § 83 (in the frame of an agreement concerning sadomasochistic practices: the national court had criminally convicted one of the parties for extremely violent sexual practices. The European Court of Human Rights ruled that this interference with the party's

A contracting party restricting a fundamental right of another party may also invoke his own right to freedom of association, which implies a large freedom to determine himself the internal organisation of the association and to choose the conditions under which new members may be admitted to the association.[126] Also, the goal of an association (such as a company supporting particular ideological convictions) may bring about restrictions of fundamental rights.[127]

As such, an association having religious, political, cultural or environmental convictions may expect from its employees that they will not, in the performance of their labour contract, defend ideas in public that are manifestly inconsistent with the beliefs propagated by the employer association.[128] Moreover, such an association could impose specific clothing prescriptions on its members.[129] Although such contractual terms could constitute a restriction of the employees' freedom of religion and of expression, laid down in Articles 9 and 10 ECHR, respectively, they seem to be acceptable if they are useful to achieve the legitimate aim pursued by the association (criterion of 'appropriateness'), if they do not go further than what is necessary to pursue the aim of the association[130] (criterion of 'necessity') and if the encroachment on the employee's fundamental rights is not disproportionate with the benefit which the employer association draws from the restriction (criterion of 'proportionality in the strict sense').[131]

Thirdly, the degree of protection of the human rights will depend on the contractual position of the party whose human rights are restricted. As such, if a contractual relation is characterised by a full equality between the contracting parties, the judge must only guarantee a minimum respect for fundamental rights.[132] In that case, the principle of the autonomy of the parties will receive more weight in the balancing of conflicting values. Equality in the performance of contracts implies that parties have concluded the contract in entire freedom. If a party is able to freely terminate a contract without harm for the other party and to engage in another contract, the protection of fundamental rights will be less extensive. However, this assumption of equality and of freedom of the parties finds its limit in the principle of human dignity, which requires a minimum level of respect for fundamental rights.[133]

---

right to respect for a private life and to dispose of his own body was pursued with a legitimate aim, namely the protection of the right to respect for a private life of the other party that did no longer agree with the sexual practices).

[126] Van Leuven (2009), p. 453.

[127] Dirix (2007), p. 63; Van Leuven (2009), p. 453.

[128] Van Gerven (2004), pp. 281–282; Van Leuven (2009), p. 454.

[129] Dirix (2007), p. 39.

[130] Dirix (2007), p. 39; Van Leuven (2009), p. 454.

[131] Van Gerven (2004), p. 282.

[132] *Pla and Puncernau v Andorra*, judgment of 13 July 2004, App. No. 69498/01 (European Court of Human Rights), § 59.

[133] Dirix (1982), p. 80; Theunis (1997), p. 179; Van Leuven (2009), p. 458.

In contrast, if a relation of power exists between the contracting parties (for instance in a labour contract or a tenancy contract), the protection of the fundamental rights of the weaker party will be more intensive. In that case, there will be less room for the principle of the autonomy of the parties. Instead, the judge must be watchful for abuses that may potentially arise from a dominant position.[134] Indeed, the stronger party knows that the other party needs the contract and will sometimes unilaterally impose restrictions on fundamental rights in the frame of the performance of the contract. Due to this unequal position between the contracting parties, the contractual relation is in that case very similar to the vertical relation between the government and a private person. This similarity justifies a higher degree of protection of the fundamental rights of the weaker party.[135]

In conclusion, not only does the proportionality test used in the public sphere of the protection of human rights fit within the criteria for the existence of an abuse of rights in the sphere of private law. Also, it provides further guidance as to how these criteria of the abuse of rights should be concretely shaped in order to constitute adequate tools for the protection of human rights in contract law relations.

3.3 Impact of the Judicial Restraint Applied in the Protection of Human Rights on the Model of Judicial Review to Find an Abuse of Rights in Private Law Relations

3.3.1 Similarity Between the Restrained Judicial Review Applied in the Protection of Human Rights and in the Finding of an Abuse of Rights in Private Law Relations

In addition to the above, there equally exists a striking congruence between the restrained judicial review carried out by the judge in evaluating an abuse of rights in private law relations and the judicial restraint pursued by the European Court of Human Rights in the evaluation of disproportionate restrictions of human rights in vertical relations.

Indeed, both in private and in public laws, the basic principle is a *contrôle marginal* of the judge.[136] As such, in the context of private law, it has been stressed that the judge may not substitute his personal view for that of the party whose behaviour he is examining (see Sect. 2.2.1 *supra*). Similarly, in a human rights context, in several cases the European Court of Human Rights has emphasised that

[134] *Fuentes Bobo v Spain*, judgment of 27 Feb. 2000, [2001] Reports VI (European Court of Human Rights), § 38 (in the frame of a labour contract).

[135] De Ly (1992), pp. 1145–1146; Dirix (1982), pp. 50–51; Theunis (1997), p. 178; Van Gerven (1989), pp. 24–25; Van Leuven (2009), pp. 458–459.

[136] Hannequart (1995), p. 130; Van Gerven and Lierman (2010), pp. 546–547; Van Leuven (2009), pp. 443–444.

it is not for the court to substitute its own assessment for that of the government, which must be allowed a sufficient margin of appreciation.[137] The court held that its supervisory function being of a subsidiary nature, it is limited to reviewing whether or not a particular solution adopted by the government can be regarded as striking a fair balance between the public interest and the individual rights at stake.[138]

Consequently, the reserved role of the judge in resolving private law disputes involving fundamental rights in the performance of contracts is comparable to the judicial review pursued by the European Court of Human Rights.[139] However, the rationale for this restrained judicial review is different. Indeed, on the one hand, the European Court of Human Rights, which deals with vertical conflicts of fundamental rights between the government and the citizens, must take into consideration the margin of appreciation left to the state. As mentioned, the degree of this discretionary power of the state can vary according to the circumstances (see Sect. 3.2.1.5 *supra*).

On the other hand, the judge who deals with horizontal conflicts concerning fundamental rights in the performance of contracts must take into account the private autonomy of the parties and their freedom of contract. These principles will grant the judge merely a 'marginal' power of review.[140] In this respect, the latter review will be more restrained than the judicial review pursued by the European Court of Human Rights in public law relations.[141] Indeed, in principle private persons are free to conclude and perform contracts at their own discretion. Thus, in principle the obligation for private persons to protect fundamental rights will be less extensive than that imposed on the government.[142]

3.3.2 Further Concretisation of the Judicial Review to Find an Abuse of Rights in Private Law Relations in Light of the Judicial Review Applied in the Protection of Human Rights

Nonetheless, the technique of a restrained judicial review in the examination of an abuse of rights in private law relations can be further concretised in light of the protection of human rights. In private law relations, the more or less restrained

[137]E.g. *Powell and Rayner v United Kingdom*, judgment of 21 Feb. 1990, [1990] Series A No. 172 (European Court of Human Rights), § 44; *Branningan and McBride v United Kingdom*, judgment of 26 May 1993, [1993] Series A No. 258-B (European Court of Human Rights), § 59; *Hatton v United Kingdom*, judgment of 8 July 2003, [2003] Reports VIII (European Court of Human Rights), § 100.

[138]*Hatton v United Kingdom*, judgment of 8 July 2003, [2003] Reports VIII (European Court of Human Rights), § 123.

[139]Van Leuven (2009), pp. 446–447.

[140]Theunis (1997), pp. 176–177; Van Leuven (2009), p. 447.

[141]De Prins et al. (2005), p. 279; Tison (2002), p. 710; Theunis (1997), p. 177; Van Leuven (2009), p. 447.

[142]Dirix (1982), p. 56.

degree of scrutiny of the judge will differ with regard to the subjective right that is abused. As such, the legal doctrine recognises that the nature of the exercised right, its object, its social value and the nature of the contractual relationship are taken into account in order to determine the level of judicial scrutiny.[143]

However, from a perspective of human rights, it must be completed that also the human right that is restricted has a decisive influence on the degree of judicial review. Indeed, the more a right has a fundamental character, the less freedom will exist for a private party encroaching on that right.[144] In such a case, the judge will be able to carry out a more intensive review yet without substituting his own opinion for that of the private person limiting the fundamental right in question. As such, the right to human dignity or the human rights affecting the intimate sphere of individuals require a stricter judicial review (see Sect. 3.2.1.5 *supra*).

Moreover, the existence of a power relation between the contracting parties will permit the judge to pursue a more intensive judicial review in order to guarantee the respect for the fundamental rights of the weaker party.[145] In this light, the judicial technique of 'practical concordance' plays a role.[146] It appears from the case law of the European Court of Human Rights that this technique seeks to avoid, to the fullest extent possible, sacrificing one fundamental right against the other. Instead, a compromise should be sought between those conflicting rights, which will respect their respective claims, by 'optimizing' each of the rights against each other.[147] In order to reach such a 'practical concordance', the court may indicate that one of the parties has an alternative to exercise his fundamental right in an equivalent way, without infringing upon the fundamental right of the other person.[148]

On the basis of this technique, in contract law relations, the judge may examine whether a person has an alternative to exercise a fundamental right in an equivalent manner. In the affirmative case, a private party engaging in a contract with that person cannot be prohibited to interfere with that fundamental right.[149] For

[143]Stijns (1990), p. 39; Stijns (2005b), p. 68.

[144]Van Gerven and Lierman (2010), p. 547; Van Leuven (2009), pp. 447 and 449.

[145]Theunis (1997), p. 178; Van Leuven (2009), p. 447.

[146]Van Leuven (2009), p. 458.

[147]De Schutter (2014), p. 518; Velaers (2007b), p. 147. See e.g. *Öllinger v Austria*, judgment of 29 June 2006, App. No. 76900/01 (European Court of Human Rights) (compromise between the applicant's right to freedom of peaceful assembly and of expression, and another association's right to protection against disturbance of its assembly).

[148]Velaers (2007b), p. 147. See e.g. *Appleby and others v United Kingdom*, judgment of 6 May 2003, [2003] Reports VI (European Court of Human Rights), §§ 47–48 (concerning the owner of a private shopping mall who refused the applicants to distribute leaflets and to collect signatures within the premises of the shopping mall. The European Court of Human Rights considered that the applicants had alternative means to communicate their views to their fellow citizens, e.g. through a campaign in the media or by obtaining individual permission from businesses within the shopping mall. Thus, the state did not fail in any positive obligation to restrict the right to private property of the owner of the shopping mall in order to protect the applicants' right to freedom of expression).

[149]Van Leuven (2009), p. 460.

instance, a school contractually prohibits the wearing of a headscarf in accordance with its constitutional freedom of education. It could be argued that this restriction does not constitute a violation of the freedom of religion anchored in Article 9 ECHR to the extent that there is another school in the proximity that allows a headscarf to be worn.[150]

Indeed, the doctrine of the 'equivalent alternative' plays an important role in the protection of fundamental rights guaranteeing the respect for democracy. As such, the essential function of the rights to freedom of religion or of expression, enshrined in Articles 9 and 10 ECHR respectively, is the promotion of democracy. In this respect, the judge must examine whether the acts of a contracting party who encroaches on these fundamental rights constitute a threat to democracy. Thus, it must be determined whether the fundamental rights could be exercised in another way, which is equivalent for the person whose rights are restricted and which results in the restriction not being a necessary threat to democracy.[151]

In conclusion, the technique of a restrained judicial review used by the European Court of Human Rights in the protection of fundamental rights may further concretise the *contrôle marginal*, which the judge traditionally applies in finding an abuse of rights in private law relations. In that way, the latter model of judicial review appears to be appropriate for the protection of fundamental rights in contract law matters.

3.4 Applications in the Belgian Case Law of the Concretised Criteria of the Abuse of Rights to Sanction Disproportionate Restrictions of Human Rights

The following part focuses on various applications in Belgian case law, which illustrate that the Belgian judiciary has concretised the traditional criteria of the abuse of rights and has modulated its technique of restrained judicial review in light of the protection of the human rights, according to the principles set out above. In particular, in the relation between contracting parties, the Belgian judge has relied on the prohibition of abuse of rights to sanction disproportionate restrictions of the right to non-discrimination, the right to human dignity, the right to privacy, the right to property and the rights to freedom of expression and of religion.

[150] Ibid.

[151] *Appleby and others v United Kingdom*, judgment of 6 May 2003, [2003] Reports VI (European Court of Human Rights), §§ 47–48; Van Leuven (2009), pp. 460–461.

3.4.1 Protection of the Right to Non-discrimination

3.4.1.1 The Anti-discrimination Laws of 2007: A Direct Horizontal Effect

In Belgian law, the right to non-discrimination is protected through a dual horizontal system. First, this right is guaranteed in an open-ended and general manner in Articles 10 and 11 of the Belgian Constitution. As mentioned, these provisions are *indirectly* applicable in horizontal relations. On the basis of the decision of the Constitutional Court of 12 February 2009, these provisions may apply through reliance on private law concepts, such as the prohibition of the abuse of rights (see Sect. 3.1.3 *supra*).

Moreover, the Belgian legislator has introduced the anti-discrimination laws of 2007,[152] which contain a limited list[153] of discrimination grounds.[154] Direct and indirect discrimination are prohibited on these grounds. The laws give a possibility for the victims to ask for the discrimination to be stopped,[155] to ask for fixed damages, to make claims before civil courts or to ask for criminal sanctions. These anti-discrimination laws are *directly* applicable in horizontal relations[156] since the laws are applicable 'in the public and the private sector'.

Applied to contract law relations, the anti-discrimination laws forbid discrimination in 'the access to and supply of goods and services that are publicly available'. Hence, the anti-discrimination laws limit the principle of freedom to contract (Article 1134 (1) Civil code).[157] Indeed, these laws forbid a discriminatory refusal to contract or discriminatory clauses.[158] Such clauses will be in breach of the laws

[152] Law of 10 May 2007 to combat certain forms of discrimination, *Belgian State Gazette* 30 May 2007 (hereafter 'General Anti-discrimination Law'); Law of 10 May 2007 to combat discrimination between men and women, *Belgian State Gazette* 30 May 2007 (hereafter 'Gender Law'); Law of 10 May 2007 to modify the Law of 30 July 1981 to punish certain racist or xenophobe acts, *Belgian State Gazette* 30 May 2007 (hereafter 'Anti-racism Law'). See for a clear overview of these anti-discrimination laws: Jansen (2011), pp. 387 *et seq.*

[153] The closed lists were not nullified by the Constitutional Court (see *supra*, Judgment of 12 Feb. 2009, No. 17/2009, B.13 *et seq.*). In a second ruling, the Court partially nullified Arts. 3 and 4.4 of the General Anti-discrimination Law regarding its omission of the ground of 'union citizenship' (Judgment of 2 April 2009, No. 64/2009, B.8.16).

[154] Discrimination is prohibited on the following grounds: Article 3 of the Anti-racism Law: *nationality, so-called race, complexion, origin or national or ethnic descent*; Article 3 of the Gender Law: *gender*; Article 4 of that law equals gender with: *pregnancy, childbirth, motherhood and trans-sexuality*; Article 3 of the General Anti-discrimination Law: *age, sexual orientation, civil status, birth, wealth, religious beliefs, ideology, political views, language, current and future state of health, handicap, a physical or genetic feature and social descent*, and, added by the Constitutional court, *union membership* (Judgment of 2 April 2009, No. 64/2009, B.8.16).

[155] Article 20 General Anti-discrimination Law, Article 18 Anti-racism Law, and Article 25 Gender Law grant the judge the power to order the cessation of the discrimination.

[156] Article 5, s. 1 Anti-racism Law, Article 6, s. 1 Gender Law, and Article 5 s. 1 General Anti-discrimination Law.

[157] De Boeck (2003), pp. 418 *et seq.*; Jansen (2011), p. 388.

[158] Dambre (2004), pp. 321 and 334–335; De Boeck (2003), pp. 424–430; Jansen (2011), p. 388.

and therefore null.[159] Given the broad formulation of the anti-discrimination laws, it is recognised that these laws equally prohibit discrimination in the performance or termination of contracts.[160]

3.4.1.2 Relevance of the Principle Prohibiting the Abuse of Rights Before the Coming into Force of the Anti-discrimination Laws

Since the anti-discrimination laws are attributed a direct horizontal effect, in contractual relations the judge can directly rely on these laws in order to sanction types of discrimination that are contained in the limited list. However, before the coming into force of the anti-discrimination laws, the judge must recur to the general principle of non-discrimination contained in Articles 10 and 11 of the Belgian Constitution, which is only granted an *indirect* horizontal effect. Thus, in contractual relations, the judge has repeatedly applied the principle of non-discrimination through reliance on the prohibition of abuse of rights.

For instance, the court has examined via the latter principle whether a private school had discriminatorily refused a girl to follow courses together with boys.[161] The girl was already registered as a student, which was held by the court to be a contractual relationship with the legal representatives of the girl, her parents. The girl had previously been admitted to follow some specific classes with boys, however, only because there was no opportunity to follow them in the neighbourhood in an all-girls school. But a possibility existed for the classes that the girl now chose to be followed together with boys. The question submitted to the court was whether the school's refusal constituted gender discrimination. The court weighed against each other the constitutional principles of non-discrimination and of the freedom of education for organising private schools (embodied in Article 24 Belgian Constitution).

The court held that, although the private school took part in the organisation of a public interest service, the refusal was not discriminatory. Thus, the school did not abuse its contractual right to refuse to allow a girl to follow classes together with boys. First, this refusal was motivated by objective organisational reasons and public interest motives, such as educational differentiation (condition of 'legitimacy'). Moreover, the court ruled that the instrument used to pursue the school's educational project, namely offering separate education for boys and girls, was not disproportionate to the harm caused to the girl (the criterion of 'proportionality in the strict sense'). For this, the court took into account the presence of a neighbouring school organised by the same school association.

---

[159]Article 13 Anti-racism Law, Article 15 General Anti-discrimination Law, and Article 20 Gender Law.

[160]Stijns and Jansen (2013), p. 11, footnote 75; Van Oevelen and Cauffman (2013), pp. 126–127.

[161]Judgment of 22 Oct. 1992, [1992–93] Rechtskundig Weekblad 541 (Civil Court of First Instance of Antwerp); see for an analysis of this case: Van Gerven (2004), pp. 282–283.

This example illustrates that the interests that a contracting party may have in restricting the other party's human right determine the intensity of protection of that human right (see Sect. 3.2.3 *supra*). In this case, the contracting party that restricted the other party's constitutional right to non-discrimination could itself invoke a constitutional right, namely the freedom of organising education. In the balancing of these conflicting values and given the concrete circumstances of the case, the judge gave more weight to the latter constitutional right. Moreover, this example demonstrates that the judge carried out a more intensive judicial scrutiny given the power relation that existed between the school and a private person. Indeed, by taking into consideration the neighbourhood of another school offering similar classes, the court applied the judicial technique of the 'equivalent alternative' (see Sect. 3.3.2 *supra*).

In other cases, the Belgian judge has evaluated the discriminatory character of the termination of a contract on the basis of the general principle prohibiting the abuse of rights. As such, the court ruled that a landlord had abused his right to unilaterally terminate a tenancy contract because he had terminated the contract for the sole reason of the tenant belonging to an ethnic minority. The landlord was refused to exercise his right to terminate the contract in such an illegitimate manner, all the more since the tenant found himself in a social and financial distressful situation (condition of 'legitimacy').[162]

In addition, the court held that an employer had abused his right to terminate a labour contract since the employer had dismissed a saleswoman for the unique reason that she had been converted to Islam and that she wore wide clothing in the store.[163] The employer feared potential negative reactions by his customers, but so far the customers had not criticised the appearance of the employee. In addition, the saleswoman could not be reproached on the grounds of any fault on her behalf. In the view of the court, the employer had discriminated on the basis of religious beliefs by imposing more demanding standards on the employee than on other saleswomen. Thus, the court forbade the employer to rely on his contractual right to dismiss the employee since he did not have a legitimate aim or any sufficient personal interest (conditions of 'legitimacy' and of 'appropriateness').

In these two examples, the contracting party that restricted the other party's right to non-discrimination could not himself invoke a constitutional right. Instead, the party relied on his right to terminate the contract, which can be drawn from the basic principle of autonomy of the parties. In these cases, in the balancing of the opposing interests the judge let the right to non-discrimination prevail, which appears to have a more fundamental nature (see Sect. 3.2.3 *supra*). Also, the power relation that existed between the contracting parties in the frame of the tenancy contract or the labour contract can explain the more intensive judicial

[162] Judgment of 12 March 1980, [1981] Mouvement communal 5 (Justice of Peace of Tubize).

[163] Judgment of 26 Oct. 1992, [1993] Sociaalrechtelijke kronieken 84 (Labour Court of First Instance of Charleroi). See on these cases: Vanderschot (2006), pp. 62–63; Van Oevelen (1995), p. 393.

protection of the weaker party, namely the tenant or the employee, who had become the victim of discrimination.

3.4.1.3 Relevance of the Principle Prohibiting the Abuse of Rights After the Coming into Force of the Anti-discrimination Laws

Next to this traditional case law, also after the coming into force of the anti-discrimination laws of 2007, the principle prohibiting the abuse of rights remains relevant in order to protect contracting parties against types of discrimination that are not enclosed in the limited list. Indeed, these other grounds of discrimination are sanctioned on the basis of the open-ended principle of non-discrimination embodied in Articles 10 and 11 of the Belgian Constitution, which can only be applied in an *indirect* manner in private law relations.

A recent example of the protection of the right to non-discrimination via the principle of the prohibition of abuse of rights is the decision of 7 October 2011 of the Belgian Court of Cassation.[164] In this case, a paediatrician asked the hospital where he was employed to be granted the advantageous status of 'integrated physician' (*statut de médecin intégré*). His colleagues of the paediatric department had already been attributed such a status. The court of appeal had established that in order to grant the requested status, the hospital must either conclude a new contract or modify the existing contract with the physician. Indeed, there previously existed a contractual relationship between the paediatrician and the hospital. However, afterwards the hospital had merged with another hospital. Following this merger, in a framework agreement the merged hospital had engaged itself to 'harmonise' the pecuniary status of the specialist physicians within a 3-year period. All physicians could associate with this beneficial status of 'integrated physician' within that period under the condition that the merged hospital accepted that status. In this case, the merged hospital refused to grant the paediatrician the requested status. Hence, the latter alleged before the court that this refusal constituted an abuse of rights.

The court of appeal ruled that the merged hospital did not abuse his right to refuse the requested status. However, the Court of Cassation overruled this decision and held that 'the refusal to contract can constitute an abuse of rights if the freedom not to conclude a contract is applied in a manner which manifestly exceeds the limits of a normal exercise of that freedom by a careful and cautious person'.

Hence, the Court of Cassation has applied the generic criterion of the abuse of rights to the freedom to contract (see Sect. 2.2.1 *supra*). It must be emphasised that before this decision, the majority in Belgian doctrine defended the opinion that only subjective rights could be subject to an abuse, as opposed to freedoms.[165] Indeed,

[164]Judgment of 7 Oct. 2011, [2011] 1 Pasicrisie 2148 (*Cour de cassation*).

[165]Van Gerven and Lierman (2010), pp. 390, 404–405 and 423; Van Gerven and Van Oevelen (2015), p. 76. See also Cornelis (2000), p. 304; Swaenepoel (2011), pp. 368–369. For France: Ghestin et al. (1994), p. 755.

for an abuse of rights it must be established that the holder of a right exercises the right within its formal limits but in a way that is manifestly improper.[166] Thus, only rights that are sufficiently well-defined are enclosed within the scope of application of the prohibition of abuse of rights.[167] From that perspective, freedoms are not susceptible to abuse since they are undetermined by nature. Yet it can be considered that the freedom not to conclude a contract has an increasingly well-delineated character due to strict social and economic legislation or framework agreements imposing limits on the refusal to contract.[168] On that basis, the Court of Cassation accepted for the first time that a refusal to contract may amount to an abuse of rights.

It follows that a discriminatory refusal to contract may constitute an abuse of rights if the criteria for an abuse of rights are fulfilled.[169] In this respect, the above case can be analysed in light of the principle of non-discrimination. Indeed, by refusing to grant the status of 'integrated physician' the merged hospital treated the paediatrician differently from his colleagues of the same department, who had obtained such a status. Since this type of discrimination is not included in the closed list of the anti-discrimination laws, these laws do not apply. However, such an unequal treatment is prohibited according to the indirect horizontal application of Articles 10 and 11 of the Belgian Constitution.

Consequently, the Court of Cassation rightly regarded the discriminatory refusal to grant the requested status as an abuse of rights to the extent that it was pursued without any legitimate or proportionate aim.[170] As to the sanction, the victim of such an abusive refusal to contract could ask for the reparation of the damages caused by that abuse (i.e., a reparation by equivalent; see Sect. 2.3 *supra*).[171]

3.4.2 Protection of the Right to Human Dignity

There equally exists important case law in which the Belgian judge recurred to the criteria to find an abuse of rights in order to sanction disproportionate restrictions to the fundamental right to human dignity. This right is enshrined in Articles 3 ECHR prohibiting torture or inhuman or degrading treatment or punishment and 23 of the Belgian Constitution, which proclaims that each person has the right to pursue a dignified life. This right implies, among others, the right to a free choice of labour and the right to decent accommodation.

[166] Cornelis (2000), p. 306; Stijns (1990), p. 39. For France: Ghestin et al. (1994), p. 755.

[167] Stijns (1990), pp. 39–40; Stijns and Jansen (2013), p. 5.

[168] Stijns and Jansen (2013), p. 7.

[169] Romain (2002), pp. 229 *et seq.*

[170] Stijns and Jansen (2013), p. 13; Van Oevelen and Cauffman (2013), p. 104.

[171] A reparation *in natura* would amount to a forced conclusion of the contract, which seems to be incompatible with the freedom to contract. In this sense: De Boeck (2003), p. 432; Stijns and Jansen (2013), p. 8; Van Oevelen and Cauffman (2008), p. 455.

For instance, the court has protected the right to conduct a dignified life with regard to an eviction procedure that was carried out in the frame of a tenancy contract. The landlord had evicted a tenant, a poor single woman with two children who had rented a social housing, at the beginning of the winter and without any due reason. The court ruled that such a behaviour constituted a forbidden inhuman treatment in application of Article 3 ECHR. In view of the court, the landlord had abused his alleged contractual right to order the eviction of the tenant since he had exercised that right without any personal or reasonable interest and in a way that was humanly degrading for the tenant (condition of 'legitimacy').[172]

Moreover, in various cases the court ruled that the landlord's contractual right to terminate a tenancy contract following a wrongful occupation of the premises by the tenant must be limited in view of the principle of respect for human dignity, anchored in Article 23 of the Belgian Constitution. It emerges from these cases that a landlord abuses his right to terminate a tenancy contract if he does so in a manifestly disproportionate manner in view of the human needs of the tenant (criterion of 'proportionality in the strict sense'). In these circumstances, the court has repeatedly ruled that the termination of the contract should be postponed or even precluded.[173]

Also in the frame of supply agreements, the prohibition of inhuman treatment contained in Article 3 ECHR has been regularly invoked against a supplier of electricity, who had suspended the delivery following a default of payment by the client. In that way, the supplier had used his contractual right to suspend the obligation of delivery because of the non-fulfilment of the client's own obligation to pay. In these cases, the client argued that the suspension of the delivery of goods of primary need constituted an inhuman or degrading treatment, which was prohibited on the basis of Article 3 ECHR. In several cases, the court has rejected this reasoning through reliance on the theory of the abuse of rights. The court ruled that the supplier had not abused his right to suspend the delivery since he had not acted in a brutal or unexpected way but had undertaken multiple steps to settle the dispute amicably.[174] Thus, it appears that in view of the court, the suspension of the delivery was not manifestly disproportionate to the harm resulting for the client (criterion of 'proportionality in the strict sense').

---

[172] Judgment of 27 Oct. 1981, [1982] Journal des juges de paix 171 (Justice of Peace of Tubize); see for an analysis: Van Leuven (2006), pp. 180–181. Moreover, the court found that the landlord had violated Article 8 ECHR for evicting the tenant for the sole reason that he had accommodated people who were not mentioned in the tenancy contract.

[173] Judgment of 15 Feb. 1995, [1997] Journal des juges de paix 164 (Justice of Peace of Uccle); Judgment of 6 March 1995, [1996] Revue générale de droit civil belge 296 (Justice of Peace of Ixelles); Judgment of 15 March 1995, [1997] Journal des juges de paix 166 (Justice of Peace of Uccle); see for a discussion: De Vos (2010), pp. 158–159.

[174] Judgment of 17 Dec. 1982, [1985] Journal des tribunaux 529 (Civil Court of First Instance of Nivelles); Judgment of 29 Feb. 1984, [1985] Journal des tribunaux 529 (Civil Court of First Instance of Brussels); Judgment of 25 Feb. 1988, [1989] Revue de jurisprudence de Liège, Mons et Bruxelles 1132 (Civil Court of Appeal of Brussels); Judgment of 20 Nov. 1990, [1994] Iuvis 193 (Civil Court of Appeal of Mons).

However, in another case the court held that the supplier had suspended the delivery of electricity in a premature manner since the qualification of a paid amount of money was still discussed, which could eventually be seen as an advanced payment. Moreover, the client was the owner of a restaurant, who depended on the furnishing of electricity for the pursuance of his business. Thus, in the view of the court, the supplier exercised his right to suspend the delivery in an abusive way, namely without any legitimate interest and with the intention to harm the client (condition of 'legitimacy'). As a result, the supplier must pay damages to the client.[175]

The above examples show that if a power relation exists between the contracting parties, which is generally the case in the frame of tenancy or supply contracts, this may justify a higher degree of judicial review and a more intensive protection of the fundamental rights of the weaker party, namely the tenant or the client.

A last remarkable example of the protection of the right to human dignity in contractual relations is the recent decision of the Belgian Court of Cassation of 14 October 2010.[176] The case concerned a creditor who was entitled to a maintenance allowance on the basis of a settlement agreement, concluded prior to a divorce by mutual consent. The court of first instance had ruled that the creditor had abused her right to ask for the payment of the allowances in the concrete circumstances: the agreement on which these allowances were based was almost 30 years old, meanwhile the creditor had set up a new household and enjoyed an income that was equivalent to that of the debtor, and as a result of the payments, the income of the debtor ended up lower than the minimum living wages for a single person, without the debtor being to blame for the situation. Thus, the court of first instance held that further payment of the allowances would constitute a violation of the debtor's right to a dignified life guaranteed in Article 23 of the Belgian Constitution. Hence, the court refused to allow the creditor to exercise her right to ask for the payment of the allowances. The court even abolished the maintenance allowance for the future.

The Court of Cassation confirmed this decision. The Court ruled that further performance of the settlement agreement would constitute an abuse of rights and that the abolishment of the allowances could be ordered in view of Article 23 of the Belgian Constitution and the general principle prohibiting the abuse of rights. The Court took into account the criterion of proportionality in the strict sense: the harm that the considerable payments had caused to the debtor was without any proportion to the advantages obtained by the creditor.

The abolishment of the contractually established maintenance allowance in light of the respect for human dignity seems to contrast with the traditional case law of the Court of Cassation, in which it has refused the application of the so-called

---

[175]Judgment of 17 Dec. 1985, [1986] Jurisprudence de Liège 98 (Justice of Peace of Bouillon). See for a discussion: Van Leuven (2006), p. 180.

[176]Judgment of 14 Oct. 2010, [2010] 1 Pasicrisie 2643 (*Cour de cassation*); see on this case: Stijns and Jansen (2013), pp. 29–30.

theory of hardship (*théorie de l'imprévision*). Indeed, the Court has principally rejected the possibility for the judge to modify or to abolish the content of contractual provisions on the basis of the principle of good faith in view of new and unforeseen circumstances, which make the performance of the contract more difficult.[177]

Yet this example demonstrates that the judge may apply a stricter review and grant a higher degree of protection to fundamental rights in function of the sensitive nature of these rights (see Sects. 3.2.3 and 3.3.2 *supra*). As such, the right to pursue a dignified life has considerable weight in the balancing of conflicting values and tends to leave less room for the private autonomy of the parties in the performance of contracts.

3.4.3 Protection of the Right to Privacy

In several decisions, the Belgian judge has ensured the protection of the fundamental right to privacy on the basis of the prohibition of abuse of rights in contractual relations. This right is anchored in Articles 8 ECHR and 22 of the Belgian Constitution, which proclaim the right to respect for private and family life.

For instance, a social housing company had terminated a tenancy contract in accordance with a contractual term, which provided that the company could terminate the contract if there existed serious doubts as to the effective residence of the tenant in the premises. However, in order to establish the tenant's lack of effective residence, the housing company had conducted a search of the premises without previously notifying the tenant and in his absence. Hence, the court ruled that this search amounted to an impermissible domiciliary visit, which violated the fundamental right to privacy of the tenant in application of Article 22 of the Belgian Constitution.

Thus, in view of the court, the housing company had abused his right to terminate the tenancy contract since this termination was the result of inadmissible inquisitorial methods. The court emphasised that there existed less intrusive manners to verify the effectiveness of the tenant's residence (criterion of 'necessity' or 'minimal impairment'). Consequently, the court found that the unlawfully obtained elements of proof could not be taken into consideration. The housing company was refused to rely on its contractual right to unilaterally terminate the contract.[178]

In another case, an employer had dismissed an employee whose companion had regularly behaved aggressively towards the staff and the customers, after having asked the employee to stop her private relationship with that companion. The court ruled that the employer's interference with the employee's private life pursued a

[177] Judgment of 14 April 1994, [1994] 1 Pasicrisie 365 (*Cour de cassation*); Judgment of 30 April 2004, [2004] 1 Pasicrisie 744 (*Cour de cassation*); Judgment of 20 April 2006, [2006] 1 Pasicrisie 884 (*Cour de cassation*); Stijns and Jansen (2013), p. 30; Van Ommeslaghe (2013), pp. 817–820.

[178] Judgment of 12 May 2005, [2007] Journal des juges de paix 158 (Justice of Peace of Roeselare).

legitimate purpose, namely the guarantee of safety at work (criterion of 'legitimacy'). The court held that as such, the dismissal of the employee was not abusive. However, in this case, the dismissal was followed by the sending of a fax to all members of the staff, which informed them of the employee's dismissal and prohibited them to keep any contact with her. Hence, the court ruled that in these circumstances the dismissal obtained an abusive character. Indeed, the sending of such a fax created the assumption that the employee had committed a professional fault. In view of the court, the informing of all staff members was not strictly necessary to achieve the aim of guaranteeing safety at work (criterion of 'necessity'). Thus, the employer had abused his right to terminate the labour contract and must pay damages to the employee.[179]

These examples illustrate that at several occasions, the Belgian judge has carried out a careful scrutiny and has granted significant weight to a fundamental right that touches on the intimate sphere of individuals in the balancing of the interests of contracting parties. As such, in certain situations the principle of the autonomy of the parties in the performance of contracts must yield to the fundamental right to privacy of another party.

3.4.4 Protection of the Right to Property

Likewise, the Belgian court has relied on the prohibition of the abuse of rights in order to guarantee the protection of the right to property, enshrined in Articles 1 of the First Protocol to the ECHR and 16 of the Belgian Constitution.

As such, the court has ruled that, although the government has a discretionary power to decide on the opportunity of an expropriation, it may not abuse this right by 'freezing' the normal use of a property during a period that manifestly exceeds the time that is reasonably necessary to study the feasibility of the planned expropriation activities (criterion of 'necessity'). In the case submitted to the court, the claimant had been deprived from his right to property during 45 years following different orders of expropriation. Thus, the court considered that the government had abused his right to expropriation and that, on that basis, Article 1 of the First Protocol to the ECHR had been violated. In view of the court, this violation gave rise to damages on the basis of Article 1382 Civil code.[180]

Yet, similarly, if a company of public utilities (e.g., a water company) has a right to expropriation on the basis of a contract concluded with the government, it may not exercise that contractual right in a manner that constitutes a manifestly disproportionate interference with the right to property of the citizens. Thus, the principle

[179] Judgment of 7 Aug. 2007, [2007] Revue régionale de droit 75 (Labour Court of Appeal of Liège).

[180] Judgment of 28 March 2002, [2002] Revue de jurisprudence de Liège, Mons et Bruxelles, 1107 (Civil Court of First Instance of Liège).

prohibiting the abuse of rights will reduce the disproportionate exercise of the contractual right to expropriation to an adequate use.

3.4.5 Protection of the Freedom of Expression

Moreover, in a series of cases, the Belgian judge has examined a potential infringement of the right to freedom of expression in contractual relations on the basis of the prohibition of abuse of rights. This right is anchored in Articles 10 ECHR and 19 of the Belgian Constitution.

The cases brought before the court concerned a tenancy contract or a regulation of joint ownership, which provided that it was prohibited to install satellite dishes on the outside of the rented or co-owned property. In the different cases, the tenant or the individual owner argued that this prohibition violated their right to freedom of expression because this right includes the freedom to receive information. Thus, the question arose before the court whether the landlord or the general assembly of joint owners had exercised their property right in a way that manifestly exceeded the limits of a normal exercise of that right by a careful and cautious person by prohibiting the instalment of satellite dishes ('generic criterion' of the abuse of rights).

In the various cases, the court has ruled each time that the prohibition of the instalment of satellite dishes on the exterior of the good did not constitute an abuse of rights since it did not disproportionately violate the freedom of expression of the tenant or the individual owner. Indeed, in view of the court, the tenant or the individual owner disposed of other means to receive the requested information, in particular through the instalment of a satellite dish at another place or through access to alternative distribution services.[181]

Thus, in view of the power relation existing between the contracting parties, the court applied a more intensive judicial technique and searched for an 'equivalent alternative'. Indeed, the judge examined whether the freedom of expression could be exercised in another way, which is equivalent for the contracting party whose rights were restricted and which guarantees the respect for democracy (see Sect. 3.3.2 *supra*). In the presence of an equivalent alternative, the freedom of expression can be reconciled with the principles of the autonomy of the parties and the freedom to contract.

[181]Judgment of 20 March 1997, [1998] Journal des juges de paix 295 (Justice of Peace of Wolvertem); Judgment of 23 March 2001, [2001–02] Algemeen juridisch tijdschrift 146 (Civil Court of Appeal of Ghent); Judgment of 15 April 2002, [2003] Echos 183 (Justice of Peace of Mouscron-Comines-Warneton); Judgment of 17 Dec. 2002, [2005] Tijdschrift voor Gentse rechtspraak 192 (Justice of Peace of Oostende). See for an analysis: De Vos (2010), pp. 160–162; Van Leuven (2006), pp. 188–189.

3.4.6 Protection of the Freedom of Religion

Finally, there exist different examples concerning the protection of the right to freedom of religion between contracting parties via the principle prohibiting the abuse of rights. This right is guaranteed in Articles 9 ECHR and 19 of the Belgian Constitution.

For instance, an old case concerned a regulation of joint ownership that prescribed that it was forbidden to put advertisement on the outside of the building. It was only allowed to affix a small sign on the door or the outside wall according to the dimensions that were determined by the housekeeper. However, a tenant had installed a small metal case on his door frame containing a *mezouza* with the text of the Jewish credo, in conformity with a prescription of Jewish religion. The director of the building claimed the removal of this object referring to the regulation of co-ownership. Yet the court dismissed that claim on the basis of the freedom of religion. The court took into account that the *mezouza* had only small and inconspicuous dimensions.[182] Thus, the judge implicitly applied the criterion of proportionality: given the small size of the metal case, its removal would cause disproportional harm to the tenant. Hence, by asking the removal of the *mezouza*, the director of the building had abused his right based on the regulation of co-ownership.[183]

Moreover, with regard to labour agreements, the employer must take into account the freedom of religion of his employees.[184] Yet the freedom of religion must be carefully weighed against conflicting fundamental values, which may influence the degree of protection of that right (see Sect. 3.2.3 *supra*). As such, the court has ruled that an employer did not abuse his right to terminate a labour contract since the employee was repeatedly absent without permission in order to fulfil his religious prescriptions. In view of the court, the freedom of religion does not include the right for an employee to prevent the normal functioning of the school community, which has been established on the basis of the equally fundamental freedom of education.[185] In another case, the court has ruled that a restriction imposed on the clothing of the employees, and more specifically the

[182]Judgment of 11 Feb. 1961, [1961] Journal des tribunaux 686 (Civil Court of First Instance of Brussels).

[183]Van Oevelen (1982), pp. 122–123; Van Oevelen (1995), p. 386.

[184]See the example given in section 3.4.1 concerning the discrimination on the basis of religious views: Judgment of 26 Oct. 1992, [1993] Sociaalrechtelijke kronieken 84 (Civil Court of First Instance of Antwerp); Judgment of 1 March 1995, [1996] Sociaalrechtelijke kronieken 409 (Labour Court of First Instance of Hasselt). See also Judgment of 17 Oct. 2002, [2002] Journal du droit des jeunes 44 (Labour Court of Appeal of Brussels): the court found that an employee did not abuse her right to terminate a labour contract and did not lose her right to unemployment allowances, since the position ceased to be compatible with imperative clothing prescriptions imposed by the Islamic religion to which the employee had been converted.

[185]Judgment of 18 April 1989, [1989] Limburgs rechtsleven 105 (Labour Court of Appeal of Antwerp); Van Leuven (2006), p. 188; Van Oevelen (1995), pp. 389–390.

prohibition to wear a headscarf, was not disproportionate since it was a necessary measure to pursue the legitimate aim of guaranteeing safety at work.[186]

Thus, these cases demonstrate that in the balancing of conflicting values, in particular situations the fundamental interests of the other party may justify a restriction of the freedom of religion.

4 Conclusion

In conclusion, the general principle prohibiting the abuse of rights appears to be an appropriate instrument to sanction illegitimate restrictions of human rights in contractual relations. Indeed, the model of an indirect reception of human rights in contractual relations seems to be preferable to a direct reception. Not only the application of human rights through reliance on existing concepts of private law reconciles the autonomy of the parties with the respect for human rights, but also these concepts of private law offer suitable instruments to balance conflicting fundamental values in contractual relations.

As such, it has been demonstrated that the specific criteria to find an abuse of rights in private law relations are similar to the proportionality test used to assess restrictions of human rights in vertical relations. Also, an important congruence exists between the judicial review applied in the protection of human rights in vertical relations and the *contrôle marginal* used by the judge in finding an abuse of rights in private law relations.

More importantly, it results from the discussed Belgian case law that the criteria of the abuse of rights and the judicial review applied in private law relations have been concretised or modulated in light of the specific context of human rights. As such, in the assessment of an interference with a human right in contractual relations, not only does the judge take into account the contractual right that is abused, but also he considers the nature of the human right which is restricted. In that way, the court will pursue a stricter review and offer a more intensive protection of human rights in function of the sensitive nature of the human right at issue or of the power relation existing between the parties.

Although the primary focus of this chapter has been Belgian law, it can be concluded with a comparative consideration. Indeed, it results from the above that the criterion of proportionality, which applies as a specific criterion of the prohibition of abuse of rights ('abuse-based legal orders') or of the limitative function of good faith ('reasonableness and fairness-based legal orders'), may constitute an adequate instrument to balance conflicting fundamental values in contractual

[186]Judgment of 3 June 2004, [2004] Nieuw juridisch weekblad 881 (Labour Court of Appeal of Antwerp); Van Leuven (2009), p. 470. On that basis, the court ruled that a woman had the right to refuse the position at issue on the basis of compelling religious clothing prescriptions which imposed the wearing of a headscarf.

relations. Hence, in the Civil law traditions that recognise the moderation of a manifestly improper exercise of a contractual right—on the basis of the general principle prohibiting the abuse of rights or the limitative function of good faith—the criterion of proportionality could play an important role in the evaluation of unlawful restrictions of fundamental rights between contracting parties.

As demonstrated, the enforcement of human rights through the theory of abuse of rights or the limitative function of good faith has the advantage that these principles can determine the specific sanction that must apply to an illegitimate limitation of a human right. Thus, a disproportionate infringement on a human right will be reduced to a proper interference and, if necessary, in the concrete circumstances a contracting party can be completely refused to exercise a contractual right that interferes with a human right of another party.

References

Baeck J (2007) Hoofdstuk 6: gevolgen tussen partijen. In: Commentaar met overzicht van rechtspraak en rechtsleer. Bijzondere Overeenkomsten. Kluwer, Malines, pp 1–112

Barak A (2003) Constitutional human rights and private law. In: Friedmann D, Barak-Erez D (eds) Human rights in private law. Hart Publishing, Oxford, pp 13–42

Cherednychenko O (2004) Constitutionalisation of contract law: something new under the sun? EJCL 8:1–17

Cherednychenko O (2007) Fundamental rights, contract law and the protection of the weaker party. Sellier, München

Coester-Waltjen D (2001) Constitutional aspects of party autonomy and its limits. In: Grundmann S, Kerber W, Weatherill S (eds) Party autonomy and the role of information in the internal market. De Gruyter, Berlin, pp 41–48

Cornelis L (2000) Algemene theorie van de verbintenis. Intersentia, Antwerp

Dambre M (2004) De wet bestrijding discriminatie in het huurrecht. In: De Vos M, Brems E (eds) De wet bestrijding discriminatie in de praktijk. Intersentia, Antwerp, pp 321–347

De Boeck A (2003) Doorwerking van het gelijkheidsbeginsel in het contractenrecht. De contractvrijheid in het nauw gedreven? In: UFSIA (ed) Vrijheid en gelijkheid: de horizontale werking van het gelijkheidsbeginsel en de nieuwe antidiscriminatiewet. Maklu, Antwerp, pp 413–444

De Ly F (1992) Het gelijkheidsbeginsel in het contractenrecht. Rechtskundig Weekblad 55:1141–1160

De Page H (1962) Traité élémentaire de droit civil belge, vol 1. Bruylant, Brussels

De Prins D, Sottiaux S, Vrielink J (2005) Handboek Discriminatierecht. Kluwer, Malines

De Schutter O (2014) International human rights law, 2nd edn. University Press, Cambridge

De Vos BJ (2010) Horizontale werking van grondrechten, Een kritiek. Maklu, Apeldoorn-Antwerp

Dirix E (1982) Grondrechten en overeenkomsten. In: Rimanque K (ed) De toepasselijkheid van de grondrechten in private verhoudingen. Kluwer, Antwerp, pp 36–91

Dirix E (2007) Privaatrecht en multiculturaliteit. Intersentia, Antwerp

Dirix E (2011) Heeft het privaatrecht nog een toekomst? In: Over grenzen. Liber Amicorum Herman Cousy. Intersentia, Antwerp, pp 807–815

Dürig G (1978) Grundgesetz. Kommentar. C.H. Beck, München

Eissen MA (1995) Le principe de proportionnalité dans la jurisprudence de la Cour européenne des droits de l'homme. In: Pettiti L-E, Decaux E, Imbert P-H (eds) La Convention européenne des droits de l'homme. Commentaire article par article. Economica, Paris, pp 65–81

Fauvarque-Cosson B, Mazeaud D (eds) (2008) Projet de cadre commun de référence: Terminologie contractuelle commune. Société de Législation Comparée, Paris
Flauss J-F (1992) L'abus de droit dans le cadre de la Convention européenne des droits de l'homme. RUDH 4:461–468
Fleischer H (2003) Der Rechtsmissbrauch zwischen Gemeineuropäischem Privatrecht und Gemeinschaftsprivatrecht. JZ 58:865–874
Foriers PA (1994) Observations sur le thème de l'abus de droit en matière contractuelle. Revue critique de jurisprudence belge 48:189–240
Gallez L (2005) La lutte renouvelée contre les discriminations. Revue belge de droit constitutionnel 12:399–419
Ganten TO (2000) Die Drittwirkung der Grundfreiheiten. Duncker & Humblot, Berlin
Ghestin J, Goubeaux G, Fabre-Magnan M (1994) Traité de droit civil, Introduction générale. LGDJ, Paris
Hannequart Y (1995) Le principe de proportionnalité en droit belge. In: Le principe de proportionnalité en droit belge et en droit français. Editions du Jeune Barreau, Liège, pp 129–149
Hartkamp AS (2005) Verbintenissenrecht, Deel II, Algemene Leer der Overeenkomsten. In: Asser C (ed) Handleiding tot de beoefening van het Nederlands Burgerlijk Recht. Kluwer, Deventer
Hartlief T, Stolp M (2000) De ontbinding wegens tekortkoming aan banden gelegd: de eisen van subsidiariteit en proportionaliteit als nieuw referentiekader. In: Smits J, Stijns S (eds) Remedies in het Belgisch en Nederlands contractenrecht. Intersentia, Antwerp, pp 245–270
Heinrichs H (2006) § 242. In: Palandt Bürgerliches Gesetzbuch. C.H. Beck, München
Henrard K (2008) De verhouding tussen de concepten redelijke aanpassing, indirecte discriminatie en proportionaliteit. In: Bayart C, Sottiaux S, Van Drooghenbroeck S (eds) De nieuwe federale antidiscriminatiewetten. Die Keure, Bruges, pp 257–295
Jansen S (2011) The defect of consent deceit, information duties, and discrimination legislation: The Thor Steinar cases applied in Belgian law. ERPL 19:371–393
Jansen S (2012) De invloed van het Europese antidiscriminatierecht op privaatrechtelijke verhoudingen. In: Samoy I, Sagaert V, Terryn E (eds) Invloed van het Europese recht op het Belgisch privaatrecht. Intersentia, Antwerp, pp 145–206
Krüger W (2007) § 242. In: Münchener Kommentar zum Bürgerlichen Gesetzbuch. C.H. Beck, München
Larenz K, Wolf M (2004) Allgemeiner Teil des Bürgerlichen Rechts. C.H. Beck, München
Le Tourneau P (2008) Droit de la responsabilité et des contrats. Dalloz, Paris
Leisner W (1960) Grundrechte und Privatrecht. C.H. Beck, München
Lenaerts A (2010) The general principle of the prohibition of abuse of rights: a critical position on its role in a codified European contract law. ERPL 18:1121–1154
Marchandise M (2007) La prescription libératoire en matière civile. Larcier, Brussels
Mazeaud HL, Tunc A (1965) Traité théorique et pratique de la responsabilité civile délictuelle et contractuelle. Montchrestien, Paris
McBride J (1999) Proportionality and the European Convention on Human Rights. In: Ellis E (ed) The principle of proportionality in the laws of Europe. Hart Publishing, Oxford, pp 23–35
Neville Braun N (1994) Is there a general principle of abuse of rights in European community law? In: Curtin D, Heukels T (eds) Institutional dynamics of European integration. Martinus Nijhoff, Dordrecht, pp 511–525
Nipperdey HC (1972) Freie Entfaltung der Persönlichkeit. In: Die Grundrechte, IV(2). Scherpe, Krefeld
Ost F, Van Drooghenbroeck S (2005) La responsabilité, face cachée des droits de l'homme (Introduction). In: Dumont H, Ost F, Van Drooghenbroeck S (eds) La responsabilité, face cachée des droits de l'homme. Bruylant, Brussels, pp 1–49
Raynaud J (2003) Les atteintes aux droits fondamentaux dans les actes juridiques privés. Presses Universitaires d'Aix-Marseille, Aix-en-Provence

Renauld B (2009) Sources et notions du droit de la lutte contre les discriminations. In: Wautelet P (ed) Le droit de la lutte contre la discrimination dans tous ses états. Anthemis, Liège, pp 7–61
Rimanque K, Peeters P (1982) De toepasselijkheid van grondrechten in de betrekkingen tussen private personen. Algemene doelstelling. In: Rimanque K (ed) De toepasselijkheid van de grondrechten in private verhoudingen. Kluwer, Antwerp, pp 1–33
Rochette J (1971) Les atteintes aux droits de l'homme effectuées de bonne foi. In: Liber amicorum René Cassin, vol 3. Pedone, Paris, pp 231–244
Romain JF (2002) Des principes d'égalité de traitement et de proportionnalité en droit privé, en particulier dans la théorie des troubles de voisinage et l'abus de droit (plus précisément dans le cas du refus individuel de contracter). Revue de droit de l'ULB 13:185–256
Ronse J (1977) Marginale toetsing in het privaatrecht. Tijdschrift voor privaatrecht 14:207–222
Samoy I (2004) Recente wetgeving en Europese richtlijnen: invloed op het verbintenissenrecht. In: Verbintenissenrecht. Die Keure, Bruges, pp 71–99
Schulze R (ed) (2005) Bürgerliches Gesetzbuch. Nomos, Baden-Baden
Schwarze J (2005) European administrative law. Sweet & Maxwell, London
Sottiaux S (2008) De rechtvaardigingsgronden in het federale discriminatierecht. In: Bayart C, Sottiaux S, Van Drooghenbroeck S (eds) De nieuwe federale antidiscriminatiewetten. Die Keure, Bruges, pp 227–256
Spielmann D (1995) L'effet potentiel de la Convention européenne des droits de l'homme entre personnes privées. Bruylant, Brussels
Stijns S (1990) Abus, mais de quel(s) droit(s)? Réflexions sur l'exécution de bonne foi des contrats et l'abus de droits contractuels. Journal des tribunaux 109:33–44
Stijns S (1994) De gerechtelijke en buitengerechtelijke ontbinding van overeenkomsten. Maklu, Antwerp
Stijns S (2005a) De matigingsbevoegdheid van de rechter bij misbruik van contractuele rechten in de Belgische rechtspraak van het Hof van Cassatie. In: Smits J, Stijns S (eds) Inhoud en werking van de overeenkomst naar Belgisch en Nederlands recht. Intersentia, Antwerp, pp 79–100
Stijns S (2005b) Leerboek verbintenissenrecht. Die Keure, Bruges
Stijns S, Jansen S (2013) De basisbeginselen van het contractenrecht: kroniek van de recentste evoluties. Tijdschrift voor Belgisch Burgerlijk Recht 27:2–30
Stijns S, Van Gerven D, Wéry P (1996) Chronique de jurisprudence (1985–1995). Les obligations: les sources. Journal des tribunaux 115:689–752
Stoffel-Munck P (2000) L'abus dans le contrat, essai d'une théorie. LGDJ, Paris
Sudre F (2012) Droit européen et international des droits de l'homme. Presses Universitaires de France, Paris
Swaenepoel E (2011) Toetsing van het contractuele evenwicht. Intersentia, Antwerp
Theunis J (1997) Het gelijkheidsbeginsel, juridisch interpretatiekader, met bijzondere aandacht voor "corrigerende ongelijkheden" en doorwerking in private rechtsverhoudingen. In: Alen A, Boes M, Deruyck F (eds) Doorwerking van het publiekrecht in het privaatrecht. Mys & Breesch, Ghent, pp 127–181
Tison M (2002) L'égalité de traitement dans la vie des affaires sous le regard du droit belge. Journal des tribunaux 121:697–710
Van Drooghenbroeck S (2001) La proportionnalité dans le droit de la convention européenne des droits de l'homme. Prendre l'idée simple au sérieux, Bruylant, Brussels
Van Drooghenbroeck S (2005) L'horizontalisation des droits de l'homme. In: Dumont H, Ost F, Van Drooghenbroeck S (eds) La responsabilité, face cachée des droits de l'homme. Bruylant, Brussels, pp 355–390
Van Gerven W (1982–83) Beginselen van behoorlijk handelen. Rechtskundig Weekblad 46:962–978
Van Gerven W (1987) Algemeen Deel in Beginselen van Belgisch Privaatrecht. Story-Scientia, Antwerp

Van Gerven W (1989) Handels- en economisch recht in Beginselen van Belgisch privaatrecht. Story-Scientia, Brussels
Van Gerven W (1991) Het evenredigheidsbeginsel: een beginsel met een groot verleden en een grote toekomst. In: In het nu, wat worden zal. Kluwer, Deventer, pp 75–86
Van Gerven W (1992) Principe de proportionnalité, abus de droit et droits fondamentaux. Journal des tribunaux 111:305–309
Van Gerven W (1995) Het proportionaliteitsbeginsel. In: De norm achter de regel. Hommage aan Marcel Storme. Kluwer, Deurne, pp 3–17
Van Gerven W (1997) Wederzijdse doordringing van publiek- en privaatrecht op nationaal en supranationaal niveau: van doorwerking gesproken! In: Alen A, Boes M, Deruyck F (eds) Doorwerking van het publiekrecht in het privaatrecht. Mys & Breesch, Ghent, pp 183–202
Van Gerven W (2004) Remedies for infringements of fundamental rights. EPL 10:261–284
Van Gerven W, Lierman S (2010) Algemeen Deel Veertig jaar later. Privaat- en publiekrecht in een meergelaagd kader van regelgeving, rechtsvorming en regeltoepassing. Kluwer, Malines
Van Gerven W, Van Oevelen A (2015) Verbintenissenrecht. Acco, Leuven
Van Leuven N (2006) Derdenwerking van mensenrechten in de Belgische rechtsorde. In: Wouters J, van Eeckhoutte D (eds) Doorwerking van internationaal recht in de Belgische rechtsorde. Intersentia, Antwerp, pp 167–192
Van Leuven N (2008) Les contrats et les droits de l'homme: une interaction mutuelle. In: Droit des contrats. Questions choisies. Larcier, Brussels, pp 89–161
Van Leuven N (2009) Contracten en mensenrechten. Een mensenrechtelijke lezing van het contractenrecht. Intersentia, Antwerp
Van Leuven N (2011) Les destinataires des droits constitutionnels. In: Verdussen M, Bonbled N (eds) Les droits constitutionnels en Belgique. Bruylant, Brussels, pp 111–146
Van Leuven N (2012) De invloed van het EVRM op het contractenrecht. In: Samoy I, Sagaert V, Terryn E (eds) Invloed van het Europese recht op het Belgisch privaatrecht. Intersentia, Antwerp, pp 433–465
Van Oevelen A (1982) Eerbiediging van de grondrechten en het woonrecht. In: Rimanque K (ed) De toepasselijkheid van de grondrechten in private verhoudingen. Kluwer, Antwerp, pp 94–146
Van Oevelen A (1991) Algemene rechtsbeginselen in het verbintenissen- en contractenrecht. In: Van Hoecke M (ed) Algemene Rechtsbeginselen. Kluwer, Antwerp, pp 95–157
Van Oevelen A (1995) De totstandkoming, de uitvoering, de sancties bij niet-uitvoering en de beëindiging van overeenkomsten waarin een migrant partij is. In: De Feyter K, Foblets MC, Hubeau B (eds) Migratie- en migrantenrecht. Recente ontwikkelingen. Die Keure, Bruges, pp 365–396
Van Oevelen A (2001) De sanctie van het misbruik van contractuele rechten. Rechtskundig Weekblad 65:779–781
Van Oevelen A, Cauffman C (2008) Contractvrijheid, contractweigering en antidiscriminatie. In: Bijzondere overeenkomsten, XXXIVste postuniversitaire cyclus Willy Delva. Kluwer, Malines, pp 439–517
Van Oevelen A, Cauffman C (2013) Contractvrijheid en niet-discriminatie in contractuele verhoudingen. In: Humbet P, Van De Woesteyne I (eds) Sociaal en fiscaal recht: "Elck wat wils". Kluwer, Malines, pp 93–144
Van Ommeslaghe P (1987) L'exécution de bonne foi, principe général de droit? Revue générale de droit civil belge 1:110
Van Ommeslaghe P (2010) Droit des obligations, vol 1. Bruylant, Brussels
Van Ommeslaghe P (2013) Les obligations in De Page Traité de droit civil belge, vol II/1. Bruylant, Brussels
Vande Lanotte J, Haeck Y (2005) Handboek EVRM, vol 1. Intersentia, Antwerp
Vanderschot K (2005) De sanctionering van abusieve partijbeslissingen genomen bij contractuele wanprestatie: de verschillende gedaantes van de matigende werking van de goede trouw. Tijdschrift voor Belgisch Burgerlijk Recht 19:87–99

Vanderschot K (2006) De bestrijding van discriminatie in het gemeen contractenrecht. In: Stijns S, Wéry P (eds) La loi antidiscrimination et les contrats. Die Keure, Bruges, pp 43–68

Velaers J (2003) De horizontale werking van het discriminatieverbod in de antidiscriminatiewet, enkele constitutionele beschouwingen. In: UFSIA (ed) Vrijheid en gelijkheid: de horizontale werking van het gelijkheidsbeginsel en de nieuwe antidiscriminatiewet. Maklu, Antwerp, pp 287–326

Velaers J (2007a) 'De objectieve en redelijke rechtvaardiging' als ultieme toetssteen van ongelijke behandeling in verzekeringszaken. In: Van Schoubroeck C, Cousy H (eds) Discriminatie en verzekering. Maklu, Antwerp, pp 85–112

Velaers J (2007b) De proliferatie van de zgn. klassieke 'liberale' grondrechten in de XXste en de XXIste eeuw. In: Peeters B, Velaers J (eds) De Grondwet in groothoekperspectief. Liber Amicorum Discipulorumque Karel Rimanque. Intersentia, Antwerp, pp 99–159

Verhey LFM (1992) Horizontale werking van grondrechten, in het bijzonder het recht op privacy. Tjeenk Willink, Zwolle

Viout J-O (1995) La Cour européenne des droits de l'homme et le principe de proportionnalité. In: Le principe de proportionnalité en droit belge et en droit français. Actes du colloque organisé par les Barreaux de Liège et de Lyon le 24 novembre 1994. Editions du Jeune Barreau, Liège, pp 187–197

Wéry P (2002) Les sanctions de l'abus de droit dans la mise en oeuvre des clauses relatives à l'inexécution d'une obligation contractuelle. In: Mélanges Philippe Gérard. Bruylant, Brussels, pp 127–148

Wéry P (2011) Droit des obligations. Larcier, Brussels

Westerman HP (ed) (2008) Erman Bürgerliches Gesetzbuch. Otto Schmidt, Cologne

Crystal and Mud Contracts: The Theory of Contract and the Ontology of Values

Pier Giuseppe Monateri

Abstract The aim of this chapter is to use the evolution of Italian law as an example of a typical Latin jurisdiction that passed through different ages, characterised by the adoption of different values, in order to understand the inherent ambiguity of the legal discourse on contract and values. The chapter will proceed toward a discussion of the nature of values in the context of the theory of Comparative law. The main conclusions will be (1) that there is not a pure form of contract and (2) that in order to cope with values we need to develop a theory of legal ontologies as the main target of Comparative law.

1 Introduction: Contracts and Values as Epistemological Problems

The aim of this chapter is to use the evolution of Italian law as an example of a typical Romanist jurisdiction that passed through different ages, characterised by the adoption of different values, in order to understand the inherent ambiguity of the legal discourse on contract and values.

On a general basis, contract has never been more alive than nowadays and pervasively dominates world transactions.[1] Notwithstanding its enduring presence and the complex apparatuses of technicians devoted to managing clauses and interpretation, the inquiry on the proper nature of contract, on its status and collocation within private legal taxonomies continues to be a controversial exercise.

Most economic theories and writings on contracts either implicitly or explicitly assume that contracts have a clear meaning once they are agreed to. The main issue of judicial interpretation rarely enters these economic analyses. Anyhow, this problem is normally reduced to the possible sources of ambiguity and vagueness inherent to any text, ranging from disputes concerning the meaning of contractual provisions to uncertainties about the overall parties' intent. The controversy in the

---

[1]See Monateri (2016), p. 5, with reference to Gilmore (1974).

P.G. Monateri (✉)
Department of Law, University of Turin, Turin, Italy
e-mail: monateripg@gmail.com

L. Siliquini-Cinelli, A. Hutchison (eds.), *The Constitutional Dimension of Contract Law*, DOI 10.1007/978-3-319-49843-0_5

traditional legal understanding of judicial interpretation is whether the judiciary should adhere to a strict construction of the contract or whether it should take a broader perspective of the contractual intent so that situations not explicitly covered by the language of the agreement may still lie under its scope.

The same attitude is adopted, normally, also with reference to values since it is assumed that, when properly stated, a value has a definite meaning, even if, maybe, the limits and borders of its application may turn out to be rather fuzzy.

It is then a consequence of the nature of the problems involved that a reflection on contract must raise fundamental epistemological issues and aim to dissect the underlying structure of the most accredited conceptual frameworks.

How can we critically rebuild a theory of Contract law as a separate field of law? How can we reassess the genealogy of Contract law, managing the darker legacies[2] embedded in Roman tradition? And in which sense is a Romanist contract really different from a Common law contract?

Gordley[3] organises his discussion around the need to resolve three basic problems in contract theory. The first problem is the normative justification for enforcing contracts, the second is explaining the content of a contractual obligation, and a third problem concerns the consequences that should ensue when a contract is breached.

In this chapter, we shall concentrate on the first two issues as they concern the same status of a theory of contract, independently from the remedies by which its content can be achieved in practical terms because these remedies, as different as they are in the various legal traditions, depend heavily on the solutions given to the determination of the content of the obligations of the parties and on the normative justification of their enforcement.

As it has been noted, despite the long history and the recent increase in theorising about Contract law, the nature and purpose of such theorising remains under-discussed, and many basic questions lie unanswered. Competing visions have framed the intellectual debate: autonomy theories have faced property and reliance theories, and from their impact, if not from their collision, a new creature, a hybridised form of scientific construction, has taken shape. On a parallel level, trans-historical and inter-cultural investigation paves the way for the possible corruption or contamination of the normative purity predicated to Contract law by legal science. A deeper glance claims for new taxonomies, for other schemes of intelligibility, apt to valorise the specific role played by 'contracticles', namely by different types of transactions to be found at the lowest level of generality. In this perspective, a supplementary bulk of fragmented knowledge opens meaningful fissures within the body of systematised codes. The reflection on the actual morphology of contract rules also reveals the growing influence of social justice in Private law and uncovers the failures that can be ascribed to the liberal conceptions of the classical legal thought.

---

[2]See Somma and Monateri (2003), p. 55.

[3]Gordley (2001), p. 17.

The 'interpretive stance' of the judiciary, in fact, varies according to the type of contract involved and to the place assigned to contracts within a given legal framework. So it depends not only upon the rules of interpretation but also on a variety of norms and background theories of the scope of Contract law itself. This fact is easily acknowledged in comparative legal studies, but it does not entail a different approach or the elaboration of an alternative theory. We could say that on the one side economists analyse contract and values as being indifferent to the process of elaboration of their meanings and that on the other side lawyers concentrate on these processes as losing the wider economic scope of contracts for society.

The matter becomes crucial as long as we remind ourselves that contracts are the most important pieces of elaboration of a spontaneous overall order of society but that the rules adopted for their construction can be used to 'channel' private agreements toward a specified or designed kind of societal order.

Between a purely spontaneous order and a purely planned and designed order, there is indeed an intermediate model represented by a value-oriented interpretation of private agreements, in which economic actors are left free to conclude agreements whose content can in any event be checked in courts. But what is important to notice, immediately, is that, contrary to pro-market theories, the issue of values is always present under any 'representation' of the nature of a contract, including the liberal age of the nineteenth century. Indeed, as a matter of fact, liberalism is a set of values, and so it never happened to have a pure model of contract, to which then 'values' had been applied. Even the so-called 'classical' model was already a model imbued with values producing a given meaning of private agreements. In a sense, no agreement has a pure meaning, and its meaning is always the product of interacting factors, including the values pervading the type of society in which that agreement occurs[4].

According to this appraisal of the matter, throughout the whole chapter we shall consider two main opposite models of contract:

(a) contract as a 'private affair' of the parties in privity, to be strictly construed;
(b) contract as a 'social act': a social means to achieve wanted or desired social ends, with a strong interest by society as a whole to have just and fair transactions, open to wide interventions by the judiciary to construe its text and to discover the duties of the parties involved.

The important and closely related topic is, of course, the tense relationship between freedom of contract and judicial intervention. In particular, the 'jurispathic' power[5] asserted by national courts is to be scrutinised both in its theoretical foundations and in its operational way of functioning. The judicial creation of exceptions, of cases of contractual terms' inapplicability, seems to

[4]See Grundman (2008), p. 19 et seq.

[5]Cover (1983), p. 4 et seq.

construct a kind of supra-competence of the judiciary, enhancing a new-fangled sovereign order based on a hyperbolic claim of the power of the courts.

As we said, from our standpoint there is not such a thing as a 'pure contract'. Even the appraisal of an agreement as a pure 'private affair' is a value-oriented interpretation of the brute facts of the existence of an offer and an acceptance. The liberal interpretation of contract cannot then possess a privileged stance. The matter is that the brute facts of offer and acceptance always receive a 'technical' definite meaning only through the glasses of some value-oriented viewpoint, including the liberal one.

Of course the two opposite models we have just presented are rarely to be found in their most extreme versions and can be mingled in many intermediate interpretations of what a contract is:

1. contract as a mere private ordering but associated with a more or less strong judicial protection of the weaker party;
2. contract as a 'social act' to achieve a spontaneous order, with more or less limited but not absolute power of construction by the courts, through 'signals' directed to private actors in order to orient the overall order of markets, without really designing its details.

These are two intermediate models are more easily to be found in comparative empirical analysis, but their appreciation depends, of course, on a discussion of the strongest models of which they are but softer combinations.

It is quite natural that the first model of contract, a private text to be literally construed, can be associated with the metaphor of crystal and that the second model, contract as a social act in the hands of courts, can be as easily associated with the metaphor of mud. In this second model, contract can become a swamp of unimagined duties into which a party may fall. But both models entail social risks and costs. The first model implies the risk of under-inclusion:[6] I thought that a duty was logically implied by the other duties of my counterpart and I discovered that it was not, so I paid a price I would not have paid. The second model implies the opposite risk of over-inclusion: I discover that I am under certain duties I would never have agreed to or for which I would have bargained a different price.

These risks and costs are not only private but also social because they affect the costs associated with the use of markets.[7] Social costs generated by transactions would be in this way compared with the costs associated with the opposite risks of under- and over-inclusion of duties for the parties at stake.

The two models are opposite versions of the contract not only from the political standpoint: a liberal contract *vs* a socialist or socially oriented contract. They represent also a different moral conception of justice.[8]

---

[6]Rizzo and Arnold (1987), p. 65.

[7]Coase (1988).

[8]Hesselink (2007), p. 330 et seq.

The major implication of the first model is indeed that courts cannot be allowed to check the adequacy of consideration, whereas they can consider it under the second model. So the first model contradicts openly the Aristotelian doctrine of commutative justice,[9] whereas the second model embodies it even if in a tacit way. The first model is not amoral but simply believes in the values of private autonomy to the point of barring a court from checking the price of the exchange at the cost of exploitation of the weaker party. The second model believes that justice is achieved only when the value of exchanged quantities is objectively the same, at the cost of destroying the autonomy of the subject. In this way, there is at stake not only a conflict between alternative views of the economic system but also a clash of deeply opposing conceptions of justice, which we try constantly to sterilise because we like to believe in both at the same time.

This clash of philosophies, finally, entails a different aesthetics of the contract, the former being based on an individualistic imagery associated with private agreements and the latter being imbued with a lot of social imagination, giving rise to two different narratives of what the law and the legal order are or can be. This imagery is far from being abstract; it orients the concrete interpretations given by courts in their construction of private agreements.

In this way, in the next sections, we shall analyse four main factors:

1. the existence of a general theory of contract in comparison with the idea that there are many different contracts, each deserving a varied legal regulation: labour contracts, sale of goods, construction contracts, consumer contracts and so on;
2. the rules on interpretation of contracts;
3. the use of general clauses such as good faith or fair dealing;
4. the power of the judge to review the adequacy of consideration.

These factors will be omnipresent, but our main concern, using Italy as a Latin model,[10] shall always be to see how the discourse on contract is projected and moulded, meaning not a particular theory of it, or a particular interpretation of its nature, but the building of the presupposed frame[11] through which, and within which, we speak about contract and values.

In order to analyse these factors, our chapter will be divided into three main sections. Section 2 presents the assumptions on which the ‘classical’ model of contract has been based in a nineteenth century Romanist liberal tradition, as embedded in the first Italian Civil code of 1865, which was in fact a translation of the French Code Civil, with its inner contradictions. Section 3 explores the impact that the fascist revolution had on this field, with the enactment of the actual Civil code of 1942, reorienting it toward a different set of ‘totalitarian’ values. In Sect. 4 we shall see how the evolution that occurred during the fascist era has been

[9] Gordley (2010), p. 10 et seq.

[10] Livingston et al. (2015), p. 177 et seq.

[11] Costantini (2017).

reversed from the standpoint of an almost social, if not explicitly socialist, anti-fascist republican constitution of 1948 and also the transformations that at present are undermining this approach in favour of a neo-liberal model of contracts. Finally, we shall try to sketch out our conclusions in the last Sect. 5.

2 The Liberal Model: Its Values and Inconsistencies

In the introduction we have sketched out the classical model of contract as a private affair of the parties in privity. In this section, we shall scrutinise how the principle of freedom of contract was technically framed in the liberal age of the nineteenth century within the texture of concepts derived from the Roman law tradition. It is then important to remember how this technical construct came under the rubric of the general law of obligations.

The law of obligations, in civilian jurisdictions, was thought to be the cornerstone of Private law, and the law of contract was deemed to be the cornerstone of the law of obligations. As such, it became the object of thoughtful and deep theories developed by legal scholars and followed by the courts.

According to the French *Code civil* (Article 1101), a contract is a convention by which one or more persons oblige themselves toward one or more other persons to do, not to do or to deliver something. A few articles later (Article 1108), the French code establishes that four conditions are necessary for a convention to be binding: (1) the agreement of the obliged party, (2) a fixed and precise object of her obligation, (3) a legitimate 'cause' of the obligation and, (4) when deemed necessary by the law, a solemn form of the act of obligation, normally a deed performed under a public notary.

The Italian Civil code of 1865 repeated literally these dispositions in Articles 1098–1104 *et seq.*

It is then rather easy to grasp the Romanist model of this theory of contract. A contract is one of the sources of an obligation; others may be a tort or an unjust enrichment. That is why the real matter was the obligation in itself: contract is just one of its sources, and, in such a way, the main field of Private law, contract, torts and unjust enrichment could be unified under a general theory of the obligation, forming the real intellectual hard core of the system of Private law.

According to the liberal prevailing standards of the time, contract was a private affair of the parties. To a large extent, the French doctrine reduced contract to agreement, and for the German doctrine, it became essential just to investigate the will of the parties, and their declarations, to the measure whether these external acts of expression matched their inner wills.

Needless to say, this classical model of contract was thought to be 'crystal' clear. One can be obliged only so long as, and to the extent that, he really intended to be. The resulting obligation had to correspond to the party's agreement to be obliged, and nobody could be obliged to something that he never agreed to.

It must briefly be remembered how different this classical theory of contract was in comparison to the English one: contract was not a matter of 'bargain', or 'quid pro quo', but a matter of matching wills. For this reason, gift was included into the category of contract, whereas it was not a contract for the English law because in that case there was no consideration for the undertaking of the other party. For the same reasons, bailment was also thought to be a contract. In sum, even a gratuitous undertaking was a contract, provided that the parties so agreed.

In any event, not every agreement could be a valid contract; in particular, the agreement between the parties had to contain a 'legitimate cause' of the arising obligation.

This has been a peculiar feature of the French law of contract, and it was never fully accepted in Germany, but it was followed by the Italian law, so that the matter of what is a cause, a 'causa', of the obligation became of the most striking importance. We can easily understand that an agreement without a proper object, a fixed sum of money or a specified good cannot be valid. We can also rather easily imagine that, given the liberal standards of the time, I could not be obliged if I said something as a joke or am under the effect of a seven-per-cent solution of cocaine. But what was a legitimate cause of the obligation? Was it not the will of the parties? Is not contract per se a legitimate cause of it?

Apparently, this provision had been introduced after the Revolution to allow judicial control of private transactions.[12] Since many obligations of the previous feudal system had been abolished (like feudal *corvées* or donations made for past services or forms of homages to the Lord tenant), courts were allowed to investigate the ground of private affairs, in order to avoid the position that customs linked to the old order would be protracted unduly under the form of a contract. Thus, in France, as in Italy, a donation made to compensate a past service (*donatio remuneratoria*) was reputed to be null and void[13] because this was deemed to be a way of compensating peasants for their *corvées* out of the proper form of Labour law now in force.

In this way, in France and in Italy, the cause of the obligation became a means to investigate the private affairs of the parties. It was not intended to censure their inner motives but to ascertain in an objective way if the transaction could be allowed or not, given the revolutionary nature of the new *régime* and its revolutionary struggle against the old order.

This represented a major departure from the pure Roman high classical model, where the simple matching of promise and acceptance would have produced an obligation in the form of a *sponsio*: Do you promise to give me £100? I do promise. This exchange of formal promises, on a specified object, was sufficient to produce a binding obligation. Now matters became more confused. Properly speaking, it was no longer a matter of promise but just one of declaration of intent, abandoning any possible transcendence implicit in the term promise. On the other hand, the

[12]Creutzig (1969), p. 374 et seq.

[13]On the intricate history of the *donatio remuneratoria* see Laurent (1999).

agreement of the parties could be investigated by the court under the necessity of finding in it a legitimate cause of the obligation, other than the mere agreement itself.

Needless to say, the newer theory gave rise to infinite controversies in legal writings,[14] given the difficulty of distinguishing between the objective cause of the obligation and the personal motives of the parties. An adversary of the 'cause' could easily point at the incongruence of considering a donation as a contract. In the case of a sale of goods, the cause of the contract was found in the exchange of the price for the good, but what about the case of a gift? Italian and French authors stated that in this case, the cause of the obligation consisted in the *animus liberalis,*[15] in the willingness to give something to the other party in return for nothing. So at the same time the exchange of something for something and the giving of something for nothing could be both valid causes of the obligation!

In any event, as long as liberal values prevailed in society, these theoretical discussions had little impact on the practice of the law, but a further factor of inconsistency must be added. In the Civil law systems, there has been always present a classification of 'types' of contracts.[16] In this way, the unity of the law of obligations was split into different 'boxes' represented by the various typical contracts: sale of goods, donation, contract to form a company, bailments, construction contracts and so on. This was due to the lack of a general theory of contract in Roman law being absorbed into the general theory of the obligation, and to the historical growth, especially under Greek and oriental influences, of different kinds of agreement introduced into Roman law through a piecemeal process by the jurisdiction of the Praetor.[17] With the rising importance of the cause, this element became used also to qualify the agreement reached by the parties. Since the rules for various contracts differed on many points, the courts have been allowed to re-qualify the agreements made by private citizens. The parties could have written that they concluded a contract of sale, but if the good had still to be constructed, the judge could re-qualify the convention as a construction contract and then apply to it the proper rules for that type of contract and not those chosen by the parties.

The point has been peculiarly noticed by Jim Gordley.[18] The Civil law tradition has always been rather 'Aristotelian' in this sense: the court knows the essence of a contract, so if the parties have called sale what in reality is a donation, they have been simply wrong in their explication of the essence of their own transaction, and the judge could 'correct' them by applying the rules proper to the essence of the contract. A consequence of this reasoning is that the real nature of a sale *nummo uno*, e.g. of an apartment in the city centre of Rome for just one shilling, was indeed that of a donation, with the consequence that that contract should be void as a sale

[14]See all the references in Hussard (2002).

[15]Santoro-Passatelli (2002), p. 225.

[16]See Livingston et al. (2015), pp. 201–206.

[17]Daube (1951), p. 67 et seq.

[18]Gordley (2010), p. 30 et seq.

and valid as a donation only if the proper form of the donation had been used by the parties.

This point represents a major departure from the pure facade of a liberal economy because in a Civil law jurisdiction, the judge always had the 'Aristotelian' power to investigate the nature of the agreement and so to decide if it was valid or not, and on what basis.

This Aristotelian influence on the Civil law jurisdictions is not to be underscored because it entails also the possibility to apply to contracts the principles of commutative justice, transforming it from a pure philosophical stance to a positive legal rule.

According to Aristotelian commutative justice, an exchange is just only if the quantities exchanged are rather equal since justice is a kind of right proportion.[19] Thus, a contract must be just, independently from the appreciation that the parties made of their interests. A contract for the construction of a lavish coach for a few pounds could again be declared invalid because it is contrary to contractual justice, to be interpreted not according to the parties' will but to the objective quantities exchanged. This is, in English term, the power to appreciate the adequacy of consideration. English courts refused to consider it, asserting that even if the presence of a consideration is necessary, it is not in the proper domain of courts of justice to consider its adequacy. Civil law courts took the opposite path. Since justice is the end of the law, adequacy of consideration must be appreciated by law courts.

Given all the factors considered, it is easy now to consider how the classical model was built around a bunch of inconsistencies. A contract is the agreement of the parties, and all agreements on patrimonial assets are contracts. But a 'cause' of the contractual obligation is necessary, and courts can investigate it. If the cause is illicit, the contract is void. Besides, any contract is a piece of a kind, and so a court can scrutinise it, in order to classify it properly, and then apply to it the right rules needed by its very nature, independently from what the parties have written. Moreover, a contract must be just, so that it cannot be binding if there is no adequacy of consideration.

We can, by consequence, conclude this section by asserting that the pure form of the contract as a mere private affair of the parties has never been accepted in French and Italian laws. Both the French and the Italian Civil codes have been liberal codes but with a lot of inconsistencies. The most important in our field of enquiry was that between the proclaimed principle of freedom of contract and the legal rules allowing the courts to substantially rewrite the contract for the parties, searching for the cause of the obligation, interpreting the agreement on the basis of its true essence, and to control the adequacy of consideration in order to improve the so-called contractual justice as something different from the mere agreement of the parties in privity.

---

[19]Aristotle discusses this theory in the Nicomachean Ethic, Book V, chapter 3. See Gordon (2007).

So long as all judges were sharing liberal values, these inconsistencies had little impact, but things were to change before the advent of Fascism and then with the implementation of a newer anti-fascist, and to a large extent, socialist Constitution. To sum up, it was not the text of the codes but the shared ideology of the judiciary that made these systems liberal.

3 The Totalitarian Theory of Contract and the Dark Side of 'Good Faith'

In the previous section, we have seen the inner inconsistencies of the liberal shape of the Romanist tradition, which was achieved by the code of 1865, and we have seen to what extent the liberal flavour of the rules on contract was due more to the ideology of the judiciary than to the precise text of the code. From this standpoint, it was the values shared by the courts to give room to a liberal theory of contract. Now we shall concentrate on the changes that happened during the fascist revolution, which produced a new Civil code, and tried to change the values that lie at the basis of a theory of contract.

As it is rather well known in 1922, Italy was taken over by a fascist *régime*. This happened in the context of a state of exception. The Crown, as well as the majority of conservatives, was primarily concerned with the actual possibility, after the First World War, of a communist revolution and so allowed the Duce and his party to rule the country to avoid that risk.[20] Mussolini, with all his boasts of a newer Caesar, never acquired the same power that Hitler could assume in the republican Germany; he had constantly to struggle against the counter-power of the King, who finally, and too late, put a sudden end to the *régime* in 1943, arresting him, because of the Anglo-American invasion of Sicily. Needless to say that just because of its remaining power, the Crown shared many, if not all, of the responsibilities of the fascist *régime* allowing the fascist party to take this course of action, including the enactment of the anti-Semitic racial laws of 1938.

From this standpoint, the Duce was unable to rewrite the Constitution, enacted by the Monarchy in 1848, but he could transform the structure of administration along fascist political lines of intervention and finally, in 1942, succeeded in designing a new system of codes, including the Civil code, which is still in force.

Of course the pivotal interest of Fascism concerned Public law, and the control of administration, but the pervasive nature of a totalitarian *régime* required also the reframing of the structures of civil society, and the final accomplishment of this goal was aimed at reforming the presumed liberal Civil code of 1865. It is not immaterial to see how fascist and Nazi scholars tried to review, according to their own values, the general basis and principles of the code and in particular of Contract law as the cornerstone of the economic system.

[20]See Livingston et al. (2015), pp. 2, 100 and 132.

Fascists and National Socialist scholars devoted indeed an important meeting of the Italo-German juridical Committee to the matter of contracts, which was held in Vienna in the spring of 1939.[21]

On that occasion, they discussed the principle of freedom of contract to affirm its value only within the limits imposed by the new public order created by the political regimes of the two nations. They specified that freedom of contract is abused not only in the case of explicitly illegal contracts, or in the case of immoral agreements, but also in all those cases in which a contract could be contrary to the political principles of national order or contrary to the fundamental principle of economy as laid down by State authority. Along these guidelines, the law of contracts was fully re-examined.

Such limitations were meant to underline the subordination of the parties' interests to those promoted by the 'legal system' as the objectified entity incarnating the political will of the State. According to the prevailing ideology, the relation between the parties had to be seen no more as 'antagonistic', as in capitalist countries, but as cooperative, and so a strong emphasis was given to the principle of good faith in the formation and execution of contract. As an important author said, it is important for society that the relation between the parties would not be seen as a struggle but a joint attempt to improve national economy.[22] The consequence, of course, was to give to courts the further power to check whether the parties had complied with the rules of good faith in their mutual contractual relations: a major blow to the theory of privity of contract as a private affair of the parties.

It is worth noticing that in this way the reference to good faith is not connected with the jus-rationalist *fides*: it does not lead, in fact, to suppress the principle of the freedom of contract to give prominence to the opposite principle of contractual equity. The legal system, in fact, prevails over the private act for aims placed beyond the parties' horizon and not corresponding to the intention of achieving the balance of performances.[23]

Good faith became an objective test as good faith was redesigned to be a set of unwritten rules implying a given behaviour of the parties to the contract. Such formulation is insisted upon during the works for the drafting of the *Volksgesetzbuch*, the code that was expected to supplant the BGB, the older German Civil code, on the lines traced by the new political regime. On that occasion, it was underlined in particular that the law of contract must be restricted to the exchange of goods and services, which represented, as we have seen, a major deviation from the Civil law tradition. However, in the intention of these scholars, these innovations would not represent an element of crisis in the traditional doctrine of contracts but simply an integration of the same doctrine

---

[21]See Il Comitato Giuridico Italo-germanico per la Riforma del Diritto delle Obbligazioni, *Rivista di diritto commerciale* (1938) at I, 437.

[22]See Somma and Monateri (2003), para 4 with references.

[23]Siebert (1942), p. 454, cited in Somma and Monateri (2003) fn 32.

Fascists and National Socialists recognised the importance of the free private enterprise, but as a value to be re-examined in the light of the maxims formulated by the regime. In the Italian context, such idea provoked a re-examination of the matter of contracts in less strict terms than in the German formulation. And yet it leads to promote solutions characterising a pattern of Contract law subordinated to the necessity of production and to the superior interests of the nation.[24]

To these ideas belong the descriptions of the law of obligations in terms of a glorification of the law of contracts as a sector of the legal system in which the interests of the parties were to become strictly linked with the national economic life of the nation as a whole.[25]

These remarks did not contradict the patrimonial nature of the performance (Article 1174 Civil code) and of the legal relation that is the object of the contractual relation (Article 1321 Civil code). In both cases, such nature is included in the intention of co-ordinating the regulations of contracts with the damage compensation system centred on the principle of the patrimonial liability of the debtor. The law of contract was still meant to represent an 'objective' and merely technical field of positive law.[26]

Different observations can be made with regard to the principle of good faith as a new cornerstone of the law of contract. Such reference, in fact, takes up the idea of co-operation of the parties to the obligation, and in this perspective it reveals its potential use for political purposes and interference of the courts in contractual relations.

Further possibilities of intervention derived from the above-mentioned traditional Roman approach to the different kinds of contracts, in the plural. Indeed, there are 'typical' contracts that can, as we said before, be easily classified as sale, loan or other and 'atypical agreements' that do not match standard traditional categories. The Italian Civil code of 1942, enacted under Fascism, provides that private parties can conclude contracts that do not belong to one of the 'types' provided for by the code itself if the scope of their agreement is anyhow directed to realise interests approved by the law (*interessi meritevoli di tutela* (Article 1322 Civil code)).

In this respect, it is specified that this rule intends to codify the maxim according to which the legal system acknowledges the private agreement only in as much as the effects deriving from it realise at the same time interests outside the sphere of the parties: freedom of contract is accepted insofar as it matches the national interests and insofar as it can be strictly checked in court. There was no room for an economic plan of socialist or communist flavour; parties could conduct their economic activities by private decisions, but their decisions could be scrutinised in court.

---

[24]Perlingieri (1978), pp. 5 et seq.

[25]See the 'Relazione della Commissione Reale al progetto del libro Obbligazioni e Contratti', n. 5.

[26]See the 'Relazione del Guardasigilli al progetto ministeriale delle obbligazioni', n. 17.

Similar considerations applied to the importance of the 'causa' as one of the essential requisites of contracts. Pivotal was the discipline of 'causa' of 'atypical' contracts: in the fascist idea, the supremacy of positive law on private agreements is mostly characterised as an instrument for the imposition of the will of the political power 'per se' and not as a means to affect the situation of the party whose interests the system decides to interpret. In other words: in the Fascist and National Socialist Contract law, a private citizen, even when acting as an economic agent, was never to be considered *uti singulus*, a mere individual, but always *uti civis*, an engaged political subject.

It is important to underline that both Fascism and National Socialism develop reflections regarding protection of the weaker contracting party. On the other hand, they do not deviate from the principle according to which the prevalence of the legal system of contract is a mere mark of the power of the group on the individual. The weaker contracting party, in fact, is considered as such only insofar as he is party to a bond that the outside intervention intends to examine in the perspective of the common needs and not of the balance between performances.

Such considerations are consistent in the first place with some of the proposals worked out during the drawing up of the National Socialist 'popular code', and in particular the one concerning the duty of the drafting party to formulate the general conditions of contract in accordance with the needs of society.

In this sense, the general conditions of mass contracts assume a largely different meaning compared to the one attributed to them previously, in particular by liberal scholars. The latter had considered such conditions as a sort of generalisation of the contents of bonds that certain categories of contracting parties would later conclude. The National Socialist scholars deemed such an approach not to be a sufficient break with the traditional private system and maintain that it was necessary, on the contrary, to underline the prescriptive character of the general conditions of contract.

Not all the proposals formulated by National Socialist authors implied a discipline of mass contracts having the indicated features. On the other hand, those who justified the lawmaker's intervention to reduce the scope for private autonomy without carrying out considerations regarding the matter of contractual equity are definitely prevalent.

Even the Fascist experience tackles the protection of the weaker contracting party with different attitudes. In the Civil code, some rules seem to take up models aimed at promoting values such as the balance between the performances provided for in contracts: in particular, the provision stating usurious interests to be void (Article 1815) and the one deciding on the matter of annulment for injury, pointing out the general character of such remedy and setting aside the referability of the relevant hypothesis to the vices of agreement (Article 1448).

Similar concerns seem to have inspired the discipline of the general conditions of contracts (Article 1341 Civil code) and of contracts stipulated through forms (Article 1342 Civil code). This latter is sometimes indicated as an instrument of protection of the contracting parties who are at a disadvantage because of the context in which the transaction is stipulated.

The underlining of all these aspects is a feature of Fascist and National Socialist Contract law, which refers to the economic interests of the group and in such perspective pursues objectives such as an efficient allocation of assets: *Der Vertrag hat für die Gemeinschaft die Aufgabe, an einer sinnvollen Güterverteilung und zur Erreichung immer höherer Leistungen mitzuwirken.*[27] Therefore, the invectives of certain authors that in the Fascist period point out the distance of the new ideas from the Liberal theories about the *homo oeconomicus* assume a merely propagandistic meaning, and in any case they seem to be inconsistent, as those theories are also founded on a view of the contract that sets aside the parties' horizons.

A common feeling has thus been shown between the Fascist and the National Socialist literature interested in constructing a Contract law alternative to the one inherited from the liberal scholars.

In particular, I would like, here, to stress the role displayed by the principle of good faith.

It is well known that the use of good faith for the above-mentioned aims is not a remedy conceived by the National Socialist literature. It was established, in fact, during previous periods and is present, for instance, in the first doctrinal formulations of the 'contractual grounds' (*Geschäftsgrundlage*) theory: the whole of the events integrating the implied foundation of a negotiable agreement, the breaking of which justifies an intervention aimed at re-balancing the transaction.

The theory in question is established in a period of German juridical history characterised by the intention of re-examining the cultural premises on which the civil codification is based, and in particular the intention of re-valuating the *rebus sic stantibus* clause. In the Italian context, it is precisely the recourse to this clause that allowed the courts during the Fascist period to justify certain interventions affecting the contents of a contract. As nothing was contained in the Civil code of the Kingdom of Italy on this matter, the judges used to this end the provision regarding good faith in the fulfilment of contracts (Article 1124).

A few final remarks need to be added.

The comparison with National Socialist law has allowed the highlighting of certain features characterising the Fascist doctrine of Contract law. In particular, it has allowed us to remark that such doctrine is based on the subordination of agreements to the legal system for aims outside the pursuit of interests ascribable to the parties. The comparison with the German experience has also made it clear that the prevalence of the legal system is often functional to the promotion of the economic structure decided upon by the political sovereign. This leads one to confine the matter to the cases of exchange of goods and services, through certain devices that differentiate it from contracts of a jus-rationalist character. From this point of view, the Fascist and National Socialist experiences diverge from the preceding theories about functionalisation of private action, even though they seem to imply a reconstruction of the relations between contracts and the legal

[27] Stoll (1936), p. 1; and see also Haupt (1943), p. 84.

system that is not always sensitive to the question of the balance between performances.

If these are indeed the characteristics of the Fascist law of contracts, it is necessary to specify, in the first place, that they have been introduced in the Civil law codification in force. And it is further to be underlined that this implies the presence of a juridical doctrine in some way participating in the construction of such law. It is also important to underline, as a conclusion of this section, the role that was displayed by blurred and undefined general clauses in the effort of establishing a new vision of contract in the totalitarian setting of Fascism and Nazism.

Based, as they are, on general principles and concepts, such as ‘good faith’, the policy of these regimes needed to be applied by lawyers agreeing with their political scopes because these words are indeed ‘empty vessels’, and they can be poured rather differently by interpreters with different political orientations.

4 Constitutional Turns and the Autopoiesis of Values

As we have seen in the previous section, the fascist *régime* came to an end in 1943, but it was resumed by the Germans in the north of Italy in the form of a Republic (*Repubblica Sociale Italiana*) up to the end of the war and the final surrender to the allies.

From 1945 to 1947, Italy was ruled under a provisional legislation[28] enacted in political accordance by the Heir to the Throne, the representatives of the parties united in the anti-fascist front (*Comitato di Liberazione Nazionale*, CLN) and the representatives of the allied forces of occupation. At the end of this transitional period, a Constitutional Assembly was elected and produced a newer anti-fascist Constitution, which, with some variances, is still in force.

The Italian Constitution (*Costituzione della Repubblica*) was promulgated on December 27, 1947, and defines the basic structure and functions of the State granting the legislative power and control over the executive to Parliament. The Constitutional Court (*Corte Costituzionale*), comprised of fifteen judges appointed by the President, by Parliament and by the highest courts, determines the constitutionality of all laws. For this purpose, it may only be seized by a lower court in the form of a prejudicial question. The Constitutional Court is also empowered to define the powers of the State, of the regions, to judge disputes between such institutions and to try the President and the ministers. Besides this, the Italian Constitution provides for a number of basic values that must inform not only the public administration but the whole national life, including the relations between private citizens. In this way, the individualistic state of the nineteenth century, and

[28]Livingston et al. (2015), p. 54 et seq.

the corporative state of the fascist era, has been replaced by the social state of the first Republic.

What is the most relevant here is that this Constitution resulted from a compromise between the liberal, Christian democratic and the communist parties. As such, the rigid Italian Constitution provides for different possible trends in its interpretation. Fundamental rights of property and of economic activities, as well as 'social rights', are defined in, and protected by, this Constitution, and it is clear that the Civil code has been deprived of its constitutional function. One way of viewing this change is to see fundamental Private law concepts as having been modified by the addition of social or public elements, and such terms as the 'socialisation' or the 'publicisation' of Private law are frequently encountered.

Indeed, the limitations on property and freedom of contract introduced by the Civil code of 1942 have been further expanded in the 1948 Constitution, and by the progress of its interpretation. Taken together, the property and contract provisions of the 1942 Code and the 1948 Constitution reveal a tendency toward a social conception of private interests. Related to this trend are provisions directed toward the recognition and protection of social groups and interests, the most important of which, for our field of enquiry, may be considered the protection of the weaker party in bargaining situations,[29] not to mention the introduction of an integrated and comprehensive group of provisions recognising and regulating the Labour law relation.[30]

From this perspective, Italian law provides specific rules of interpretation for clauses enclosed in contracts (Articles 1362–1371 Civil code). These rules also apply to unilateral acts and promises (Article 1324 Civil code) and are to some extent similar to those provided for wills. The rules are to be employed according to a hierarchy: only if the first does not prove satisfactory will the second apply and so on.

The first basic criterion for construing contracts requires one to seek the common intention of the parties (if there was such a common intention). Whenever there was a common understanding and the parties agreed on a certain meaning of the words contained in a clause, that common meaning is essential and binding, regardless of the literal sense of the words contained therein (Article 1362 Civil code). Thus, the common intention of the parties must prevail over the common sense of the words. Second, the meaning of a clause may be understood only by analysing the general context of the agreement (Article 1363 Civil code), which implies examining the parties' behaviour during negotiations, upon execution of the contract and with respect to performance of the contract (Article 1362 sec. 2, Civil code).

If the parties insist on opposite or different interpretations of the same contractual clause, the rules seek to find the most reasonable interpretation. First of all, no such rules apply if one of the parties claims a different meaning of a clause in bad faith. Otherwise, a clause is firstly to be interpreted so as to have some effect,

[29]See Article 1448 c.c. providing rescission in certain cases of unequal bargaining position.

[30]See Codice civile, fifth book, particularly Articles. 1060–1081, 2222–2246.

whereas the meaning that would render it ineffective is to be rejected (Article 1367 Civil code). If no reasonable interpretation may be reached, the court must construe the words according to the general practices in that specific field (Article 1368 Civil code). If the clause is contained in model forms of contract prepared by one of the parties in advance, any dubious clause is to be interpreted in the most favourable way for the other party (Article 1370 Civil code). If all other criteria have not provided a satisfactory meaning to a clause, the words are to be interpreted so as to equally balance opposite interests in the deal (Article 1371 Civil code).

All these norms are, of course, crafting a picture of Italian contract as a 'social act' with extensive power of judicial intervention on private agreements. The aim is patently to protect the weaker part and to reach the ideal of commutative justice,[31] not to mention the norms specifically derived from the European legislation on consumer protection,[32] which are not specifically within the scope of this chapter.

This is the general theory of contract, which became so designed as to assure what is labelled as contractual justice beyond the mere agreement reached by the parties,[33] and a variety of authors adopt the theory that these general Private law doctrines must further be fostered by a 'constitutionally oriented' reading.[34]

The essence of this view is that the Italian Constitution is mainly entered upon the values of the person,[35] so that the whole of legislation, including Private law, must be reviewed with the aim of implementing these values, up to the formulation of a wide doctrine of the constitutionalisation of Private law,[36] in the sense of its constitutionally oriented reading.

There is then a point that is to be noted. The norms we have cited were all norms of the 1942 Code enacted in the fascist era, and these same norms have been reinterpreted in the new Constitutional landscape without any need to change them since they had, in any event, already bypassed the individualistic assumptions of the classical liberal model.

Given this permanence of texts, and this huge shift in values, the question that may then arise is, what is the nature of values in the legal field?

What is the nature of a constitutional value? And how does it impact on Private law?

According to the classical account prevailing in many Civil law jurisdictions, a value is something underlying the principles that can be derived from the rules laid down by the Constitution.[37]

---

[31]Calvo (2013), p. 44 *et seq.*

[32]See Alpa (2014) with all references.

[33]See Sacco (1993), pp. 375 et seq. and 484 et seq.

[34]Perlingieri (2010).

[35]Baldassarre (1997).

[36]Sorrenti (2006).

[37]Dossetti (1995).

Striking as it is, this theory implies that a court is legitimated not only in making a liberal construction of constitutional provisions but also to infer from them the principles that are logically implied by them. It is not only a theory of the penumbra of the Constitution but also an attitude implying the possibility to 'know' the underlying essence of the Constitution beyond its actual wording.

In these terms, a principle is not something out of the Constitution, or something lying in its penumbra, but it is in the text of it, or it is to be logically inferred from the set of existing norms. Thus, we may infer that since there are many norms in the Italian Constitution protecting the dignity of the person, even if there is no provision strictly equivalent to Article 1 of the German Constitution,[38] the Italian Constitution is in any event also based on the principle of the protection of human dignity,[39] being the principle making coherent different norms contained in different sections taken as whole. From hence to the plan of values the step to be taken is not a giant leap. A value is the underlying transcendent element justifying in more than legal terms the principles logically inferred as legally existent from the texts of the norms.

Thus, a principle is something in force, and it can be applied to cases not expressly covered by any precise norm. A value is more an aid to interpretation: since that given principle has a transcendent foundation in a value, that value must in turn be used to interpret it, in its application to different cases. To state this in general terms, whenever a doubt may exist as to the meaning of a provision, the court must adopt the sense that is more consistent with the values introduced by the Constitution.

More than other discourses on law, the theory of autopoiesis has insisted on the constitutionalisation of the world society and on the structures of values becoming legal. I mean the incorporation within the self-referential communicative structure of the law of values coming from the moral or social communication systems.[40] In this respect, certainly the path followed by the Italian doctrine of the constitutionalisation of Private law, and henceforth of contract, may be said to fit into these theoretical orientations.

---

[38]See German Constitution Article 1 [Human Dignity]:

> (1) Human dignity is inviolable. To respect and protect it is the duty of all state authority.
> (2) The German People therefore acknowledge inviolable and inalienable human rights as the basis of every human community, of peace, and of justice in the world.
> (3) The following basic rights are binding on legislature, executive, and judiciary as directly valid law.

[39]Lipari (2004).

[40]Mattheis (2012), p. 626 et seq.

In particular, emphasis has been placed on the ‘rule of law’ as an overarching principle of ‘constitutional legality’.[41] The rule of law[42] could serve as a communication platform between the political and the legal system of the world society:[43] in this way, the two autopoietic and functionally differentiated sub-systems could communicate with each other and use these principles in the autopoiesis of the two systems.[44] This ‘platform’ would thus signify a structural coupling and a form of global constitutionalisation—at least in the language of systems theory.

In the old Kelsenian approach existed an almost ontological gap that separated law and politics, the two being located on different dimensions of the reality, the normative reality for the law and the value reality for politics.[45] But it is, according to me, just through the example of the Italian experience that we may perceive a transformational moment. This term refers to the moment when lawmaking and its actors transform the values expressed inside the political arena into legal categories and concepts.

For example, the idea of the State having an interventionist attitude in the economy (in order to protect the public) is transformed into several legal limitations (or counter-principles) to the general legal principle of freedom of contract.[46]

Surely the relationship between the legal and the political system has undergone a metamorphosis and has led to a functional synthesis between the two systems. Even if completely functionally delineated political and legal systems may be utopian, or at an ‘embryonic stage’, such structures did emerge in the Italian doctrine on contract. So is there a system-theoretical constitutionalisation of civil society? And what is the role of contract today in such a market-oriented society? Is contract really the key factor of the market, or is it that contract can become the threshold though which political or social goals, other than those purely economic, may enter into the markets to shape them into a socially oriented set of institutions?

I presume that, at the very end, the problem of ‘contract and values’ has to cope with the existence of these thresholds between different communicative systems. This fact is normally under-emphasised by authors involved in the theory of autopoiesis, and not without reason. Indeed, it is this theory that can elucidate, and bring to light, the existence of thresholds, but their very existence will naturally undermine the purity of their own theory on the separation between different communicative systems.

This is a kind of paradox that we shall try to afford in the next final section when we shall try to reach our conclusions.

---

[41]See Bodansky (2009), p. 565 et seq.

[42]We need to remember in addition that the pro-market intervention of the American Supreme Court in *Lochner vs New York* 198 US 45 (1905) was based on the theory of substantive due process as a Constitutional value to be applied even to private parties.

[43]Beaulac (2009), p. 197; and see Waldron (2006), p. 1 et seq.

[44]Zieret (2008), pp. 466–467.

[45]Kelsen (1957), p. 365.

[46]Cheshire et al. (1996), pp. 352–353.

5 Conclusion: Form and Substance and the Social Ontology of Contract

In the first paragraph, we have delineated two extreme versions of what a contract can be, from the pure market model of the contract as a private affair of the parties in privity to the model of the contract as a 'social act', an act performed by the parties where wider social interests are at stake and where more or less room for a judicial scrutiny of the content and the justification of the act is allowed. As we have seen, 'values' as such are always at stake. The so-called pure model, or classical model of the contract, is just a contract imbued with liberal pro-market values.

Then, in the second paragraph, using Italy as an exemplary Latin jurisdiction, we have deepened the way in which the classic model of the contract has been built up by jurists in a technical frame, which entailed, from its very origins, an endless tension between freedom of contract and judicial interventionism, in particular through the intrusion of the element of the *cause de l'obligation* and the ideal of Aristotelian commutative justice.

In this way, in the third paragraph, we have seen how a fascist theory of contract could become possible within the framework of the civilian tradition, using the same technical elements to serve no longer liberal values but the 'values' of the new political order for the sake of a national economy oriented toward political struggle and dominance.

Finally, in the fourth paragraph, we have displayed the way in which the same elements could be used, under a reversed scale of social values, for the aims of a social democrat political environment oriented toward the construction of a post-liberal non-individualistic society, and at the end of that paragraph we have then started a discussion about the nature of values embedded in a legal order, with particular reference to the theory of the autopoiesis of the law.

Now a first conclusion that we can draw concerns the form and substance of Contract law in its passing through different ages and different value landscapes. In particular, we have remarked on the importance of the ideology shared by the judiciary in applying a series of technical elements that tend to remain unchanged notwithstanding the political changes occurring in society. In a way, as it has been told, judges are important actors in a symbolic representation of the conflict of commitments.[47] As such, the judge is a cultural figure engaged in persuading adversaries in the spite of the arbitrariness of values, and Contract law may be an ideal context for this labour, precisely because it presents, in a highly sophisticated discourse, problems of daily life, immediate and inescapable.

This first conclusion matches with a second one that could deem to be a classical standard comparative conclusion, proving why critical thinking in the law and

[47]Kennedy (1976), p. 1777.

comparatives may often collide even when they start from opposite political standpoints.[48]

Such a second comparative conclusion can be summarised as follows:

1. From its very beginning, civilian contract possessed elements in open contradiction to the theory of the contract as a private agreement based solely on the principle and values of freedom of contract.
2. These elements are basically
   (a) the theory of the *cause de l'obligation*;
   (b) the classification of contracts in different pre-formed 'types';
   (c) the idea of an underlying 'Aristotelian' contractual commutative justice;
   (d) the underlying belief in the usefulness of general clauses and undefined principles such as good faith or fair dealing.

These elements can variously be combined together to allow the judge to rewrite the contract for the parties, and so they are basically illiberal, but they can be combined in different forms to serve a variety of political goals and social values, including, by an exercise of judicial self-restraint, liberal and pro-market values as it happened in nineteenth century French and Italian jurisdictions. This is maybe why contract is apparently deeply resistant to political understanding.

What we need then is now a theory of values that can assign to them a definite role within the pure legal framework of a legal-political tradition.

To understand this last passage, and considering the discussion we led in the previous section, my theory is now that we must pass through a reconsideration of values as 'constitutional elements' of a 'social ontology', in the sense used by John Searle.[49]

Values normally share an ontological opaqueness and an uncertain status.

What are they? They are not beings or entities. They are not living even if we adopt metaphors to speak about the birth, growth and death of values: '... values are no more, they have gone away ... new values raised ... we are expecting for the coming of new values ...'

Values should belong to the world of Sollen (ought to be) and not of Sein (being). They transcend the metaphysics of being, even if they are incorporated in the devices and apparatuses directing and capturing the behaviour of subjects. On the other side, values can be deemed to be openly subjective as a typical production of the subject as such in the forms of his ideals, beliefs and attitudes.[50]

According to my theory, this uncertain ontology of values has been mainly a product of criticism, in the form of the Kantian departmentalisation of pure reason, moral reason and aesthetics.[51]

---

[48]Muir-Watt (2000), p. 505.

[49]Searle (1995).

[50]Calabresi (1985).

[51]De Man (1986), pp. 7–8.

Something that once could have been perceived as unitary, like the vision of a *Madonna del Brunetto*, would then be split into the following:

(a) a pure consideration of the object itself as an existing object possessing certain qualities that pure reason can apprehend, as its size, location, time frame and so on;
(b) a pure consideration of their aesthetic value, as something producing passions, and fit to be used as a model or to be rejected as a deformity;
(c) a pure consideration of its moral values because of the moral ideas it can raise in the audience, inspiring attitudes and beliefs.

On this departmentalisation, Marxism introduced the idea of a political appraisal of values, in particular in the form of ideological criticism, from the standpoint of their political impact and their role in shaping a false consciousness of the real, to serve the interests of the dominating class. Thus, a *Madonna del Brunetto* could become the object of a critique for its way of representing a false ideal world to which people should conform, believing to serve some ideal value of existence, hiding the real existential situation of the audience of being entrapped into a class role at the service of some dominating power.

It is, from this standpoint, hard to deny that the legal discourse on contract has been largely dominated by aesthetic ideologies in favour of or against a pure market society.[52] In this way, the legal discourse on contract, far from being autopoietic, produced different narrative plots: from the rise and fall of freedom of contract of Atiyah[53] to the 'age of anxiety' of Gilmore,[54] with different stances, from the defence of Roman contract by Gordley[55] to the attack on Roman Contract law by the World Bank.[56]

Here I am interested not in solving these conflicts but rather in surfacing their structure. So the question becomes: what is the social ontology of values in relation to contract theory?

According to the simplistic but clear-cut formula used by Searle, the structure of a social ontology is given in the following form:

'X counts as Y in C'.

Where X is a social object, Y is its representation, and C is a given context.

This given, it is rather simple to see values as part of the constitutive ontological elements of C.

We can grasp the above-mentioned abstract algebra substituting its cold variables with the objects of our enquiry, transforming it into the following:

C = system of values;

---

[52]Polanyi (1944).

[53]Atiyah (1979).

[54]Gilmore (1974).

[55]Gordley (2016).

[56]See the World Bank Policy Research Working Papers, 2003, n° 3136, Legal Institutions and Financial Developments.

X = offer and acceptance;

Y = the result of what a contract is in a given system.

Offer and acceptance are here used to represent the brute facts of an agreement and as such are to be interpreted as a synecdoche for the whole range of possible brute behaviours of the parties at stake. 'Contract' is then the outcome that C assigns to these brute facts in the form of a cluster of complex meanings.

If you like, we could state the same thing using a different paradigm, more critical, more post-modern or more lacanite, like saying that a 'contract' is what the Big-Other is imposing upon us when we bargain or agree with another.

Here I bypass easily the critique that there aren't indeed 'brute facts'. There are. A production chain is a brute factual reality, as is the fact that Joe Smith entered John Doe's shop at 5h20 p.m. is a brute fact, simply true or false. What is never pure is the meaning of facts, and especially the meaning of a chain of facts, since it is already always the outcome of an interpretation.

As a matter of fact, it is part of my conclusions that, in this sense, there is no pure form of contract because we need always a C assigning a Y to an X. So even contract as a pure agreement based on freedom of contract, in the purest liberal sense, is not the pure form of contract, upon which newer and different values that intervened in the political process or are inferred from Constitutions are being overimposed.

Contract as a mere private affair, to be strictly construed, is a peculiar form of contract, but it is not the platonic form of a contract. As a matter of history, it came on the stage much later than the Roman contract. The nineteenth century hard contract was an invention, a historical artefact that emerged, tended to disappear, and is now experiencing a newer life. It is a revenant.

So contract has never been pure in any sense; it has always been embedded into a value-structured social ontology, performing different social goals. From this, perhaps the most relevant conclusion to be traced is about the nature of historical legal studies and of Comparative law as a discipline, where history shows the archaeology of given social formations, and Comparative law studies the different social ontologies having a legal meaning, whatever we may intend for 'legal'.

What Comparative law as such can do is to depict 'models' and to explain how these models work in terms of their constituent parts, remembering that their workings depend on the social meaning assigned to them by the uncanny presence of structures of meaning that bypass the boundaries separating different communicative systems.

This explains why a construct as a contract may last for a very long span of time remaining quite unchanged even if it assumes a totally different social or economic significance.

The model of Roman contracts, based as it is on the contrasting elements of 'agreement', 'causa', 'default rules of the type' and 'good faith', could acquire a pagan, Christian, liberal, socialist, fascist, social-democrat, left-liberal or pro-market meaning. And what it is, its substance, depends not on its constituent parts but on the system C of meaning assignment. Substance belongs to the Big-Other.

It is true, on the other side, that a model based on agreement and consideration works differently, and that historically displayed a major resistance to being used for political goals different from liberalism. But since there is no such thing as a crystal structure of the Common law, for the very reason that it is at best unwritten, it is always possible that, in the long process of discovering what the Common law really is, newer theories on adequacy of consideration could emerge, as theories of unconscionability have done. And we cannot exclude that in the future, even in Common law jurisdictions, good faith will finally appear as a standard by which to judge the behaviour of the parties and to interpret their texts, not to mention the always underlying ideal of commutative justice as necessarily present in every exchange. Neither can we exclude the reverse: that the civilian systems will finally abandon, under the pressure of international entities, these attitudes, and will change, for instance, precisely as now French law did, the very notion or importance of the *cause de l'obligation*.

I would finally underline that this 'Aristotelian' ideal, so important in determining judicial intervention in defining the content of a contract, is not so purely Greek and philosophical as it seems to be. The whole of classical economics is based, after all, on the assumption that market exchanges are to be just. I mean that the price paid is correct. A market where goods are regularly sold at a price that is too low or too high will necessarily evolve toward the right market price for those goods, but for external interferences. If it does not happen, it means that information on that market is too asymmetrical and that some of the buyers or the sellers are constantly deceived and exploited. As long as a market must represent the objective scarcity of a commodity, such asymmetrical markets will be of no use to society, and it should rather, from the standpoint of efficiency, proceed through political allocations. Thus, there is no sharp line dividing the philosophical question of justice from the economic efficiency of markets, and indeed the considerations were united in Louis de Molina and the works of the Second Scholastic.[57] This is particularly true if we introduce the assumption that, on an efficient market, all actors must be rational. If they are, their agreements will never be unjust because they possess all the relevant information, can discount any strategic behaviour and can produce complete contracts covering all possible contingencies. And besides, their undertakings will always possess a legitimate and objective rationale, *id est* a legitimate and objective cause of their obligations.

This is said not only to restate what we know, that consumer protection is a legal answer to possible market failures due to an asymmetrical distribution of information, but also to assert what is a bit less obvious: that, in theory, a system based on pure agreements and strict interpretation should, in the very end, produce the same results of a system based on 'causal' contracts and a judiciary check of good faith and adequacy of consideration, if all actors are rational.

This is less obvious, and I cannot be here so analytic as to prove this result, but it is more than a pure speculation. A rip-off economy could not endure even if it could

[57]See Hayek (1976), pp. 178–179.

survive in the short run, but a judicial check is a long process, so it is very doubtful that a judicial intervention could do better than pure market forces as, on the reverse, it is very dubious that market forces will not produce, and maybe more speedy, the same results as judicial controls. It is one of the mysteries of market forces, to be still fully investigated objectively, without the usual boring mantras constantly recited by pro-marker theorists, that these forces really tend to produce justice ... but for the political power acquired by some lobbying groups to capture regulations in their favour, altering the market mechanisms. After all, this is the 'theological' mystic of the market, which is giving it a legitimacy that otherwise it could not possess. Nobody wants a constant production of injustice, and from this standpoint we should reconsider the way in which the 'invisible hand' of the market was theorised during the Scottish enlightenment as a secularisation of the religious concept of providence.

All this may change abruptly only in totalitarian versions of contract theory, when the political interests of the nation, or of a particular class, are put as a decisive factor for the determination of the content of contracts and their enforcements. In any event, liberal countries may also find themselves at war and may have the temporary necessities to improve regulations altering markets and their standard outcomes. This is conceded even by Hayek in his discussion of the spontaneous order.[58] One simply cannot manage a war or an emergency situation by the means of the spontaneous order. What totalitarian regimes tried to do, as in Italy, was to alter the structure of contract because they thought they would last for a long time, but they did not, and they did not succeed in altering the structure of contract either. Finally, the fascist and post-fascist structure of contract remained the same old Roman one. Even social democratic values changed for a while points of interpretation of contracts but had to leave its basic structure unchanged. Of course regulation can be imposed, and prices can become state controlled, but that is another story. It regards not the structure of contract but the limits allowed to the bargaining process, and the impact of regulation on legislation or on the law in general, which is a rather different topic.

My final conclusion is then twofold.

On the one side, a conclusion is that we cannot have a theory of contract without having a conscious theory of the values that must be associated with it. We cannot have a contract without values, whatever these may be. If these values are liberal, then we will have a liberal contract as one of the possible uncanny incarnations of its nature.

On the other side, contract, and the social order produced by contracts, possesses this uncanny and elusive nature. It appears to be something we cannot completely govern more than it governs us.

After all, contract is one of the few values—as we are told—that even the Devil is always bound to respect.[59] Part of this elusive nature is also part of the mysteries,

[58]Hayek (1976), p. 107 et seq.

[59]Obvious reference is here to Marlow's and Goethe's Doctor Faust.

or liturgies, of the *Oikonomia*[60] and of its modern, particularly Scottish, derivation from secularised religious concepts.

Maybe, in plunging further into the details of the origin of the two different modern models of contract, the British and the Continental, we could one day reach the conclusion that ... all the major concepts of the theory of contract have been once theological conceptions.

References

Agamben G (2011) The kingdom and the glory: for a theological genealogy of economy and government (trans: Chiesa L, Mandarini M). SUP, Stanford

Alpa G (2014) I contratti del consumatore. Giuffré, Milano

Atiyah PS (1979) The rise and fall of freedom of contract. OUP, Oxford

Baldassarre A (1997) Diritti della persona e valori costituzionali. Giappichelli, Torino

Beaulac S (2009) The rule of law in international law today. In: Palombella G, Walker N (eds) Relocating the rule of law. Hart, Oxford, pp 197–223

Bodansky D (2009) Is there an international environmental constitution? Indiana J Global Leg Stud 16:565–584

Calabresi G (1985) Ideals, beliefs, attitudes, and the law: Private law perspectives on a Public law problem. Syracuse University Press, New York

Calvo R (2013) L'equità nel diritto privato. Giuffré, Milano

Cheshire GC, Fifoot CHS, Furmston MP (1996) Law of contract. Butterworths, London

Coase R (1988) The firm, the market and the law. University of Chicago Press, Chicago

Costantini C (2017) The unburiable contract. Grant Gilmore's discontinuous parabola and the literary construction of American Llegal style. In: Monateri PG (ed) Comparative Contract law. Edward Elgar, Cheltenham

Cover RM (1983) Nomos and narrative. Harv Law Rev 97:4–68

Creutzig J (1969) Quelques remarques sur le problème de l'obligation abstraite. Revue Internationale de Droit Comparé 21:373–383

Daube D (1951) The peregrine praetor. J Roman Stud 41:66–70

De Man P (1986) The Resistance to theory. University of Minnesota Press, Minneapolis

Dossetti G (1995) I valori della costituzione. Edizioni San Lorenzo, Reggio Emilia

Gilmore G (1974) The death of contract. Ohio State University Press, Columbus

Gordley J (2001) Contract law in the Aristotelian tradition. In: Benson P (ed) The theory of Contract law: new essays. Cambridge University Press, Cambridge

Gordley J (2010) The philosophical origin of modern contract Doctrine. OUP, Oxford

Gordley J (2016) In Defence of Roman Contract. In: Monateri PG (ed) Comparative Contract law. Edward Elgar, Cheltenham

Gordon JS (2007) Aristoteles über Gerechtigkeit – Das V. Buch der Nikomachischen Ethik. Verlag Karl Alber, Freiburg

Grundman S (2008) Constitutional values and European Contract law. Kluwer Law International, Alphen aan den Rijn

Haupt G (1943) Vertragsfreiheit und Gesetz. Zeitschrift der Akademie für Deutsches Recht 9:80–91

Hayek FA (1976) Law, legislation and liberty, vol 2. The University of Chicago Press, Chicago

[60] Agamben (2011).

Hesselink MW (2007) European Contract law: a matter of consumer protection, citizenship, or justice? Eur Rev Private Law 15:323–348
Hussard E (2002) L'économie du contrat. Revue juridique de l'Ouest 15:7–65
Kelsen H (1957) What is justice? justice, law, and politics in the mirror of science. University of California Press, Berkeley
Kennedy D (1976) Form and substance in Private law adjudication. Harv Law Rev 89:1685–1778
Laurent M (1999) Les actes de précaire, instruments de transferts patimoniaux (France du Nord et de l'Est, VIIIe-XIe siècle). Mélanges de l'Ecole française de Rome. Moyen-Age 111:607–647
Lipari N (2004) Diritto e valori sociali: legalità condivisa e dignità della persona. Studium, Roma
Livingston MA, Monateri PG, Parisi F (2015) The Italian legal system. SUP, Stanford
Mattheis C (2012) The system theory of Niklas Luhmann and the constitutionalization of the world society. Goettingen J Int Law 4:625–647
Monateri PG (ed) (2016) Comparative Contract law. Edward Elgar, Cheltenham
Muir-Watt H (2000) La fonction subversive du droit comparé. Revue internationale de droit comparé 52:503–527
Perlingieri P (1978) Scuole civilistiche e dibattito ideologico: introduzione allo studio del diritto privato in Italia. Rivista di diritto civile 69:1–44
Perlingieri P (2010) Funzione giurisdizionale e costituzione italiana. ESI, Napoli
Polanyi K (1944) The great transformation. Beacon Press, Boston
Rizzo MJ, Arnold FS (1987) An economic framework for statutory interpretation. Law Contemp Probl 50:165–180
Sacco R (1993) Il contratto. UTET, Torino
Santoro-Passatelli F (2002) Dottrine generali del diritto civile. Jovene, Napoli
Searle JR (1995) The construction of social reality. Free Press, New York
Siebert W (1942) Contrato y libertad de contratación en el nuevo sistema del Derecho alemán. Revista de derecho privado: 454
Somma A, Monateri PG (2003) The Fascist theory of contract. In: Gorges C, Ghaleigh NS (eds) Darker legacies of law in Europe: the shadow of National Socialism and fascism over Europe and its legal traditions. Hart, Oxford
Sorrenti G (2006) L'interpretazione conforme a costituzione. Giuffré, Milano
Stoll H (1936) Vertrag und unrecht. Mohr, Tübingen
Waldron J (2006) The rule of international law. Harv J Law Publ Policy 30:1–15
Zieret KA (2008) Weltrecht und regionale Differenzierung. Rechtstheorie 39:453–475

Decolonising South African Contract Law: An Argument for Synthesis

Andrew Hutchison

Abstract South Africa is an example of a 'mixed' legal system. The fascinating synthesis of Roman-Dutch and English Contract laws is a key feature of this system and has often been remarked upon by scholars. The new frontier of debate in this country, however, is as to the role of the Constitution in shaping the Common law of contract and effecting transformation of our commercial landscape. The question in this regard of how to apply the Bill of Rights to the common law seems to have been settled at indirect horizontality. A related and pressing concern is how to incorporate indigenous African Customary law perspectives into the law of contract. All of these revisionist aims must, however, leave South Africa as a viable country in which to invest and do business. This paper was inspired by the 2015 'decolonisation' movement and will explore ways in which to effect (in a commercially viable manner) the goal of decolonisation of Contract law, which is arguably mandated by the Constitution. In the light of this, one must ask, what is the future of South Africa's traditional Roman-Dutch common law of contract?

1 Introduction

Student protests rocked South African universities in 2015 and 2016, with a central call being for 'decolonisation'.[1] This term, which seems to have been inspired (inter alia) by the writing of the Afro-Caribbean scholar, Fanon, seeks to effect real

This work is based on the research supported by the National Research Foundation. Any opinion, finding and conclusion, or recommendation expressed in this material is that of the author and the NRF does not accept any liability in this regard.

[1]This movement, which started at the University of Cape Town as a call for the removal of a prominent statue of British colonialist Cecil John Rhodes in March, spread very quickly to other South African universities, with the general call being for transformation of institutions perceived as being Eurocentric. In October and November 2015 there were nationwide student protests against increases of student fees, which arose at the University of the Witwatersrand and spread to all major universities around the country within a week. Protests continued intermittently through 2016 at most South African universities, particularly once it became clear that fees for tertiary

A. Hutchison (✉)
Department of Commercial Law, University of Cape Town, Rondebosch, Cape Town, South Africa
e-mail: andrew.hutchison@uct.ac.za

L. Siliquini-Cinelli, A. Hutchison (eds.), *The Constitutional Dimension of Contract Law*, DOI 10.1007/978-3-319-49843-0_6

transformation in post-apartheid South Africa, both of university culture and curriculum.[2] In a legal context, this could arguably entail revisiting the content and sources of the legal system brought to the country and initially developed by successive colonial governments. Such a decolonisation process underlines what is indigenous and African in South African law and questions that which has been imported. (African Customary law continues to be practised by a large proportion of the black population of the country.)[3] Also at the heart of the decolonisation movement are broader social justice concerns. South Africa is a country where inequality is rife, with the divisions largely (although not exclusively) following racial lines.[4] Another possibility, consonant with the protesters' philosophy, is to draw on the experience of other African countries in formulating laws in a post-colonial setting.[5]

The choice of the term 'decolonisation' to describe the process argued for in this chapter is intended to provide a tentative response to the student movement's demands from the perspective of a participant in the academic discourse of South African Contract law. The usage of this term is not intended to carry a technical meaning but rather to mark an attempt to capture the ethos of a more Afropolitan vision of Contract law, to be reached through a process of synthesis of indigenous African and received (European) contract laws. Of course, any argument about what is 'African' or 'Afropolitan' risks positing a stereotypical view of a broad range of peoples residing in a large country on a very diverse continent. The present author has nevertheless used broad trends drawn from the discourse of African scholars, as well as the Constitutional Court, in describing a generalised position on what an indigenous African view of law might entail. In defence of this method, the present author would argue that what is set out below is intended to provide a framework for future legal research and development of the law, recognising the plural nature of South African legal sources and systems, rather than an anthropological account of African customs or law. Future research into what a living African Customary law (or laws) of contract might entail will hopefully reveal a more scientifically derived vision of the true nature of indigenous African contracting.

---

education would remain a reality going forward and would be subject to inflationary increases in 2017.

[2]For an influential theoretical account of decolonisation, see Fanon (1967). See also: Fanon (2008). In the South African context, see Biko (2004) for another statement of the black consciousness ideal.

[3]Himonga and Bosch (2000), p. 306.

[4]See by way of example: Massie et al. (2014), pp. xxii–xxvi; Piketty (2014), pp. 326–328.

[5]This chapter will use Nigeria as an example here, since it is Anglophone and hence accessible to the author. Nigeria is particularly relevant since it is, at the time of writing, Africa's largest economy. See: Staff Writer, The Economist (2014).

Reference will also be made to other SADC countries which base their Private law largely on South African law, such as Zimbabwe, Namibia and Botswana. For the influence of South African law in these countries, see: Zimmermann and Visser (1996), pp. 3–4.

A big driver of change in the South African context is the democratic Constitution and particularly, from the point of view of the law of contract, the horizontally applicable Bill of Rights contained therein.[6] Given the history of this country, transformation of society from an authoritarian culture to a caring and human-rights-based one is a core constitutional goal, along with redress of historic inequalities.[7] Thus, the decolonisation process resonates with the broader constitutional aims of effecting changes to the existing framework to bring about greater distributive justice.[8] This paper will explore possible ways, in line with the existing constitutional jurisprudence, in which the South African law of contract can be decolonised while still maintaining the country as a secure destination for investment and commercial activity.

South Africa's colonial history began in 1652 with the arrival of the Dutch at the Cape.[9] These settlers brought with them their law and set up a local governing structure.[10] Later, from 1795, except for a brief interlude between 1803 and 1806, the English took over the colonial administration of the country.[11] South Africa's status as a collection of separate jurisdictions continued until 1910, when South Africa's four composite territories formed a union to become one country.[12] This was achieved by means of the South Africa Act (1910) of the British Parliament.[13] Following the Statute of Westminster (1931), the Union Parliament became the supreme and sovereign legislative power in South Africa.[14] The apartheid government, elected in 1948, withdrew from the British Commonwealth in March 1961 and became a republic later that year.[15] White minority rule was maintained until a transition to democratic rule was negotiated with the representatives of the black liberation struggle, with the official date of the first black majority government coming into power being the 27 April 1994.[16] On this date, the so-called interim Constitution[17] took effect, with the 'final' Constitution being enacted in 1996 and coming into force on 4 February 1997.[18] This 1996 Constitution is now

[6]On horizontal application see text and accompanying notes 72–76 in Sect. 3 below.

[7]See by way of example: Mureinik (1994), Langa (2006) and Ackermann (2000).

[8]See by way of example: Klare (1998) and Davis and Klare (2010). For a work tracing the influence of Aristotle on contract law, see: Gordley (1991) (see pp. 12–13 for a discussion of distributive justice in this context).

[9]Hahlo and Kahn (1968), p. 567. The settlement was financed and administered by the Dutch East India Company ('VOC'). Initially the intention was to found a refreshment station for passing ships, but after a short period, the first 'freeburghers' began to farm independently, which began the process of permanent European settlement. See generally in addition: Fagan (1996), pp. 35–37.

[10]Hahlo and Kahn (1968), pp. 567–575; Fagan (1996), pp. 35–41.

[11]Hahlo and Kahn (1968), pp. 567, 575–578; Fagan (1996), pp. 46–51.

[12]Hahlo and Kahn (1968), pp. 567, 575–578; Fagan (1996), pp. 46–49; Hutchison (1991), p. 28.

[13]Hutchison (1991), p. 28.

[14]Ibid.

[15]Ibid., pp. 28–29.

[16]See generally: De Vos and Freedman (2014), pp. 15–23.

[17]Act 200 of 1993 (hereinafter the 'interim Constitution').

[18]De Vos and Freedman (2014), pp. 20–25.

the supreme law of the country, with the Constitutional Court being tasked with the final say on the implementation thereof.[19]

The modern South African common law remains tainted in the eyes of some due to its origins in largely European sources and the subsequent interpretation of these by a colonial, and later an apartheid, judiciary.[20] This body of Contract law is, however, as shall be shown below, in many ways a local and unique synthesis.[21] The existence of a home-grown law of contract distinguishes South Africa from many other African states, such as Nigeria, which uses English law (nominally as it stood in 1900) as its modern source of Contract law in a commercial setting.[22] Since democracy in South Africa, the Constitutional Court has elected to work within the constraints of the existing framework of Contract law but has been grappling with how to effect transformation in the business sphere through development of the common law.[23,24] Indeed, the question of how to incorporate the values of the African majority remains a vexing one.[25] African Customary law is a valid and binding source of law under the final Constitution, but it only applies 'when applicable', which is assessed with reference to the nature of the transaction and the parties involved.[26] To the extent that a 'Customary law of contract' exists, it would thus only pertain subject to the recognised rules on choice of law in South Africa.[27] If Customary law is to influence the common law of contract, there must be a cross-pollination of ideas from Customary law to the generally

---

[19]Sections 2; 165–173 Constitution of the Republic of South Africa, 1996 (hereinafter the 'final Constitution'). Note: the hierarchy of the South African court structure was changed by the Constitution Seventeenth Amendment Act, 2012 (in force since August 2013), in terms of which the Constitutional Court is now the apex court in all matters.

[20]For an example of recent black consciousness scholarship making this type of argument, see: Sibanda and Mosaka (2015). See also in a different context: Barnard-Naudé (2016).

[21]On the fact that the South African common law in general is a local synthesis, see Hahlo and Kahn (1968), Chapter 17; Fagan (1996) and Price (1947). For a negative view of this synthesis, see Chanock (2001), pp. 155–169.

[22]See Mwalimu (2009), pp. 399–401. Asein (2005), p. 101 hints at a certain hostility to the colonial origins of the received English Common law. The alternative appears to be only Customary law, however, which in the current Nigerian law is subject to 'any law for the time being in force' (Ibid., p. 129, citing Section. 20(1) of the Cross River State High Court Law).

[23]See in particular: *Barkhuizen v Napier,* [2007] (5) SA 323 (Constitutional Court); *Everfresh Market Virginia (Pty) Ltd v Shoprite Checkers (Pty) Ltd,* [2012] (1) SA 256 (Constitutional Court); *Paulsen and Another v Slip Knot Investments 777 (Pty) Ltd,* [2015] (3) SA 479 (Constitutional Court). These cases are discussed below in Sect. 3.

[24]In this chapter, 'common law' (lower case) will be used to refer to the body of South African law built up through judicial development of the historic sources. 'Common Law' (upper case) will be used to refer to the English Common Law and the legal family originally based thereon.

[25]Zimmermann and Visser (1996), pp. 12–15. The Constitutional Court's position on this question is discussed below in Sect. 3.

[26]Section 211(3) final Constitution. See further: Himonga and Nhlapo (2014), pp. 82–87; Bennett (2004), pp. 42–43. It should be noted that the exact meaning of the phrase 'when applicable' in Section. 211(3) remains (to date) a little uncertain.

[27]See Himonga and Nhlapo (2014), pp. 82–87.

applicable common law. This would create a truly South African law of contract and would address the notable lacuna of African thinking from the historic South African legal discourse on this topic.[28] In an age of decolonisation, this is highly appropriate.

This chapter will begin with an account of the traditional Roman-Dutch common law of contract in South Africa in Sect. 2. Next, it will consider the subsequent development of the common law under the transformative mandate of two successive Constitutions in Sect. 3, with particular emphasis on how to include African values in this process. Legislative development of specific regimes dealing with employment and consumer law will largely not be discussed, although these are also part of the constitutionalisation of Contract law.[29] In Sect. 4, the nature of African Customary law in this country and the question of whether a Customary law of contract exists will be considered. Since the focus of the Constitutional Court in developing the common law of contract has been on underlying values, notably fairness, reasonableness and good faith, this will be the central thread used as a case study throughout the three primary studies on common, Customary and Constitutional laws.[30] Section 5 will deal with the issue of how to decolonise the South African law of contract and the inter-linked question as to the future of the traditional Roman-Dutch-based law of contract in this country. The chapter will conclude with an argument for a new synthesis of ideas and sources in Sects. 6 and 7.

2 The Traditional Common Law of Contract

The South African law of contract is based on uncodified Roman-Dutch law, as expounded by the so-called old authorities of the Netherlands.[31] Dutch statutes and precedents are largely only incorporated to the extent that these are discussed by these institutional writers.[32] Of particular relevance are legal texts from the province of Holland, dating from the seventeenth and eighteenth centuries, up until the Dutch codification in 1806.[33] This bedrock of old legal principles has traditionally

[28]Compare Zimmermann and Visser (1996), pp. 12–15; compare the argument of Sachs (1989).

[29]See on Labour law (inter alia): Labour Relations Act 66 of 1995, Employment Equity Act 55 of 1998, Basic Conditions of Employment Act 75 of 1997, Broad-Based Black Economic Empowerment Act 53 of 2003. On Consumer law, see (inter alia): Consumer Protection Act 68 of 2008, National Credit Act 34 of 2005, Rental Housing Act 50 of 1999.

[30]The Constitutional Court's position of 'fairness' in contracting will be explored in Sect. 3 below.

[31]Fagan (1996), p. 41.

[32]Ibid.; Hahlo and Kahn (1968), p. 579.

[33]Hahlo and Kahn (1968), pp. 578–596; Fagan (1996), pp. 41–45. It should be noted that the bald statement made here sums up what has in the past been a hotly contested terrain. There were both narrow views of Roman-Dutch law, namely that only the writers of the province of Holland during the above period were binding, with other Dutch writers of the period, or even other European writers of *ius commune* generally, being of mere persuasive authority. Hahlo and Kahn at

been considered to form the residual common law of South Africa, dealing with core areas of Private law, such as the law of persons, things and obligations.[34] The English colonial administration introduced (*inter alia*) the doctrine of precedent and law reporting, however, which added a layer of English procedure onto the civilian roots.[35] This placed the development of the common law squarely within the control of the courts. Due to important historic factors, such as the inaccessibility of legal sources written in Latin or Dutch; the fact that many legal practitioners were primarily schooled in the English Common law; and the lack of contextual suitability of a centuries old system of law in a contemporary commercial setting, the English law of contract was often referred to by South African courts.[36] Indeed, certain forms of specific contract, notably the contract of insurance, saw English law being adopted almost verbatim by the South African legislature and courts.[37] English doctrines such as estoppel by representation, rectification, rescission of contract for innocent misrepresentation and the doctrine of undue influence were furthermore grafted onto the Roman-Dutch framework by the courts to form our distinctive mixed system of Contract law.[38]

The role of the (then apex) Appellate Division has been highlighted in this process. This court, formed in 1910 upon the union of the four territories making up present-day South Africa, was staffed with jurists who were able to read the foreign language sources of Roman-Dutch law and to derive therefrom the basic legal principles that form the bedrock of South African Contract law today.[39] This combination of historical factors led to the development of a South African law of contract, which has links to the law of ancient Rome and the subsequent development of that system to accommodate local custom by writers of the *ius commune* of medieval Europe, along with certain key features of the English Common law system, as illustrated above. This is truly a fascinating legal synthesis, and it was created here in South Africa by our own legal practitioners.[40]

---

pp. 580–581 set out this viewpoint. Fagan at pp. 43–44 argues for a broader view based on the fact that national boundaries were not clearly observed by writers in the period in question, plus the fact that South Africa courts have traditionally selected the version of the law which best suits the particular policy argument being furthered in a given case.

[34]Compare Hahlo and Kahn (1968), p. 586fn5, which reflects the historic fact that most South African law schools (at the time of writing) taught these concepts as Roman-Dutch Law I, II, III, et cetera, rather than under their more conventional subject titles, as used around the world. This was the position at the University of Cape Town until 1995. Thereafter the title 'Private Law' was used for these courses, until 2001 when a new curriculum introduced titles such as Law of Property, Law of Contract, Law of Succession etc.

[35]Hahlo and Kahn (1968), pp. 575–578.

[36]Fagan (1996), p. 57; Chanock (2001), pp. 156–159.

[37]General Law Amendment Act 8 of 1879 (Cape Colony); General Law Amendment Ordinance 5 of 1902 (Orange Free State); Fagan (1996), p. 56.

[38]See generally: Zimmermann (1996).

[39]Fagan (1996), p. 60; Chanock (2001), pp. 160–167; Corder (2010), pp. 572–575.

[40]For praise of South Africa's Roman-Dutch common law see: Hahlo and Kahn (1968), p. 596 ('one of the world's great legal systems'). For a negative view that one of the major underlying

This type of rosy Eurocentric picture has been painted by many South African scholars down the years, who would rather ground the common law of this country in ancient European sources than in the harsh realities of the colonial context of our land. Chanock argues that this is not the full picture and that South African Contract law was created in this country with specific biases necessary to maintain the colonial and later white minority sovereign status quo, particularly with regard to questions surrounding the subjugation of the black population.[41] Chanock sets out a revisionist history of South Africa's Roman-Dutch common law, with reference (inter alia) to the doctrine of good faith in contract, as well as to specific contractual regimes, such as employment and credit agreements.[42] Chanock's views implicate the traditional position on notions such as inequality of bargaining power and fairness in contracting.[43] While the present author sees value in the judicially created version of South African Contract law and in the (future) comparative development of the common law of contract with regard to worldwide trends in legal systems based on European 'parent' models (as shall be argued below), Chanock's views on South African legal history do seem to have some purchase with regard specifically to the historic treatment of the doctrine of contractual good faith.

The purpose of this section of the paper is not to reiterate praise for South Africa's unique blend of Common and Civil laws but to demonstrate the potential for decolonisation of Contract law. This will be done by tracing (very briefly) the history of notions of fairness in contracting through the history of South African Contract law. This should simultaneously illustrate the rich European roots of the existing South African common law, as well as the deliberate choice that has been made between competing authorities, to move towards a system of law that has the capabilities of upholding the interests of the dominant commercial classes in society. This thread will then be built upon in the following sections to show the scope for constitutional change and indeed decolonisation.

Others have traced the historical pedigree of the doctrine of good faith in South African law, so I will be brief here.[44] African notions of good faith will be dealt with in Sect. 4, so I will set out the European history only here. The origins of contractual good faith (or *bona fides*) in Roman law lie in the Roman distinction between contracts by stipulation, which required certain procedural formalities for validity, and consensual contracts that were created by agreement alone.[45] A party to a contract by stipulation could protect himself against the fraud of his counterpart

---

motivators for development of a South African version of Roman-Dutch law was resistance to British imperialism and a desire to subjugate the local black population by means of (*inter alia*) the law of contract, see Chanock (2001), pp. 155–176.

[41]Chanock (2001), pp. 172–176.

[42]Ibid., pp. 155–184.

[43]Ibid., pp. 169–184.

[44]The two key texts (in the opinion of this author) on the history of the doctrine of good faith in South Africa are Zimmermann (1996) and Hutchison (1999).

[45]Zimmermann (1996), pp. 218–220; Hutchison (1999), pp. 215–217.

by requesting that the *praetor* insert into the procedural formula a standard clause known as the *exceptio doli*, which could be relied on to challenge bad faith conduct by his opposite number.[46] Consensual contracts were said to rest on good faith (*bona fides*), which meant that the *exceptio doli* was unnecessary here.[47] By the time of the formative Roman-Dutch law period in the seventeenth century, this distinction had fallen away and all contracts were said to be consensual, or *bona fidei* contracts.[48] Hence, the system of contracting brought to the Cape by the first European settlers was firmly based on good faith, as has been noted by many judgments of the Appellate Division and its successor, the Supreme Court of Appeal.[49]

In twentieth-century South African Contract law, the defence known as the *exceptio doli generalis*, the historical relevance of which has been outlined above, enjoyed what Zimmermann has termed a 'surprising afterlife'.[50] Indeed, this defence was used as a 'passport' for the importation of many equitable devices, largely from English law, by serving as a Roman-Dutch peg on which to hang the desired English doctrine.[51] The status of the *exceptio doli generalis* as an independent defence to attack conduct as not being in good faith remained controversial, however. This device was dealt a mortal blow in 1988 in the *Bank of Lisbon* case, in which the majority of the Appellate Division buried it as a 'superfluous, defunct anachronism'.[52] In the same decision, the majority of court also ruled that good faith was not an independent ground on which to challenge a contract.[53] The idea of fairness in contracting lived on, however, and in the very next year (1989), a doctrine of 'unconscionability' was developed by the same court in *Sasfin v Beukes* under the public policy rule.[54] The appearance of fairness in this new guise, referred to in *Sasfin* as 'doing simple justice between man and man', gave hope to those who supported good faith in Contract law.[55] The Supreme Court of Appeal reiterated its

---

[46]Zimmermann (1996), pp. 218–220; Hutchison (1999), p. 216.

[47]Ibid.

[48]Habersack and Zimmermann (1999), p. 219; Hutchison (1999), p. 216.

[49]*Paddock Motors (Pty) Ltd v Igesund,* [1976] (3) SA 16 (Appellate Division), p. 28; *Tuckers Land and Development Corporation (Pty) Ltd v Hovis,* [1980] (1) SA 645 (Appellate Division), pp. 651–652; *Bank of Lisbon and South Africa Ltd v De Ornelas,* [1988] (3) SA 580 (Appellate Division), pp. 601–602; *Eerste Nasionale Bank van Suidelike Afrika Bpk v Saayman NO,* [1997] (4) SA 302 (Supreme Court of Appeal), pp. 318–331 (per Olivier JA); *Brisley v Drotsky,* [2002] (4) SA 1 (Supreme Court of Appeal), para 22.

[50]Zimmermann (1996), p. 236.

[51]Ibid. The 'passport' metaphor is taken from *Connock's (SA) Motor Co Ltd v Sentraal Westelike Ko-operatiewe Maatskappy Bpk,* [1964] (2) SA 47 (Transvaal Provincial Division), p. 49.

[52]*Bank of Lisbon and South Africa Ltd v De Ornelas,* [1988] (3) SA 580 (Appellate Division), p. 607. Zimmermann (1996), pp. 234–235 notes that the only case in which the *exceptio doli generalis* was successfully invoked as a defence in its own right, was in the high court decision in *Rand Bank Ltd v Rubenstein,* [1981] (2) SA 207 (Witwatersrand Local Division).

[53]*Bank of Lisbon and South Africa Ltd v De Ornelas,* [1988] (3) SA 580 (Appellate Division), p. 607. Zimmermann (1996), pp. 609–610.

[54]*Sasfin (Pty) Ltd v Beukes,* [1989] (1) SA 1 (Appellate Division), p. 7H–9G.

[55]Jansen JA in a dissenting judgment in *Bank of Lisbon and South Africa Ltd v De Ornelas,* [1988] (3) SA 580 (Appellate Division), pp. 617F–G had already linked the underlying basis of the

Bank of Lisbon position, however, in *Brisley v Drotsky* in 2002.[56] There, the Supreme Court of Appeal stated that good faith was not an independent ground on which to challenge a contract, although it did underlie the law of contract as a whole and found expression in its more technical rules (such as those on misrepresentation) and in the interpretation of contracts.[57] This is where the doctrine of good faith remains at present, even under the final Constitution, although the Constitutional Court appears to be flirting with developing a doctrine of objective reasonableness as shall be demonstrated in Sect. 3.[58]

In sum then, it is clear that under the guidance of the Appellate Division, the doctrine of good faith in Contract law, which was inherent in the Roman-Dutch system of contracting, and which could thus easily have been selected from the available sources to form a strong component of our modern system of contracting, was not selected. Instead, the courts have favoured a position on good faith that is closer to the strict English Common law position but without the tempering effect of a separate branch of law based on equity.[59] This of course aids contractual and commercial certainty but does little to protect the position of weaker contracting parties. Indeed, even the English developed a parallel system of consumer Contract law by legislation from the 1970s, whereas in South Africa this is only a comparatively recent development, undertaken as part of the constitutional mandate.[60] An emphasis has been placed on sanctity of contract and *caveat subscriptor* in most decisions, as is demonstrated (for example) by the case history in controversial areas of contracting such as exemption clauses and non-variation clauses.[61] Chanock's view, discussed above, is that this was evidence of a deliberate policy

---

exceptio doli generalis, namely the 'sense of justice of the community' to the 'defences based on public policy'. See further: Lubbe (1991).

[56]*Brisley v Drotsky,* [2002] (4) SA 1 (Supreme Court of Appeal), paras 11–22. Confirmed in: *Afrox Healthcare Bpk v Strydom.* [2002] (6) SA 21 (Supreme Court of Appeal), paras 31–32; *South African Forestry Co Ltd v York Timbers Ltd,* [2005] (3) SA 323 (Supreme Court of Appeal), paras 26–31. For more recent statements by the SCA to this effect see the cases cited in note 111 below.

[57]*Brisley v Drotsky,* [2002] (4) SA 1 (Supreme Court of Appeal), para 22. Note that this statement is taken from Hutchison (2001), pp. 743–744. Compare the creative use by the SCA of good faith at the interpretation stage in *South African Forestry Co Ltd v York Timbers Ltd,* [2005] (3) SA 323 (Supreme Court of Appeal), paras 32–36.

[58]See the cases cited in notes 23 above and 85 below. See Price and Hutchison (2015).

[59]For an introduction to the English position on good faith see: Whittaker and Zimmermann (2000), pp. 39–48, but note the recent English case law developments discussed below in the text accompanying notes 211–212.

[60]On English Consumer law, see (inter alia): Consumer Credit Act, 1974; Unfair Contract Terms Act, 1977; Sale of Goods Act, 1979. Compare SA statutes cited above note 29.

[61]See: *Brisley v Drotsky,* [2002] (4) SA 1 (Supreme Court of Appeal) (on non-variation clauses) & *Afrox Healthcare Bpk v Strydom,* [2002] (6) SA 21 (Supreme Court of Appeal) (on exemption clauses). Hutchison (2001), Lubbe (2004) and Bhana and Pieterse (2006). Note that the position on exemption clauses with regard to consumer contracts has been alleviated by the Consumer Protection Act 68 of 2008 (see Chapter 2, part G). The case law on mistake in contract has sometimes seen a relaxation of the *caveat subscriptor* rule, however, based on the doctrine of reasonable reliance. See in particular: *Sonap Petroleum (Pty) Ltd v Pappadogianis* [1992] (3) SA 234 (Appellate Division).

of preferring capital over labour and commercial over consumer interests, as was required by a nascent regime of oppression to subjugate the majority of the population.[62] While this may not be the conventional view, and notions of contractual certainty can validly be defended on sound commercial grounds, it is clear that a policy choice has been made here, and it is an individualistic, pro-business one.[63]

Contractual certainty and business interests are indeed vital in a developing economy, which needs economic growth in order to uplift the population, but it must be acknowledged that this involves a policy choice, which can only be defended in the current South African climate if there is a hiving off of consumer and employment laws (as indeed there has been post democracy). The fact remains that there is a strong basis in the Roman-Dutch sources of South African law for a doctrine of good faith, which has been diluted by the subsequent development of Contract law in order to promote (sometimes) competing values of freedom of contract and contractual certainty. The 'underlying' value of good faith could instead be foregrounded if this was found to be in line with a new African policy direction that the now apex Constitutional Court wished to follow.[64]

3 The Constitutional Law of Contract

The mandate of both the democratic South African Constitutions is (and was) indisputably the transformation of law and society, to undo the injustices of colonialism and Apartheid and to create a new societal construct with a strong element of social justice.[65] Indeed, elements of human dignity, equality and freedom are foregrounded in the final Constitution and are central values underlying the Bill of Rights.[66] Central to the goal of transformation is the notion of substantive equality, which takes into account differences between people, particularly historical disadvantage, in the formation of law and policy.[67] 'Freedom' needs to be balanced against 'dignity', in the sense that these values can sometimes pull in

[62]Chanock (2001), pp. 169–184.

[63]For defences of the necessity of contractual certainty, see in particular the following articles by Supreme Court of Appeal Justices, writing in their personal capacity: Brand (2009), Lewis (2013) and Wallis (2016).

[64]The key Constitutional Court cases on contract law will be discussed below and are listed in note 23 above and note 85 below.

[65]This purpose is expressed in the Preamble to the final Constitution. Compare also Chapter 2's Bill of Rights, which includes not only civil and political rights, but also socio-economic rights. For discussion in law journals, see: [Former Chief Justice of the Constitutional Court] Langa (2006); [Former Deputy Chief Justice of the Constitutional Court] Moseneke (2009).

[66]Sections 7(1), 36(1), 39(1) final Constitution.

[67]Ibid, Section 9(2). See further: Employment Equity Act 55 of 1998 & Broad-Based Black Economic Empowerment Act 53 of 2003.

different directions.[68] This would be the case, for example, if 'freedom' implied 'freedom of contract', whereas 'dignity' entailed a sense of 'innate human worth', should a plaintiff's rights arising out of a validly concluded contract infringe the basic well-being of the defendant.[69] 'Dignity' can, however, have several different interpretations, from Kantian autonomy to a more collective notion, centred on group solidarity.[70] This is relevant in an excursus such as the present, which attempts to marry (Western) individualism with the African notion of *ubuntu*.[71] Elements of both individual and collective rights can be found within the South African Bill of Rights, which necessitates a value judgement in application.

With regard to the application of the Bill of Rights to the common law, the Constitutional Court has vacillated between direct and indirect approaches.[72] This is perhaps a result of the fact that the text of both the interim and later final Constitutions is open to interpretation in this regard.[73] Under the interim Constitution, the Constitutional Court had analysed the position in several leading constitutional democracies and ultimately based its finding on the German position of indirect horizontality.[74] The text of the final Constitution was amended in a manner that undercut this decision, however.[75] Room was left in the text for continued

[68]For a brief general discussion of freedom versus dignity, which explains potential conflict and the resolution thereof, see: Meyerson (1997), pp. 10–15. For a view that freedom and dignity are inter-linked and not in antithesis, see: Du Bois (2008).

[69]Compare: Lubbe (2004), pp. 420–423.

[70]Du Bois (2008), Ackermann (2000), Cowen (2001) and Feldman (1999). In a specifically contractual context, see: Lubbe (2004), pp. 420–423.

[71]This will be explored in Sect. 5 below.

[72]Interim Constitution: *Du Plessis v De Klerk,* [1996] (3) SA 850 (Constitutional Court), paras 42–49 (indirect application to the common law under the relevant sections of the interim Bill of Rights). Final Constitution: *Carmichele v Minister of Safety and Security,* [2001] (4) SA 938 (Constitutional Court), paras 33–40, 50–60; *S v Thebus,* [2003] (6) SA 505 (Constitutional Court), paras 23–32; *K v Minister of Safety and Security,* [2005] (6) SA 419 (Constitutional Court), paras 15–19; *Barkhuizen v Napier,* [2007] (5) SA 323 (Constitutional Court), paras 23–30. All of these cases favoured indirect application under Section 39(2). See however: *Khumalo v Holomisa,* [2002] (5) SA 401 (Constitutional Court), paras 29–33 (direct application of the Bill of Rights under Section 8 of the final Constitution to a defamation claim). Currie and De Waal (2013), pp. 46–47 argue that *Khumalo* is the only decision in which the Constitutional Court applied the Bill of Rights directly to the common law. In the subsequent *Barkhuizen* decision, the Constitutional Court was invited to use direct application, but chose instead indirect application. These authors thus reach the logical conclusion that this is the preferred method of the Constitutional Court. There is much debate on this point in the law journals, see by way of example: Woolman (2007), Fagan (2010), Bhana (2013) and Du Bois (2015).

[73]Sections 7 and 35(3) of the interim Constitution; Sections 8 and 39(2) of the final Constitution. For discussion, see the sources listed in the previous note.

[74]*Du Plessis v De Klerk,* [1996] (3) SA 850 (Constitutional Court), para 60.

[75]Section 8 of the final Constitution differed from Section 7 of its predecessor in that the 'judiciary' is expressly bound by the Bill of Rights in Section 8(1) and Sections 8(2)–(3) go on to spell out that natural and juristic persons are also bound and that the common law must be developed to give effect to fact. See: Woolman (2005) and Van der Walt (2001).

indirect application, though, and when the first case developing the Common law of contract was decided, it was this option that the Constitutional Court opted for.[76]

In the seminal 2007 *Barkhuizen* decision, in which a 90-day time bar clause in an indemnity insurance policy was challenged on the basis of the right of access to court,[77] the majority judgment of the Constitutional Court (per Ngcobo J) preferred to test the contract against the Bill of Rights indirectly, via the public policy rule, than by direct application of the constitutional right to the term in question. In this regard, the majority adopted a two-stage test in determining 'fairness': both a term in a contract and the enforcement thereof had to be valid under the public policy rule.[78] Public policy in turn was defined as follows:

> Public policy represents the legal convictions of the community; it represents those values held most dear by society. . . .Since the advent of our constitutional democracy, public policy is now deeply rooted in our Constitution and the values that underlie it.[79]

And

> Notions of fairness, justice and equity, and reasonableness cannot be separated from public policy. Public policy takes into account the necessity to do simple justice between individuals. Public policy is informed by the concept of *ubuntu*.[80]

An alternative basis for the claim, namely that the insurance company was in breach of a term of 'good faith' implied by law, was not upheld by the majority of the court.[81] Although the judgment held that the 'concepts of justice, reasonableness and fairness constitute good faith',[82] it went on to hold that 'good faith is not a self-standing rule, but an underlying value that is given expression through existing rules of law' (with reference to the Supreme Court of Appeal decision in *Brisley*).[83] Ngcobo J expressly left open the question whether this limited role for good faith was appropriate, on the ground that the facts submitted in the pleadings constituted insufficient basis for a determination on this issue.[84]

Since *Barkhuizen*, there have been a number of Constitutional Court decisions that involved the application of the common law of contract in the new constitutional dispensation.[85] The court has shown a willingness to develop (or at least consider developing) the common law in some fairly drastic ways. Thus, in the

---

[76]Section 39(2). See *Barkhuizen v Napier,* [2007] (5) SA 323 (Constitutional Court), paras 23–30.

[77]Section 34 final Constitution.

[78]*Barkhuizen v Napier,* [2007] (5) SA 323 (Constitutional Court), para 56.

[79]Ibid., para 28.

[80]Ibid., para 51.

[81]Ibid., paras 79–83.

[82]Ibid., para 80.

[83]Ibid., para 82.

[84]Ibid., paras 82–83.

[85]*Everfresh Market Virginia (Pty) Ltd v Shoprite Checkers (Pty) Ltd,* [2012] (1) SA 256 (Constitutional Court); *Maphango v Aengus Lifestyle Properties (Pty) Ltd,* [2012] (3) SA 531 (Constitutional Court); *Botha v Rich NO,* [2014] (4) SA 124 (Constitutional Court); *Cool Ideas 1186 CC v Hubbard,* [2014] (4) SA 474 (Constitutional Court); *Malan v City of Cape Town,* [2014] (6) SA 315 (Constitutional Court); *Paulsen and Another v Slip Knot Investments 777 (Pty) Ltd,* [2015]

Everfresh case, the majority of the Constitutional Court expressed support in principle for the idea that there may be an enforceable duty to negotiate (where a clause in a commercial lease agreement created a right to renew the lease, subject to agreement on rental) even in the setting of a commercial contract between two juristic persons.[86] This support in principle was expressly based on 'good faith' and '*ubuntu*':

> Were a court to entertain Everfresh's argument, the underlying notion of good faith in contract law, the maxim of contractual doctrine that agreements seriously entered into should be enforced, and the value of *ubuntu*, which inspires much of our constitutional compact, may tilt the argument in its favour.[87]

Ultimately, the majority left this matter undecided, however, due to a procedural concern that this (constitutionally inspired) argument had been raised in this the apex court for the first time, leaving them without the benefit of the views of lower courts, and hence instead denied the applicant leave to appeal.[88] A very interesting *dictum* (for present purposes) was made in the minority judgment in *Everfresh*, namely:

> The development of our economy and contract law has thus far been shaped predominantly by colonial legal tradition represented by English law, Roman law and Roman-Dutch law. . . .[T]he majority of people in our country places a higher value on negotiating in good faith than would otherwise have been the case. Contract law cannot confine itself to colonial legal tradition alone.[89]

Indeed, the good faith question, left open by the Constitutional Court in *Barkhuizen*, remains open to date, although there has been increasing lip service that has been paid to this concept by subsequent decisions.[90] Following the dicta in *Everfresh* outlined above, in *Botha v Rich NO*, principles of contractual fairness and good faith were used to invalidate a cancellation of a contract for the purchase of land on instalments and to enforce transfer of that property to the natural person purchaser.[91] The unanimous court made the following statements:

> . . .[O]ur law of contract, based as it is on the principle of good faith, contains the necessary flexibility to ensure fairness. In *Tuckers Land and Development Corporation* it was pointed

(3) SA 479 (Constitutional Court); *Makate v Vodacom Ltd* [2016] (4) SA 121 (Constitutional Court); *Nkata v Firstrand Bank Ltd* [2016] (4) SA 257 (Constitutional Court).

[86] *Everfresh Market Virginia (Pty) Ltd v Shoprite Checkers (Pty) Ltd,* [2012] (1) SA 256 (Constitutional Court), para 72.

[87] Ibid.

[88] Ibid., paras 74–80.

[89] Ibid., para 23.

[90] See the dictum in *Everfresh Market Virginia (Pty) Ltd v Shoprite Checkers (Pty) Ltd,* [2012] (1) SA 256 (Constitutional Court) cited above in the text accompanying note 86; and those in *Botha v Rich NO,* [2014] (4) SA 124 (Constitutional Court) cited below in the text accompanying notes 92–93.

[91] *Botha v Rich NO,* [2014] (4) SA 124 (Constitutional Court), paras 23, 49–51.

out that the concepts of justice, reasonableness and fairness historically constituted good faith in contract.[92]

> Bilateral contracts are almost invariably cooperative ventures where two parties have reached a deal involving performances by each in order to benefit both. Honouring that contract cannot therefore be a matter of each side pursuing his or her own self-interest without regard to the other party's interests. Good faith is the lens through which we come to understand contracts in that way.[93]

Broader questions of substantive equality and the inter-linked question of fairness in contracting for the emergent class of black businesspersons were expressly referred to in the main judgment in *Paulsen* in 2015.[94] Here the majority of the Constitutional Court undid a long-standing common law precedent concerning whether the *in duplum* rule in commercial credit agreements was suspended by the institution of legal proceedings.[95] (The *in duplum* rule at South African common law holds that when arrear and unpaid interest has accrued to an amount equal to the outstanding capital sum, interest will cease to run but that any payment made thereafter will go to decrease interest first, rather than the capital amount, whereafter interest may again accrue back up to the *duplum* amount.)[96] The majority, over a very strong dissenting judgment,[97] held that allowing interest to run afresh upon the commencement of litigation would have a chilling effect on the access to credit of debtors, many of whom may be historically (if no longer presently) disadvantaged.[98] On the issue of sanctity of contract and the fact that the obligation to pay interest was sourced in a validly concluded contract, the main judgment of Madlanga J states:

> To say *pacta sunt servanda* should prevail here because debtors like the Paulsens are 'stout-boned' and should be held to bargains they concluded open-eyed, misses the point. The plain reality is that in South Africa debtors are typically not as financially resourced as the large corporates that dominate the credit market. That there may be some 'stout-boned' debtors does not detract from this economic reality.[99]

---

[92]Ibid., para 45 (references omitted—*Tuckers Land and Development Corporation (Pty) Ltd v Hovis,* [1980] (1) SA 645 (Appellate Division) is cited above at note 49).

[93]Ibid., para 46.

[94]*Paulsen and Another v Slip Knot Investments 777 (Pty) Ltd,* [2015] (3) SA 479 (Constitutional Court), paras 66, 73–75 (per Madlanga J).

[95]Ibid., paras 89–94 (per Madlanga J); 106,119 (per Moseneke J); Cameron J dissenting. *Standard Bank of SA Ltd v Oneanate Investments (Pty) Ltd (in Liquidation),* [1998] (1) SA 811 (Supreme Court of Appeal) stated the prior position and was overruled by the majority of the Constitutional Court in *Paulsen*.

[96]See for example: *Nedbank Ltd and Others v National Credit Regulator and Another,* [2011] (3) SA 581 (Supreme Court of Appeal), para 37.

[97]*Paulsen and Another v Slip Knot Investments 777 (Pty) Ltd,* [2015] (3) SA 479 (Constitutional Court), paras 120–150 (per Cameron J).

[98]Ibid., paras 66–94 (per Madlanga J); 103,106, 119 (per Moseneke J).

[99]Ibid., para 73.

It bears reiteration at this point that the debtors in this case were directors of a company and had stood surety for its obligations.[100] The transaction was not subject to the relevant consumer credit statute.[101] The decision of the majority judgments meant the difference between a liability for the sureties to pay R72 million (as argued by the finance company, based on interest having run again from the time of initial institution of legal proceedings) and R24 million (as ordered by the Constitutional Court, based on a capping of interest even after the institution of legal proceedings, which had already progressed through two previous court hearings).[102]

The main judgment indeed grounded its finding on the *in duplum* rule, which was clearly a policy decision, on an interpretation of the relevant Roman-Dutch institutional writers.[103] The discussion of competing Roman-Dutch viewpoints by a present-day Constitutional Court justice evidences the continuing relevance of this source of the law in the modern era, particularly since this historic source was argued to be the correct statement of South African law, as opposed to the previous rule developed from the same sources by the Supreme Court of Appeal in 1998.[104] This only lends credence to the view that Roman-Dutch sources are merely available to be exploited by judges as a legitimating basis for whatever policy-based interpretation of the law they wish to adopt.[105] This also lends support to the view that a synthesis of values is being developed here in crafting a uniquely South African system of Contract law to suit our present-day climate.

What is clear at the present date of writing is that the Constitutional Court is attempting to transform the common law of contract. This is done by ensuring greater scope for fairness *inter partes*, upholding the dignity of the weaker party at the expense of the freedom of contract of the stronger party. What is not clear is exactly what the new doctrine of contractual fairness entails. In *Barkhuizen*, the Constitutional Court was clear that it was dealing with unconscionability based on the public policy rule,[106] but the concept has become more amorphous due to

[100]For an account of the facts, see *Paulsen and Another v Slip Knot Investments 777 (Pty) Ltd,* [2015] (3) SA 479 (Constitutional Court), paras 1–11.

[101]Ibid., paras 32–41.

[102]Ibid., paras 1, 102.

[103]Ibid., paras 42–58. The two writers involved were Huber and Van der Keesel—these two sources were in conflict on the question in issue, while the SCA in *Oneanate* had chosen the Huber view that interest runs afresh from the institution of legal proceedings, the Constitutional Court preferred the view of Van der Keesel that it did not. Based on the view that there was a conflict in the Roman-Dutch law sources, it is hard to see how a choice between these was not based on policy grounds. While Madlanga J maintained that he was not developing the common law (paras 55–58), Moseneke J in the majority judgment disagreed with this argument (paras 112–113), although he concurred in the ultimate order made by Madlanga J.

[104]Ibid., paras 55–58 (per Madlanga J).

[105]Hahlo and Khan (1968), p. 580; Chanock (2001), p. 166. Both of these views relate to the development of the South African common law prior to democracy, but it is submitted that the arguments are relevant to the present point.

[106]See text above and *Barkhuizen v Napier,* [2007] (5) SA 323 (Constitutional Court), paras 23–30.

successive *dicta.*[107] Judicial discretion in cases involving alleged unfairness has increased, and only time will tell exactly how the doctrine will be concretised.[108] At present, the indirect application of the Bill of Rights prevents public law from overtaking the common law of contract as the governing system for contractual disputes, but it is unclear as to exactly what the duty of good faith in contract (as a distinct concept from public policy) entails.[109] Thus, while it is clear that the Constitutional Court views good faith as important, and inter-linked to African notions such as *ubuntu*, it has not yet come out and stated that good faith/*ubuntu* is an enforceable duty in all contracts.[110] It would appear then that this value continues to merely underlie the law of contract, an interpretation that the Supreme Court of Appeal, as the next court down in the hierarchy, has been at pains to promote.[111] Indirect application of the values underlying the Bill of Rights does necessitate a clear definition of which values are relevant and what these entail, however, and it is herein that there lies scope for the development of the doctrine of good faith, possibly subsumed under the African value of *ubuntu* but still subject to clearly defined limits. This will be the focus of the inquiry into African Customary law in the next section.

4 The African Customary Law of Contract

African Customary law has been a source of law long ignored by the core areas of South African jurisprudence.[112] In a historical overview of South African law published in 1968, Hahlo and Kahn devote only a few lines to this branch of the law, whereas Roman-Dutch law and its history occupy about half of the total book's length.[113] African Customary law traditionally applied only to those culturally subject to it and, even then, subject to a 'repugnancy clause' whereby a judicial

[107]Compare the discussions of the role of good faith in *Barkhuizen*, *Everfresh* and *Botha* covered above, along with the dicta on the role of '*ubuntu*' in *Everfresh* in particular (see note 86 and accompanying text).

[108]Compare the arguments of Brand (2009), Lewis (2013) and Wallis (2016).

[109]For an argument that Public law (in the form of human rights dispensations) should not render the Private law of contract redundant, with reference to various European legal systems, see: Cherednychenko (2007), pp. 541–549.

[110]A close reading of judgments such as *Barkhuizen*, *Everfresh* and *Botha* indicates the Constitutional Court still views good faith/*ubuntu* as values underlying the common law and given expression to through rules, such as that on public policy.

[111]*Bredenkamp v Standard Bank of South Africa Ltd,* [2010] (4) SA 468 (Supreme Court of Appeal), paras 52–53; *African Dawn Property Finance 2 (Pty) Ltd v Dreams Travel and Tours CC and Others,* [2011] (3) SA 511 (Supreme Court of Appeal), para 28; *Potgieter v Potgieter NO and Others,* [2012] (1) SA 637 (Supreme Court of Appeal), para 32.

[112]Chanock (2001), pp. 291–293.

[113]Hahlo and Kahn (1968), p. 579 (on 'bantu law'); pp. 329–596 (on Roman-Dutch law).

officer could pronounce upon the moral acceptability of a given rule.[114] This led to the development of a parallel branch of the law, which Chanock describes as the 'common law B', with its own courts.[115] Modern Customary law scholars point towards this system of colonial/white minority administration as the cause of the creation of a distorted 'official' Customary law—existing in written sources such as the law reports and legislation.[116] In contrast with this former contested 'official' Customary law, the Constitutional Court has confirmed that today the true version of Customary law is recognised as being the 'living' Customary law, as practised on the ground by African communities.[117] Given the fact that this law exists largely in oral tradition and cultural practices, there remain difficulties of proof of the living Customary law, which has to be established in each case through evidence.[118] This is also partly to blame for the creation by the white minority administration of an official Customary law for a judicial system that depended on written sources.[119] Today, the final Constitution recognises African Customary law as a valid source of South African law in its own right, although subject to the supreme Constitution, like all other sources.[120] As stated above, African Customary law applies 'when applicable', which is to be determined with reference to whom the parties to the dispute are and the nature of the underlying transaction or circumstances.[121] Rules on choice of law have been developed to deal with competing Customary laws of different communities or competition between the common and Customary laws.[122] It should also be noted that the final Constitution entrenches the right to culture, which is viewed as giving a right to live by African customary traditions and practices as Customary law envisages.[123] There have been several Constitutional Court decisions on Customary law, which have developed the so-called living

[114]Section 11(1) Black Administration Act 38 of 1927; Section 54A(1) Magistrates' Courts Act 32 of 1944 (1986–1988 by amendment of this Act); Section 1 Law of Evidence Amendment Act 45 of 1988. Today African Customary law applies 'where applicable' under Section 211(3) of the final Constitution, but is subject to the Constitution itself in terms of the supremacy clause (Section 2).

[115]Chanock (2001), pp. 243–357.

[116]Himonga and Nhlapo (2014), pp. 24–25; Bennett (2004), pp. 5–7.

[117]*Alexkor Ltd and Another v The Richtersveld Community and Others,* [2004] (5) SA 460 (Constitutional Court), paras 51–57; *Bhe and Others v Magistrate, Khayelitsha, and Others (Commission for Gender Equality as Amicus Curiae); Shibi v Sithole and Others; SA Human Rights Commission and Another v President of the RSA and Another,* [2005] (1) SA 580 (Constitutional Court), paras 40–46, 156–157; *Shilubana and Others v Nwamitwa,* [2009] (2) SA 66 (Constitutional Court), paras 42–49; *MM v MN and Another,* [2013] (4) SA 415 (Constitutional Court), paras 23–25; Himonga and Nhlapo (2014), p. 31.

[118]Himonga and Nhlapo (2014), pp. 32–33; Bennett (2004), pp. 48–49.

[119]Himonga and Nhlapo (2014), pp. 60–61; Bennett (2004), pp. 5–7, 44–48; Chanock (2001), pp. 291–293.

[120]See Sections 2, 30, 31, 39(2)–(3) and 211 final Constitution.

[121]Ibid., Section 211(3). See Himonga and Nhlapo (2014), pp. 81–87.

[122]Himonga and Nhlapo (2014), pp. 72–76, 81–87.

[123]Sections 30–31 final Constitution. Bennett (2004), pp. 78–90.

Customary system.[124] (It may, however, be argued that this simply gives rise to a new official Customary law different to practices on the ground.)[125] Customary Contract law has only been considered in the democratic era in the context of disputes subject to the common law of contract, however.[126] In the following paragraphs, this paper will describe certain typical forms of contract-like obligation in the context of Customary law. The main argument advanced in this paper is for Customary law to inform the development of the common law of contract; there will be only limited discussion of a potential development of the parallel system of Customary Contract law itself.[127]

Certain South African texts on African Customary law contain a chapter on contracting.[128] The emphasis here falls on obligations that are created by agreement and that give rise to certain rights and duties on the parties to those agreements. These obligations tend to arise in the context of certain types of transaction yet are largely non-commercial in nature.[129] Thus, the recent text edited by Himonga and Nhlapo states that African Customary law contractual obligations exist in a family or community context.[130] The foremost of these is the 'contract' of *lobolo*, in terms of which a prospective husband makes a payment in money or cattle to the family

---

[124]See by way of example the cases cited in note 117 above. For a particularly good example of the development of the 'living' Customary law see *MM v MN and Another,* [2013] (4) SA 415 (Constitutional Court), where the court developed the Customary law rules surrounding marriage in the light of the Constitution, to give an earlier wife a say as to whether her husband married a second wife. In other cases, like *Bhe*, the Constitutional Court developed the living Customary law by amending the Intestate Succession Act, rather than developing Customary law itself. See Sibanda and Mosaka (2015), pp. 274–280 for a critical account of this process.

[125]Himonga and Nhlapo (2014), pp. 32–33. Compare *Bhe and Others v Magistrate, Khayelitsha, and Others (Commission for Gender Equality as Amicus Curiae); Shibi v Sithole and Others; SA Human Rights Commission and Another v President of the RSA and Another,* [2005] (1) SA 580 (Constitutional Court), para 215.

[126]The clearest statement is by Yacoob J in *Everfresh Market Virginia (Pty) Ltd v Shoprite Checkers (Pty) Ltd,* [2012] (1) SA 256 (Constitutional Court), para 23, but see also Moseneke J in the same case at paras 71–72. See further: *Barkhuizen v Napier,* [2007] (5) SA 323 (Constitutional Court), para 51 on *ubuntu* informing public policy.

[127]Note that Himonga and Nhlapo (2014) contains a chapter 10 on Customary Contract law, as does Joubert (2009), paras 230–243. An examination of these chapters reflects that the type of transaction discussed mostly relates to ties of kinship, particularly marriage, and there is little clear statement of general principles of contract law. Thus while the Constitution requires that recognition be given to these transactions and that they be developed where necessary, there is little scope for the displacement of the common law of contract in a commercial setting. Rather this paper will argue for a cross-pollination of the customary value of *ubuntu* into the common law of contract.

[128]See sources in note 127 above. See further: Elias (1956), pp. 144–155. These accounts have been described as 'official' Customary law, however: Mqeke (2003), p. 118 (cited in Himonga and Nhlapo (2014), p. 195).

[129]The few examples given below should illustrate this point, see further the chapters in note 127 above.

[130]Himonga and Nhlapo (2014), p. 187.

head of his prospective wife as a precondition to a valid customary marriage.[131] This is an obligation, in the sense that Customary law and values require this payment to be made and indeed view the validity of the subsequent marriage as conditional upon payment, yet it is intended to secure familial bonds and ensure good faith, rather than act as commercial transaction.[132] In order to make a payment of *lobolo*, a prospective husband may also enter into various quasi-credit agreements with a benefactor within the community, which would give rise to an obligation to pay back the borrowed amount to such person when the husband is able to do so.[133] The customary understanding in most of these arrangements is that the income from the future *lobolo* of a daughter born of the resultant marriage would be used to settle any debt that is still outstanding.[134] (Customary law knows no concept of prescription.)[135]

Other contracts are also identified, such as the *sisa* contract, in terms of which a less well-off member of the community takes over part of the herd of the livestock of a better-off member and cares for this himself in exchange for the milk and produce of the herd.[136] Ownership of the livestock, including offspring born to these, remains with the lender.[137] Bekker identifies this as a form of insurance to the better-off party (since herds are spread over a greater area), as well as a form of social assistance to the less well-off party.[138]

The emergent impression, however, is that these are specific forms of transaction and there is no general underlying system of Contract law. Furthermore, the context of these transactions is firmly rooted in the family or community setting, which means that transposing the resultant principles of 'contract' to an arms-length commercial context between strangers or juristic persons is inappropriate. The basis of these rules is custom or tradition, and they are clearly designed to operate only within the context of a certain type of cultural transaction.

There are, however, more modern and commercial examples of contractual obligation observed by the African community. A key one of these is the so-called *stokvel*, which is a form of rotating savings and credit association.[139] This is a transaction in which a group of people form a club and all members make regular contributions to a joint account, which is then drawn on by members, either in turn

[131]Ibid., pp. 188–191. For the present statutory definition of '*lobolo*' (or the equivalent in other official African languages) see Section 1, Recognition of Customary Marriages Act 120 of 1998.

[132]Himonga and Nhlapo (2014), p. 189. For an anthropological account of the social value of *lobolo*, see: Yarbrough (2014).

[133]Himonga and Nhlapo (2014), pp. 190–193; Bekker (2009), para 238.

[134]Himonga and Nhlapo (2014), pp. 190–193; Bekker (2009), para 238.

[135]Himonga and Nhlapo (2014), pp. 208–209; Bekker (2009), para 243.

[136]Himonga and Nhlapo (2014), pp. 194–195; Bekker (2009), para 241.

[137]Himonga and Nhlapo (2014), pp. 194–195; Bekker (2009), para 241.

[138]Bekker (2009), para 241.

[139]For useful South African studies of this concept, see: Verhoef (2001), Schultze (1997a, b) and Mashigo and Schoeman (2012). For an international overview, which includes South Africa, see: Ardener (1964).

or when required.[140] There are several ways in which such clubs function, and these institutions play an important role as a mechanism of saving, credit and insurance in poorer communities.[141] Again, enforcement of debts due to a *stokvel* is usually ensured through peer pressure, rather than formal judicial intervention.[142] In the literature on this phenomenon, which cuts across disciplines, from economics to anthropology to law, there is a common thread that the communal nature of this type of mechanism provides both the enforcement mechanism as well as an underlying motivation for settling claims, particularly when a club member suffers hardship and is allowed by her peers to draw upon the communal pot.[143] This community orientation of a more recently developed customary contractual institution reflects the similar basis of the more traditional customary contracts.[144] It is to this value of communal well-being, referred to in the South African literature and case law as *ubuntu*, to which this paper now turns.[145]

The philosophical concept known as *ubuntu* in South Africa has been used by the Constitutional Court in a variety of contexts, including, as has been shown above, Contract law.[146] Often the concept is expressed in the phrase *ubuntu ngumuntu ngabantu*, or 'a person is a person through other people'.[147] This notion is said to entail a sense of communal well-being, with the emphasis on group rather than individual interests.[148] Hence, the Constitutional Court has used *ubuntu* to emphasise restorative justice, which was used to justify outlawing the death penalty[149] and has been put forward as a rationale for using an apology as a remedy for a defamation suit, rather than an award of monetary damages.[150] In a contractual setting, the exact meaning of this term remains a little vague, but it is usually used in the same sentence as concepts such as 'fairness, justice and reasonableness'.[151]

140Verhoef (2001), pp. 263–272; Schultze (1997a), pp. 20–24.

141Ibid.

142Verhoef (2001), p. 264; Mashigo and Schoeman (2012), p. 56, Ardener (1964), p. 216.

143Verhoef (2001), pp. 272–273 (referring to the concept of '*ubuntu*'); Schultze (1997a), p. 23; Mashigo and Schoeman (2012), p. 56.

144Compare Elias (1956), pp. 144–156.

145For a summary of the leading case law on '*ubuntu*', as well as a collection of essays on the topic, see: Cornell and Muvangua (2012). Another South African publication dedicated exclusively to *ubuntu* is: Diedrich (2011).

146Ibid. The use of *ubuntu* as a value under the final Constitution has been argued to be based on the following provision at Section 39(3): 'The Bill of Rights does not deny the existence of any other rights or freedoms that are recognized or conferred by common law, Customary law or legislation, to the extent that they are consistent with the Bill.' See: Himonga (2013).

147For example, see: Mokgoro (2012), p. 317.

148Ibid., pp. 317–318; Himonga (2013), pp. 173–180; Keep and Midgley (2007), pp. 31–33.

149*S v Makwanyane*, [1995] (3) SA 391 (Constitutional Court). For a philosophical discussion of the role of *ubuntu* in this decision, see: Metz (2010).

150*Dikoko v Mokhatla*, [2006] (6) SA 235 (Constitutional Court), paras 62–70 (per Mokoro J), 112–121 (per Sachs J).

151Compare *Barkhuizen v Napier*, [2007] (5) SA 323 (Constitutional Court), para 51 (in setting out the content of public policy under the final Constitution).

Bennett has argued that this concept is an African form of equity, and the equation in contractual setting with good faith or fairness is easily drawn.[152]

An investigation into the African literature on the concept reveals that the exact meaning of *ubuntu* is a contested terrain. Emeritus Constitutional Court Justice Mokgoro has drawn attention (in her personal writing) to the difficulty of defining the concept in the abstract and in a foreign language.[153] Mokgoro argues that *ubuntu* is an 'expansive, flexible and philosophically accommodative idea' and that 'it is one of those things that you know when you see it'.[154] She does, however, identify elements of this concept: 'group solidarity, conformity, compassion, respect, human dignity, humanistic orientation and collective unity'.[155] 'Community' indeed features as a central component of most attempts to define this concept.[156] What are the limits of 'community' in this context? Himonga has drawn attention to the competition in the African sources between those who view the African worldview as predominantly community-orientated and those who still acknowledge a role for individuality.[157] She recognises differences between a 'Western' worldview, based on respect for individual rights, and an 'African' view, which stresses communal interests and rights.[158] She maintains, however, that even within the 'African' worldview there is scope for a more moderate version of community, which 'recognizes the equal worth of the individual and community'.[159] This philosophical view is backed up by Gyekye, who takes a moderate view of community:

> [I]mplicit in the communitarianism's recognition of the dual features of the self – the self as an autonomous, assertive entity capable of evaluation and choice *and* as a communal being – is a commitment to the acknowledgment of the intrinsic worth of the self and the moral rights that can be said necessarily to be due to it.[160]

Gyekye does, however, add that 'individual rights, the exercise of which is meaningful only within the context of human society, must therefore be matched with social responsibilities'.[161]

In the South African context, Himonga has derived from the contested terrain around the meaning of *ubuntu* an argument that this concept underlies the protection of socio-economic rights, which are entrenched in the Bill of Rights.[162] This is

[152]Bennett (2011), p. 18. Bennett notes that *ubuntu* is a broader concept than good faith or public policy, however.

[153]Mokgoro (2012), p. 317.

[154]Ibid., pp. 317–318.

[155]Ibid., p. 318.

[156]See by way of example: Mokgoro (2012), pp. 317–318; Himonga (2013), pp. 173–177; Keep and Midgley (2007), pp. 31–33; Metz (2010), pp. 83–85.

[157]Himonga (2013), pp. 174–177.

[158]Ibid., p. 176.

[159]Ibid., p. 177.

[160]Gyekye (1997), p. 64.

[161]Ibid., p. 65.

[162]Himonga (2013) (with reference to the right to healthcare, contained in Section 27 of the final Constitution).

underscored by an understanding of the right to 'dignity' as going beyond requiring one to 'respect each member of society' to 'ensuring that every member is given an opportunity to exercise his or her right to dignity to the full'.[163] With this background in mind, one can guess that the intention of the Constitutional Court was to use *ubuntu* in the sense of social responsibility to temper the Common law's protection of individual contractual rights in order to effect the transformative and redistributive ambitions of the Constitution. Thus, *ubuntu* would require the protection of the vulnerable in society in line with the human-rights-based mandate to revise Contract law. This author accepts the validity of this use of *ubuntu* but would like to draw on the notion that individual interests and freedoms are not repugnant to the African worldview, in order to derive a narrower concept of 'contractual *ubuntu*'. This concept decolonises South African Contract law by adopting African terminology and philosophy for a commercial setting yet should moderate the content of some views of what *ubuntu* entails, in order to achieve greater legal certainty. 'Contractual *ubuntu*' indeed may have strong parallels in the common law concept of good faith, although this too remains a nebulous concept in the present state of South African law. Comparative suggestions of what 'good faith' may entail are suggested below in Sect. 6, which could be reinterpreted through the African lens of communitarian social responsibility as set out above.

Where does that leave arm's length commercial contracts? There are two options here, in line with the parallel systems of common law and Customary law applicable in South Africa. The first is to develop the living Customary law of contract, such that it exists. Perhaps two parties, who both culturally identify with African Customary law, could choose for their commercial contract to be governed by the African Customary law of contract. This would of necessity involve a development of the living Customary law of contract, but as we have seen in the case of *stokvels*, some commercial transactions are part of an indigenously developed system of contracting and have been given effect to in the courts.[164] The second option is for the African Customary law of contract to remain a community-orientated construct, operating largely outside the commercial sphere, but for a notion of 'contractual *ubuntu*' to inform the common law of contract in a process of cross-pollination of ideas.[165] The question here, however, is would two commercial parties, even if they ascribed to an 'African' worldview, wish for their commercial interests to be left to the vagaries of a governing notion of *ubuntu*, which in the event of a dispute could only be determined by a presiding judicial officer in line with her subjective notions of 'knowing it when she sees it'?[166] A necessity is for a narrower notion of

[163]Keep and Midgley (2007), p. 35.

[164]For a reported decision involving a *stokvel*, see: *Mndi v Malgas*, [2006] (2) SA 182 (Eastern Cape High Court). It should be noted that much of the literature on *stokvels* draws attention to the fact that these obligations are typically enforced outside of the courts, resorting rather to social pressure. See text accompanying notes 142–143 above.

[165]Compare the argument of Keep and Midgley (2007), p. 48.

[166]Compare Mokgoro (2012), pp. 317–318, discussed above. For a negative view on the potential of *ubuntu* to operate in a commercial contractual setting, see: Wallis (2016).

'contractual *ubuntu*' to operate in a commercial setting, which must be given definite content in order to preserve contractual certainty and the sanctity of contracts. This type of argument presupposes, however, that the existing value system underlying the common law of contract is also worth retaining, albeit in synthesised form. In this regard, a brief examination of the law of contract of the leading post-colonial economy in Africa, Nigeria, will be used to demonstrate the continuing value of the received system of law.

Nigerian law has been shaped into the Common law mould due to its former status as a British colony.[167] Successive Nigerian statutes during the colonial period made provision for a 'reception' of the English Common law, which displaced the existing Customary law.[168] Following independence in 1960, this position was maintained, so that English Common law as it stood on 1 January 1900 remains a large part of the law of Nigeria.[169] The Nigerian law of contract is indeed squarely based on the English Common law,[170] although Asein argues that today Nigeria draws on its own legal policy, as well as the Common law of other countries within that family, to develop its own Nigerian Common law.[171] A glance at the leading Contract law text suggests that the English influence is pervasive and lasting, however.[172] Nigeria has a supreme Constitution, passed in 1999, which contains a justiciable Bill of Rights.[173] There is little guidance in this document as to whether these rights should apply to Contract law, however.[174] Customary law remains a binding source of Nigerian law but is subordinated to other branches of the law, including the received English Common law.[175] Hence, a contract would only be subject to Nigerian Customary law if that was appropriate for the parties and the transaction concerned.[176] Furthermore, Nigerian parties may expressly choose for their contract not to be governed by the Customary law.[177] The emergent picture is one of a nation that has chosen to follow the Common law of contract for historic and pragmatic reasons. Indeed, the Nigerian Supreme Court stated in 2002:

---

[167]Asein (2005), p. 3.

[168]Ibid., pp. 100–102. Malemi (1999), p. 46.

[169]Asein (2005), pp. 101–102; Malemi (1999), pp. 46–47.

[170]Mwalimu (2009), pp. 400–401.

[171]Asein (2005), pp. 107–112.

[172]Sagay (1985).

[173]Constitution of the Federal Republic of Nigeria, 1999. The Bill of Rights can be found in chapter four of this enactment.

[174]See in particular the property clause (Section 44), which refers to contracts only to exempt them from a prohibition on the compulsory taking of property; and the application clause (Section 46), which states that any person who alleges a contravention of the Bill of Rights may approach a High Court for redress.

[175]Asein (2005), pp. 129–138.

[176]Mwalimu (2009), pp. 400–401.

[177]Ibid., p. 401.

> Nigeria does not cease to be Nigeria because it has chosen a particular mode for ensuring the procedural completeness of its legal system, just as Nigeria does not cease to be Nigeria by choosing the English language. . . .Our legal system draws much of its strength from being part of a common law system having its roots in the past while remaining organic.[178]

To the present author, this statement supports an argument that commercial contracting is a universal process, hence the continuing value of the English Common law of contract in Nigeria, subject to the requirement that this received law would have to be applied in its new setting with the necessary local modifications.[179] This is particularly relevant to a country like South Africa, which is today grappling with the question of decolonisation. While it is the view of the present author that the Nigerian position with regard to the subordination of Customary law and the lack of a human-rights-informed law of contract is not ideal,[180] it does speak to the pragmatic value in retaining the received system of (contract) law. This argument will be explored below in Sect. 5.

5 Decolonisation and the Future of Roman-Dutch Contract Law in South Africa

On the question of appropriate balance between the sources of South African law, I believe that there is merit in the decolonisation movement's call for the release of South African law from colonial constraints. The question is as to how exactly this should take place. Following the revolution in France, the civil law was codified to capture the ethos and aims of the new government.[181] This was not a new law developed from scratch, however, but rather built on the earlier work of pre-revolutionary scholars such Pothier.[182] In the same way, it would be counter-productive for South Africa to begin from scratch with a new system of law altogether.[183] As a reading of a standard textbook on Customary law reveals, this system is not appropriate for the governance of every aspect of the modern state and this includes the area of contracting.[184] Indeed, the South African law of contract is

[178] *Caribbean Trading and Fidelity Corporation v Nigerian National Petroleum Corporation,* [2002] 34 WRN 11 (Supreme Court of Nigeria), cited in Asein (2005), p. 99.

[179] Compare Mwalimu (2009), pp. 399–400 and the *dictum* of Lord Denning to this effect in *Nyali Ltd v Attorney-General,* [1955] 1 All ER 646 (House of Lords), pp. 652–653.

[180] The lack of a strong constitutional dimension to Nigerian contract law is in line with the present English position, however, see below notes 213–214 and accompanying text.

[181] Robinson et al. (2000), pp. 263–264.

[182] Ibid., pp. 264–265.

[183] Compare the argument of Sachs (1989), pp. 5–6.

[184] Himonga and Nhlapo (2014) refer to law on marriage and persons; succession; contract; delict; criminal law; traditional leadership and dispute resolution procedure. Compare Bennett (2004) who has substantive chapters on traditional leadership, family, marriage, children, succession and land tenure.

used by many of our neighbours, such as Zimbabwe and Namibia, which similarly maintain this Roman-Dutch-based system despite their hard-won freedom from colonial forces.[185] The reason for this is simple: South African Contract law has been developed over time into a system that is capable of operating in the modern commercial context. There is an extensive body of case law, supported by considerable academic writing in the form of books and journals. To discard all this knowledge at this stage would be impractical and would incur costs for which South Africa simply does not have room in its budget. In addition, the resultant phase of legal uncertainty would damage the commercial outlook in a country that is in dire need of economic investment. In short, it is not viable solution.

This is where the South African Constitution becomes relevant. In simple, everyday language, it captures the aspirations of the new democratic order and the desire to correct all that was wrong with colonial and apartheid South Africa. While the common law of contract is not dismissed by the final Constitution, there is a clear mandate to develop this to take account of the values in the Bill of Rights.[186] In addition, certain sections of the Bill of Rights call for legislation to give effect to those rights—the results of which, including the Labour Relations Act (1995), have transformed certain areas of South African contract dramatically and totally overhauled its common law roots.[187] Later developments such as the National Credit Act (2005) and the Consumer Protection Act (2008) continue this mandate, although not directly called for by the Constitution. The Constitutional Court has shown a willingness to intervene radically in the existing framework of Contract law beyond these measures, in order to effect transformation.[188] This is the social justice that decolonisation calls for, and it is happening at present in the South African courts, albeit incrementally, as is appropriate for judicial development of the common law.

On the transformation front, there has also been a strong drive to make the judiciary more representative both in race and gender of South Africa's population.[189] Thus, if Roman-Dutch law is to continue as the major underlying basis of South African Contract law, it must be because an increasingly black judiciary, with no ancestry in Europe and no connection to European sources of law other than an historic colonial imposition of these, sees value in such a system. It may be for reasons of expediency that Roman-Dutch law remains the basis of South African Contract law.[190] Perhaps these sources will be manipulated by the bench to further policy goals, as was argued above to have been done by the Constitutional Court in *Paulsen*. It may also be, however, that the Roman system has survived 2,000 years because it is a rational and sound system of law, which is logically classified and

[185] Zimmermann and Visser (1996), pp. 3–4.

[186] Compare the discussion in section three above.

[187] Section 23 final Constitution calls for legislation to give effect to fair labour practices.

[188] See Sect. 3 above.

[189] This is required by Section 174(2) of the final Constitution.

[190] This is in line with the argument of Sachs (1989). See also: Van Niekerk (1998).

expounded in clear principles.[191] It should be noted that the Roman system of law has had far wider influence than the Roman Empire ever extended, simply because it presented a useful and adaptable precedent, which could be employed by many subsequent legal systems in new contexts.[192] Roman-Dutch law was a blend of Roman principles with contemporary Dutch Customary law—a process of modernisation and development that continued in its afterlife in South Africa.[193] Indeed, courts applying South African law have remarked on more than one occasion on the fact that Roman-Dutch law is a living system of law, capable of adapting to the context in which it must operate.[194]

The argument of this paper is thus simple: Roman-Dutch Contract law today operates in a decolonised setting and, as such, must adapt to the demands of those whose interests it is now at last called upon to fully serve. No longer imposed by a colonial administration, Roman-Dutch law must now woo a new demographic of lawyers, who will adapt it to serve their purposes. One of the simplest ways of doing this is to take the African normative system, based on the philosophy of *ubuntu*, and transpose it into the setting of Roman-Dutch Contract law. In order not to subordinate one source of law to another, this new synthesis should properly be referred to simply as 'South African Contract law'.

Thus, Roman-Dutch law will continue to provide the basic framework of the new South African Contract law, but historic sources will probably decline in relevance as these are reinterpreted by the new dispensation. While remaining a binding source of South African law, historic Roman-Dutch law must now prepare to be appropriated, developed and ultimately rebranded in service of the decolonisation of South African Contract law.

In the following Sect. 6, this paper will explore some views in the world literature on what a duty of good faith entails, in order to attempt to derive from this appropriate content for 'contractual *ubuntu*'. The aim here is to create a synthesis in which commercial interests (and along with these the economic prosperity of the country) are protected but through which Contract law is nevertheless decolonised by an infusion of African values.

---

[191]Zimmermann (1990), pp. vii–xi.

[192]Hugo Grotius *Epistolae ad Gallos* CLVI (1633), cited in Zimmermann (1990), p. v.

[193]Hahlo and Kahn (1968), pp. 514–517; Price (1947), p. 494.

[194]For example: *Blower v Van Noorden,* [1909] TS 890 (Transvaal Supreme Court), p. 905: 'There come times in the growth of every living system of law when old practice and ancient formulae must be modified in order to keep in touch with the expansion of legal ideas, and to keep pace with the requirements of changing conditions.' See also: *Pearl Assurance Co v Union Government,* [1934] AD 560 (Privy Council), p. 563.

6 Synthesis

Contractual certainty remains the lodestar of the common law of contract, and this should not change in order to effect a loosely conceived and ill-thought-out objective of decolonisation.[195] This paper will assume that commercial contracting is indeed a universal phenomenon and that concepts found in the parent legal systems of Europe, such as public policy and good faith, are merely open norms to be given content to in a localised setting. In this way, issues such a desire to promote social justice or protect a weaker contracting party are as much a concern in Europe as they are in South Africa.[196] Moreover, these open norms are already to be found in South African law; thus, we need merely to re-appropriate them, with new names if this is deemed necessary, in order to give them a content that is appropriate in a decolonised South African setting.

Lessons can be learnt here from the German experience, where the German Constitutional Court has, since the promulgation of the *Grundgesetz* following World War II, made inroads into the established German law of contract in order to undo an oppressive regime that entrenched existing rights in society.[197] Germany has been a world leader in this field, developing the concept of *mittelbare Drittwirkung* (indirect horizontality) in order to develop their system of Private law while keeping a separation from public law.[198] The interesting feature of the German approach to constitutionalising Contract law is that this is done through the medium of open norms, such as good faith and public policy.[199] This appears to be the model that the South African Constitutional Court is following, although there is little reference to Comparative law in the line of cases following *Barkhuizen*.

Seen in this light, the South African Constitutional Court's notion of public policy is simply a channel for constitutional values and a means by which the law of contract can be transformed in accordance with policy goals. Good faith is an important component of the public policy rule, along with *ubuntu* and constitutional values.[200] A clearly defined concept of 'good faith' could thus help to give content to what the Constitutional Court envisages as the exact scope of contractual fairness in this country. The traditional scope of good faith in the South African Common law was dealt with in Sect. 2 above. In Sect. 3, however, this paper argued that the Constitutional Court seems to view a greater role for the doctrine, although the exact parameters thereof remain a little hazy. Some guidance from the Comparative

---

[195] Compare the argument of Wallis (2016).

[196] Compare: Mak (2008); Cherednychenko (2007); Study Group on Social Justice in European Private Law (2004).

[197] Mak (2008), pp. 9–12; Lewan (1968); Oeter (1994); Habersack and Zimmermann (1999).

[198] Apart from the sources cited in note 197 above, see for a South African discussion: *Du Plessis v De Klerk,* [1996] (3) SA 850 (Constitutional Court), paras 39–41.

[199] Mak (2008), pp. 70–83; Cherednychenko (2007), p. 115.

[200] *Barkhuizen v Napier,* [2007] (5) SA 323 (Constitutional Court), para 51 read with para 80. Compare the discussion in Kruger (2011).

law, particularly those systems where good faith plays an important role, may therefore be helpful in this regard.

As a key example of a Civil law system, in the German law of contract, good faith is recognised as an overarching obligation at all stages of contracting and has also been used as a peg on which to hang new developments of more technical rules of contracting, such as the rules on fundamental change of circumstances, developed from the 1920s onwards.[201] Similar statements can be made about Dutch and Italian laws.[202]

Even in the Common law realm, where the role of good faith in contracting has traditionally been more controversial, some countries seem to also be developing in this direction.[203] This represents an interesting form of convergence on this theme between different legal families. In Common law countries, 'good faith' is in some jurisdictions incorporated as an implied term to commercial contracts.[204] Although the Supreme Court of Canada, for example, restricts this to a subjective notion of honesty, good faith was described as an 'organising principle' of the law of contract.[205] In Australia, courts may be moving even further in this direction.[206] Another leading Common law jurisdiction with an entrenched policy of good faith is the United States, where statute/model law implies a duty of 'good faith and fair dealing' into all contracts.[207] Thus, 'good faith' is expressly more than just honesty, but there does not seem to be uniformity in the interpretation of the more objective obligation of 'fair dealing'.[208] Some view it as a duty simply to exercise rational

---

201 Whittaker and Zimmermann (2000), pp. 18–32.

202 Ibid., pp. 52–55; Mak (2008), pp. 35–37.

203 In addition to the references supplied in notes 204–212 below, see: Paterson (2009).

204 See in particular the brief summary of the US position in Summers (2000). For the Australian position, see: Peden (2009) and cases cited below in note 206. See further the cases cited in notes 205 and 211–212 below for the position in Canada and the UK.

205 *Bhasin v Hrynew* 2014 SCC 71 (Supreme Court of Canada), paras 33, 63, 73–74. The court was careful to state at para 86 that: 'The duty of honest performance ... should not be confused with a duty of disclosure or of fiduciary loyalty. A party to a contract has no general duty to subordinate his or her interest to that of the other party.'

206 See: *Vodafone Pacific Ltd v Mobile Innovations Ltd,* [2004] NSWCA 15 (New South Wales Court of Appeal), paras 189, 125. See further: *Alcatel Australia Ltd v Scarcella,* [1998] 44 NSWLR 349 (New South Wales Court of Appeal); *Burger King Corporation v Hungry Jack's Pty Ltd,* [2001] 69 NSWLR 558 (New South Wales Court of Appeal) in support of this view. The question whether a duty of good faith should be recognised in the performance of all contracts had previously been left open by the High Court of Australia in *Royal Botanic Gardens v South Sydney City Council,* [2002] 186 ALR 289.

207 US Uniform Commercial Code (Revised version: 2008) §1–201(20), read with §1-304; Restatement (Second) Contracts §205; Summers (2000) and Perillo (2009), pp. 412–417.

208 For a general discussion of the law on good faith in commercial contracts (especially franchising) see: Hadfield (1989–1990). By way of case law example, see: *Bak-A-Lum Corporation of America v Alcoa Building Projects Inc,* [1976] 351 A 2d 349 (Supreme Court of New Jersey); *Taylor Equipment Inc v John Deere Company,* [1996] 98 F 3d 1028 (US Court of Appeals, 8th circuit); *United Airlines Inc v Good Taste Inc,* [1999] 982 P 2d 1259 (Supreme Court of Alaska).

business judgement,[209] whereas others have interpreted it as a duty to take into account the legitimate interests of an opposing contractual party.[210] Finally, in the parent system of English law itself, despite some murmurings about a greater role for good faith,[211] the appellate courts seem set against this.[212] It is also to be noted that English Contract law has largely escaped constitutional review thus far, outside of clear infringements of the Human Rights Act,[213] such as where there is unfair discrimination.[214]

With regard to giving content to the South African open norms, be they public policy, good faith or *ubuntu*, courts should learn from the Comparative law, particularly that of the more closely defined Common law realm, and expressly attempt to give content to these norms. If *ubuntu* entails upholding relations within a community and preserving a collective sense of dignity, this would foreground the speedy settlement of contractual disputes in order to preserve relationships, as well as preferring solutions that lead to upliftment of those in need. A more individualised sense of *ubuntu* could simply be a duty to act in a socially responsible manner, which could be linked to duties such as honesty and reasonableness, duties that the Constitutional Court seems to view as incumbent upon contracting parties. Of course, our courts would have to determine whether reasonableness entails only a contractual term or conduct being justifiable according to business judgement (and hence defensible on grounds of rationality) or something more than this, such as a

---

209 Hadfield (1989–1990), pp. 980–984.

210 *United Airlines Inc v Good Taste Inc,* [1999] 982 P 2d 1259 (Supreme Court of Alaska), per Matthews CJ dissenting.

211 *Socimer International Bank Limited (in liquidation) v Standard Bank London Ltd,* [2008] EWCA Civ 116 (England and Wales Court of Appeal (Civil Division)), para 66 (good faith as a fetter on an exercise of a contractual power); *Yam Seng Pte Ltd v International Trade Corporation Ltd,* [2013] EWHC 111 (England and Wales High Court (Queen's Bench Division)), para 131 (English law prepared to recognise good faith as a term implied on the facts, although not a term implied by law).

212 *Interfoto Picture Library Ltd v Stiletto Visual Programmes Ltd,* [1988] 2 WLR 615 (Court of Appeal (Civil Division)), p. 621; *Walford v Miles,* [1992] 2 AC 128 (House of Lords), p. 138. In a follow up to *Yam Seng Pte Ltd v International Trade Corporation Ltd,* [2013] EWHC 111 (England and Wales High Court (Queen's Bench Division)), the Court of Appeal chose not to read in an implied duty of good faith, since this would be in conflict with the express terms of the contract, see: *Mid Essex Hospital Services NHS Trust v Compass Group UK and Ireland Ltd (t/a Medirest),* [2013] EWCA Civ 200, paras 105–112. For a brief overview of the English position, see: Steyn (1997) and Whittaker and Zimmermann (2000).

213 Human Rights Act, 1998. See generally: du Bois's chapter in this volume; Hoffman (2011). For a comparison of the UK and South African human rights regimes and their impact on private in each of these countries, see: A Price (2012).

214 MacQueen (2004), pp. 380–383; Rose (2011), p. 301. The obligations of a landlord under the Rent Act 1977 were developed on constitutional grounds in *Ghaidan v Godin-Mendoza,* [2004] UKHL 30. There, the rights of the same sex partner of a deceased tenant to a statutory tenancy were recognized by the House of Lords, where the Rent Act referred only to the rights of a 'wife or husband'. In *Wilson v Secretary of State for Trade and Industry,* [2003] UKHL 40 the House of Lords declined to strike down a provision of the Consumer Credit Act, 1974 in a challenge based on the Human Rights Act, 1998. See further on these cases: du Bois's chapter in this volume; Van Zyl Smit (2011), p. 66.

duty to act in a manner commensurate with fiduciary loyalty.[215] An intermediate construct, which balances individualism with the collective elements of *ubuntu* in the sense of social justice, would require a party to have regard to the 'legitimate interests' of her counterpart, which should be enough to ensure social responsibility.[216]

Concerns of promoting harmony and social cohesion, which operate in a community context, are not easy to transpose into a commercial setting, where relations are at arm's length. It is here that a distinction should be drawn between conventional commercial contracts and more niche areas, like consumer or employment contracting, which have rightfully been hived off and dealt with in specialist statutory regimes.[217] Rather than generalised values reflecting a bygone pre-commercial era, contractual *ubuntu* should take into account the need to effect social justice in South Africa and the fact that the best way to ensure this, along with the protection of socio-economic rights, is through solid economic growth. Contractual certainty is key here, and the development and use of open norms in Contract law should hence not be too vague and restrictive of contractual sanctity. This may sound like expropriation of some of the core tenets of *ubuntu* under a banner of Western individualism, but this interpretation could also be based on a more individualist reading of an ever-evolving African social philosophy, as well as on the pragmatic reasons of sound business practice. This has been demonstrated above with reference to Nigeria, which has favoured European Contract law over indigenous Customary Contract law.

7 Conclusion

South African Contract law has always been a blend of various legal ideas. Originally, it contained a bedrock of uncodified Roman-Dutch law, onto which various English law doctrines were welded. The parallel system of African Customary law contains certain contract-like transactions but no system of rules adaptable for a commercial end. African Customary law is observed by a significant proportion of the South African population, however, and its accompanying value system remains relevant to most who identify themselves as black South Africans. The colonial and Apartheid governments largely sidelined Customary law as a source of law, leaving its development up to specialist courts.[218] There was certainly no cross-pollination of ideas from Customary law into the Common law.

---

[215]The term 'fiduciary loyalty' is borrowed from *Bhasin v Hrynew,* [2014] SCC 71 (Supreme Court of Canada), para 86.

[216]Compare in this regard the concept of 'reasonable expectations of honest men' set out in Steyn (1997).

[217]See statutes cited in note 29 above.

[218]Himonga and Nhlapo (2014), chapter 1; Bennett (2004), pp. 34–42.

This position will change in the future, however. A new generation of post-apartheid lawyers in South Africa have studied Customary law, as well as the Common law of contract, and there is no reason why a process of synthesis should not take place.[219] This is particularly true if this new generation of lawyers are strong proponents of decolonisation and of appropriating the sphere of commercial law for their own ends. This paper has put forward an argument as to one way in which the common law of contract can be decolonised: namely, harnessing the transformative power of the Constitution to introduce African ideas into Contract law through its open norms. 'Contractual *ubuntu*' may then inform the public policy rule for determining the validity of contract terms and the enforcement thereof, as per existing Constitutional Court *dicta*. Alternatively, 'contractual ubuntu' could be an enforceable duty in its own right, as a general rule of Contract law, which would impose certain duties of good faith on both of the contracting parties. This would ensure respect for legitimate interests, without giving blanket discretion to judicial officers to determine contractual disputes based on that officer's personal sense of fairness. This system works in many Civil law countries, notably Germany, and is a good model for South Africa to follow. Decolonisation of South African law should thus involve a new class of South African lawyers taking ownership of the historic South African Contract law, including the Roman-Dutch sources, and reinterpreting these to fashion its own construct of a commercially viable system of South African Contract law.

Acknowledgements The author would like to express his thanks to Chuma Himonga, Alistair Price, Caroline Ncube, Tom Bennett, and Dale Hutchison for their comments on a draft of this chapter. The views expressed herein remain my own and should not (necessarily) be ascribed to those who provided comments.

References

Ackermann L (2000) Equality and the South African Constitution: the role of dignity. HJIL 60: 537–556

Ardener S (1964) The comparative study of rotating credit associations. JRAI 94:201–229

Asein J (2005) Introduction to Nigerian legal system, 2nd edn. Ababa Press, Lagos

Barnard-Naudé J (2016) The pedigree of the common law and the unnecessary Constitution: a discussion of the Supreme Court of Appeal's Decision on *RH v DE*. SALJ 133: 16-28

Bekker J (2009) Law of contract. In: Joubert W (ed) The law of South Africa, vol 32. LexisNexis, Durban, pp 238–243

Bennett T (2004) Customary law in South Africa. Juta, Cape Town

[219] African Customary law was introduced as an optional course by the University of Cape Town Law Faculty for the first time in 1977 (it had previously been covered at UCT as part of a course on African government and law in the Faculty of Humanities), but only became a compulsory for the LLB in 2001 after a curriculum review.

Bennett T (2011) Ubuntu: an African equity. In: Diedrich F (ed) Ubuntu, good faith and equity: flexible legal principles in developing a contemporary jurisprudence. Juta, Cape Town, pp 3–23
Bhana D (2013) The horizontal application of the Bill of Rights: a reconciliation of sections 8 and 39 of the Constitution. SAJHR 29:351–375
Bhana D, Pieterse M (2006) Towards a reconciliation of contract law and constitutional values: *Brisley* and *Afrox* revisited. SALJ 123:865–895
Biko S (2004) I write what I like. Picador, Johannesburg
Brand F (2009) The role of good faith, equity and fairness in the South African law of contract: the influence of common law and the Constitution. SALJ 126:71–90
Chanock M (2001) The making of South African legal culture 1902–1936. CUP, Cambridge
Cherednychenko O (2007) Fundamental rights, contract law and the protection of the weaker party. Sellier, Munich
Corder H (2010) A century worth celebrating. SALJ 127:571–580
Cornell D, Muvangua N (eds) (2012) Ubuntu and the law. Fordham University Press, New York
Cowen S (2001) Can "dignity" guide South Africa's equality jurisprudence. SAJHR 17:34–58
Currie I, De Waal J (2013) The Bill of Rights handbook, 6th edn. Juta, Cape Town
Davis D, Klare K (2010) Transformative constitutionalism and common and customary law. SAJHR 26:403–509
De Vos P, Freedman W (eds) (2014) South African constitutional law in context. OUP, Cape Town
Diedrich F (ed) (2011) Ubuntu, good faith & equity: flexible legal principles in developing a contemporary jurisprudence. Juta, Cape Town
Du Bois F (2008) Freedom and the dignity of citizens. Acta Juridica 112–148
Du Bois F (2015) Contractual obligation and the journey from natural law to constitutional law. Acta Juridica 281–312
Elias T (1956) The nature of African customary law. MUP, Manchester
Fagan E (1996) Roman-Dutch law in its South African historical context. In: Zimmermann R, Visser D (eds) Southern cross: civil law and common law in South Africa. Juta, Cape Town, pp 33–64
Fagan A (2010) The secondary role of the spirit, purport and objects of the Bill of Rights in the common law's development. SALJ 127:611–627
Fanon F (1967) The wretched of the earth. Penguin, London
Fanon F (2008) Black skins, white masks. Grove Press, New York
Feldman D (1999) Human dignity as a legal value – part I. Public Law 682–702
Gordley J (1991) The philosophical origins of modern contract doctrine. Clarendon, Oxford
Gyekye K (1997) Tradition and modernity: philosophical reflections on the African experience. OUP, New York
Habersack M, Zimmermann R (1999) Legal change in a codified system: recent developments in German suretyship law. Edinb Law Rev 3:272–293
Hadfield G (1989–1990) Problematic relations: franchising and the law of incomplete contracts. SLR 42:927–992
Hahlo H, Kahn E (1968) The South African legal system and its background. Juta, Cape Town
Himonga C (2013) The right to health in an African cultural context: the role of *ubuntu* in the realization of the right to health with special reference to South Africa. J Afr Law 57:165–195
Himonga C, Bosch C (2000) The application of African customary law under the Constitution of South Africa: problems solved or just beginning. SALJ 117:306–341
Himonga C, Nhlapo T (eds) (2014) African customary law in South Africa: post-Apartheid and living law perspectives. OUP, Cape Town
Hoffman D (ed) (2011) The impact of the UK Human Rights Act on private law. CUP, Cambridge
Hutchison D (ed) (1991) Wille's principles of South African law, 8th edn. Cape Town, Juta
Hutchison D (1999) Good faith in the South African law of contract. In: Brownsword R, Hird N, Howells G (eds) Good faith in contract: concept and context. Aldershot, Ashgate, pp 213–242

Hutchison D (2001) Non-variation clauses in contract: any escape from the *Shifren* straitjacket? SALJ 118:720–746
Joubert W (ed) (2009) The law of South Africa, vol 32: indigenous law, 2nd edn. Durban, LexisNexis
Keep H, Midgley R (2007) The emerging role of *ubuntu-botho* in developing a consensual South African legal culture. In: Bruisma F, Nelken D (eds) Explorations of legal cultures. The Hague, Elsevier, pp 29–56
Klare K (1998) Legal culture and transformative constitutionalism. SAJHR 14:146–188
Kruger M (2011) The role of public policy in the law of contract, revisited. SALJ 712–740
Langa P (2006) Transformative constitutionalism. Stell Law Rev 16:351–360
Lewan K (1968) The significance of constitutional rights for private law: theory and practice in West Germany. ICLQ 17:571–601
Lewis C (2013) The uneven journey to uncertainty in contract. THRHR 76:80–94
Lubbe G (1991) *Bona fides*, billikheid end die openbare belang in die Suid-Afrikaanse kontraktereg. Stell Law Rev 1:7–25
Lubbe G (2004) Taking fundamental rights seriously: the Bill of Rights and its implications for the development of contract law. SALJ 121:395–423
MacQueen H (2004) Delict, contract, and the Bill of Rights: a perspective from the United Kingdom. SALJ 121:359–394
Mak C (2008) Fundamental rights in European Contract law: a comparison of the impact of fundamental rights on contractual relationships in Germany, the Netherlands, Italy and England. Wolters Kluwer, Austin
Malemi E (1999) The Nigerian legal system. Princeton, Lagos
Mashigo P, Schoeman C (2012) Stokvels as an instrument and channel to extend credit to poor households in South Africa. JEF 5:49–61
Massie K, Collier D, Crotty A (2014) Executive salaries in South Africa: who should have a say on pay? Jacana Media, Johannesburg
Metz T (2010) Human dignity, capital punishment, and an African moral theory: toward a new philosophy of human rights. JHR 9:81–99
Meyerson D (1997) Rights limited. Juta, Cape Town
Mokgoro Y (2012) *Ubuntu* and the law in South Africa. In: Cornell D, Muvangua N (eds) *Ubuntu* and the law. Fordham University Press, New York, pp 317–323
Moseneke D (2009) Transformative constitutionalism: its implications for the law of contract. Stell Law Rev 20:3–13
Mqeke RB (2003) Customary law and the new millennium. Lovedale Press, Alice
Mureinik E (1994) A bridge to where? Introducing the interim Bill of Rights. SAJHR 10:31–48
Mwalimu C (2009) The Nigerian legal system, vol 2: private law. Dorrance, Pittsburgh
Oeter S (1994) Fundamental rights and their impact on private law – doctrine and practice under the German Constitution. Tel Aviv Univ Stud Law 12:7–32
Paterson J (2009) Implied fetters on the exercise of discretionary contractual powers. Monash Law Rev 35:45–73
Peden E (2009) Implicit good faith – or do we still need an implied term of good faith? JCL 25: 50–61
Perillo J (2009) Calamari and Perillo on contracts, 6th edn. Thomson Reuters, St Paul
Piketty T (2014) Capital in the twenty-first century. Belknap Press of HUP, Cambridge
Price T (1947) The future of Roman-Dutch law in South Africa. SALJ 64:494–505
Price A (2012) The influence of human rights on private common law. SALJ 129:330–374
Price A, Hutchison A (2015) Judicial review of exercises of contractual power: South Africa's divergence from the common law tradition. RabelsZ 79:822–851
Robinson O, Fergus T, Gordon W (2000) European legal history. Butterworths, London
Rose F (2011) Commercial law. In: Hoffman D (ed) The impact of the UK Human Rights Act on private law. CUP, Cambridge, pp 300–320

Sachs A (1989) The future of Roman-Dutch law in a non-racial democratic South Africa: some preliminary observations. SA Constitutional Studies Centre, Institute of Commonwealth Studies, London
Sagay I (1985) Nigerian law of contract. Sweet & Maxwell, London
Schultze W (1997a) The origin and legal nature of the *stokvel* – part 1. South Afr Merc Law J 9: 18–29
Schultze W (1997b) The origin and legal nature of the *stokvel* – part 2. South Afr Merc Law J 9: 153–170
Sibanda S, Mosaka T (2015) *Bhe v Magistrate, Khayelitsha*: a cultural conundrum, Fanonian alienation and an elusive constitutional oneness. Acta Juridica:256–280
Staff Writer (2014) Nigeria: Africa's new number one. The Economist (12 April). Available at: http://www.economist.com/news/leaders/21600685-nigerias-suddenly-supersized-economy-indeed-wonder-so-are-its-still-huge. Accessed 13 Nov 2015
Steyn J (1997) Contract law: fulfilling the reasonable expectations of honest men. LQR 113: 433–442
Study Group on Social Justice in European Private Law (2004) Social justice in European Contract law: a manifesto. Eur Law J 10:653–674
Summers R (2000) The conceptualisation of good faith in American contract law: a general account. In: Zimmermann R, Whittaker S (eds) Good faith in European Contract law. CUP, Cambridge, pp 118–141
Van der Walt J (2001) Progressive indirect horizontal application of the Bill of Rights: towards a co-operative relation between common law and constitutional jurisprudence. SAJHR 17: 341–363
Van Niekerk G (1998) A common law for Southern Africa: Roman law or indigenous African law. CILSA 31:158–173
Van Zyl Smit J (2011) Statute law: interpretation and declarations of incompatibility. In: Hoffman D (ed) The impact of the UK Human Rights Act on private law. CUP, Cambridge, pp 66–90
Verhoef G (2001) Informal financial service institutions for survival: African women and *stokvels* in Urban South Africa, 1930–1998. Enterp Soc 2:259–296
Wallis M (2016) Commercial certainty and constitutionalism: are they compatible? SALJ 133: 545-568.
Whittaker S, Zimmermann R (2000) Good faith in European Contract law: surveying the legal landscape. In: Zimmermann R, Whittaker S (eds) Good faith in European Contract law. CUP, Cambridge, pp 7–62
Woolman S (2005) Application. In: Woolman S, Roux T, Bishop M (eds) Constitutional law of South Africa, 2nd edn. Juta, Cape Town, pp 31-1–31-161
Woolman S (2007) The amazing, vanishing Bill of Rights. SALJ 124:762–794
Yarbrough M (2014) Very long engagements: legal consciousness and the persistent authority of bridewealth in a South African community. New York Law School Review. Available at: http://www.nylslawreview.com/wp-content/uploads/sites/16/2014/10/Yarbrough.pdf. Accessed 5 Nov 2015
Zimmermann R (1990) The law of obligations: Roman foundations of the civilian tradition. Juta, Cape Town
Zimmermann R (1996) Good faith and equity. In: Zimmermann R, Visser D (eds) Southern cross: civil and common law in South Africa. Juta, Cape Town, pp 217–260
Zimmermann R, Visser D (1996) Introduction: South African law as a mixed legal system. In: Zimmermann R, Visser D (eds) Southern cross: civil and common law in South Africa. Juta, Cape Town, pp 1–30

Curbing the Abuse of a Dominant Position Through Unfair Contract Terms Legislation: Australian and UK Comparison

Philip H. Clarke

Abstract The doctrines of freedom and sanctity of contracts have combined in Anglo-Australian law to enable dominant contracting parties to abuse their position by foisting unfair contract terms upon those with whom they deal. However, since the heyday of these doctrines in the late nineteenth century, the courts have gradually abridged this power using a variety of equitable and common law doctrines and principles. More recently, unencumbered by constitutional restrictions, parliaments in Australia and the UK have passed legislation specifically aimed at preventing such abuse by rendering ineffective unfair contract terms. This chapter examines this legislation and its justifications and following a comparative analysis makes some suggestions for reform.

P.H. Clarke (✉)
Deakin University, Geelong, VIC, Australia
e-mail: philip.h.clarke@gmail.com

L. Siliquini-Cinelli, A. Hutchison (eds.), *The Constitutional Dimension of Contract Law*, DOI 10.1007/978-3-319-49843-0_7

1 Introduction

This essay looks at the legislative attempts in Australia[1] and the United Kingdom[2] to curb the ability of dominant[3] parties to abuse their position by foisting unfair terms on those with whom they contract.[4] In neither country is there a constitutional restriction on the power of the legislature to do this, akin, for example, to that imposed on the States by the 10th Amendment of the United States Constitution. As a result, although the doctrines of freedom and sanctity of contract have exerted a restraining influence in this respect, in both countries Parliament has been able to intrude into contractual relationships in the pursuit of securing just and fair outcomes.

In Australia and the UK, unfair contract terms legislation is a relatively recent innovation. It draws inspiration from the European Council's 1993 directive

[1]In Australia, this legislation is contained in the Australian Consumer Law ('ACL') appearing as Part 2–3, 'Unfair Contract Terms'. The ACL is set out in Schedule 2 of the Competition and Consumer Act 2010 ('CCA'). The ACL applies to goods and services (the meanings of which are discussed below) other than financial services. In relation to financial services, unfair contract terms are governed by Subdivision BA of Division 2, Part 2 the Australian Securities and Investments Commission Act 2001 ('ASIC Act') which for all intent and purposes the same as Part 2–3 of the ACL. For this reason, primary reference will be made to the ACL provisions. In one Australian jurisdiction (Victoria) unfair terms were first regulated by amendments to the Fair Trading Act 1999 ('FTA'), introduced in 2003. However, these were repealed following the introduction of the ACL.

[2]In the United Kingdom, the legislation that is the primary concern of this essay is contained in Part 2 of the Consumer Rights Act 2015 ('CRA') headed 'Unfair Terms', which came into operation on 1 October 2015. However, reference will also be made to the Unfair Contract Terms Act 1977 ('UCTA'). Despite the breadth of its title, this Act is restricted to controlling the use of exclusion clauses, rather than addressing unfair terms generally.

[3]For present purposes, a party is regarded as occupying a dominant position *vis-à-vis* those with whom it deals if it is able to contract on its own terms. Dominance may derive from its ability to pressure or influence the other party, or from the lack of alternatives open to the latter, or from the latter's urgent need, or their inclination to contract without reading or understanding the terms on which they are doing so, or their lack of ability or opportunity to do otherwise. As understood, the focus of dominance is the relationship between contracting parties and thus differs from market power which focusses on the power of a contracting party to act independently of its competitors. It is important because there is evidence that unfair contract terms can be as prevalent in competitive markets as they can be in those that are not: see, for example, The Law Commission and the Scottish Law Commission (2002) Unfair terms in contracts: a joint consultation paper, para 2.7 ('The Law Commissions' joint consultation paper (2002)'); Productivity Commission (2008) Review of Australia's consumer policy framework. Inquiry report, Volume 2, p. 422 ('Productivity Commission report').

[4]A dominant party may abuse its position in other ways; for example, by not fulfilling its fiduciary duties, or exerting undue influence over the other party, to secure a transaction that is not substantively unfair. The focus of this essay, however, is on the use of such a position to secure a contract on terms that are unfair to the other party.

on unfair terms[5] and constitutes a further whittling away of the doctrines of freedom and sanctity of contracts. However, there are notable differences in the scope and the content of this legislation and, as a result, in the extent to which reliance is still placed upon market forces to prevent unfair outcomes. After surveying the rules that enable dominant parties to abuse their position and the existing devices employed by the law to curb such abuse, the essay will consider the policy reasons for addressing unfair contracts. It will then compare and evaluate Australian and UK unfair contract terms legislation with a view to determining how successful it might be and whether its ability to curb abuses of a dominant position could be enhanced.

2 Abuse of a Dominant Position and Existing Curbs

The doctrine of freedom of contract provides the foundation in Anglo-Australian law for dominant parties to abuse their position. This stipulates that contractual obligations can be assumed only voluntarily, that individuals are free to choose with whom they contract and, most importantly, that, with certain narrow public policy exceptions,[6] the parties negotiating a contract are free to agree on whatever terms they choose. Once they have done so, the closely allied doctrine of the sanctity of contract prescribes that their contract should, on moral and economic grounds, be enforced according to its terms. When the parties are evenly matched and their negotiations robust, comprehensive and honest, freedom of contract reinforces the operation of free markets and accords with the personal freedoms that underpin western democracies. In Australia and the United Kingdom, it also receives practical support from the established common law rule, often referred to as the rule in *L'Estrange v Graucob*,[7] that in the absence of misrepresentation, or the availability of a plea of *non est factum*, a person who signs a document, including a contractual document, is bound by its terms regardless of whether they had been read or understood.[8] Were the law otherwise, the courts reason, it would 'make chaos of every-day business transactions' and preclude third parties from assuming the 'legal efficacy of the instrument' thereby causing 'serious mischief'.[9]

Anglo-Australian law also adopts a similarly *laissez faire* attitude to the existence of power: it is lawful to occupy a dominant position (most relevantly for

[5]Council Directive 93/13/EEC of 5 April 1993 on unfair terms in consumer contracts ('ECD 93').

[6]Early examples were the refusal to enforce freely negotiated contracts in restraint of trade and contracts to commit a crime.

[7]*L'Estrange v Graucob Ltd,* [1934] 2 KB 294 (Court of Appeal (UK)).

[8]See, for example, *Parker v South Eastern Railway Co,* [1877] 2 CPD 416 (Court of Appeal (UK)), especially at p. 421; *L'Estrange v Graucob Ltd,* [1934] 2 KB 294 (Court of Appeal (UK)); *Wilton v Farnworth,* [1948] 76 CLR 646 (High Court of Australia) especially at p. 649; and *Toll (FGCT) Pty Ltd v Alphapharm Pty Ltd,* [2004] 219 CLR 165 (High Court of Australia).

[9]See *Wilton v Farnworth,* (1948) 76 CLR 646 (High Court of Australia), p. 649; and *Toll (FGCT) Pty Ltd v Alphapharm Pty Ltd,* [2004] 219 CLR 165 (High Court of Australia), para 47.

present purposes, a dominant market position) and to seek to acquire such a position as long as no anti-competitive means are used to do so. Further, what is anti-competitive in this regard is being increasingly narrowly defined.[10] Combined with freedom and sanctity of contract, this has meant that dominant contracting parties have been able, with relative impunity, to insist upon terms that are harsh and oppressive by making it clear to those with whom they contract that they must either 'take it or leave it'. And such conduct has not been isolated. The use of contracts to deliver goods and services is now so ubiquitous and inequality of bargaining power so prevalent that most consumers and many businesses have no realistic option other than to meet their needs by contracting and to accept whatever terms are dictated to them. Furthermore, without needing to be overtly dictatorial, dominant parties are often able to contract on their own unfair terms because they can be confident that when those terms are recorded in a signed document, the rule in *L'Estrage v Graucob* will bind the other party to them, regardless of whether they have been read or understood.

However, since its zenith towards the end of the nineteenth century,[11] the extent to which freedom of contract has been able to facilitate abusive conduct has been curtailed by judicial decision[12] and legislation.[13] In some cases, this has occurred as a result of the law recognising collateral interests and values such as the desire to prohibit discrimination or to ensure that potential liability is covered by insurance.[14] Most instances, however, are attributable to recognition that the doctrine's key premises—that contracts are freely entered into, are freely negotiated and as a result produce fair outcomes—are rarely present in practice.

Judicial curbs on the abuse of a dominant position contract have occurred primarily through the application of general common law and equitable principles and have focused on ensuring procedural fairness in the negotiation process. Thus, vitiating factors such as duress, undue influence, misrepresentation and unconscionable conduct are now readily invoked to make contracts voidable where the dominant party has used illegitimate pressure to secure the other party's agreement, or has failed to perform their fiduciary obligations when dealing with them, or has taken advantage of their special disadvantage, or has misled them in some way. Such conduct will enable the latter to impugn the contract regardless of whether it is

---

[10]See The Harper Panel (2015) Competition policy review: Final report, especially to s 46.

[11]For example, in *Printing and Numerical Registering Co v Sampson,* [1875] LR 19 Eq 462 (Court of Appeal (UK)), p. 465 Jessel MR argued that the most important public policy consideration was that 'men of full age and competent understanding shall have the utmost liberty of contracting, and that their contracts when entered into freely and voluntarily shall be held sacred and shall be enforced by courts of justice'.

[12]The seminal work tracking this is Atiyah (1979).

[13]For example, legislation prohibiting racial and other forms of discrimination when contracting; legislation preventing contracts excluding or restricting the operation of statutory terms; and legislation making it compulsory to take out certain forms of insurance.

[14]For example, compulsory third party car insurance and workers compensation schemes.

substantively unfair, although being of this nature may be evidence that there has been procedural irregularity in the transaction.

Attempts to curb the abuse of a dominant position by addressing substantive unfairness have, until recently, been more circumspect, focusing primarily on preventing the use of penalty clauses and unfair reliance on exclusion clauses.[15] To this end, the courts have consistently declared penalty clauses to be void[16] and have created numerous obstacles to the use of exclusion clauses. Legislation has also prevented exclusion clauses being used to exclude or restrict consumers' reliance on the implied term regimes created by sales of goods or credit legislation[17] or a person's liability for death or personal injury resulting from negligence.[18] On the other hand, in the case of non-consumer transactions and liability for negligence causing other forms of loss or damage, legislation has regulated, rather than precluded, the use of exclusion clauses.[19] However, the courts have eschewed direct assaults on the efficacy of such clauses[20] and have made it clear that (outside the areas now governed by legislation) a carefully drafted clause that unambiguously forms part of a contract can provide protection from the even most egregious breaches of contract or other civil duty.[21] As a result, dominant parties, careful to avoid procedural unfairness, have retained considerable opportunity to abuse their dominant positions by dictating terms that are unfair to the weaker parties with whom they contract. And there is evidence that dominant parties have

[15]An Australian exception to this is the prohibition, since 2011, of unconscionable conduct in s 21 of the ACL. The matters to which a court may have regard when determining whether this section has been contravened (set out in s 22) make clear that as well as procedural matters, the content of the terms and conditions of the contract can be considered. Equivalent provisions dealing with financial services appear in the equivalent sections of the ASIC Act.

[16]The common law in the UK and Australia makes void contractual provisions that penalise one party, rather compensate the other, should certain events occur, or not occur: see *Dunlop Pneumatic Tyre Co Ltd v New Garage and Motor Co Ltd,* [1915] AC 79 (House of Lords) and *Andrews v Australia and New Zealand Banking Group Ltd,* [1912] HCA 30 (High Court of Australia).

[17]For the UK see ss 6(1) and (2) UCTA; the latter has since been repealed and replaced by s 31 of the CRA. For Australia see s68 Trade Practices Act 1974 ('TPA'); this has been replaced by s 64 of the ACL.

[18]See s 2(1) UCTA.

[19]Section 2(2) UCTA requires an exclusion clause to satisfy 'the requirement of reasonableness' to be effective. The Australian TPA, ss 68A and 68B allowed exclusion clauses to limit liability in certain ways in cases, respectively, of the supply of non-consumer goods or services or recreational services. These provisions have been replaced by s 64A of the ACL and s139A of the CCA, respectively.

[20]See, for example, *Suisse Atlantique Societe d'Armement Maritime SA v NV Rotterdamsche Kolen Centrale,* [1967] 1 AC 361 (House of Lords) and *Photo Production Ltd v Securicor Ltd,* [1980] AC 827 (House of Lords).

[21]See for example, *South Australian Railways Commissioner v Egan,* (1973) 130 CLR 506 (High Court of Australia) in which Menzies J described the exclusion clause under consideration as one in which 'not one oppressive provision which could be found has been omitted'; however, it was still found to protect the Commissioner. See also, *Photo Production Ltd v Securicor Ltd,* [1980] AC 827 (House of Lords).

done so. To this extent, the doctrine of freedom of contract has remained alive and well. However, unfair contract terms legislation in the UK and Australia now seeks to address this situation directly.[22]

3 The Rational for Unfair Contracts Term Legislation

The principal rationale advanced for introducing unfair contract terms legislation is that it curbs unethical behaviour and promotes fair contractual dealings. Unfair contract terms are seen as morally objectionable; they offend the community's sense of what is just, right and proper and for this reason should be rendered void. To this extent, the legislation reflects similar values to those that have traditionally underpinned judicial responses to duress, undue influence and unconscionable conduct. This sentiment is reinforced by the fact that the net effect of unfair terms is to transfer wealth, in one form or another, from the weaker to the dominant contracting party. Indeed, this is the most common explanation for dominant parties wishing to use them.[23] While the overall extent of this transfer is impossible to quantify with precision, a 1999 estimate of the savings to consumers attributable to the work of the UK Office of Fair Trading in removing unfair terms was that, in the case of one mortgage company, it saved consumers £65.2 million a year and in the case of eight mobile phone companies, it saved them between £60 and £80 million a year.[24]

Two further observations can be made about the moral condemnation of unfair terms. First, in the UK and now in Australia, it has not reached the level required to make it an offence to use or enforce them. Although there are precedents for doing this,[25] these have not been followed in the legislation under consideration. Second, a significant element of the moral objection to unfair terms is that, typically, weaker parties have no practical opportunity to read or understand or negotiate about them and thereby to take them into account when deciding whether or not to enter into a contract at all, or with whom to do so. Consequently, the legislation has been

[22]Australia also addressed this situation by enacting more robust prohibitions of unconscionable conduct. These cover substantive as well as procedural unconscionability: see Part 2-2 of the ACL.

[23]Another possible explanation, noted in the Productivity Commission report, p. 152, is that they are used to deter 'problematic behaviour by small groups of consumers' thereby benefiting consumers as a whole. However, it is not clear why this objective cannot be achieved by using fair terms, specifically targeted at such behaviour.

[24]National Audit Office (1999) ('The National Audit Office's report').

[25]In Australia's first foray into unfair contract terms legislation, Part 2B of the Victorian FTA, using, or attempting to enforce, a 'prescribed unfair term' in a standard form consumer contract *was* made an offence by s 32Z. This provision was repealed in 2010 when the Act was brought into line with the ACL. The original bill introducing the ACL included provisions that would have made it an offence to include a prohibited term in a standard form consumer contract. However, this was removed following recommendations of the Senate Standing Committee on Economics.

framed so as not to apply where this objection is thought to be inapplicable. Thus, exemptions exist in relation to terms dealing with the upfront price and the main subject matter of the contract, and the legislation applies only to consumer contracts or, in the case of Australia, to consumer and small business contracts.

There are also economic justifications for unfair term legislation. First, as the Australian Productivity Committee has noted, 'unfair acts can undermine trust and social capital generally, increasing the cost of all kinds of transactions between people'.[26] This is particularly relevant to e-commerce where confidence that 'at a distance' transactions will produce mutual benefits is a significant factor in consumers' willingness to use this means of meeting their needs. Second, unfair terms will often allocate the risks associated with a transaction away from the party best able to efficiently address those risks. One example is the use of exclusion clauses to protect a manufacturer from liability should its products prove to be defective in some way; such clauses shift the risk (and consequences) of this occurring from the party best able to take preventive measures (the manufacturer) to the purchaser who cannot do so.[27] This situation is made worse where the latter is unaware that their contract has this effect and fails to insure against the risks it entails. Such 'low cost harsh terms' contracts make the market 'inefficient in that many customers would have preferred better terms even if this would have meant then having to pay somewhat higher prices'.[28] Third, unfair terms may produce market failure where suppliers who efficiently address business risk cannot, as a result of incurring the cost of doing so, compete on price with those who contractually, and quite possibly without their knowledge or understanding, transfer those risks to their customers. Market failure will occur when the efficient firms are forced to vacate the market to those that are less efficient. This is especially likely in those markets characterised by little or no repeat business.[29]

Although there are strong in principle arguments in favour of unfair contract terms legislation, it has been recognised that there are countervailing considerations that should be taken into account when it is being framed. As well as a residual sympathy for the value of freedom of contract, these include the initial and ongoing

---

[26]Productivity Commission report, p. 415. See also, House of Representatives, Treasury Legislation Amendment (Small Business and Unfair Contract Terms) Bill 2015, Explanatory Memorandum, ('Explanatory Memorandum') which argued at para 3.154 that 'reducing the incidence of unfair contract terms is expected to provide a significant benefit to the Australian economy'.

[27]Whilst there are now limits on this occurring in relation to consumers and in respect of personal injury it is still possible in other cases; see for example, *Maxitherm Boilers Pty Ltd v Pacific Dunlop Ltd* [1998] 4 VR 559 (Court of Appeal (Victoria)).

[28]The Law Commissions' Joint consultation paper (2002). An example of this situation is the practice, common amongst car rental firms, of making consumers bear the risk of loss or damage to the vehicle hired, regardless of whether this was attributable to their fault, thereby shifting the insurance burden to the consumer. This practice was recently found to be unfair under Australia's unfair contracts term legislation: see *ACCC v CLA Trading Ltd* [2016] FCA 377 (Federal Court of Australia).

[29]See Productivity Commission report, pp. 419–420.

costs that dominant parties will incur to ensure compliance[30] and the distinct possibility that the benefits to the weaker party of not being afflicted by unfair terms will be moderated by them having to pay higher prices and experience reduced supply.

4 The Scope of Unfair Terms Legislation in Australian and the UK

4.1 Who Is Bound and Who Can Invoke?

Table 1 shows who is bound by the unfair contract terms legislation in Australia and the UK and who can invoke its provisions. For completeness, it also includes reference to the European Council Directive.

Two issues arise concerning who is bound by these provisions, namely, are they restricted to businesses and are they restricted to suppliers? In relation to the first issue, ECD 93 and the CRA are expressly restricted to businesses. This follows from the definition of 'seller or supplier' in ECD 93[31] and 'trader' in the CRA.[32]

Table 1 Persons covered

	ECD 93	CRA 2015	ACL/ASIC	UCTA 1977
Who is bound	Sellers or suppliers acting in their trade, business or profession	Traders—persons acting in trade, business, craft or profession	Anyone supplying a consumer or contracting with small business under a standard form contract	Anyone contracting on their standard terms or who is covered by the acts governing the sale of goods or hire purchase
Who can invoke	Consumers—natural persons not acting in a trade, business or profession	Consumers—individuals acting for purposes wholly or mainly outside their trade, business, craft or profession	Individuals who acquire wholly or predominantly for personal domestic or household use or consumption and small businesses	Anyone who has contracted on the other party's standard terms or who can invoke the implied term provisions in the acts governing the sale of goods or hire purchase

[30]In Australia it was estimated that the net annual compliance cost of extending its unfair contract terms regime to include small businesses would be approximately '$50 million in the first year, with no ongoing compliance costs': see Explanatory Memorandum para 3.172.

[31]See Article 2(c) ECD 93.

[32]See ss 2(2) and 76(2) CRA.

On the other hand, the ACL and UCTA are not restricted in this manner. However, the requirement in the ACL[33] and s 3(1) of the UCTA that supply be pursuant to a standard form contract is likely to have the same effect in practice. While a private individual *could* use a standard form contract to supply a consumer (when selling a house, for example), this is not likely to be a common occurrence. Section 6 of the UCTA is potentially wider in scope in so far as it applies to anyone who supplies pursuant to a contract for the sale or hire of goods; again, however, this is unlikely to be significant in practice.

In relation to the second issue, ECD 93 and the CRA only bind suppliers, that is, sellers, suppliers or traders that contract to supply a consumer.[34] They do not bind persons *acquiring* goods or services, with the result that monopsonists that insist upon unfair terms when doing so are not covered. On the other hand, the ACL is capable of binding those that acquire, as well as those that supply. In the case of consumer contracts, this is of little practical significance as very few unfair acquisition contracts are likely to come within the definition of 'a consumer contract' in s 23(3). However, in the case of small business contracts, it is very significant. Indeed, one of the principal objectives of the ACL's recent[35] extension to small business contracts is to curb the ability of dominant businesses to force small business suppliers into accepting low prices and harsh terms in the former's standard acquisition contracts.[36] With that in mind, the definition of a 'a small business contract' in s 23(4) of the ACL was drafted so as to cover contracts of acquisition, as well as contracts of supply, and so can bind those who acquire, as well as those who supply. Similarly, the UCTA is capable of applying to exclusion clauses used by those acquiring goods or services, as well as by those who supply them.[37]

As will be immediately apparent from Table 1, another important difference between the various provisions is in relation to who can invoke the protection they afford. Thus, whereas ECD 93 and the CRA provisions protect only consumers, the UCTA can be invoked by consumers and businesses, regardless of their size, and the ACL can be invoked by consumers and by businesses—but only if they have fewer than 20 employees.[38] This reflects one of the more contentious debates in this area, namely, whether the legislation should protect businesses, as well as consumers.

[33]See s 23(1)(b) ACL.

[34]This is because both include within their definition of 'unfair' a requirement that the term be detrimental to 'the consumer': see Article 3(1) ECD 93 and s 62(4) CRA. In the case of the CRA this is reinforced by the requirements that the contract be between a 'trader' and a 'consumer' and only the consumer can choose not to be bound by the unfair term: see ss 61(1) and 62(1) CRA.

[35]These came into effect on 13 November 2016.

[36]For examples of this, see the contracts under consideration in *ACCC v Coles Supermarkets Australia Pty Ltd* [2014] FCA 1405 (Federal Court of Australia).

[37]See ss 3(1), 6(1)(1A), 7(1)(4A), 8 and 10 UCTA.

[38]See s 24(4)(b) ACL.

In their 2002 joint consultation paper, *Unfair Terms in Contracts*,[39] the Law Commission and the Scottish Law Commission provisionally recommended that revised unfair contract terms legislation should extend to all businesses.[40] In doing so, they noted that the courts would take into account the size of the business and whether the contract in question was unusual for the business. The case for such an extension was that 'in the business-to-business context standard form contracts cause problems which are similar to, if not so severe, as those affecting consumer contracts'.[41] In particular, businesses often face the same practical difficulties as consumers do in being able to ascertain, evaluate and understand the terms presented to them and often have just as little bargaining power vis-à-vis the businesses with whom they contract. Indeed, the ability of a dominant contracting party to adopt a 'take it or leave it' position can make some businesses *more* vulnerable to unfair contract terms than consumers. This is because, with very few exceptions, consumers will usually have the option of purchasing a substitute product, purchasing elsewhere or not purchasing at all, whereas a business facing a supplier or customer with substantial market power may have no commercially viable alternative than to deal with them and accept their terms.[42]

In reaching this conclusion, the Commissions rejected the option of restricting the extension to small businesses on the ground that this would 'create even more complexity' and 'would cause difficulties for business'.[43] However, their consultees disagreed. While most opposed the proposed extension to *all* businesses, many agreed that small businesses needed greater protection. As a result, in their report, the Commissions recommended that small businesses (defined as those with nine or fewer employees) should receive the same protection as consumers but only in relation to standard, as distinct from negotiated, terms.[44] Despite the support it received, this recommendation was not accepted, with the result that the position in the UK is that

- the revised unfair contract terms legislation—Part 2 of the CRA—applies only to consumer contracts, and only consumers are not bound by an unfair term in such a contract[45];

---

[39]The Commissions' terms of reference were to consider whether the UCTA and The Unfair Terms in Consumer Contracts Regulations 1999 ('the UK Regulations 1999') should be replaced with new legislation, whether the Regulations (or their replacement) should extend to businesses and whether more accessible language could be used.

[40]The Law Commissions' joint consultation paper (2002), para 5.25.

[41]Ibid., para 5.17.

[42]*South Australian Railways Commissioner v Egan,* [1973] 130 CLR 506 (High Court of Australia) provides an example. Here the contract was described as one from which 'not one oppressive provision which could be found was omitted. [It was] so outrageous that it is surprising that any contractor would undertake work for the railways Commissioner upon its terms'. But, of course Mr Egan did!.

[43]The Law Commissions' joint consultation paper (2002), para 5.36.

[44]Ibid., paras 5.30 and 5.40.

[45]See s 62(1)(2) CRA.

- the UCTA has been retained to deal with exclusion clauses in terms that protect businesses. However, to avoid overlap, it has been amended so that its key provisions do not apply to consumer contracts; these are governed by the CRA.[46]

In Australia, unfair contract terms provisions were included as Part 2-3 of the ACL when it was introduced in 2010. However, although the 2009 exposure draft legislation was capable of applying those provisions to business contracts, the final legislation restricted them to 'consumer contracts'.[47] Nevertheless, subsequently, for the kinds of reasons advanced by the Law Commissions in their report, pressure developed to extend them to small businesses.[48] In 2015, this resulted in the ACL being amended to include small business contracts.[49] As a result, the position in Australia is that the unfair contract terms provisions of the ACL apply to the following:

- Consumer contracts—these are defined as contracts made by 'an individual' who acquires goods, services or an interest in land 'wholly or predominantly for personal, domestic or household use or consumption'.[50] This makes the *purpose* for which the individual acquires the goods, services or interest in law the critical factor rather than the inherent nature of what is being acquired.
- Small business contracts—these are defined by reference to the size of the business (it must employ 'fewer than 20 persons') and the size of the contract (the upfront price must not exceed $300,000, or $1,000,000 if the contract has a duration of more than 12 months).

Although, at the time of writing, the extension of the ACL's unfair contract terms provisions to small businesses was yet to come into effect, a number of observations can be made about it and difficulties anticipated.[51] First, it will often be difficult for a business to know whether the contract it is making falls within the

[46]See ss 3(1), 6(1)(1A), 7(1)(4A), 8 and 10 UCTA.

[47]Although the intent appear to have been to restrict use of the provisions to consumers, they do not actually do so. This is because, although the definition of consumer contract in s 23(3) requires the supply or sale to be to an individual, the provisions do not restrict reliance upon them to that individual. Consequently, an unfair term in a standard form contract developed and forced upon a business by an individual is vulnerable to a complaint by the business. This is also the case with the small business amendments discussed below with the result that protection would be available to a large firm that had been made subject to an unfair contract term by a small business with market power. This could arise where the small business was, for example, the sole manufacturer of a component essential to the large firm's operations, thus making the latter vulnerable should it need the component urgently. Although, in practice, occurrences of this kind of situation are likely to be rare, it does illustrate the kind of unfortunate distinctions the legislation creates.

[48]See the discussion in the Explanatory Memorandum at paras 3.34–3.67.

[49]Treasury Legislation Amendment (Small Business and Unfair Contract Terms) Act 2015. These amendments came into effect on 13 November 2016.

[50]See s23(3) ACL.

[51]The following observations derive from advice the author provided to the Institute of Public Accountants in 2015.

definition of a 'small business contract'. This is most likely to be because it will not know whether the other party 'employs fewer than 20 persons' and because, in any case, 'employee numbers is not the straight forward concept it might at first appear'.[52] Some attempt is made to address this in s 23(5) of the ACL. However, the terms used are vague and involve information about the other party's employees to which the business will not have ready access, and even if it does, at the margins at least, they will often be contestable. Second, the monetary limit of the definition will exclude small businesses that make only a few large contracts each year, rather than numerous smaller ones, for example, an agricultural producer selling an annual crop. In this connection, it is suggested that a small business that makes only a few contracts each year with a customer occupying a dominant position in the relevant market is likely to be in a far more vulnerable position than most consumers.[53] Third, the monetary limit will make it possible for a dominant party to avoid the provisions where it is possible to aggregate the contracts it makes so that they exceed that limit. Given the ability of a dominant firm to pressure the small business into accepting its terms in the first place, it is not unrealistic to anticipate that they could also pressure them into aggregating its supply or acquisition contracts. Fourth, the monetary limit will create undesirable distinctions within the provisions between consumer and business contracts. For example, the definition of 'consumer contract' in s 23(3) means that they will cover the acquisition by an individual of a multi-million-dollar home acquired for personal use. On the other hand, the monetary limit would prevent them from applying to a small businesses' acquisition of business premises for, say, $301,000. Similarly, a consumer's purchase of a $350,000 car for personal use would be covered, but a businesses' purchase of a $350,000 commercial vehicle would not.

4.2 *What Subject Matters and Types of Contract Are Covered?*

Prima facie, the subject matter coverage of the various unfair contract terms provisions is substantially the same in Australia and the UK. However, as the following summary indicates, there are differences in the contracts they exclude from that coverage:

- ECD 93 is expressed in terms that appear to make it applicable only to terms relating to the sale or supply of goods or services. This follows from the reference to goods and services in Article 3 and the preamble to the Directive.

[52]The Law Commission and the Scottish Law Commission (2005) Unfair terms in Contracts: Report on a reference under s3(1)(e) of the Law Commissions Act 1965 ('The Law Commissions' 2005 report'), para 5.47.

[53]See, for possible examples, the contracts under consideration in *ACCC v Coles Supermarkets Australia Pty Ltd*, [2014] FCA 1405 (Federal Court of Australia).

However, it has been assumed that it also applies to contracts relating to land, and this is the interpretation given to the *Unfair Terms in Consumer Contracts Regulations 1999*, implementing it in the UK.[54]

- The CRA, with a number of specific exceptions or qualifications, applies to all consumer contracts regardless of the subject matter. However, contracts of employment and apprenticeship are excluded by s 61(2), and the bar on the exclusion or restriction of liability for negligence created by s 65 does not apply to contracts of insurance, contracts relating to the creation or transfer of an interest in land[55] or settlement contracts.[56]
- The ACL applies to contracts for the supply of 'goods or services' or the 'sale or grant of an interest in land'.[57] This apparently universal coverage is qualified, however, by the exclusion by s 28 of contracts of marine salvage or towage, charter parties, contracts for the carriage of goods by ship, contracts that are the constitution of a company or other body and (in relation to small businesses contracts) contracts to which a prescribed Australian law applies. In addition, it does not apply to 'financial services' or a 'financial product' that, instead, are covered by equivalent provisions in the ASIC Act.[58] This excision of financial services and products from the ACL is unfortunate as it can be the source of uncertainty and confusion about which act applies without producing any obvious benefits.[59]
- The UCTA provisions governing the use of contract terms to exclude or restrict liability for negligence (s 2), or breach of contract (s 3), are also drafted in apparently universal terms. However, they are then limited by the exclusion of a miscellaneous group of subjects listed in Schedule 1.[60] On the other hand, s 8, dealing with misrepresentation, is of universal application, whereas Sects. 6 and 7 apply only to contracts relating to the supply of goods.

---

[54]The Law Commissions' joint consultation paper (2002), para 3.44. The UK Regulations 1999 were replaced by the CRA on 1 October 2015. However, any contracts entered into before that date are still be governed by them.

[55]See s 66(1)(a)(b) CRA.

[56]Ibid., s 66(2).

[57]See s 23(3)(4) ACL.

[58]See s 131A(1) CCA.

[59]For a recent example, see *ACCC v CLA Trading Pty Ltd* [2016] FCA 377 (Federal Court of Australia), paras 12–35.

[60]See s1(2) UCTA and Schedule 1(1)–(4). These are: insurance; interests in land; intellectual property; the formation, dissolution or constitution of a company or the rights and obligations of its members; and securities. Also, ss 2(2), 2(3), 3 and 7 do not apply to contracts of marine salvage or towage, charter parties and contracts for the carriage of goods by sea. On the other hand, s 2 (1) does apply to such contracts. Sections 2(1) and (2) do not apply to employment contracts except in favour of the employee.

Table 2 Terms covered

	ECD 93	CRA 2015	ACL/ASIC	UCTA 1977
Negotiated or standard terms	Terms must not be 'individually negotiated'.[a]	It applies to terms whether or not they were negotiated.[b]	It applies only to terms in a 'standard form contract'.[c]	Sections 2, 5, 7 and 8 apply to terms whether or not they were negotiated.[d] Section 3 applies only to 'written standard terms of business'.[e]
Burden of Proof	If in issue, the supplier bears the burden of showing that the term was individually negotiated.[f]	Not applicable	If it is alleged that a contract is a standard form contract, this is presumed unless the other party proves otherwise.[g]	Not applicable
Notices	Not covered	Notices covered similarly to terms	Not covered	Notices excluding or restricting liability for negligence covered[h]
Terms excluded or saved	Terms reflecting mandatory legislative provisions or the provisions or principles of international conventions to which the State or the EU is a party[i]	Terms reflecting mandatory legislative provisions or the provisions or principles of international conventions to which the UK or the EU is a party[j]	Terms defining the main subject matter, the upfront price, or that are required or expressly permitted by law are excluded.[k]	The following terms are saved:[l] terms a statute authorises or requires expressly or by necessary implication, terms made to comply with an international agreement to which the UK is a party.

[a]See Article 3(1) ECD 93. A term is not 'individually negotiated' if it was drafted in advance and the consumer was not able to influence its substance. The fact that some part of a term, or the contract were negotiated, does not prevent the overall assessment being that it was not negotiated: see Article 3(2)
[b]See the absence of such a requirement in ss 61 and 62 CRA
[c]See s 23(1)(b) ACL. When deciding if a contract is a standard form contract it may take into account any matters it considers relevant; but it must take into account those listed in s. 27(2). These focus on the relative bargaining power of the parties, whether the contract was pre-prepared and nature and the degree of negotiation
[d]These sections deal terms excluding or restricting liability for negligence, breach of the statutory or other obligations applying to the supply of goods and misrepresentation
[e]This section deals with standard terms that seek to exclude or restrict the author's liability for breach of contract, or to allow them to render substantially different performance or no performance at all
[f]See Article 3(3) ECD 93
[g]See s 27(1) ACL
[h]See s 2 UCTA
[i]See Article 1(2) ECD 93
[j]See s 73(1) CRA
[k]See s 26(1) ACL. The exclusion of terms relating to the main subject matter and price is considered below and compared with the approach taken in the UK
[l]'Saved' in this context means that the term is not removed, its effect is not restricted and reliance upon it is not prevented: see Section 29(1) UCTA

4.3 What Terms Are Covered?

Table 2 shows the terms covered by the various acts; in particular, whether they are restricted to those that are contained within a contract, or to those that are not negotiated between the parties. It also indicates who bears the burden of proof on the latter issue and what terms are excluded from the scope of the provisions.

It is clear from Table 2 that in relation to the terms covered, there are significant differences between the current position in the UK and that in Australia. The most notable is that the principal UK act, the CRA, applies to negotiated and non-negotiated terms, whereas the Australian ACL applies only to standard form contracts. In both cases, this represents a move away from a previous position. In the UK, the precursor to the CRA[61] followed ECD 93 in restricting coverage to non-negotiated terms. However, after identifying problems with this restriction, the Law Commissions recommended that new unfair contract terms legislation apply as well to negotiated terms[62]; this was implemented in the CRA. The arguments for taking this approach were that it would reduce uncertainty about whether a term was covered; would protect consumers who, despite pre-contractual negotiation, were still effectively forced to accept the dominant party's unfair terms; and would prevent negotiation being used as a means of avoiding the legislation.[63] It was also noted that where genuine negotiation has occurred, it is unlikely that the term would be judged unfair and that, in any case, most negotiation would relate to price, or the main subject matter, and be exempt from coverage for that reason.[64] Australia, however, moved in the other direction. Thus, while Part 2B of the Victorian Fair Trading Act 1999 made any unfair term void,[65] following the recommendation of the Productivity Commission,[66] the ACL was restricted to 'standard form contracts'. In making this recommendation, the Commission argued that by their very nature, negotiated agreements would 'eliminate any terms seen as unfair' and that the parties to negotiated contracts 'are usually sufficiently sophisticated to ensure acceptable contract outcomes and can reasonably be expected to have their "eyes

[61]The UK Regulations 1999.

[62]The Law Commissions' 2005 report, para 3.55. The Law Commissions repeated this advice in 2013 in their report, The Law Commission and the Scottish Law Commission (2013) Unfair terms in consumer contracts: Advice to the Department for Business, Innovation and Skills. ('The Law Commissions' 2013 report'), para 7.66.

[63]In evidence to the Commissions, the Office of Fair Trading noted the UK Regulations 1999 could be avoided by 'businesses making a practice of regularly imposing unfair terms which had a bespoke or negotiated element'. Concern was expressed that 'regulators could be precluded from taking action against a term negotiated in this way on the grounds that it is an individually negotiated term': See Law Commissions' report at para 3.156.

[64]Ibid., paras 3.52 and 3.53.

[65]On the other hand, only using in relation to a consumer 'a standard form contract containing a prescribed unfair term' an offence: see s 32Z FTA.

[66]Productivity Commission report, p. 161.

wide open'".[67] Unfortunately, the Commission appears to have also been influenced by the fact that the UK provisions at the time also excluded negotiated terms and to have been unaware that the Law Commissions had recommended, based on experience with those provisions, that this exclusion should be removed. Its conclusion is also at odds with one of the principal objections to unfair terms, namely, that they are 'offered on a "take it or leave it" basis by a party with greater bargaining power',[68] as this power can be exercised in relation to negotiated terms just as well as it can with those that are not.

A feature of the ACL is that, unlike ECD 93 and the UK regulations implementing that Directive,[69] its 'negotiated terms exclusion' is achieved by limiting the unfair contract terms provisions to a 'standard form contract'.[70] This term is not defined as such; rather, the courts are left to determine whether a particular contract is of this nature by taking 'into account such matters as it thinks relevant'.[71] However, when doing so, s 27(2) requires the court to have regard to a list of five matters, with provision made for the regulations to add to this list in the future. These make it clear that the term 'standard form contract' is misleading in so far as a contract can be of this nature even though its terms are unique to the parties and have never been used before or since.[72] For example, it would almost certainly catch a contract containing entirely novel terms that a dominant party prepared in advance and required the other to accept on a 'take it or leave it' basis. However, although s 27(2) makes it clear that negotiation about the 'upfront price payable', or defining 'the main subject matter of the contract', will not prevent a contract from being a standard form contract, it is unclear what degree of negotiation about other matters will have this effect. For example, could a dominant party avoid scrutiny by initially proposing outrageously unfair terms that it anticipates will meet resistance from the other party and then moderate its demands slightly to a point at which it is able to force somewhat less unfair terms upon that party because of weakness of her position?[73] Because of the potential for situations such as this to arise, it can be anticipated that the ACL's 'standard form contract' requirement will be a source of unfortunate uncertainty and litigation, especially after the small business contract provisions come into operation. This could be avoided by amending the ACL so

[67]Ibid. The Commission also reasoned that 'egregious terms' in a negotiated contract could be addressed by the law relating to unconscionable conduct; in particular by what is now Part 2-2 of the CCA. Its conclusion was that 'the inclusion of negotiated contracts would involve risks that exceed the likely benefits'.

[68]See Explanatory Memorandum at para 3.21.

[69]See s 5(1) of the UK Regulations 1999.

[70]See s 23(1)(b) ACL.

[71]Ibid., s 27(2).

[72]This contrasts with the definition of 'standard form contract' in s 32U of the FTA (Victoria) which required the contract to be one 'drawn up for general use in a particular industry'.

[73]It is noted that in *St Albans City Council v International Computers,* [1996] EWCA Civ 1296 (Court of Appeal (UK)), the Court of Appeal held that the mere discussion of a term is not sufficient to make it a negotiated term.

that, like the CRA, it applies to contracts whether or not they are negotiated, leaving that matter to be relevant only in relation to the issue of whether the contract was unfair.

In relation to the standard form contract requirement, for the purpose of proceedings, s 27(1) of the ACL presumes that a contract is of that nature unless it is proved otherwise. In doing so, it follows the approach taken in Article 3(2) of ECD 93. The ACL and ECD 93 are also the same in dealing only with unfair terms when these are contained in a contract. On the other hand, the CRA also applies to unfair notices to the extent that they relate 'to rights or obligations as between a trader and a consumer' or purport 'to exclude or restrict a trader's liability to a consumer',[74] and the UCTA applies to notices that seek to exclude or restrict a person's liability for negligence.

As Table 2 indicates, ECD 93, the CRA and the UCTA have similar provisions preventing them from applying to terms that reflect mandatory domestic legislation, or binding international agreements. Likewise, the ACL contains an equivalent provision in respect of domestic legislation. However, the ACL also, in effect, entirely excises terms that define the main subject matter of the contract, or that sets the upfront price payable. While this is in line with the special treatment given to those terms by ECD 93 and the CRA, it also reflects the more extreme position taken in relation to them by the ACL, namely, to entirely exempt them from scrutiny, rather than merely to exclude them from a fairness assessment.[75]

5 The Test of Unfairness

Unsurprisingly, at the core of unfair contract terms legislation is the concept of 'unfair'. This involves a judgement being made in each case about the nature of the individual term in question, having regard to factors prescribed in the legislation. However, in the UK but not it would seem in Australia, the view has been taken that some terms are so inherently objectionable that they are rendered ineffective per se, that is, without an individual unfairness assessment being necessary. Table 3 summarises the definitions of unfairness used in Australia and the UK, the factors made relevant to assessing whether a term is unfair, the indicative examples of terms that are potentially unfair, the terms that are per se unfair and the burden of proof.

The approach to identifying unfair terms taken in the UK and Australia is essentially the same as that prescribed in ECD 93. This involves three components; first, a definition of 'unfair'; second, a requirement that the courts have regard to a

[74]See s 61(4) CRA.

[75]The Law Commissions have referred to this as the difference between an 'excluded term' and an 'excluded assessment' approach: see The Law Commissions' 2013 report at paras 3.80–3.109.

number of prescribed matters when determining whether a term is unfair; and, third, a non-exhaustive list of examples of the kinds of terms that may be unfair.

5.1 *Definition of 'Unfair'*

ECD 93 defines an unfair term as one that 'contrary to the requirement of good faith . . .causes a significant imbalance in the parties' rights and obligations arising under the contract, to the detriment of the consumer'.[76] Although used in UK Regulations 1999, this definition was eschewed by the Law Commissions in their review of UK law. Instead, they recommended the adoption of a 'fair and reasonable' test,[77] and that reference should not be made in this test to good faith,[78] or to a significant imbalance in the rights and obligations of the parties, as this was considered unhelpful.[79] However, those recommendations were not adopted, and what is now s 62(4) of the CRA replicates the definitions used in ECD 93 and the Regulations. The ACL, on the other hand, while incorporating the 'significant imbalance' and 'detriment' elements of ECD 93, contains no 'good faith' requirement but does include a requirement that the term not be 'reasonably necessary in order to protect the legitimate interest of the party who would be advantaged by the term'.[80] This novel element appears designed to recognise that there may be cases in which an otherwise unfair term is justified because it is no more than is reasonably necessary to protect a legitimate interest of the party it advantages. Doing so thereby obviates the need for the ACL to qualify its list of examples of unfair terms in the manner that occurs with the comparable list in ECD 93 and the CRA[81] and to do so in terms that are broad enough to apply to new terms and situations that were unforeseen when the list was drafted.

5.2 *Factors to Be Considered*

When assessing whether a term is unfair, ECD 93, UK Regulations 1999 and the CRA require a court to consider the nature of the subject matter of the contract, the circumstances existing at the time the term was agreed upon and all of the other terms of the contract or another contract on which it depends.[82] The ACL

[76]See Article 3(1) ECD 93.

[77]The Law Commissions' joint consultation paper, para 3.91.

[78]Ibid.

[79]Ibid., para 4.90.

[80]See s 24(1)(b) ACL.

[81]This is the effect of Part 2 of the Annex to ECD 93 and Part 2 of Schedule 1 of the CRA.

[82]See Article 4(1) ECD 93; the UK Regulations 1999, reg. 6(1); and s 62(5) CRA.

Table 3 Definitions of 'Unfair' and related matters

	ECD 93[a]	CRA 2015	ACL/ASIC	UCTA 1977
Definition of 'unfair'	Contrary to the requirement of good faith, it (1) causes a significant imbalance in the parties' rights and obligations (2) to the consumer's detriment.[b]	Contrary to the requirement of good faith, it (1) causes a significant imbalance in the parties' rights and obligations (2) to the consumer's detriment.[c]	There is no contrary to good faith requirement. It requires (1) imbalance in rights and obligation, (2) imbalance is not needed to protect legitimate interests, (3) it would be detrimental to a party.[d]	The terms covered are ineffective except in so far as they are reasonable,[e] defined as 'fair and reasonable' having regard to the circumstances.[f]
Factors that must be considered when assessing the fairness of a term	The nature of the goods or services, all the circumstances at the time the contract was made, all the other terms[g]	The nature of the subject matter, all circumstances at the time the contract was made, all the other terms[h]	The (1) transparency of the term and (2) the contract as a whole	If relevant, (1) the relative bargaining power (2) inducements or opportunity to contract elsewhere without the term, (3) knowledge of the term, (4) whether it was reasonable to expect compliance with the obligation excluded and (5) whether the goods were a special order for the customer
Examples of potentially unfair terms—indicative and non-exhaustive	Listed in the Annex	Listed in Schedule 2[i]	Listed in s 25	Not listed
Terms that are rendered ineffective per se	None	Consumer terms or notices excluding or restricting liability for death or personal injury resulting from negligence[j]	None	Any term or notice excluding or restricting liability for death or personal injury resulting from negligence [k]

(continued)

Table 3 (continued)

	ECD 93[a]	CRA 2015	ACL/ASIC	UCTA 1977
Burden of proof on the issue of unfairness	No reference to this issue.	No reference to this issue.	Burden is on the party advantaged by a term to prove that it was reasonably necessary to protect a legitimate interest.[l]	The supplier bears the burden of proving that the term was reasonable.
Duty of the court in proceedings relating to the terms of a consumer contract	No such requirement	If it has sufficient material to do so, the court must consider whether the term is fair even if this issue is not raised by the parties.[m]	No such requirement	No such requirement

[a]The UK Regulations 1999 implemented the Directive in identical terms: see regs. 5(1), 6(1) and Schedule 2
[b]See Article 3 ECD 93
[c]See s 62(4) CRA. Section 62(6) provides essentially the same in relation to notices
[d]See s 24(1) ACL
[e]See ss 2(2), 3(2), 6(1A), 7(1A) and 8 UCTA
[f]Ibid., Section 11(1)
[g]See Article 4 ECD 93
[h]See s 62(5) CRA. Section 62(7) provides essentially the same in relation to notices
[i]Ibid., s 63(1)
[j]See ss 65(1) and (2) CRA. Some limits on the scope of this s are imposed by s 66. s 63(6) also makes a terms unfair per se if it makes the consumer bear the burden of proof in respect to compliance by a distant supplier or an intermediary with the Distance Marketing Directive
[k]See ss 2(1) and (3) UCTA
[l]See s 24(4) ACL
[m]See s 71 CRA

equivalent, although likely to produce the same outcome, is expressed quite differently. It *permits* a court to have regard *any* matter the court thinks relevant but then *requires* it to take into account 'the extent to which the term is transparent' and 'the contract as a whole'.[83] For this purpose, a term is defined as being transparent if it is 'expressed in reasonably plain language; ... legible; ... presented clearly; and readily available to any party affected by the term'.[84] The inclusion of transparency as a factor that must be taken into account and the meaning assigned to it closely mirrors the recommendations of the Law Commissions,[85] who argued that 'plain

[83]See s 24(2) ACL.

[84]Ibid., s24(3).

[85]See the Law Commissions' 2005 Report, para 3.97–3.101.

and intelligible language was a vital aspect of fairness'.[86] Furthermore, although the ACL does not so provide expressly, it would appear that a court could find a term to be unfair '*principally* or *solely* because it was not transparent' as they recommended.[87] The inclusion in each provision of a requirement that the court consider all of the other terms of the contract reflects accepted wisdom that because a term's apparent unfairness may be counterbalanced by benefits conferred by other terms, the unfairness of a term cannot be determined in isolation from the rest of the contract. For example, a term imposing severe conditions on the transferability of an airline ticket may not, on balance, be unfair where those conditions exist to enable the supplier to provide the consumer with other benefits such as a lower price.[88]

5.3 Examples of Terms That May Be Unfair

As Table 3 shows, other than the UCTA, each provision contains a list of terms that may be considered unfair. These lists are seen as a source of information for regulatory authorities, consumers and suppliers about the types of terms that are at risk of being judged unfair. In the case of suppliers, this is particularly useful as it indicates the kind of terms that it may be wise to avoid, or treated judiciously, especially in the absence of counterbalancing terms benefiting the other party. However, the lists are indicative only; they do not prohibit the use of the terms listed, nor do they create a presumption that a term on the list is unfair. The CRA and ACL permit additions to be made to the list by, respectively, a statutory instrument or regulation.[89]

The origin of the lists is the Annex to ECD 93. The terms listed there were adopted by UK Regulations 1999, and a slightly modified and updated version was included as Schedule 2 of the CRA. The list in the ACL, although expressed in clearer language, is substantially the same. However, there are two minor variations; first, as noted above, the presence of s 24(1)(b) in the definition of unfair makes it unnecessary for the list to be qualified in the same manner as those in UK Regulations 1999 and the CRA. Second, the ACL's list does not explicitly refer to a term excluding or limiting a supplier's liability for a consumer's death or personal injury,[90] although this situation would appear to be covered by the breadth of s 25 (K), which refers to 'a term that limits, or has the effect of limiting, one party's right to sue another party'.

---

[86] Ibid. para 3.98.

[87] Ibid., para 3.102.

[88] See *Jetstar Airways Pty Ltd v Free,* [2008] VSC 539 (Supreme Court (Victoria)).

[89] See s 63(3) CRA and s 25(n) ACL.

[90] This is the first example given in each of the other lists.

5.4 Terms That Are Unfair Per Se

The scheme of the unfair contract terms provisions under consideration is to subject the terms they cover to a fairness test; only if the term fails that test is it not binding. However, to varying degrees, the UCTA, CRA and ACL create exceptions to this approach in respect of terms that are considered so objectionable that they should be rendered void per se, that is, without the need for an individual fairness assessment to be made of them. These per se provisions are directed at terms falling into the following categories:

- Terms seeking to reduce the statutory protection conferred on consumers—the CRA and the ACL contain provisions imposing various obligations on suppliers in favour of the consumers with whom they deal. To prevent the supplier avoiding, or reducing, these obligations by the use of a term in the contract of supply, such terms are rendered void per se. In the case of the CRA, this is absolute and effected by provisions in Part 1 of the CRA,[91] rather than those in Part 2 dealing with unfair terms. In the case of the ACL, it is also absolute and effected in a similar manner.[92] However, the latter has two minor exceptions. First, reflecting the ACL's broader definition of 'consumer', a term limiting in prescribed ways the supplier's liability in respect of non-consumer goods or services will not be void, provided that reliance on the term is fair and reasonable. In respect of that precondition, a court is required to have regard to all the circumstances of the case and, in particular, to a list of matters that was clearly inspired by Schedule 2 of the UCTA.[93] Second, a term in a contract for the supply of recreational services may exclude, restrict or modify liability for breach of the consumer guarantees created by the ACL in respect of liability for death, personal injury or disease, provided this is not caused by the supplier's reckless conduct.[94]
- Terms excluding, or restricting, a trader's liability for death or personal injury resulting from negligence—Section 65(1) of the CRA creates a per se prohibition of a trader using a term in a consumer contract, or notice, to exclude or restrict liability of this nature, and s 65(2) prevents a *volenti non fit injuria* defence being raised merely because a person agreed to, or was aware of, such a term. Although these provisions apply only to terms in a consumer contract or notice, they are not limited to terms directed at consumers. For example, they would prevent a term in a consumer contract excluding or restricting the trader's liability to a child of the consumer, as well as to the consumer themselves. However, there are a number of exceptions to the scope of these provisions

[91]See s 31(1) CRA in relation to the supply of goods; s 47(1) in relation to the supply of digital content; and s57(1) in relation to the supply of services.

[92]See s64 ACL (relating to suppliers) and s 150 (relating to manufacturers).

[93]Ibid., s 64A.

[94]See s 139A CCA.

created by s 66 to cover liability that may arise in connection with a land, insurance or settlement contract, or out of granting non-commercial access to premises for recreational purposes. There is no equivalent provision in the ACL.

- Terms or notices excluding or restricting any liability for death or personal injury resulting from negligence—Section 2(1) of the UCTA creates a *per se* prohibition of any person seeking to invoke a contract term or a notice of this nature in relation to any other person; it is not restricted to terms that would protect business suppliers or traders or to terms that would disadvantage consumers. It is reinforced by s 2(3), which precludes such a term or notice being used to create a *volenti non fit injuria* defence. However, to prevent overlap with the CRA, these provisions do not apply to a term in a consumer contract or notice.[95] Also, as noted earlier, Schedule 1 of the UCTA provides that s 2 does not apply to a miscellaneous list of contracts. Again, there is no equivalent provision in the ACL.

5.5 *Burden of Proof*

In relation to the burden of proof, different positions are adopted in the UK and Australia. In the UK, the UCTA provides that it is for the party claiming that a contract term or notice is enforceable because it satisfies the reasonableness requirement to show that it does so, rather than for the other party to show that it is not. This is unlike ECD 93 and UK Regulations 1999, which are silent on this issue. Faced with this difference, in 2005 when considering new legislation in this area, the Law Commissions[96] recommended that in proceedings involving a consumer, the business seeking to rely on a term should bear the burden of proving that it was fair. This was on the ground that the latter would be better placed to explain why the term was fair and likely to have more resources with which to do so. On the other hand, where proceedings were brought by an enforcement authority, they recommended that the authority should bear the burden of proof.[97] However, when the Commissions revisited this issue in 2013, they adopted a different position, influenced by decisions of the Court of Justice of the European Union to the effect that national courts are obliged, of their own motion, to consider the issue of unfairness regardless of whether the parties have raised the matter.[98] With this in mind, they recommended that new legislation should not include any provisions regarding the burden of proof but, rather, should provide that ‘in proceedings brought by individual consumers, the court should be required to consider the

[95] See s 2(4) UCTA.

[96] The Law Commissions’ 2005 report, para 3.130.

[97] Ibid., para 3.163.

[98] See the discussion in The Law Commissions’ 2013 report, paras 7.68–7.69 and 7.89.

fairness of a term even if the consumer has not raised the issue of unfairness'.[99] This approach was adopted in the CRA, although extended to all proceedings and not just those brought by consumers.[100] However, the court is under this duty only if it considers that it has before it sufficient material 'to enable it to consider the fairness of the term'.[101] In so qualifying the court's duty, the legislation highlights a significant problem with the Commissions' changed position, namely, that it may often *not* be the case that 'the only evidence that is required is to present a copy of the term to the court so that it is 'able to read the term and decide for itself whether the term is fair'.[102] Having regard to the CRA's definition of unfairness and the matters to which a court must have regard when determining fairness, this issue has the potential to be complex and contested, placing individual consumers at a significant disadvantage. For the reasons they advanced in 2005, it is regrettable that the Commissions resiled from their initial recommendations and that their revised position was adopted.

In Australia, the ACL adopted a more nuanced position. On the issue of whether a term is unfair, the party claiming that it is of this nature bears the burden of proving, on the balance of probabilities, two of the three elements of the definition of unfairness prescribed by s 24(1). On the other hand, the third element (that the term is not reasonably necessary to protect a legitimate interest of the party it advantages) is presumed in their favour, unless proved otherwise. The ACL also does not impose a duty on the court to consider unfairness in the absence of this being raised by one of the parties. However, this omission may not be significant in so far as Australian judges have an inherent power to raise matters not in issue between the parties and have them addressed should they be of the opinion that this is called for by the facts before them. Nevertheless, it is regrettable that the ACL has not comprehensively placed the burden of proof on the party contending that a term is fair.

6 The Subject Matter and Price Exclusions

Perhaps the most controversial aspects of UK and Australian unfair contract terms legislation are the subject matter and price exclusions. These derive from 4(2) of ECD 93, which provides that the 'assessment of the unfair nature of the terms shall relate neither to the definition of the main subject matter of the contract nor to the adequacy of the price ...'. The European Commission did not initially wish to include this provision in the Directive but was persuaded to do so on the ground that

[99]Ibid., para 7.94.

[100]See s 71(2) CRA.

[101]Ibid., s 71(3).

[102]The Law Commissions' 2013 report, para 7.92.

it deals with matters that are best left to the market place.[103] Nevertheless, it allowed Member States to adopt more stringent provisions, and several have taken this opportunity and have not included exclusions of this nature in their domestic legislation.[104] On the other hand, the UK has followed the Directive, an approach that has also been adopted in Australia.[105] This is because the price and subject matter were seen as matters about which suppliers compete and consumer are alert and so are best left to market forces.[106] To do otherwise, it is argued, would interfere with freedom of contract and damage price competition.[107] Furthermore, because suppliers have different cost structures, determining whether a price was unfair could often give rise to arguments that the courts and authorities are ill-equipped to resolve, and in any case should suppliers charge exorbitant prices, this could be addressed in individual cases by the law of unconscionable conduct.[108]

The price and subject matter exclusions are predicated on the terms involved being expressed in clear and accessible language so that consumers are not unfairly surprised by what they provide and are able to make ready comparisons between what is being offered by competing suppliers. Terms of this nature have the virtue of simultaneously protecting consumers and promoting competition and for this reason should not be subjected to a fairness assessment. Unfortunately, it has proved difficult to legislatively differentiate such terms from those that are not of this nature and that should, therefore, be vulnerable to such an assessment. Thus, for example, the UK's first attempt to do this, the 1999 Regulations,[109] was found by the Law Commissions to be 'fundamentally uncertain' and to have 'generated considerable litigation',[110] and their initial approach to remedying this situation by drawing a distinction between 'main' or headline' prices and charges that are 'incidental' or 'ancillary' only was rejected by the Supreme Court.[111] Their second attempt, therefore, focussed directly on the heart of the matter by restricting the exclusions to terms that were 'transparent and prominent', an approach that was seen as a practical way of distinguishing between terms that 'consumers take into account in their decision to buy the product and those which become lost in the small print'.[112] This approach was adopted in s 64 of the CRA, which can be summarised as follows:

---

[103]Ibid., para 2.3.

[104]Ibid., para 3.8.

[105]The UK provision is s 64 of the CRA; the Australian provisions are s 26 of the ACL and s 12BI of the ASIC Act 2001.

[106]The Law Commissions' joint consultation paper, para 4.63.

[107]The Law Commissions' 2005 report, para 3.57.

[108]Ibid.

[109]Essentially, the UK Regulations 1999, reg. 6(2), adopted the wording of the Directive.

[110]The Law Commissions' 2013 report, para 2.4.

[111]*The Office of Fair Trading v Abby National plc*, [2009] UKSC 6 (Supreme Court (UK)).

[112]The Law Commissions' 2013 report, paras 5.18, 3.59 and 3.79.

- A term in a consumer contract is not to be assessed for fairness to the extent that it specifies the 'main subject matter of the contract'.[113] To that extent only, the exclusion is of the whole term.
- On the other hand, a price term in a consumer contract is not to be assessed only as regards the 'appropriateness of the price payable ... by comparison with' what is supplied under the contract.[114] This does not exclude the whole term; it excludes only an assessment of the 'appropriateness of the price payable', in other words, of whether the consumer has paid too much for what they received. All other aspects of a price term, such as those regarding the timing or method of payments or the variation of the price, remain subject to a fairness assessment. This different treatment of subject matter and price terms (the difference between the 'excluded term' and the 'excluded assessment' approach) was adopted to maintain compatibility with the Directive.[115]
- Price is not defined in the CRA. However, the Law Commissions recommended that it should mean 'money consideration' in line with s 2(1) of the Sale of Goods Act 1979 and did not seek to distinguish between 'main' and 'ancillary' prices.[116]
- These exclusions, however, apply only if the term is 'transparent and prominent'. This means that it must be

(a) 'expressed in plain and intelligible language and (in the case of a written term) is legible'; and
(b) 'brought to the consumer's attention in such a way that an average consumer would be aware of the term'. For this purpose, an 'average consumer' is one who is 'reasonably well-informed, observant and circumspect'.[117]

- These exclusions also do not apply to the terms listed in Part 1 of Schedule 2 of the Act—the 'Grey list'.[118] This exposes to a fairness assessment a number of terms relating to the main subject matter, or price, that may meet the transparency and prominence requirements but which experience has shown to have the potential to exploit consumers because of 'their behavioural biases'.[119] It seeks to address an insight from behavioural economics, namely, that consumers do not always act rationally, indeed, that they are predictably irrational. This is something of which unscrupulous suppliers can take advantage by including certain types of unfair terms in their contracts, confident that they will be ignored by consumers. Examples include terms that significantly over-compensate the supplier should the consumer not proceed with the contract, or permitting the

[113]See s 64(1) CRA.
[114]Ibid.
[115]See The Law Commissions' 2013 report, para 3.100.
[116]Ibid., para 4.61–4.65.
[117]See s 64(2)–(5) CRA.
[118]Ibid., s 64(6).
[119]See the discussion in The Law Commissions' 2013 report, paras 3.46–3.58.

supplier to unilaterally and without a valid reason alter its terms, subject matter or the price payable. Inclusion on this list does not mean that the term is necessarily unfair; it merely allows it to be assessed when this may not otherwise have been possible.

Reflecting the policy position described above, the Australian ACL also seeks to exclude subject matter and price terms from being rendered ineffective on the grounds that they are unfair. However, although the provisions designed to achieve this outcome resemble those in the CRA, there are also noticeable differences. Some of these appear to have been designed to avoid the difficulties experienced with UK Regulations 1999; whether they will succeed remains to be seen.

The ACL exclusions are contained in s 26(1) of the ACL, which provides that s 23 (the provision rendering unfair terms void) does not apply

> to a term of a consumer contract to the extent, but only to the extent, that the term:
>
> (a) defines the main subject matter of the contract; or
> (b) sets the upfront price payable under the contract; or
> (c) is a term required, or expressly permitted, by a law of the Commonwealth, a State or a Territory.

Paragraph 26(1)(c) is similar in effect to s 73(1) of the CRA and has been noted above in connection with Table 2 outlining which terms are covered by the legislation. Paragraph 26(1)(a) is virtually identical to s 64(1)(a) of the CRA, the only difference being the use of the word 'defines' rather than 'specifies'. Importantly, both subject matter exclusions operate only 'to the extent' that the term specifies or defines the main subject matter of the contract so that a term that goes beyond this remains vulnerable to a fairness assessment. This is important because otherwise it may have been possible for a supplier to avoid a fairness assessment of an objectionable provision by incorporating it into a main subject matter term, for example, by describing the goods or services being supplied but then going on to give the supplier the option to unilaterally supply substitute goods or services instead. The 'to the extent that' restriction makes it clear that the fairness of that option can be assessed.[120]

On the other hand, there are significant differences regarding how clear terms must be to qualify for exclusion under the ACL and in the approach it takes to the exclusion of price terms.[121] These are summarised as follows:

- Unlike s 64 of the CRA, s 26 of the ACL does not require terms to be 'transparent and prominent' before they are excluded. While such a requirement may be inappropriate in relation to a term covered by paragraph 26(1)(c), its omission in relation to the subject matter and price exclusions means that they have the

[120]This is made clear by s 25(g) ACL and CRA item 12, part 1, Schedule 2.

[121]The ACL contains a number of other provisions relating to price including prohibitions against making false representations about price, bait advertising, multiple pricing and component pricing.

potential to operate prejudicially to consumers in a manner not possible in the UK.

- Whereas s 64(1)(b) of the CRA excludes only making an assessment of the appropriateness of the price, s 26(1)(b) excludes the price term to the extent that it sets the upfront price payable. Whether there is any practical difference between these approaches is unclear; for example, while a term fixing the time at which the price is payable is not covered by s 64(1)(b), this is less obvious in relation to s 26(1)(b) as in some cases such a term may be considered part of setting the price.
- For the purpose of the price exclusion, s 26(2) of the ACL defines price as 'consideration' rather than a money payment. This broadens the exclusion by giving it the potential to apply to other forms of consideration than money, which, when combined with the absence of a 'transparent and prominent' requirement, could result in certain price terms not being subject to a fairness assessment despite not reflecting the rationale for their exclusion. Using an Australian historical example, it would exclude from examination John Batman's 1835 'purchase' of 600,000 acres in what is now Victoria from the local inhabitants in exchange for 20 pairs of blankets, 30 tomahawks, 100 knives, 50 pairs of scissors, 30 looking glasses, 200 handkerchiefs, 100 pounds of flour and 6 shirts.[122]
- Section 26(1)(b) excludes a price term only to the extent that it 'sets the upfront price'. This appears to be an attempt to make the exclusion apply only to terms setting the main or headline price, that is, the price that attracts consumers' attention and that they use when making product comparisons and purchasing choices and not to those terms relating to price that are obscured from them by being located in the fine print, or that reveal the quantum of the price only after the consumer has become bound.[123] This latter aspiration is reinforced by the definition of 'upfront price' in s 26(2), which requires it to be 'disclosed at or before the contract is entered into'. However, although the timing aspect of this requirement may be clear, it is open to at least two criticisms. First, if it is indeed an attempt to distinguish headline prices from those that are ancillary only, then it runs counter to the conclusion of the Law Commissions,[124] influenced by the decision of the UK Supreme Court in *Abbey National*,[125] that in practice it will often be impossible to do this because of the complex nature of the consideration

---

[122]See the Batman Land Deed, National Museum of Australia. In an early example of setting aside unfair contracts, this agreement was shortly afterwards rendered void by a proclamation issued by the Governor of New South Wales.

[123]For a brief outline of the rationale for this provision see the Explanatory Memorandum for the Trade Practices Amendment (Australian Consumer Law) Bill 2009, paras 2.67–2.76 which argues (at para 2.73) that a consideration of whether a payment 'forms the upfront price may be the transparency of the disclosure of such a payment, or the basis upon which such payment may be determined'.

[124]See The Law Commissions' 2013 report, para 4.61.

[125]*The Office of Fair Trading v Abby National plc,* [2009] UKSC 6 (Supreme Court (UK)).

consumers exchange for the goods or services they receive, especially in the case of service and finance transactions. Second, and more importantly, the ACL's requirement that the price be 'disclosed' is significantly weaker than the CRA's requirement that it be 'transparent and prominent', especially having regard to the meaning that the CRA gives to those words in s 64. Assume, for example,[126] that a contract between a consumer and a financial institution, recorded in a lengthy printed contract, provides that the consumer will not be paid interest on money deposited with the institution in exchange for receiving a package of financial products; in such a case, it would seem that the term has set the upfront price (interest foregone) as this is 'disclosed' (made known, revealed, exposed to view[127]) in the contract before it was concluded and hence would be excluded from being vulnerable to a fairness assessment under s 24.[128] However, to be similarly excluded under the CRA, it would be necessary for this term to also be expressed in 'plain and intelligible language' and brought to the consumer's attention in such a way that an average consumer would be aware of the term'—neither of which will necessarily have occurred in this example.[129]

- The definition of upfront price in s 26(2) of the ACL specifically excludes any consideration 'that is contingent of the occurrence or non-occurrence of a particular event'. This would exclude, for example, terms requiring a consumer to pay compensation should they decide not to proceed with a contract or permitting a supplier to retain money paid in advance by the consumer should the contract be terminated prematurely or charging a higher rate of interest should the consumer miss a repayment. In such cases, the fairness of the term could be assessed under s 24. As a result of taking this approach, the Australian Grey list (s 26 of the ACL) contains only two terms covering price, one directed at penalties and the other at terms varying the upfront price. The CRA, on the other hand, contains no equivalent; instead, it lists a number of price-related terms on its Grey List, thereby subjecting them to a fairness consideration in that manner.

---

[126]This example is based on a scenario outlined in *The Office of Fair Trading v Abby National plc* [2009] UKSC 6 (Supreme Court (UK)), p. 42.

[127]See the meaning assigned to 'disclose' in Moore (1999).

[128]It is noted that as the product involved is a financial service, the relevant Australian provisions would actually be ss 12BG and 12 BI of the ASIC Act 2001.

[129]This exposes another difference between the ACL and the CRA: whereas the former includes transparency (defined in terms similar to those used in s 64(3) and (4) of the CRA) as a factor a court must take into account when determining whether a term is unfair, the CRA does not do this. On the other hand, as discussed in the text, whereas to qualify for exclusion under s 64 of the CRA, a term must be 'transparent and prominent', there is no such requirement in the ACL. Confusingly, the CRA does, however, obligate traders to ensure that the written terms of a consumer contract or consumer notice are transparent, and 'transparent' appears to have the same meaning here as in s 64: see ss 68 and 64(3).

7 The Consequences of the Terms Being Unfair

The consequences of a term being unfair is summarised in Table 4.

Under the CRA, the principal effect of the term unfair is that it is not binding on the consumer.[130] However, as it is not rendered void, a consumer can still rely upon an unfair term should they choose to do so.[131] Also, the unfairness of a contract term will not necessarily affect the validity of the rest of the contract; this will continue ‘so far as practicable, to have effect in every other respect’.[132] Finally, including an unfair term in a consumer contract, or seeking to rely upon one, is not an offence. However, a regulator may apply for an injunction (or interdict in Scotland) against a person if the regulator thinks that the person is ‘using, or proposing or recommending the use of’ an unfair term or a term or notice that is not transparent.[133]

Table 4 Consequences of a term being unfair

	ECD 93	CRA 2015	ACL/ASIC	UCTA 1977
Effect of the term on the consumer	Not binding on the consumer	Not binding on the consumer	Void	Ineffective to exclude or reduce their cause of action
Effect of the term on the supplier		Remains bound if the consumer so chooses	Being void, the supplier is also not bound	Ineffective to protect against liability
Effect on the remainder of the contract	Remains binding if severance is possible	Remains binding if severance is possible	Remains binding if severance is possible	Not mentioned but applying ordinary contract principles, would remain binding if severance is possible
Criminal consequences			Not directly	None
Other enforcement powers	Public action is required to prevent the continued use of unfair terms	Injunction may be obtained in relation to unfair terms	Declarations and injunctions may be obtained if a term has been declared unfair	None

[130]For a term in a consumer contract, see s 62(1) CRA; for a term in a consumer notice see s 62(2).

[131]See s 62(3) CRA.

[132]Ibid., s 67.

[133]Ibid., s 70 and Schedule 3, para 3. ‘Regulator’ is defined in para 8 of this Schedule. The investigative powers available to regulators and in particular to an ‘Unfair Terms enforcer’—the persons or bodies who may enforce provisions about unfair contract terms—are set out in Schedule 5.

The effect of the ACL's provisions is similar. An unfair term is void and severable. As a result, it will not bind the consumer but will leave the rest of the contract unaffected if the contract is capable of operating independently.[134] However, as the unfair term is void, rather than merely not binding on the consumer, the consumer does not have the option of choosing not to be bound by the term while still enforcing it against the supplier.

As the ACL does not prohibit including, or seeking to rely upon, an unfair contract term, its general penalty and enforcement provisions are inapplicable. However, s 250 empowers a court on the application of a party to a consumer contract, or the regulator, to declare that a term of the contract is unfair. Once such a declaration has been made, should the supplier apply or rely on the term, or purport to do so, an injunction can be obtained restraining them from doing so in such terms as the court thinks appropriate. Such an injunction can be obtained by the regulator or any other person.

8 Conclusion

Unfair contract terms legislation is a significant and valuable curb on the ability of dominant contracting parties to impose unfair terms on those with whom they deal. Although the current Australian and UK provisions are still in their infancy, experience with their precursors suggests that businesses will respond to them positively by excising unfair terms from their contracts[135] and that consumers will benefit.[136] However, the comparisons made above identify a number of areas in which one jurisdiction may benefit by following the lead of the other. These include the following:

- extending the CRA to protect (at the very least) small businesses—the Law Commissions recommended this in 2005, and it is now the position under the ACL. Such an extension should also be accompanied by expanding the CRA so that it binds those who *acquire* on unfair terms as well as those who *supply* on such terms; in other words, enabling suppliers as well as consumers to choose not to be bound by them;
- extending the ACL to cover negotiated contracts, as well as those that are 'a standard form'. This is the position under the CRA and the reasons advanced by

[134]Ibid., s 23(1) and (2).

[135]In evidence to the Australian Productivity Commission, Consumer Affairs Victoria said that its experience with Victoria's unfair terms legislation was that 'many hundreds of terms have been amended and amended on a voluntary basis by businesses': see Productivity Commission report, p. 424.

[136]See The National Audit Office's report for estimates of consumer benefits derived from the work of the Office of Fair Trading in relation to unfair terms, outlined above.

the Law Commissions in 2005 and 2013 for taking this approach are equally applicable to the ACL;

- adding transparency and prominence to matters listed in s 62(5) of the CRA so they can be considered when determining whether a term is unfair. Although not clear, the reference to these matters in s 64 may suggest that they are not to be considered in relation to that issue. Section 24 of ACL takes that approach;
- the exclusion provisions of the ACL being tightened by requiring, as does the CRA, the terms to be transparent and prominent before they can avoid a fairness assessment.

References

Atiyah P (1979) The rise and fall of freedom of contract. OUP, Oxford

Moore B (ed) (1999) The Australian Oxford dictionary. OUP, Oxford

National Audit Office (1999) Report by the Comptroller and Auditor General: the Office of Fair Trading: protecting the consumer from unfair trading practices. TSO, London

Productivity Commission (2008) Review of Australia's consumer policy framework. Inquiry report, vol 2. Productivity Commission, Melbourne, p 422

The Harper Panel (2015) Competition policy review: Final report

The Law Commission and the Scottish Law Commission (2002) Unfair terms in contracts: a joint consultation paper

The Law Commission and the Scottish Law Commission (2005) Unfair terms in contracts: report on a reference under section 3(1)(e) of the Law Commissions Act 1965

The Law Commission and the Scottish Law Commission (2013) Unfair terms in consumer contracts: advice to the Department for Business, Innovation and Skills

The Influence of Constitutional Law in German Contract Law: Good Faith, Limited Party Autonomy in Labour Law and Control of Contractual Terms

Béatrice Schütte

Abstract In German law, an influence of Fundamental rights in Contract law has been recognised since the mid-1950s. How this influence was effected and whether it was a direct or indirect effect was discussed for approximately 30 years. The prevailing approach today, in both court practice and academia, is that the effect is an indirect one. Only under the scope of Article 9 III *Grundgesetz* is the effect in Contract law a direct one. Some legal academics also mention the State's duty of protection in relation to the Fundamental rights. The aim of this article is to review the influence of Fundamental rights in German Contract law. The different dogmatic approaches discussed over the years and their respective development will be reviewed and contrasted with the current situation. Various examples will be used to illustrate the types of cases where the influence of Fundamental rights becomes particularly relevant. These examples include good faith, the control of contractual terms and limited party autonomy in Labour law. These will be substantiated with examples from court practice.

1 Introduction

In international terms, the influence of Fundamental rights in Private law is referred to as the 'constitutionalisation of Private law'.[1] Legal academics often comment that this 'constitutionalisation of Private law' has reached its most advanced stage in Germany.[2]

According to Article 1 III GG,[3] the three State powers are bound by the Fundamental rights as directly applicable law. However, shortly after the German

[1]Smits (2006), p. 9.

[2]Cherednychenko (2007), p. 4.

[3]The *Grundgesetz*, literally 'Basic Law', is the German Constitution. In this chapter, its provisions will be referred to with the abbreviation 'GG'.

B. Schütte (✉)
Aarhus University, Aarhus, Denmark
e-mail: schuette.beatrice@gmail.com

L. Siliquini-Cinelli, A. Hutchison (eds.), *The Constitutional Dimension of Contract Law*, DOI 10.1007/978-3-319-49843-0_8

Grundgesetz entered into force, a discussion commenced concerning if, and to what extent, Constitutional law and particularly the Fundamental rights provisions have influence on Private law. In other words, whom do they bind and what is their effect? More precisely, this question refers to whether and under which conditions the Fundamental rights not only applied vertically, between the State and its citizens, but also horizontally between its citizens.[4] If they applied horizontally, it would mean that natural persons and legal entities would have to take the Fundamental rights into account when establishing legal relations with others.[5] Different approaches emerged regarding the 'if' and the 'how' of the influence of Constitutional law on Private law. The claim of influence of Constitutional law on Private law has been generally criticised by some legal academics.[6]

It is not possible for Contract law to influence Constitutional law as the latter is superior to the former. This can be drawn directly from the wording of Articles 93 I Nrs. 2, 3, 4 a, 4b and 100 I of the *Grundgesetz*.[7] Today, the fact that Constitutional law influences Contract law means that a complete shift has occurred since the nineteenth century, when Private law ranked higher in the hierarchy.

In this chapter, the historical development of the influence of Constitutional law on Contract law in Germany will be described, as well as the dogmatic approaches taken and how they emerged. With the assistance of the examples of good faith and control of contractual terms, as well as limited private autonomy in Labour law, it will be illustrated how this influence is observed in practice.

2 General Remarks on the *Grundgesetz* and the Fundamental Rights in German Law

The German Constitution is the fundamental legal framework of the country. Not only is it the binding norm and a political yardstick that underlies the execution of public force; it is also an expression of the legal culture in Germany.[8] The section of the Constitutional law concerning Fundamental rights has particular influence on German Contract law. The notion of Fundamental rights in this context goes beyond the respective section of the *Grundgesetz*, as codified in Article 1-19 GG. It also includes the rights equivalent to them (grundrechtsgleiche Rechte), which are those mentioned in Article 93 I no. 4 lit. a GG, where the violation can be

[4]Von Münch and Kunig (2012), Vorbemerkungen (Preliminary remarks) Articles 1–19, marginal no. 15; Hufen (2014), p. 97.

[5]Stern (1988), p. 1513.

[6]More details below at para 6.

[7]Ipsen (2014), p. 157. Necessarily, the Constitution needs to rank above all other law in order to ensure its applicability upon all of the law. Grimm (2003), marginal no. 28.

[8]Schmidt-Bleibtreu et al. (2014), Das GG als Grundlage staatlicher Rechtsordnung, marginal no. 198.

claimed by means of a constitutional complaint.[9] The Fundamental rights are the most essential part of the *Grundgesetz*. First and foremost, they are subjective defensive rights, protecting certain freedoms, civil rights and liberties, as well as legal assets that are at each individual's disposition from interventions, limitations and violations by the State.[10] They have a so-called *status negativus*. That means, if the State infringes these rights, the individual can claim remedy and a prohibitory injunction. The *status negativus* refers not only to direct interferences with protected interests of the individual, such as arrest, search or expropriation but also to factual or indirect infringements, which can be of manifold character.[11] It is always relevant in cases where the protective scope of the Fundamental rights is endangered or limited, and thus the individual is at a disadvantage.[12]

According to the Federal Constitutional Court, the Fundamental rights constitute a general regime of values that underlies the entire legal order.[13] They contain guidelines and incentives for legislation, administration and the judiciary. This was first held in the *Lüth* ruling, discussed below.[14] However, the first findings in this field date back to the time of the Weimar Republic. They were developed based on the subjective quality of the Fundamental rights, the so-called institutional guarantees. They were intended to protect certain historically developed legal concepts that at the same time either constitute Fundamental rights or are closely related to them. In today's *Grundgesetz*, these can be found in several provisions, including Article 2 I GG regarding private autonomy, Article 6 GG regarding marriage and family and the parents' custody of their children, Article 14 GG regarding property and the law of inheritance or Article 19 IV GG concerning the guarantee of legal protection.[15] The theory of the Fundamental rights as a system of values can be traced back to the State theory of Rudolf Smend, who in his main work 'Verfassung und Verfassungsrecht' (Constitution and Constitutional Law) formulated the doctrine of integration.[16]

The legislator regulates Private law as such, the courts apply and substantiate the law, and thus it is necessarily bound by the Fundamental rights. The legislator itself is obliged to follow the Fundamental rights, according to Article 1, Section 3 GG.[17]

---

[9]Maunz and Dürig (2015), Article 1 III, marginal no. 9. The rights equivalent to the Fundamental rights are those granted by Article 20 IV GG (the right to resistance), Article 33 GG (the equal citizenship and the eligibility to public office), Article 38 GG (the active and passive right to election), Article 101 GG (the right to a lawful judge), Article 103 GG (the right to a fair trial) and Article 104 GG (legal requirements concerning deprivation of liberty and prohibition of torture).

[10]Schmidt-Bleibtreu et al. (2014), Das GG als Grundlage staatlicher Rechtsordnung, marginal no. 198.

[11]Stern and Becker (2016), Die Funktionen (Dimensionen) der Grundrechte, marginal no. 34.

[12]Ibid., marginal no. 35.

[13]Merten and Papier (2006), § 55, marginal no. 7.

[14]Schwabe (1975), p. 446.

[15]Stern and Becker (2016), Die Funktionen (Dimensionen) der Grundrechte, marginal nos. 37, 38.

[16]Rennert (2014), p. 34.

[17]Article 1 s 3 GG: The following basic rights shall bind the legislature, the executive and the judiciary as directly applicable law. All English translations of legal provisions in this chapter are taken from www.gesetze-im-internet.de.

In court proceedings, the judges execute the State's sovereign power in relation to the parties to the trial. The judges are, therefore, bound to apply the Fundamental rights relevant for the respective case by Article 1 III GG and are obliged to guide the trial complying with the rule of law. In this context, the judge is mainly, but not exclusively, bound by the procedural Fundamental rights found in Articles 19 IV, 101 and 103 GG.[18] If a judge ignores the influence of the provisions of Constitutional law in Private law, he will violate the Constitutional law by failing to recognise the objective content of the Fundamental right. Furthermore, through his ruling in his position as a public authority, he also violates the Fundamental right that the citizen is entitled to have taken into account.[19]

3 Historical Development

In Germany, the first movements with the aim of establishing of a democratic constitution took place in the nineteenth century. However, it was not until the era of the Weimar Republic that a democratic constitution containing codified Fundamental rights was enacted. A nation state is required for a Constitution.[20] And up until this point, Germany was not generally considered to be a single nation as it more resembled a collection of smaller kingdoms, duchies and the like. The Weimar Constitution entered into force in 1919 and was based on the democratic principle.[21] It contained both 'Basic Rights and Basic Duties of the Germans'.[22] Among the Basic duties was the duty to serve in the army. The duties of going to school and the duty of all citizens to contribute to carrying the public burden in accordance with personal assets, as well as the duty to perform community service, existed as prescribed by law.[23] The rights contained in the Weimar Constitution were merely declaratory and not enforceable by court proceedings. Furthermore, the Weimar Constitution did not have any influence on the development of Private law.[24]

The enactment of the *Grundgesetz*[25] in 1949 marked a clear cut with the darkest chapter in German history. When the new Constitution was drafted, the

[18]Pieroth et al. (2014), marginal no. 194; *Vielleicht,* [1979] BVerfGE 52, 203 (Federal Constitutional Court).

[19]Ibid., marginal no. 200.

[20]Grimm (2003), § 1, marginal no. 28.

[21]Schneider (2003), § 5, marginal no. 21. Article 1 of the Weimar Constitution read 'All state power originates from the people'.

[22]The title of the second part was 'Grundrechte und Grundpflichten der Deutschen'.

[23]Schneider (2003), § 5, marginal no. 32.

[24]Brüggemeier (2006), pp. 60–61.

[25]The *Grundgesetz* was intended to be of preliminary character and to be valid until East and West Germany would be unified. This can also be read from Article 146 GG. Mußgnug (2003), § 8, marginal no. 53.

responsible committee put every possible effort into enacting a law that would help prevent the reoccurrence of any similar events as seen under the former national socialist regime. In contrast to the Constitution of the Weimar Republic, one of the main objectives was to enact Fundamental rights that were not merely 'declamations, declarations and directives' but also 'directly applicable Federal law upon which every single German, every inhabitant of our country shall be enabled to file a claim before the courts'.[26] However, it is not claimed that the *Grundgesetz* introduced provisions concerning Human rights from scratch. Rather, it recognises a pre-State duty of all State powers to protect those rights.[27] Their placement at the very beginning of the Constitution stresses their absolute priority in relation to all of the other constitutional provisions. The first recognition of Fundamental rights in the domain of private law in the post Basic law era took place in 1954, when the Federal High Court of Justice held that the general right to personality from Article 1 I and 2 I GG was a private right to be respected by everyone.[28] However, in this judgment, the Federal High Court of Justice did not elaborate on what kind of dogmatic basis this conclusion was set.[29] According to Brüggemeier, it was the intention of the judges to break with the traditional focus on economic interests and to also consider the personal interests of the parties.[30] Criticism of the Private law and its lack of social aspects, and in particular the protection of the weaker party, had already been made before the German Civil code[31] entered into force.[32]

---

[26]Mußgnug (2003), § 8, marginal no. 56. According to Dreier, this assumption was not correct. 'Empty words' were only such Fundamental Rights which were fully subject to the power of the legislator. The practical enforcement was limited because the common and particularly important remedy of filing a constitutional complaint that is used today, did not exist in the Weimar Republic. See Dreier (2013), Vorbemerkungen vor Article 1 GG, marginal no. 16.

[27]Badura (2015), p. 91.

[28]Stern (1988), p. 1526; *Leserbriefe*, [1954] BGHZ 13, 334 (Federal Constitutional Court): Violation of the general right to personality by publication of private letters in a newspaper. The general right to personality mainly plays a role in cases involving tort law. See for example *Herrenreiter,* [1958] BGHZ 26, 349 (German Federal Court in Civil Matters); *Soraya,* [1973] BVerfGE 34, 269 (Federal Constitutional Court); *Caroline von Monaco/Hannover*, [1999] BVerfGE 101, 361 (Federal Constitutional Court). All three cases deal with compensation for non-pecuniary damage for violation of personality rights. With the abovementioned judgment, the Federal High Court of Justice supported the approach of direct horizontal effect. Later, the court changed its practice and based the extended protection of personality rights on the State's duty to protect human dignity, Article 1 I 2 GG. See Canaris (1984), p. 231.

[29]Brüggemeier (2006), p. 64.

[30]Ibid., p. 59.

[31]*Bürgerliches Gesetzbuch* ('BGB').

[32]Martinek (2005), pp. 5–6.

4 The Horizontal Effect of Fundamental Rights: Drittwirkung von Grundrechten

The influence of Fundamental rights on Private law is addressed under the German term *Drittwirkung von Grundrechten*—horizontal effect of the Fundamental rights. This term was introduced by Hans Peter Ipsen.[33] In the early 1970s, there was already consensus that the Fundamental rights have a horizontal effect. However, there was still discussion concerning the development of the effect and whether it was direct or indirect.[34] An argument in favour of a general horizontal effect of the Fundamental rights, be it direct or indirect, is the principle of the unity of the legal order.[35] In a constitutional state, the Constitution guarantees the unity of the legal order. Furthermore, in the *Lüth* judgment, the Federal Constitutional Court held that the system of values provided by the Fundamental rights constitutes a decision of general principle that applies to all areas of law.[36] The unity of the legal order implies that legal terms with the same wording must be interpreted in the same way, independent from the area of law from which they belong. Furthermore, violations should be treated consistently across all areas of law. For example, what is forbidden according to Criminal law cannot be permitted under Private law.[37]

The questions concerning the horizontal effect of the Fundamental rights is very relevant in relation to Contract law as the *Grundgesetz* guarantees its most essential component, namely the positive and negative freedom of contract, as part of the more comprehensive private autonomy. In other words, the individual has the freedom to conclude or not to conclude a contract and to freely determine the content of any such contracts entered into. Private autonomy is foremost a defensive right, meaning that any requirements made by the public authorities constitute an infringement, and so legal provisions imposing limitations need to be justified in light of the Constitution.[38]

The private autonomy enables self-determination on the part of the individual with regard to the organisation of legal relations. It is a fundamental principle and of

[33]Hans Peter Ipsen was a professor of Constitutional law and became particularly renowned after the Second World War as an expert in European law. He faced criticism for starting his career as a doctoral student under the Nazi regime. He was a member of both the NSDAP and SA. See Stern (2015), pp. 718 and 719; Ruffert (2009), p. 389.

[34]Schwabe (1971), p. 9.

[35]Christensen and Fischer-Lescano (2007), p. 83. The legal concept of the unity of the legal order was subject to various criticisms. For example, it has been argued that the courts use it as a means of legitimation and to hype ordinary techniques of judicial argumentation. (See Ibid. p. 70). On the other hand, it has been argued that it is just a rhetorical tool that is used when it seems tactically appropriate. An actual unity of the legal order, conceptual or normative, cannot even be achieved by dogmatic means for each area of law, thus it is definitely condemned to failure with regard to the legal order as a whole. See Felix (1998), p. 9, with further references.

[36]*Lüth,* [1958] BVerfGE 7, 198 (Federal Constitutional Court).

[37]Christensen and Fischer-Lescano (2007), p. 71.

[38]Maunz and Dürig (2015), Article 2, marginal no. 101.

essential value to society, and so it is granted by the Constitution through Articles 1 I and 2 I GG as a part of the general freedom of action and the right to personality.[39] The individual as '*homo oeconomicus*' is entitled to draft his legal relations on his own authority.[40]

Critics fear an increasing limitation to the private autonomy of the individual by various means, including the application of consumer protection rules or the substantiation of comprehensive clauses in order to abolish alleged or actual imbalances between the parties to a contract, as well as the extension of duties of information or protection.[41]

The situation is slightly different if public authorities act under Private law. In this context, one has to distinguish between fiscal acts on the one hand, such as the purchase of office material, and on the other hand the use of Private law in relation to tasks that belong under the remit of Administrative law, the so-called Administrative Private law.[42] In the latter field, it is undisputed that the Fundamental rights are directly binding. This can be determined from the wording of Article 1 III GG.[43] Furthermore, the Fundamental rights have a direct horizontal effect when it comes to limitations envisaged by law that can only be substantiated by empowered third parties, as is the case with cancellation periods or participation rules in Labour law, or under the provisions of the law of landlord and tenant.[44] However, there is discussion concerning fiscal acts and whether authorities are directly bound to the Fundamental rights or whether the theory of indirect effect applies.[45] The indirect horizontal effect only applies when the infringement of a Fundamental right originates from a private person.[46]

4.1 The Direct Horizontal Effect of Fundamental Rights: Unmittelbare Drittwirkung von Grundrechten

The traditional approach regarding the influence of the Fundamental rights on Contract law was the so-called theory of the direct horizontal effect of Fundamental rights, first proposed by Hans Carl Nipperdey[47] and applied for a long time in the

[39]Olzen (2015), marginal no. 49.

[40]Maunz and Dürig (2015), Article 2, marginal no. 101.

[41]Olzen (2015), marginal no. 49.

[42]Säcker et al. (2012), § 242, marginal no. 66.

[43]Von Münch and Kunig (2012), Vorb. Article 1, marginal no. 20; Pieroth et al. (2014), marginal no. 187.

[44]Maunz and Dürig (2015), Article 1 III, marginal no. 59.

[45]Pieroth et al. (2014), marginal no. 187.

[46]Maunz and Dürig (2015), Article 1 III, marginal no. 59.

[47]Hans Carl Nipperdey was the first President of the Federal Labour Court and had a significant influence in the legal development in the early years of the Federal Republic of Germany. Hollstein (2005), p. 249.

continuous practice of the Federal Labour Court.[48] There was already consensus that numerous Fundamental rights constitute general values for the entire legal order. Nipperdey then concluded that they were directly binding for Private law relations and not only through legal acts.[49] In this context, the Fundamental rights constitute a prohibition regime. Thus, the Fundamental rights become statutory prohibitions in the sense of § 134 BGB[50] in the domain of Contract law, and in tort law they are absolute rights under the scope of § 823 I BGB and protective statutes under the scope of § 823 II BGB.[51,52] Legal scholars argued in favour of a direct effect so that the legislator would be bound by the Constitution.[53] The judges at the Federal Labour Court held that the Fundamental rights had undergone a change to their meaning and that a significant number of the rights not only granted freedoms towards the State but were also principles of social life.[54] Furthermore, it was argued that the State not only interfered with Fundamental rights but also protected threatened positions granted by the Fundamental rights and thus acted as a moderator to colliding private interests.[55] Additionally, the wording of Article 1 II GG was taken as an argument in favour of the direct horizontal effect, as the provision reads: 'The German people therefore acknowledge inviolable and inalienable human rights as the basis of every community, of peace and of justice in the world.' Fundamental rights as basis of every community is read as an indicator of their direct applicability inter partes.[56] Another argument is derived from Article 1 III GG and proposes that if the State powers are bound directly by Fundamental rights, then the actions of citizens should also be bound by Fundamental rights.[57]

This approach has been criticised for limiting the autonomy of the parties. As any legal transactions affect Fundamental rights, such as Article 2 or 14 GG, norms like § 138 BGB would be out-ruled and replaced by the much stricter control mechanism of suitability, necessity and proportionality.[58] The main argument advanced against the direct effect is that the Fundamental rights as such are a

---

[48]Pieroth et al. (2014), Grundrechte Staatsrecht II, marginal no. 190.

[49]Richardi et al. (2009), § 12, marginal no. 8; Enneccerus and Nipperdey (1959), p. 93.

[50]§ 134 BGB: A legal transaction that violates a statutory prohibition is void, unless the statute leads to a different conclusion.

[51]§ 823 I BGB: A person who, intentionally or negligently, unlawfully injures the life, body, health, freedom, property or another right of another person is liable to make compensation to the other party for the damage arising from this.

§ 823 III BGB: The same duty is held by a person who commits a breach of a statute that is intended to protect another person. If, according to the contents of the statute, it may also be breached without fault, then liability to compensation only exists in the case of fault.

[52]Nipperdey (1961), p. 15; Canaris (1984), p. 202.

[53]Hager (1994), p. 374.

[54]Von Münch and Kunig (2012), Vorb. Arts. 1–19, marginal no. 17.

[55]Hufen (2014), p. 97.

[56]Christensen and Fischer-Lescano (2007), p. 265.

[57]Dürig (1956), p. 158.

[58]Canaris (1984), p. 209.

regime of defensive rights for the individual against the State.[59] The only provisions having direct effect on third parties are Article 9 III 1 GG and Article 9 III 2 GG.

Critics further argued that the wording of important constitutional provisions indicated that only the State was the intended addressee of the Fundamental rights. As such, it was argued that according to Article 1 I 2 GG, the State power must respect and protect human dignity. Furthermore, the three State powers are bound to the Fundamental rights according to Article 1 III GG.[60] The same applies to the legal reservations: the addressee is clearly the legislator.

Another argument against the necessity of a direct effect is that there is no such superior–inferior relationship between private persons as there is between the State and its citizens. Only the State can use enforcement measures like administrative acts or penalties.[61] Some scholars completely reject any horizontal effect.[62] In contrast, one can argue that compared to the nineteenth and early twentieth century, the social reality has significantly changed. Individuals face not only State power but also other potentially dominant parties, such as employers.[63]

4.2 *The Indirect Horizontal Effect of Fundamental Rights: Mittelbare Drittwirkung von Grundrechten*

The idea of indirect horizontal effect of the Fundamental rights was first mentioned in academic publications by Günther Dürig.[64] In this context, indirect effect means that the Fundamental rights neither apply directly to Private law, nor are they statutory prohibitions in the sense of § 134 BGB. Instead, they have impact on Private law by providing a system of values. The provisions of Private law cannot be contradictory. Dürig's approach was aimed at safeguarding private autonomy and the independence of Private law.[65] According to his approach, the Private law legislation is from a constitutional point of view an aliud in relation to public law orders and permissions.[66] Therefore, in the field of Private law in a case of an infringement of Fundamental rights, one could only argue with § 134 BGB if the Constitution itself mentioned nullity.[67] The Fundamental rights influence Private

[59] Hager (1994), p. 373.

[60] Canaris (1984), p. 204.

[61] Ibid., p. 206.

[62] Jörn Ipsen has argued that private individuals are not the addressees of Fundamental rights. From a dogmatic point of view he deems the concept of horizontal effect both unnecessary as well as likely to cause significant confusion. Still, he acknowledges that the Fundamental rights are being applied when interpreting the comprehensive clauses. See Ipsen (2012), marginal no. 70.

[63] Merten and Papier (2006), § 55, marginal nos. 3, 4.

[64] Dürig (1956), p. 162.

[65] Cherednychenko (2007), p. 4.

[66] Canaris (1984), p. 210.

[67] As for instance in Article 9 III GG. Dürig (1956), p. 162.

law through the so-called comprehensive clauses, which are legal provisions that are formulated with a wide scope so that they have to be substantiated in court practice.[68] The best-known examples are good faith as codified in § 242 BGB and *bonos mores* according to § 138 BGB. This has given rise to the question as to why only the comprehensive clauses, and not other Private law provisions, are relevant as an 'entrance door' for the Fundamental rights, particularly since the Federal Constitutional Court later also applied the yardstick of Fundamental rights to Private law legislation.[69] The Court held that the Fundamental rights extend their influence mainly through those provisions containing binding law and are therefore a part of the *ordre public*, i.e., those principles that are also binding inter partes for reasons of public interest.[70] In simple terms, this means that the Private law provisions remain decisive in conflicts between private parties. However, they must be interpreted in light of the Fundamental rights, so that the underlying constitutional values will be sufficiently considered.[71]

4.2.1 *Lüth* as a Ground-Breaking Decision

The adoption of the approach of the indirect horizontal effect, 'mittelbare Drittwirkung', in court practice started with the renowned *Lüth* judgment handed down by the Federal Constitutional Court in 1958.[72] This judgment is considered to be the most important judgment in German Fundamental rights practice and is seen as a milestone on the way to giving the Fundamental rights the importance they have today in German Law.[73] The core issues of this case concerned Tort law and not Contract law, and the question of how the freedom of opinion was to be taken

[68]Von Münch and Kunig (2012), Vorb. Articles 1–19, marginal no. 17. The Fundamental rights influence through the comprehensive clauses is not a phenomenon exclusively seen in Private law. The same occurs in both Criminal and Administrative law where there are provisions containing comprehensive terms. As for Criminal law, one can mention public nuisance (*grober Unfug*) and the criterion of reliability (*Zuverlässigkeit*) in Industrial law. For each individual case, the court is required to substantiate whether certain behaviour amounts to nuisance or what it takes to be deemed reliable. See Schwabe (1975), p. 448.

[69]Ladeur (2009), p. 545.

[70]Ibid., p. 549.

[71]Smits (2006), p. 12.

[72]*Lüth,* [1958] BVerfGE 7, 198 (Federal Constitutional Court).

[73]Christensen and Fischer-Lescano (2007), p. 53. Two further decisions are deemed important for the relevance of Fundamental rights today: The *Elfes* Judgment (*Elfes,* [1957] BVerfGE 6, 32 (Federal Constitutional Court)) and the Pharmacy Judgment (*Apotheken,* [1958] BVerfGE 7, 377 (Federal Constitutional Court)). The former deals with the general freedom of action and the question as to whether it had to be interpreted in a wide or a narrow scope. The latter takes up the freedom of profession. The Federal Constitutional Court introduced a three-level system for limitations to be made to the freedom of profession and the requirements for the limitations on the respective levels to be justified in the light of Constitutional law. Christensen and Fischer-Lescano (2007), p. 53.

into consideration. The director of the Senate in Hamburg, Erich Lüth, had called for a boycott regarding a movie of the director Veit Harlan, called *Unsterbliche Geliebte* (Immortal Lover). Veit Harlan had previously been known as the director of the movie *Jud Süß*. Its content was clearly anti-Semitic, and the National Socialists used it for their propaganda.[74] Based on § 826 BGB,[75] the District Court of Hamburg prohibited Lüth from calling for boycott. Lüth filed a constitutional complaint. According to the Federal Constitutional Court, a call for boycott is not necessarily an act *contra bonos mores*, and it may possibly be justified considering all relevant circumstances.

Therefore, the judgment of the District Court of Hamburg may have violated Lüth's Fundamental right to freedom of expression if the applied Private law provisions are influenced by the Fundamental right to a degree that they are no longer suitable as a base for the judgment.[76] The court stressed the fundamental significance of the freedom of expression for the free democratic constitutional structure and held that it would not be adequate to allow this Fundamental right to be limited by a legislative act and thus by court rulings based on those acts. As a consequence, any law that limits the freedom of expression, as well as the rulings based on those laws, must be viewed in the light of the respective Fundamental right.[77] The Federal Constitutional Court has since upheld the concept of the indirect effect.[78] The *Lüth* judgment was also the starting point of attributing the Fundamental rights a '*status positivus*'.[79] However, the Court did not elaborate on the discussion as to whether the horizontal effect of the Fundamental rights was a direct or indirect one, arguing that in this particular case an indirect horizontal effect would solve the problem.[80]

---

[74]In the years 1948 and 1950, Harlan had been accused of crimes against humanity and of defamation as the movie provoked a mass incitement enabling the mass crimes of National Socialism against the Jews. He was deemed not guilty as the court held that after the beginning of World War II it was no longer possible to reject an assignment made by the then Ministry of Propaganda without facing the danger of imprisonment or being brought to a concentration camp. See 'Strafverfahren gegen Veit Harlan' in: Henne and Riedlinger (2005).

[75]§ 826 BGB is a Tort law provision: 'A person who causes damage to another intentionally by acting '*contra bonos mores*' is liable to compensation.' This is particularly relevant in cases of fraudulent behaviour.

[76]*Lüth,* [1958] BverfG 7, 198 (202, 203) (Federal Constitutional Court).

[77]Maunz and Dürig (2015), Article 5, marginal nos. 105–107.

[78]Fröhlich (2005), p. 3.

[79]Rennert (2014), p. 32. Another judgment handed down by the Federal Constitutional Court regarding calls for boycott and the horizontal effect of the fundamental rights was the *Blinkfüer* case (*Blinkfüer,* [1969] BVerfGE 25, 256 (Federal Constitutional Court)). *Blinkfüer* was a Hamburg-based weekly magazine that also contained TV and radio programme content of the GDR. After the construction of the wall between East- and West-Germany in 1961, the publishing house Springer, also based in Hamburg, and which dominated the newspaper and magazine market, asked shops to stop selling magazines containing Eastern German TV and radio programme content.

[80]*Lüth,* [1958] BVerfGE 7, 198 (204) (Federal Constitutional Court); See also Christensen and Fischer-Lescano (2007), p. 64.

The practice of the Federal Constitutional Court was mainly focused on the Fundamental rights codified in Articles 2 I, 3 I, 3 II and III, 5 I and II, 12 I and 14 I GG that had significant influence in Private law. Article 2 I GG is relevant for private autonomy.[81] The interpretation of a legal provision in light of the Constitution must not attribute it a completely new normative content. If it is necessary to redefine a rule, the old rule has to be declared unconstitutional and it is up to the legislator whether or not it is to be substituted by a new rule that meets the constitutional requirements.[82]

The indirect horizontal effect was also called *Ausstrahlungswirkung*, i.e., the Fundamental rights 'radiate' into Private law.[83] In other words, the effect of Constitutional law not only is limited to the creation of Private law but also concerns its interpretation.[84] Some legal academics, including Claus-Wilhelm Canaris, argue against any horizontal effect of the Fundamental rights, claiming that they only refer to the State.

4.2.2 The Development of the Indirect Horizontal Effect after the *Lüth* Judgment

Currently, the prevailing approach regarding the influence of Constitutional law on Contract law is the indirect horizontal effect mentioned above. There are several arguments in favour of this approach. One of them is the wording of Article 1 III GG, which only mentions the three State powers.[85] Furthermore, referring to the historical development of the Basic law, the objective was to enact the Fundamental rights in their classic sense, which means that they should regulate the relationship between the State and its citizens and limit the State's omnipotence.[86] The Federal Labour Court used to mostly follow the theory concerning the direct effect on third parties, but from the mid-1980s it started to change its practice.[87] Nowadays, it is exceptional to observe a direct effect of Constitutional law on Contract law.[88] It is generally acknowledged that Article 1 I GG, the right to human dignity, has a direct

[81]Stern and Becker (2016), Einleitung – die Hauptprinzipien des Grundrechtssystems des Grundgesetzes, marginal no. 38.

[82]Schmidt-Bleibtreu et al. (2014), Vorbemerkungen (Preliminary remarks) Article 1, marginal no. 21.

[83]The English term 'radiation' for *Ausstrahlung* is, for instance, used in Rödl (2013), p. 1024 and Kumm (2006), p. 350.

[84]Brüggemeier (2006), p. 72.

[85]Article 1 III GG: The following basic rights shall bind the legislature, the executive and the judiciary as directly applicable law.

[86]Pieroth and Schlink (2014), marginal no. 191.

[87]Hager (1994), p. 373.

[88]One of those exceptions is to be found in Article 9 III GG, see Sect. 7.3.

effect on private persons. The State's duty of protection applies as soon as a person takes measures that affect another citizen's human dignity.[89] Some provisions of the Basic Law refer directly to Private law or to Private law relationships. This is also used as an argument in favour of the indirect effect, by arguing that the fact that some provisions mention Private law explicitly suggests that it is meant to be an exception.[90] In general, one can infer that the legal content of the Fundamental rights influences Private law through the legal provisions that directly dominate it. Private law rules dating from the time before the *Grundgesetz* entered into force need to be interpreted in its light, and new laws must be drafted taking it into consideration.[91]

The influence of the Fundamental rights as a regime of values manifests specifically in those provisions that are mandatory and cannot be modified by private agreement.

Legal academics even talk about the emergence of a so-called 'constitutional private law'.[92] This is based on the assumption that the Federal Constitutional Court develops in its practice solutions for legal problems that are part of Private law. It creates Private law principles, which through the binding character attributed through § 31 BVerfGG achieve the rank of Constitutional law and may therefore be considered to be constitutional Private law.[93]

The question of the indirect effect or ripple effect of the Fundamental rights is closely linked to the fact that the Federal Constitutional Court is limited in its ability to revise the rulings made by the ordinary jurisdiction as it is not intended to be a superior Court of Appeal.[94] Its judgments concern only the question as to whether the respective Fundamental rights or Constitutional law in general have been sufficiently considered in the decisions of the ordinary courts in relation to their meaning and scale, provided they are of significant relevance to the underlying issues of the case.[95] This can be also determined from § 90 I of the Code on the Federal Constitutional Court (Bundesverfassungsgerichtsgesetz, BVerfGG). In order for a judgment handed down by the ordinary courts to have a lasting effect on protected Fundamental right positions, there should be a thorough review by the Federal Constitutional Court as to whether the interference with the Fundamental right can be justified in light of the Constitution.[96]

---

[89] *Schwangerschaftsabbruch II*, [1993] BVerfGE 88, 203 (263) (Federal Constitutional Court); Hoffmann et al. (2014), p. 91.

[90] Pieroth et al. (2014), marginal no. 191.

[91] *Lüth,* [1958] BverfG 7, 198 (205) (Federal Constitutional Court).

[92] Ipsen (2014), p. 157.

[93] Ibid., p. 158.

[94] Jarass and Pieroth (2014) Article 2, marginal no. 57.

[95] *Einsicht in Patentunterlagen,* [1964] BVerfGE 18, 85 (93) (Federal Constitutional Court); *Wettbewerbsverbot für Handelsvertreter*, [1990] BVerfG NJW 1990, 1469 (Federal Constitutional Court).

[96] *Deutschland Magazin – DGB,* [1976] BVerfG NJW 1976, 1677 (Federal Constitutional Court); *Springer/Wallraff*, [1984] BVerfG NJW 1984, 1741 (Federal Constitutional Court).

In the 1970s, Schwabe criticised a certain inconsistency in the practice of the Federal Constitutional Court with regard to the application of the doctrine of the horizontal effect of the Fundamental rights. In this context, he mentioned a number of decisions where this question could have been addressed, but either it was ignored completely or the judges held that the horizontal effect was not relevant in the particular case.[97]

General criticism against the theory of the indirect horizontal effect concerns the strict alignment between the Fundamental rights and the comprehensive clauses in Private law.[98] According to Canaris, there is no reasonable justification why the Fundamental rights should exclusively develop their influence through the comprehensive clauses. It is just as feasible that provisions with determined facts are intended to foster the implementation of Fundamental rights, and there is also no guarantee that there is always an appropriate comprehensive clause for each case.[99]

5 The Doctrine of Protective Duties

Alongside *Drittwirkung*, legal academics have more recently started to discuss the '*Schutzpflichtentheorie*', the theory concerning the State's duty of protection.[100] The State must protect the Fundamental rights of the individual through both Private law legislation and court practice. Some scholars also argue with the protection of the socially weaker party. However, this approach further extends the State's protective duties to the protection from infringement of the Fundamental rights originating from other individuals.[101]

For the first time, the State's duty to protect the Fundamental rights was mentioned in the Federal Constitutional Court's first ruling on the legality of abortion within the first three months of pregnancy,[102] where the Court explicitly mentioned a duty of protection of developing life.[103] With time, this approach became more important to the Court's practice and its relevance to legal academics also increased. The Federal Constitutional Court drew back on the protective duties in later important decisions, including those concerning terrorism,[104] peaceful use of

[97]Schwabe (1975), p. 442

[98]Canaris (1984), p. 223.

[99]Ibid.

[100]The approach was brought forward by Claus Wilhelm Canaris; Ruffert (2009), p. 389.

[101]Canaris (1984), p. 226. Some legal academics argue that the theory of protective duties has nothing to do with the horizontal effect of the Fundamental rights. Canaris (1984), p. 226.

[102]See *Schwangerschaftsabbruch I*, [1975] BVerfGE 39, 1 (41 *et seq.*) (Federal Constitutional Court).

[103]Stern and Becker (2016) Einleitung – die Hauptprinzipien des Grundrechtssystems des Grundgesetzes, marginal no. 49.

[104]*Schleyer*, [1977] BVerfGE 46, 160 (164) (Federal Constitutional Court).

nuclear power[105] and traffic noise.[106,107] The Federal Constitutional Court also argued with the protective duties in 1990 in the *Handelsvertreter* (commercial agent)[108] judgment. The Court had to check the constitutionality of a provision of the Commercial Code (§ 90 a II 2 HGB), according to which a commercial agent lost his claim for compensation for the period of prohibition of competition in the situation of an extraordinary termination of the contract. The Federal Constitutional Court deemed the provision unconstitutional, stating that it infringed the commercial agent's right to free choice of profession under Article 12 GG. The judges held that the State had a duty to protect the agent's rights arising under Article 12 GG.[109] The concept was revisited again in cases concerning prenuptial contracts and surety contracts where there was a significant imbalance between the parties.[110]

There is now a consensus that the objective function of the Fundamental rights implies the State's duty to protect them. Therefore, the State must also protect those rights from being violated by private persons. In other words, it constitutes a duty to not only omit infringements of those rights but to also actively undertake certain measures. This can be done by means of regulation.[111] The State institutions have an extensive margin of discretion as to how to comply with these duties. This also depends on the proximity and extent of the threat, on the type and importance of the interests of both the State and the private persons at stake, as well as the existing regulations and the measures that have already been taken.[112] Today, it is an important part of the Fundamental rights doctrine in almost the entire European Constitutional law.[113] The approach of the duty of protection is also relevant in connection with the multi-functionality of the Fundamental rights and is an important base for the future when considering the defence from threats to crucial legal interests.[114] The subject matter of the protective duty is determined based on the respective Fundamental right.[115] The protective duties are rarely found in the wording of the

---

[105]*Mülheim-Kärlich*, [1979] BVerfGE 53, 30 (57 *et seq.*) (Federal Constitutional Court).

[106]*Straßenverkehrslärm*, [1988] BVerfGE 79, 174 (201 *et seq.*) (Federal Constitutional Court).

[107]Schmidt-Bleibtreu et al. (2014), Vorbemerkung vor Article 1. Allgemeine Grundrechtslehren marginal no. 23.

[108]*Wettbewerbsverbot für Handelsvertreter*, [1990] BVerfGE 81, 242 (255) (Federal Constitutional Court).

[109]Ladeur (2009), pp. 554–555.

[110]Maunz and Dürig (2015), Article 1 III, marginal no. 107.

[111]Stern and Becker (2016), Einleitung – die Hauptprinzipien des Grundrechtssystems des Grundgesetzes, marginal nos. 47, 48.

[112]Schmidt-Bleibtreu et al. (2014), Vorbemerkung vor Article 1. Allgemeine Grundrechtslehren, marginal no. 23.

[113]Stern and Becker (2016), Einleitung – die Hauptprinzipien des Grundrechtssystems des Grundgesetzes, marginal no. 50.

[114]Ibid., marginal no. 54.

[115]Schmidt-Bleibtreu et al. (2014), Vorbemerkung vor Article 1. Allgemeine Grundrechtslehren marginal no. 23.

provisions of the Constitution. One example is Article 1 I 2 GG, according to which the State powers have the duty to respect and to protect human dignity.[116]

According to Papier, in connection with the protective duties, it could be considered an indirect horizontal effect when a judge in a private law case applies the objective system of values provided by the Fundamental rights as he acts in compliance with his protective duties. This approach describes even more exactly than the indirect horizontal effect how the Fundamental rights actually radiate into Private law. Not only does it include the legislator's duty to create Private law in accordance with the Fundamental rights but also the duty of the courts to interpret Private law in this way. Within the theory of the protective duties, there is no limitation to comprehensive clauses, as there is under the scope of the doctrine of the indirect horizontal effect.[117]

Under the principles of the democratic system, the legitimate legislator has a margin of discretion but is still bound to the requirements established by the Fundamental rights, such as the guarantee of private autonomy. However, he must also respect the duty of protection with regard to foreign control and thus must ensure that it is not only the principle of the survival of the fittest that applies.[118]

6 Criticism of the Horizontal Effect of Fundamental Rights

The fact that Constitutional law influences other areas of law also gives rise to criticism. It is claimed that introducing a constitutional provision, according to which individuals are also bound to the Fundamental rights, would have the same effect as upholding the doctrine of indirect horizontal effect.[119] It is also argued that there is hardly any difference between the direct and the indirect effects in terms of the final result. This is deemed to be so particularly because German Private law is fully constitutionalised. In addition, it is also being proposed that the Fundamental rights should have not only a horizontal effect but also a general effect in society.[120]

According to Kumm, a change in the Constitution to introduce a provision according to which individuals are also bound to the Fundamental rights would not change anything in practice.[121] However, on the contrary, Canaris argues that it is necessary to have the applicability of the Fundamental rights between private persons regulated by the Constitution if it is intended that these rights could also be

[116]Kumm (2006), p. 350.
[117]Merten and Papier (2006), § 55, marginal no. 10.
[118]Maunz and Dürig (2015), Article 2, marginal no. 107.
[119]Kumm (2006), p. 346.
[120]Rödl (2013), p. 1016.
[121]Kumm (2006), p. 352.

limited by individuals.[122] Other academics have even claimed that there is no room for any horizontal effect of the Fundamental rights as their substance is already represented in the operation of the Private law.[123]

7 Examples

In the following sections, some examples of the indirect effect of Constitutional law on Contract law will be shown. The influence on Contract law is mostly considered to mean that freedom of contract is the most relevant expression of private autonomy and is subject to certain limitations.[124]

The most relevant fields of influence are the general provisions, which include good faith, interpretation of declarations of the intention to create legal relations (§ 133 BGB), contracts (§157 BGB) and acting *contra bonos mores* (§ 138 BGB). The borderlines between those fields are often blurred and not defined, particularly between good faith and acting *contra bonos mores*, as those two provisions supplement each other. Furthermore, any legal transaction that is immoral does not meet the requirements of good faith.[125] The Fundamental rights mainly extend their influence in cases where the parity of negotiation is obstructed because one of the parties significantly predominates the drafting of the contract. In these situations, one of the main functions of Private law is to intervene and to adjust the contract to reach an equitable result.[126]

7.1 Good Faith, § 242 BGB

The principle of good faith is codified in § 242 BGB,[127] and a discussion as to whether Constitutional law has a direct or an indirect effect is not relevant because for both approaches constitutional values have to be considered when applying the provision.[128] The principle of good faith has major significance for all kinds of legal relations. It is one of the most important comprehensive clauses and is an ethical legal principle. Good faith is not at the disposition of the parties to a contract.[129] The concept outlined in § 242 BGB is open so that the scope of its application is not

[122] Canaris (1984), p. 204.
[123] Rödl (2013), p. 1022.
[124] Looschelders (2014), marginal no. 49.
[125] Westermann (2014), § 242, marginal no. 23.
[126] Looschelders (2014), marginal no. 52.
[127] § 242 BGB: An obligor has a duty to perform according to the requirements of good faith, taking customary practice into consideration.
[128] Bamberger and Roth (2014), § 242, marginal no. 22.
[129] Stürner (2015), § 242, marginal no. 2.

limited, and the legal consequences are not defined.[130] However, it implies a requirement to balance the interests of all parties to the legal relationship. The requirements of good faith will be met if every party to the contract acts in fair and just manner considering the respective prevailing common usage. The parties must be faithful to each other and may neither abuse nor betray the appropriate trust.[131] By these means, the moral concepts of social ethics shall find their way into the law.[132] While the immorality of a contract under the scope of § 138 BGB leads to its nullity, the situation concerning good faith is different, according to § 242 BGB. Good faith is an inherent limit to private autonomy, which enables the courts to control the defined and definite terms of a contract.[133] When interpreting and applying the general provisions, the courts are obliged to ensure that a contract will not serve as means of heteronomy. If the contract places one of the parties at a significant disadvantage, it has to be clarified whether this is the consequence of unequal positions during the negotiations. If that is the case, the contract must be adjusted within the means of these general provisions.[134]

Section 242 BGB has several different functions: these are the supplementing function, the limiting function, the corrective function and the authorisation function. In regard to the supplementing function, good faith constitutes a number of side duties and protective duties related to each specific contract. The protective duties do not concern the contractual performance.[135]

The limiting function refers to the improper exercise of a right in its various versions, such as the abuse of a right, *venire contra factum proprium*, or forfeiture.[136] The corrective function led to the development of several contractual principles, for example those principles connected to the concept of frustration of contract.[137] The authorisation function refers to the fact that § 242 BGB contains a general authorisation to develop principles of equity in judge-made law. However, it does not empower the judges to decide cases based on the principles of equity while ignoring the legal situation as set out in the contract or under the law.[138] Prior to the thorough revision of the German law of obligations, which entered into force in 2002, the concept of good faith also served to justify *culpa in contrahendo* or positive infringement of contract. These are now codified.[139]

Furthermore, § 242 BGB still serves as a legal basis for the control of contractual terms in areas that, according to § 310 IV BGB, cannot be subject to general

[130] Westermann (2014), § 242, marginal no. 12.

[131] Ibid., marginal no. 3.

[132] Olzen and Looschelders (2015), § 242, marginal no 142.

[133] *Bürgschaft*, [1993] BVerfG NJW 1994, 36 (39) (Federal Constitutional Court).

[134] Ibid.

[135] Stürner (2015), § 242, marginal no. 6.

[136] Olzen and Looschelders (2015), § 242, marginal no. 203; Stürner (2015), § 242, marginal no. 7.

[137] Stürner (2015), § 242, marginal no. 8.

[138] Prütting et al. (2015), § 242, marginal no. 24; Stürner (2015), § 242, marginal no. 9.

[139] Westermann (2014), § 242, marginal nos. 7, 11.

standard terms and conditions. These include partnership contracts, prenuptial contracts, labour contracts and collective Labour law contracts.[140] Prior to the enactment of § 307 BGB, the control of standard contract terms was based on § 242 BGB.[141]

A number of Fundamental rights have an influence on Contract law due to § 242 BGB. Court practice reveals that these are mostly those rights affecting party autonomy, which is a crucial consideration in Private law.[142] Among these are the general rights to legal personality, as derived from Articles 1 I GG and 2 I GG. The courts have used these provisions to justify, for instance, the right to insight of an individual's medical file.[143] Furthermore, the Federal Constitutional Court interpreted the freedom of profession, granted in Article 12 I GG, in such a way that the State is obliged to ensure a minimum protection of employees in dismissal situations since by its nature the employer–employee relationship is a superior–inferior relationship, and the protection of the weaker party is an essential component of the social welfare state.[144] The freedom of faith and conscience, as provided by Article 4 GG, is granted without any limitations so that the level of protection offered by the *Grundgesetz* is very high. However, the level of protection is not necessarily superior to contractual duties. The interests at stake for both parties need to be cautiously balanced for each individual case. As a consequence, an employee can claim regular breaks for prayers only if this does not cause unbearable obstructions to the work routine.[145]

In addition to the Fundamental rights, under the scope of § 242 BGB, the principle of social justice and the welfare state is also relevant. Primarily, this refers to relations between the State and the citizen, but it can also be considered when one party to a contract is significantly weaker than the other. In such a situation, the stronger party may be obliged to consider the situation of the weaker party. However, this does not constitute a general duty. More exactly, depending on the case, it is necessary to thoroughly balance the interests of all of the parties involved while at the same time considering private autonomy and the general principle that each individual is responsible for his or her own assets.[146]

The principle of good faith is not only relevant upon the conclusion of a contract. The Fundamental rights can extend their indirect horizontal effect through § 242 BGB also upon the abusive termination of the contract.[147] This can,

[140]Ibid., marginal no. 25.

[141]Säcker et al. (2012), § 242, marginal no. 24. Other legal concepts that are nowadays codified were based on § 242 before their enactment. Well-known examples include '*culpa in contrahendo*', § 311 II no. 1 BGB or interference with the basis of the transaction, § 313 BGB. Ibid. at 29.

[142]Westermann (2014), § 242, marginal no. 32.

[143]Säcker et al. (2012), § 242, marginal no. 57.

[144]Ibid., marginal no. 59.

[145]Ibid., marginal no. 66.

[146]Bamberger and Roth (2014), § 242, marginal no. 23; Westermann (2014), § 242, marginal no. 39.

[147]Scholz (2013), p. 139.

particularly concerning labour contracts, occur if the reasons for the termination are completely extraneous or discriminatory. In the latter case, § 242 BGB only applies if the discrimination is not covered by § 138 BGB, or the General Act on Equal Treatment, for example. It may also be necessary to consider other factors, such as the trust earned during many years of service in the same company. Furthermore, the Federal Constitutional Court regularly insists on paying special attention to mothers, as well as to handicapped and older employees.[148]

The termination of a contract due to inconvenient political activity of the other party to the contract may be contradictory to Article 3 I GG, which contains the obligation for equal treatment, and more exactly Article 3 III GG, which prohibits discrimination due to an individual's political conviction. For example, there have been cases where the landlord has voided a rental contract for a clothing store due to the fact that the brands sold were connected to right-wing extremist groups or where the chairman of a right-wing extremist political party was denied access to a hotel despite having a reservation.[149] In the case of the rental contract, the Federal High Court of Justice held that the tenant had been under an obligation to inform the landlord beforehand about the exact kind of clothing he planned to sell, including the specific brands, as this would have been relevant to the landlord's decision of whether or not to conclude the contract. In this context, the Court applied § 242 and referred to the private autonomy of the parties. In this particular case, the tenants had only mentioned the sale of 'outdoor clothing'.[150]

In the second case, concerning the denied access to a politician of an extremist party, the Federal High Court of Justice ruled that in general, an entrepreneur is free to decide to whom he grants access to his premises, according to the principle of private autonomy. Therefore, the hotel owner is generally entitled to impose a ban on certain individuals. The rights granted under the scope of Article 3 GG are not violated if political activities are the reason for the ban. However, if there is already a valid contract in place for the accommodation, there are very strict requirements for one party to be able to void the contract. In the aforementioned case, the politician had previously been staying at the same hotel and had on those occasions always kept his political convictions to himself. Therefore, the Federal High Court of Justice held that the booked accommodation could not be cancelled. The situation would have been different if he had previously disturbed the other guests, for example by shouting extremist slogans or by using extremist insignia.[151]

However, one must take into account that the prevailing principle in Private law is that of private autonomy, so that there is primarily no common duty of equal treatment of contracting partners.[152] In contrast to the authorities, private persons

[148]Säcker et al. (2012), § 242, marginal no. 60.

[149]Scholz (2013), p. 139.

[150][2010] BGH NJW 2010, 3362 (Bundesgerichtshof).

[151][2012] BGH NJW 2012, 1725 (Bundesgerichtshof).

[152][2012] BGH NJW 2013, 1519 (Bundesgerichtshof).

are able to choose with whom to contract freely, according to their own preferences. Nevertheless, it may become relevant if the party subject to the discrimination is at risk concerning their fundamental rights (*grundrechtstypische Gefährdungslage*). The Federal High Court of Justice assumes that to be the case if one party to the contract is significantly more powerful socially, for example in the situation of the employer in relation to the employee.[153]

In a situation where a private bank wished to terminate a bank giro contract due to the political activities of the client, the Federal High Court of Justice held that it was not abusive and, therefore, Article 3 I GG did not have any effect between the parties through § 242 BGB.[154]

7.2 Control of Contractual Terms

Constitutional law provisions may need to be considered when it comes to the control of contractual terms. When considering the influence of Constitutional law on Contract law, the lines between the issues of good faith and control of contractual terms are blurred and not well defined.

In this field, § 138 BGB can be particularly relevant, and so contracts that are *contra bonos mores*, i.e. against good conscience or public policy, are void. The legal norm consists of two sections: The content of the first section is mentioned above. The second section states that a legal transaction is void if a person exploits the predicament, inexperience, lack of sound judgement or considerable weakness of will of another individual and causes himself or a third party, in exchange for an act of contractual performance, to be promised or granted pecuniary advantages that are clearly disproportionate to the performance. *Bonos mores* is a grey legal concept, which means that there is no exact definition, but it describes the prevailing moral values in society.[155] This is why the actual content of the concept can be subject to change throughout the years, and it can also be different according to the geographical placement. The main purpose of § 138 BGB is to void legal transactions that are unacceptable to the legal community.[156] The provision in this context limits the private autonomy, as granted by Article 2 I GG.[157] Before the application of § 138, it is necessary to interpret a contract in accordance with §§ 133, 157 BGB.[158] If more than one interpretation is possible, it is necessary to pay

[153]Scholz (2013), p. 139.

[154][2012] BGH NJW 2013, 1519 (1522) (Bundesgerichtshof).

[155]Bassenge et al. (2016), § 138, marginal no. 2.

[156]Säcker et al. (2012), §138, marginal no. 1.

[157]Westermann (2014), § 138, marginal no. 1.

[158]The provisions concern the interpretations of declarations of intention, § 133, and contracts, § 157. § 133 BGB reads 'When a declaration of intent is interpreted, it is necessary to ascertain the true intention rather than adhering to the literal meaning of the declaration'. And in § 157 it reads

attention to the objective of safeguarding the contract. The option to adjust the contract under the scope of § 242 would still be available, applying the principles of good faith in order to avoid the harsh consequence of nullity under § 138 BGB.[159]

The principles of good conscience or public policy often play a role in situations where the parity between the contracting parties is significantly unbalanced, for example if one party completely dominates the contract and the other party is essentially deprived of their private autonomy.[160] Constitutional values play an important role in the legal and social order in a liberal and social State under the rule of law and so is a predominant element of public policy.[161] With regard to indirect horizontal effect, the concept of 'bonos mores' is primarily relevant in relation to the protection of human dignity, Article 1 GG, freedom of religion and conscience, and the right to marriage and family life.[162]

Other relevant provisions include § 134 BGB, concerning statutory prohibition, and § 307 BGB,[163] concerning the control of standard contractual terms. According to § 134 BGB, a legal transaction that violates a statutory prohibition is void, unless the statute leads to a different conclusion. It has already been mentioned that the direct horizontal effect of the Fundamental rights would turn those rights into statutory prohibitions. This applies to all types of legal transactions and is also a rule that limits private autonomy.[164] In relation to *bonos mores*, § 134 is the more specialised provision as it is substantiated by the respective statutory prohibition. If certain behaviour has been prohibited by the legislator, it must be taken into due account and stressed by applying § 134 BGB, instead of arguing that at least the transaction is void as under § 138 BGB.[165] This rule applies when either the content of a legal transaction or its actual performance violates a statutory prohibition.[166] When there are standard contractual terms involved, § 307 BGB is the more specialised norm and must be applied before § 138.[167] The control of standard contractual terms under § 307 BGB applies to consumer contracts when there are pre-formulated contractual terms in use.[168] The control applies to the objective content of the term, which must be determined by means of interpretation if

'Contracts are to be interpreted as required by good faith, taking customary practice into consideration'.

[159] Westermann (2014), § 138, marginal no. 2.

[160] Stürner (2015), § 138, marginal no 12.

[161] Westermann (2014), § 138, marginal no. 12 a.

[162] Ibid.

[163] § 307 BGB: '(1) Provisions in standard business terms are ineffective if, contrary to the requirement of good faith, they unreasonably disadvantage the other party to the contract with the user. An unreasonable disadvantage may also arise from the provision not being clear and comprehensible.'

[164] Supra at p. 7; Bassenge et al. (2016), § 134, marginal nos. 1, 12.

[165] Säcker et al. (2012), §138, marginal no. 4.

[166] Olzen and Looschelders (2015), § 134, marginal nos. 1, 2.

[167] Säcker et al. (2012), BGB, §138, marginal no. 5.

[168] Bassenge et al. (2016), § 307, marginal no. 3.

necessary. Under the scope of § 307 BGB, the inappropriate discrimination of one party to the contract is prohibited. The colliding interests need to be balanced depending on the type of contract, the interests of the contracting parties at stake and the general policies in the respective sector. The other party to the contract is inappropriately discriminated against if the person introducing the standard contractual terms seeks to push through their own interests at all costs while ignoring the other party's interests or concerns.[169]

The control of contractual terms has been particularly relevant for surety contracts. The Federal Constitutional Court has intervened where the surety was provided by financially weak spouses, partners[170] or children. The reason for the different approach to these types of surety contracts is the emotional bond between the guarantor and the debtor, which makes the former commit to an overwhelming financial burden.[171]

For example, the Federal Constitutional Court accepted a constitutional complaint filed by a 21-year-old unemployed woman, arguing that her private autonomy granted by Article 2 I GG had been violated as she had been persuaded to enter into such a contract. Furthermore, she was considered to be economically weak and inexperienced and to have been taken advantage of. Therefore, the judges had to consider to what extent the civil courts were obliged under the terms of Constitutional law, to control the content of such contracts if the surety is given by poor family members.[172] The Court established a duty for Private law courts to react adequately to unbalanced contractual relations by using the measures provided by Civil law, especially the provisions of good faith and *bonos mores*.[173] However, in this context it is sometimes argued that the same result can be reached without relying on the Constitution but merely adhering to the principle of social responsibility and solidarity in Contract law.[174] The lower instance courts and the Federal High Court of Justice previously disagreed on this point. While the former used to deem the conclusion of such surety contracts as *contra bonos mores*, the latter held that surety contracts could not automatically be immoral just because the guarantor faced the danger of entering into excessive debts. The guarantor's lack of business experience was not a reason to impose duties of information and guidance on the bank.[175]

This particular decision by the Federal Constitutional Court even gained attention outside of Germany and was discussed within the topic of the constitutionalisation of Private law.[176] The majority of legal academics disagreed with the

[169]Ibid., marginal no. 12.

[170]Partners were included in 2009. See [2009] BGH NJW 2009, 2671 (2672) (Bundesgerichtshof).

[171]Stürner (2015), § 138, marginal no. 8.

[172]*Bürgschaft,* [1993] BVerfG NJW 1994, 36 (39) (Federal Constitutional Court).

[173]Säcker et al. (2012), § 765, marginal no. 17.

[174]Brüggemeier (2006), p. 74.

[175]*Bürgschaft,* [1993] BVerfG NJW 1994, 36 (37) (Federal Constitutional Court).

[176]See for instance Cherednychenko (2004), p. 7; Smits (2006), p. 10.

practice of the Federal High Court of Justice. Subsequently, IX. Civil Senate, responsible for banking law, adjusted its policy.

Before the adjustment of this court practice, the Federal Constitutional Court held that surety contracts were immoral if they included an extraordinarily high risk or if the guarantor had no economic interest of their own in the loan agreement and would, based on the income, never be able to pay off the debt.[177]

This approach is still subject to criticism. It is still argued that it is a common part of private autonomy and freedom of contract that one may commit to obligations that have a significant inherent risk and include detrimental burdens.[178]

Fundamental rights can also play a role in the assessment of prenuptial contracts. In 2001, the Federal Constitutional Court handed down a judgment concerning such a contract concluded in the 1970s between a pregnant woman and her future husband.[179] Both parties to the contract renounced their right to maintenance after a future possible divorce, including in a situation of financial need. They agreed on a monthly maintenance payment of 150 German marks to support the child. The parties contracted out of any further claims to support the child. The couple's son was born in 1976, and in 1989 the couple divorced. One year later, the son successfully filed a claim for information concerning the financial status of his father and claimed further maintenance. The father appealed and claimed that he should be contracted out of his duties exceeding the payment of the agreed 150 German marks per month. The Court of First Instance (Amtsgericht) rejected the father's claim, stating that the corresponding terms of the prenuptial agreement had been *contra bonos mores*.

The father first successfully appealed the decision, but the Federal Constitutional Court finally ruled in favour of the mother.[180] The ruling of the Higher District Court (Oberlandesgericht) had violated the mother's rights guaranteed by Articles 2 I and 6 IV GG[181] since the judges failed to recognise the relevance of these provisions. One of the prerequisites of private autonomy granted through Article 2 I GG is that the individual party to a contract has full self-determination. The interests of both parties need to be balanced.

According to the provisions of Article 6 GG, the spouses are free to regulate their personal relationship during their wedded life and also for the time following a divorce. However, the State must intervene when a prenuptial contract does not express the idea of the marriage being a partnership where husband and wife are equal but instead expresses a clear dominance of one party over the other. The courts must then use the general provisions of Private law to control the terms of the contract

[177] *Bürgschaft,* [1993] BVerfG NJW 1994, 36 (38) (Federal Constitutional Court).

[178] Prütting et al. (2015), § 765, marginal no. 31; Gröschler (2015), § 765, marginal no. 23.

[179] *Unterhaltsverzichtsvertrag,* [2001] BVerfG NJW 2001, 957 (Federal Constitutional Court).

[180] Ibid.

[181] Article 6 IV GG: Every mother shall be entitled to the protection and care of the community.

and to adjust the contract, if necessary.[182] By failing to do so in this case, the Court had violated the woman's rights granted through Articles 2 I GG and 6 GG.

7.3 Limited Private Autonomy in Labour Law, Article 9 III Grundgesetz

The freedom of association was already known in German law before the Grundgesetz entered into force. In the German Empire of 1871, the freedom of association was granted under the Association Act, but the Constitution of the Empire did not contain any Fundamental rights. The Weimar Constitution granted the freedom of association as a Fundamental right.[183] When it comes to Labour law contracts, Article 9 III GG is of particular relevance. According to Article 9 I GG, all Germans enjoy freedom of association (Vereinigungsfreiheit). For example, they have the right to form corporations and other associations. Article 9 III GG is relevant to questions concerning the influence of Constitutional law on Contract law, which grants the right to form coalitions (Koalitionsfreiheit), and associations to safeguard and improve working and economic conditions.[184] In relation to Article 9 I GG, Article 9 III[185] is *lex specialis*. Freely formed employers' associations and trade unions shall help arrange the working life without any State influence.[186] This right applies to every individual and so is not dependent on citizenship. Freedom of coalition refers to these employer's associations and trade unions.[187] It also enables competition between the trade unions. The right applies to everyone regardless of citizenship or profession, including public officials, judges and soldiers.[188]

According to both the general practice of the Federal Constitutional Court and the prevailing academic approach, Article 9 III GG is a so-called double Fundamental Right. Therefore, it not only protects the freedom of the individual to form and to join coalitions, the individual freedom of coalition, but it also grants the

[182] *Unterhaltsverzichtsvertrag,* [2001] BVerfG NJW 2001, 957 (958) (Federal Constitutional Court).

[183] Von Münch and Kunig (2012), Article 9, marginal nos. 4, 5.

[184] 'Working conditions' encompass all those aspects that are related to the labour relationship, for example, salary, working hours, and regulations concerning holidays and health and safety at work. See Dreier (2013), Article 9, marginal no. 75.

[185] Article 9 III GG: The right to form associations to safeguard and improve working and economic conditions shall be guaranteed to every individual and to every occupation or profession. Agreements that restrict or seek to impair this right shall be null and void; measures directed to this end shall be unlawful. Measures taken pursuant to Article 12a, to paras. (2) and (3) of Article 35, to para. (4) of Article 87a, or to Article 91 may not be directed against industrial disputes engaged in by associations within the meaning of the first sentence of this paragraph in order to safeguard and improve working and economic conditions.

[186] Schmidt-Bleibtreu et al. (2014), Article 9, marginal no. 5.

[187] Badura (2015), p. 306.

[188] Schmidt-Bleibtreu et al. (2014), Article 9, marginal no. 23.

coalitions their organisational structure and their work, which is called the collective freedom of coalition.[189] This collective freedom of association enhances the individual freedom. Article 9 does not apply to associations founded by the State and ordered by law, whether they are of a Private law or Public law nature. Therefore, it does not protect the individual from being integrated into a corporation under Public law.[190] Article 9 III GG differs from other Fundamental rights as its effect on Private law is a direct one.[191] It protects the coalitions, not only from interference by the State but also from unlawful infringements originating from competing organisations and other private powers, provided that the pressure imposed on the protected activities is significant.[192] This is already implied by Article 9 III 2 stating that 'agreements that restrict or seek to impair this right shall be null and void; measures directed to this end shall be unlawful'.[193] This concerns not only contracts but also all types of agreements and acts of legal relevance.[194] As a consequence, private autonomy is limited in the field of Labour law contracts. The freedom of coalition counteracts the weakness of the individual employee, so that associated employees have a better standing when negotiating their working conditions.[195]

Freedom of coalition exists not only in a positive context but also as a negative freedom, for example the freedom not to join any coalition at all or to leave the coalition.[196] Therefore, agreements under Private law obliging an employer to remain a member of a certain employers' association are void according to Article 9 III 2 GG, as ruled by the Federal Labour Court in 2006.[197] The Court held that not all forms of pressure aimed at membership maintenance constitute a violation of Article 9 III. Furthermore, it is not permitted to place unreasonable obstacles to resigning from an association. A 3-month notice period was deemed reasonable, whereas a 6-month period was found to be unreasonable. The association may not claim back any financial support given during the period of a strike.[198] A member of an employers' association cannot resign without notice during collective bargaining as this would change the situation for the collective wage agreement and disrupt the balance of interest between the parties. Therefore, the Federal Labour Court

[189]Müller-Glöge et al. (2016), Article 9 GG, marginal no. 39. Dreier (2013), Article 9, marginal no. 69.

[190]Schmidt-Bleibtreu et al. (2014), Article 9, marginal no. 4.

[191]Maunz and Dürig (2015), Article 9, marginal no. 171.

[192]Schmidt-Bleibtreu et al. (2014), Article 9, marginal no. 43.

[193]According to Ipsen, Article 9 III is a private law provision of constitutional rank. Ipsen (2014), p. 158. He disagrees with the approach of horizontal effect, be it direct or indirect, and argues that a Private law subject cannot unilaterally limit another Private law subject in its freedom of action. Ipsen (2012), marginal no. 707.

[194]Maunz and Dürig (2015), Article 9, marginal no. 332.

[195]Stern and Becker (2016), Article 9, marginal no. 28.

[196]Ibid., marginal no. 38.

[197]*Negative Koalitionsfreiheit,* [2006] BAG NJW 2007, 622 (Federal Labour Court).

[198]Müller-Glöge et al. (2016), Article 9 GG, marginal no. 38.

requires the opponent trade union to be informed clearly and in due time. Otherwise, resignation is void and irrelevant concerning any industrial dispute.[199]

Under the scope of Article 9 III GG, it is forbidden to establish so-called closed shop systems that require a potential employee to be member of a trade union in order to be hired. The preferential treatment of members of a certain employer's association or trade union is also unlawful.[200]

The negative freedom of coalition does not protect against the external effects of the collective fostering of interests through the associations. In other words, it is possible that non-members are treated differently from association members. Non-members cannot request that their employers treat them in the same way as members. This does not violate the negative freedom of coalition.[201] Neither is there any room for the application of the Labour law principle of equal treatment.

However, by a special decision made by the secretary of employment and social affairs, a collective wage agreement can be declared commonly valid so that it also applies to employees that are not members of trade unions.[202] The Federal Constitutional Court stated that Article 9 provides employers and employees with the possibility to freely solve the problems emerging from their colliding interests. Many disputes concerning Labour law and Article 9 III GG concern the ways associations present themselves and the related advertising. Article 9 III GG enables the arrangement of working and economic life in such a way that the State steps back from its legislative competence and leaves the necessary regulation of details in labour contracts to the coalitions.[203]

Concerning possible limitations to the freedom of coalition, it is disputed whether Article 9 II GG[204] also applies to Article 9 III. Those arguing in favour of the applicability say that the freedom of coalition is a specialised form of the freedom of association.[205] When considering the limitation of criminal law, one must take into account that this does not enable the State to enact special criminal law legislation focusing on coalitions.[206] Furthermore, there are no reservations to the freedom of coalition,[207] but this does not mean that it is granted without limits.[208] The freedom of coalition may be limited if it is necessary to protect the

[199]Ibid., marginal no. 38 a.

[200]Badura (2015), p. 307.

[201]Müller-Glöge et al. (2016), Article 9 GG, marginal no. 35.

[202]Badura (2015), p. 311.

[203]Schmidt-Bleibtreu et al. (2014). Article 9, marginal no 27.

[204]Article 9 II GG: '(2) Associations whose aims or activities contravene the criminal law, or that are directed against the constitutional order or the concept of international understanding, shall be prohibited.'

[205]Von Münch and Kunig (2012), Article 9, marginal no. 110; Maunz and Dürig (2014), Article 9 GG, marginal no. 335.

[206]Von Münch and Kunig (2012). Article 9, marginal no. 110.

[207]The fact that there are no reservations to the freedom of coalition is used as an argument against the applicability of Article 9 II GG to Article 9 III.

[208]Stern and Becker (2016), Article 9 GG, marginal no. 88.

concerns of public welfare that are also on a constitutional level.[209] However, it has yet to be fully clarified to what extent the legislator has the right to shape the freedom of coalition. According to the Federal Constitutional Court, only those limitations that are necessary for the protection of legal interests are permitted. In this context, it has been criticised that there is no clear separation between the terms embodiment and infringement, which leads to the assumption that only the legal interests of constitutional rank can justify limitations to the freedom of coalition being weakened.[210]

8 Conclusion

It is evident that German Constitutional law, and more precisely the Fundamental rights, have an influence on Private law. In the past, there has been a dogmatic discussion as to whether the influence was direct or indirect. However, today there is consensus that the effect is indirect, but there are a few exceptions, particularly concerning Article 9 III GG, where the direct horizontal effect is explicitly implied by the wording of the provision. It has also been argued that the relationship between Constitutional law and Contract law has also been fully constitutionalised, although there are doubts that it actually goes that far. However, Article 20 I GG mentions the fact that the Federal Republic of Germany is also a social welfare state. Therefore, it is correct to place upon the courts a duty to ensure that citizens are not kept to obligations that in the long term are likely to endanger their financial situation, if the contractual negotiations were significantly unbalanced with the result of them being placed at a major disadvantage.

Of course, the question can be asked whether it is necessary to rely on the Fundamental rights at all in order to solve some of these cases. Concerning the decision on surety contracts, one could argue that the bank has side duties according to § 241 II BGB,[211] which are likely to be violated in the case discussed above. Given the fact that the bank employee suggested that the claimant's signature was a mere formality, one may even be able to assume fraudulent behaviour as a consequence of which the contract could be voided according to § 123 BGB.[212] On the other hand, it would be the guarantor bearing the burden of proof in the surety case.

---

[209] Von Münch and Kunig (2012), Article 9, marginal no. 111.

[210] Ibid., marginal no. 112.

[211] § 241 II BGB: 'An obligation may also, depending on its contents, oblige each party to take account of the rights, legal interests and other interests of the other party.'

[212] § 123 BGB:

> (1) A person who has been induced to make a declaration of intent by deceit or unlawfully by duress may avoid his declaration. (2) If a third party committed this deceit, a declaration that had to be made to another may be avoided only if the latter knew of the deceit or ought to have known it. If a person other than the person to whom the declaration was to be made

Similar situations may arise in other contractual cases if there is a similar relationship between the parties during the contractual negotiations.

In summary, the indirect horizontal effect, and particularly when combined with the State's protective duties, presents a healthy compromise concerning the application of Fundamental rights in Private law. In contrast, the direct horizontal effect goes too far in its limitations to private autonomy and, completely ignoring any horizontal effect, opens all of the floodgates (to use the terminology of Tort law) in favour of those having the superior position in contractual negotiations.

References

Badura P (2015) Staatsrecht, 6th edn. C.H. Beck, Munich

Bamberger HG, Roth H (eds) (2014) Beck'scher Online Kommentar zum BGB. C.H. Beck, Munich

Bassenge P et al (eds) (2016) Palandt Bürgerliches Gesetzbuch, Kommentar, 75th edn. C.H. Beck, Munich

Brüggemeier G (2006) Constitutionalisation of Private Law – the German perspective. In: Barkhuysen T, Lindenbergh S (eds) Constitutionalisation of Private Law. Martinus Nijhoff Publishers, Leiden/Boston, pp 59–82

Canaris C-W (1984) Grundrechte und Privatrecht. Archiv für die civilistische Praxis, pp 201–246

Cherednychenko OO (2004) The constitutionalization of contract law: something new under the sun? EJCL 8(1):1–17

Cherednychenko OO (2007) Fundamental rights and private law: a relationship of subordination or complementarity? ULR 3(2):1–25

Christensen R, Fischer-Lescano A (2007) Das Ganze des Rechts. Duncker & Humblot, Berlin

Dreier H (ed) (2013) Grundgesetz Kommentar, 3rd edn. Mohr Siebeck, Tübingen

Dürig G (1956) Grundrechte und Zivilrechtsprechung. In: Maunz T (ed) Vom Bonner Grundgesetz zur gesamtdeutschen Verfassung. Festschrift zum 75. Geburtstag von Hans Nawiasky. Isar Verlag, Munich, pp 157–190

Enneccerus L, Nipperdey HC (eds) (1959) Allgemeiner Teil des Bürgerlichen Rechts, Vol 1, 15th edn. J.C.B. Mohr, Tübingen

Felix D (1998) Einheit der Rechtsordnung: Zur verfassungsrechtlichen Relevanz einer juristischen Argumentationsfigur. Mohr Siebeck, Tübingen

Fröhlich A (2005) Sind Privatpersonen an die Menschenrechte gebunden? In: Beiträge Nürnberger Menschenrechtszentrum 2005. Available at: http://www.nmrz.de/wp-content/uploads/2009/11/Sind_Privatpersonen_an_die_Menschenrechte_gebunden.pdf. Accessed 7 Apr 2016

Grimm D (2003) Ursprung und Wandel der Verfassung. In: Isensee J, Kirchhof P (eds) Handbuch des Staatsrechts, Historische Grundlagen, § 1, Vol 1. C.F. Müller, Heidelberg, pp 3–44

Gröschler P (ed) (2015) Soergel Bürgerliches Gesetzbuch, Vol 11/2, 13th edn. Kohlhammer, Stuttgart

Hager J (1994) Grundrechte im Privatrecht. Juristenzeitung, pp 373–383

acquired a right as a direct result of the declaration, the declaration made to him may be avoided if he knew or ought to have known of the deceit.

§ 123 I BGB is applicable when the creditor calls the surety a mere formality. See Gröschler (2015), § 765, marginal no. 20.

Henne T, Riedlinger A (eds) (2005) Das Lüth-Urteil aus rechtshistorischer Sicht. Berliner Wissenschafts Verlag, Berlin
Hoffmann C, Schulz SE, Borchers KC (2014) Grundrechtliche Wirkungsdimensionen im digitalen Raum - Bedrohungslagen im Internet und staatliche Reaktionsmöglichkeiten. MultiMedia und Recht, pp 89–95
Hollstein T (2005) Um der Freiheit willen – die Konzeption der Grundrechte bei Hans Carl Nipperdey. In: Henne T, Riedlinger A (eds) Das Lüth-Urteil aus rechtshistorischer Sicht. Berliner Wissenschafts Verlag, Berlin, pp 249–269
Hufen F (2014) Staatsrecht II Grundrechte, 4th edn. C.H. Beck, Munich
Ipsen J (2012) Staatsrecht II, Grundrechte, 15th edn. Verlag Franz Vahlen, Munich
Ipsen J (2014) Verfassungsprivatrecht? Juristenzeitung 69(4):157–162
Jarass HD, Pieroth B (2014) Grundgesetz für die Bundesrepublik Deutschland, Kommentar, 13th edn. C.H. Beck, Munich
Kumm M (2006) Who is Afraid of the Total Constitution? Constitutional Rights as Principles and the Constitutionalization of Private Law. German Law J 7(4):341–369
Ladeur K-H (2009) Die Drittwirkung der Grundrechte im Privatrecht – 'Verfassungsprivatrecht' als Kollisionsrecht. In: Calliess G-P et al (eds) Soziologische Jurisprudenz, Festschrift für Günther Teubner zum 65. geburtstag. De Gruyter Recht, Berlin, pp 543–558
Looschelders D (2014) Schuldrecht Allgemeiner Teil, 12th edn. Verlag Franz Vahlen, Munich
Martinek M (2005) Vertragsrechtstheorie und Bürgerliches Gesetzbuch. Saarbrücker Bibliothek, Vortrag anlässlich der Saartage 2005 an der Keio University (Tokyo)
Maunz T, Dürig G (eds) (2015) Grundgesetz. Loseblatt-Kommentar. C.H. Beck, Munich
Merten D, Papier H-J (eds) (2006) Handbuch der Grundrechte in Deutschland und Europa – Vol II: Grundrechte in Deutschland, Allgemeine Lehren I. C.F. Müller, Heidelberg
Müller-Glöge R, Preis U, Schmidt I (eds) (2016) Erfurter Kommentar zum Arbeitsrecht, 16th edn. C.H. Beck, Munich
Mußgnug R (2003) Zustandekommen des Grundgesetzes und Entstehen der Bundesrepublik Deutschland. In: Isensee J, Kirchhof P (eds) Handbuch des Staatsrechts, Historische Grundlagen, § 8, Vol 1. C.F. Müller, Heidelberg, pp 315–344
Nipperdey HC (1961) Grundrechte und Privatrecht, Kölner Universitätsreden. Scherpe Verlag, Krefeld
Olzen D (2015) Einleitung zum Schuldrecht. In: Olzen D, Looschelders D (eds) J. von Staudingers Kommentar zum BGB. Sellier/deGruyter, Berlin
Olzen D, Looschelders D (eds) (2015) J. von Staudingers Kommentar zum BGB. Sellier/deGruyter, Berlin
Pieroth B et al (eds) (2014) Grundrechte Staatsrecht II, 30th edn. C.F. Müller, Heidelberg
Prütting H, Wegen G, Weinreich G (eds) (2015) BGB Kommentar, 10th edn. Luchterhand, Berlin
Rennert D (2014) Die verdrängte Werttheorie und ihre Historisierung - zu 'Lüth' und den Eigenheiten bundesrepublikanischer Grundrechtstheorie. Der Staat 53:31–59
Richardi R et al (eds) (2009) Münchener Handbuch zum Arbeitsrecht, 3rd edn. C.H. Beck, Munich
Rödl F (2013) Fundamental Rights, Private Law, and Societal Constitution: On the Logic of the so-called Horizontal Effect. Ind J Glob Leg Stud 20:1015–1034
Ruffert M (2009) Die Rechtsprechung des Bundesverfassungsgerichts zum Privatrecht. Juristenzeitung, 389–398
Säcker FJ et al (eds) (2012) Münchener Kommentar zum BGB, vol 1, 7th edn. C.H. Beck, Munich
Schneider H (2003) Die Reichsverfassung vom 11. August 1919. In: Isensee J, Kirchhof P (eds) Handbuch des Staatsrechts, Vol 1, Historische Grundlagen, § 5. C.F. Müller, Heidelberg, pp 177–234
Schmidt-Bleibtreu B, Hoffmann H, Hennecke HG (eds) (2014) Kommentar zum Grundgesetz, 13th edn. Carl Heymanns Verlag, Cologne
Scholz D (2013) Politische Betätigung als Ausschlussgrund im Privatrechtsverkehr, Juristische Rundschau, 137–141

Schwabe J (1971) Die sogenannte Drittwirkung der Grundrechte. Wilhelm Goldmann Verlag, Munich
Schwabe J (1975) Bundesverfassungsgericht und "Drittwirkung" der grundrechte. Zur Verfassungsrechtsprechung, Archiv des Öffentlichen Rechts, pp 442–470
Smits JM (2006) Private Law and Fundamental Rights: a Sceptical View. In: Barkhuysen T, Lindenbergh S (eds) Constitutionalisation of Private Law. Martinus Nijhoff Publishers, Leiden/Boston, pp 9–22
Stern K (ed) (1988) Das Staatsrecht der Bundesrepublik Deutschland III/1. C.H. Beck, Munich
Stern K (2015) Hans Peter Ipsen. In: Häberle P, Kilian M, Wolff HA (eds) Staatsrechtslehrer des 20. Jahrhunderts: Deutschland – Österreich – Schweiz. Walter de Gruyter, Berlin/Boston, pp 717–734
Stern K, Becker F (eds) (2016) Grundrechte-Kommentar, 2nd edn. Carl Heymanns Verlag, Cologne
Stürner R (ed) (2015) Jauernig Bürgerliches Gesetzbuch, Kommentar, 16th edn. C.H. Beck, Munich
Von Münch I, Kunig P (eds) (2012) Grundgesetz Kommentar Band 1, 6th edn. C.H. Beck, Munich
Westermann HP (ed) (2014) Erman BGB Kommentar, 14th edn. Verlag Dr. Otto Schmidt, Cologne

Agreements on Personality Rights in the Portuguese Legal System

Elsa Dias Oliveira

Abstract The rules and principles enshrined in the Portuguese Constitution are binding. The country's Civil law, and specifically the Contract law, must therefore be in accordance with it. However, the way that private individuals shall be bound by these constitutional rules and principles has been under discussion.

In the Portuguese legal system, agreements on personality rights are possible if in accordance with the law. The subject matter of these contracts, mostly governed by the Civil law, concerns personality rights, such as the right to one's image. And the legal interests subject to personality rights are also the subject of Fundamental rights enshrined in the Constitution. It follows, perforce, that it is necessary to define how the Constitutional law has an impact on these matters in the Civil law.

1 Introduction

In the Portuguese legal system, the Civil law, which includes Contract law, must not contain norms that contravene the provisions of the Constitution or the principles enshrined therein. Also the courts, in matters that are submitted for judgment, may not apply such rules contrary to the Constitutional law.

The way private individuals shall be bound to the constitutional rules and principles is not clear and it has been the subject of a great deal of discussion. In this chapter, there will be an analysis of the impact of the Constitutional law on the Civil law in general and on the Contract law specifically.

Agreements on personality rights are possible in the Portuguese legal system, if in accordance with the law. The subject matter of these contracts, ruled mostly by the Civil law, are personality rights, such as the right to one's image, to one's privacy, to one's name, and the subjects of these rights are legal interests such as image, privacy, name. These legal interests are also the subject of Fundamental rights enshrined in the Constitution. An assessment will be made here of the interconnection between the Constitutional law and the Civil law in terms of the protection of personality interests and how this affects the agreement itself. A

E.D. Oliveira (✉)
Faculty of Law, University of Lisbon, Lisbon, Portugal
e-mail: elsaoliveira@fd.ulisboa.pt

L. Siliquini-Cinelli, A. Hutchison (eds.), *The Constitutional Dimension of Contract Law*, DOI 10.1007/978-3-319-49843-0_9

specific agreement will also be under discussion, this being the one related to the commercial use of the image of professional sportsmen and sportswomen. In the Portuguese legal system, these agreements are governed by a special law, and it is important to define the relation between these rules and the general ones.

One may also have to deal with a clash of rights whenever it is not possible to reconcile the personality rights—or other rights or freedoms—of different holders. An analysis will also be made of how the Portuguese legal system regulates this problem and the possible solutions given to it.

2 The Impact of the Constitutional Law on the Contract Law

The Portuguese legal system in force is the Constitution of the Portuguese Republic of 2 April 1976, revised by Constitutional laws No. 1/82 of 30 September, No. 1/89 of 8 July, No. 1/92 of 25 November, No. 1/97 of 20 September, No. 2/2001 of 12 December, No. 1/2004 of 24 July and No. 1/2005 of 12 August.[1]

The entire Portuguese legal system falls within the scope of the Constitution, where the fundamental principles are enshrined. Civil law,[2] including Contract law, must also observe and comply with these principles. And constitutional rules and principles that have a significant impact in the Contract law legal scheme can be easily identified. As examples of these rules, one could cite Article 1 of the Constitution, according to which Portugal is a sovereign Republic, based on the dignity of the human person; in Articles 24 *et seq.*,[3] personal rights, freedoms and guarantees are set out; consumer rights are set out in Article 60; under Article 61, the right to private economic enterprise is accorded; in Article 62, the right to private property and to its transmission is guaranteed. In this context, it is also worth noting the importance of Article 13 (principle of equality), according to which all citizens possess the same social dignity and are equal before the law.

The rules and principles enshrined in the Constitution are not just simple guidelines but real binding rules with which the legislation—Contract law specifically and Civil law in general—must be in accordance. Also the courts, as well as other public bodies, may not apply unconstitutional rules.[4]

---

[1]The translation of the Constitution Articles into English was taken from http://www.tribunalconstitucional.pt/tc/en/crpen.html.

[2]Mota Pinto (2005), p. 69.

[3]As set forth in Article 24 [right to life], para 1, human life is inviolable; according to Article 25 [right to personal integrity], para 1, every person's moral and physical integrity is inviolable; according to Article 26 [other personal rights], para 1, everyone is accorded the rights to personal identity, to the development of personality, to civil capacity, to a good name and reputation, to their image, to speak out, to protect the privacy of their personal and family life, and to legal protection against any form of discrimination.

[4]Mota Pinto (2005), p. 73.

In order to avoid unconstitutional laws being enacted, the President of the Republic, as set forth in Article 278, paragraph 1, of the Constitution, may require the Constitutional Court to undertake a prior evaluation of the constitutionality of the laws that he has before him to sign.[5] Furthermore, according to Article 204 of the Constitution, the courts may not apply norms that contravene the provisions of the Constitution or the principles enshrined therein.[6] Another guarantee of respect for the Constitutional law is given in Article 280, paragraph 1, of the Constitution,[7] under which an appeal may be made to the Constitutional Court against court decisions that refuse the application of any norm on the grounds of its unconstitutionality or that apply a norm for which the issue of unconstitutionality has been raised during the proceedings.

Article 281 of the Constitution also sets out the abstract review of constitutionality and legality. And in Article 283 of the Constitution, unconstitutionality by omission[8] is set out.

It can be seen from these examples that the Constitution has an unarguable impact on Civil law in general and specifically on Contract law.

3 Fundamental Rights and Personality Rights

In the Portuguese legal system, there are different personality rights, each one related to a personality interest[9] such as life, physical integrity, psychological integrity, privacy, image, voice and so on. Because these legal interests are so important to each individual's existence, development as a person and expression of

---

[5]See Gomes Canotilho and Vital Moreira (2010), pp. 921 *et seq.*; Blanco de Morais (2011), pp. 21 *et seq.*; Miranda (2013), pp. 305 *et seq.*; Melo Alexandrino (2015), pp. 295 *et seq.* According to Article 278, para 2, '[t]he representatives of the Republic may also ask the Constitutional Court to undertake the prior consideration of the constitutionality of any norm contained in a regional legislative decree that is sent to them for signature'. And, under paragraph 4, also '(...) the Prime Minister or one fifth of all the Members of the Assembly of the Republic in full exercise of their office may ask the Constitutional Court to undertake the prior consideration of the constitutionality of any norm contained in any decree that is sent to the President of the Republic for enactment as an organic law'.

[6]See Gomes Canotilho (2003), pp. 917 *et seq.*; Gomes Canotilho and Vital Moreira (2010), pp. 517 *et seq.*; Miranda (2013), pp. 244 *et seq.*; Melo Alexandrino (2015), p. 303.

[7]See Gomes Canotilho and Vital Moreira (2010), pp. 936 *et seq.*; Blanco de Morais (2011), pp. 595 *et seq.;* Miranda (2013), pp. 252 *et seq.*; Melo Alexandrino (2015), pp. 298 *et seq.*, 303.

[8]According to Article 283 of the Constitution,

> [a]t the request of the President of the Republic, the Ombudsman, or, on the grounds of the breach of rights of the autonomous regions, presidents of the Legislative Assemblies of autonomous regions, the Constitutional Court shall consider and verify whether there is a failure to comply with the Constitution due to the omission of legislative measures needed to make constitutional norms executable.

[9]The expression 'personality interest' is used in this work as the translation of 'bem de personalidade', which means, in the Portuguese legal system, the legal interests intimately related to the person, essential to the person to exist, to develop himself or herself as a person, and such

his or her identity, they are subject to personality rights, which are usually legally taken to be subjective rights.[10] This means that the personality rights holder has legal authority to enjoy his or her personality interests—such as privacy, image, name, voice—as well as to prevent other persons taking advantage of these most exclusive interests without authorisation.

In Portuguese Civil law, personality rights are expressly set out in the Civil code, mainly in Articles 70 *et seq.*: the right to one's name (Articles 72 to 74), the right to the confidentiality of one's letters and other writings (Article 75 to 78), the right to one's image (Article 79), the right to privacy (Article 80). In accordance with Article 70, paragraph 1, the protection of each person against any threat or actual bodily or moral injury is set out in more general terms. Portuguese authors are divided on the interpretation of Article 70, paragraph 1. Some of them advocate the existence of a general right of personality that coexists with the special personality rights mentioned above.[11] Other authors, with whom I agree, consider that since not all of the personality rights are expressly set out in the law, Article 70, paragraph 1, of the Civil code establishes a general rule that allows for the protection of all relevant personality interests.[12] This does not mean that there is a general right of personality but, in a different way, that there are as many personality rights as personality interests that deserve legal protection. And this protection is guaranteed by Article 70, paragraph 1.[13]

The legal characterisation of a right as a personality right ensures to its holder that in the case of threat to or actual injury of the personality interests, the plaintiff can seek judicial remedies. According to Article 70, paragraph 2, of the Civil code, these remedies may be damages—mostly compensatory damages—and/or injunctions adequate to prevent the injury threatened or to put an end to an actual injury or even to alleviate the impact of the injuries.

---

interests include life itself. Other personality interests, such as image, allow the identification of the individual and express their uniqueness.

[10]See Gomes da Silva (1944), pp. 34 *et seq.*; Gomes da Silva (1965), pp. 156 *et seq.*; Carvalho (1981), p. 83, note 81; Amaral Cabral (1989), p. 381; Mota Pinto (1993), p. 482; Capelo de Sousa (1995), pp. 606 *et seq.*; Menezes Leitão (1996), p. 745, note 76; Oliveira Ascensão (2000), pp. 82 *et seq.*; Carvalho Fernandes (2001), p. 218; Trabuco (2001), pp. 405 *et seq.*; Menezes Cordeiro (2011), p. 101; Pais de Vasconcelos (2006), pp. 64 and 153; Pais de Vasconcelos (2015), pp. 37 *et seq.* Alternately, Antunes Varela (2000), p. 534; Cabral de Moncada (1995), pp. 74 *et seq.* Leite de Campos (1992), p. 59, claims that since the person does not have total power over these interests (e.g., one cannot commit suicide), the personality rights are not really subjective rights.

[11]See Antunes Varela (1982–1984), pp. 142 *et seq.*; Ribeiro de Faria (1990), p. 417, note 2; Mota Pinto (1993), p. 495; Capelo de Sousa (1995), pp. 198 *et seq.*, 513 *et seq.*, 577 *et seq.*, 605 *et seq.*; Mota Pinto (1999), p. 173; Trabuco (2001), pp. 394 *et seq.*; Mota Pinto (2005), pp. 209 *et seq.*; Pais de Vasconcelos (2006), pp. 64 *et seq.*; Sinde Monteiro (2007), p. 464; Pais de Vasconcelos (2015), pp. 40 *et seq.*

[12]Menezes Cordeiro (2011), pp. 103 *et seq.*; Oliveira Ascensão (2000), pp. 80 *et seq.*, 87 *et seq.*; Oliveira Ascensão (2002), p. 15; Melo Alexandrino (2007), p. 32.

[13]Dias Oliveira (2012), p. 34.

Articles 24, 25, 26, 27 of the Constitution contain stipulations regarding the Fundamental rights to life, to personal integrity, to personal identity, to the development of personality, to a good name and reputation, to one's image and so on.

So the personality interests subject to personality rights are also subject to Fundamental rights and, in this way, also constitutionally guaranteed and protected.[14]

Some of these Fundamental rights take specific form in other Articles of the Constitution and are therefore guaranteed. Among the Articles are Article 32, paragraph 8; Article 34, paragraph 1; Article 35, paragraph 1; Article 37, paragraph 4; and Article 42, paragraph 2.[15]

4 The Protection of Personality Interests Under Constitutional Law and in Civil Law

The protection of personality interests under Constitutional law and in Civil law are not detailed separately. Instead, they are interconnected.

One of the problems that has been under discussion is the definition of the impact of Constitutional law in Civil law and, specifically, in the legal relations between private persons. This is above all important if in these relations the private persons are bound by the rules and principles enshrined in the Constitution, *maxime* the ones related to fundamental personal rights, freedoms and guarantees under Articles 24 *et seq*.

Portuguese authors have been divided on this subject. Currently, in the light of Article 18, paragraph 1, of the Constitution, the constitutional precepts with regard to rights, freedoms and guarantees are directly applicable to and binding on public and private entities.

At first glance, one would not have many doubts about the way that the Article is to be interpreted since it is written that these precepts are directly applicable and bind private persons. That is why in accordance with some authors, in fact a minority of them, these rules would have a direct impact on and a direct application to the relations between private persons (*teoria da eficácia imediata*).[16]

Other authors, in fact the majority, consider that the constitutional rules and principles only have an indirect impact on the relations between private persons (*teoria da eficácia mediata*). Fundamental rights and the rules related to them are

[14]Miranda (2014), pp. 73 *et seq*.

[15]See Menezes Cordeiro (2011), pp. 141 *et seq*.; Mota Pinto (2000), p. 156.

[16]Gomes Canotilho and Vital Moreira (2007), pp. 384 *et seq*. See, about this theory, Reis Novais (2006), pp. 73 *et seq*.; Miranda and Medeiros (2010), pp. 335 *et seq*.; Vieira de Andrade (2012), pp. 234 *et seq*.; Miranda (2014), pp. 337 *et seq*.

usually seen as rights of defence against the State and not against another fellow citizen.[17] Since in Article 18, paragraph 1, of the Constitution it is not explicit how private persons are bound to these rules, these authors maintain that it is essentially through Civil law rules that this application is made. The interpretation of all Civil law rules and of general clauses in particular in accordance with the Constitutional law ensures the impact of this law in the relations between private persons.[18] One example of these general clauses that can be given is Article 70, paragraph 1, of the Civil code on personality rights.

According to a third theory (*teoria dos deveres de proteção*), which presents several similarities with the second one above, it is the State's duty to legislate in order to assure that private persons are accorded the respect of Fundamental rights in their relations with other private persons. The courts would also have an important role when the ordinary law is not enough to guarantee the respect of these rights. In this case, in matters submitted for judgment, the courts should decide in accordance with the constitutional rules on Fundamental rights.[19]

Actually, the interpretation of Civil law rules must be made according to the Constitutional law on Fundamental rights. This procedure is most relevant when general clauses are applied since the legal concepts within are not narrow and so, when interpreting the law according to Constitutional law, the coherence of the whole legal system is also assured.

So bearing in mind that in Article 1 of the Constitution it is written that Portugal is a Republic based on the dignity of the human person, one must conclude that all the rules of the Civil code should be interpreted and applied in accordance with this principle. Likewise, if the Fundamental rights to life, to personal integrity, to the development of personality, to a good name and reputation, to one's image, to privacy are set out in Articles 24, 25, 26 of the Constitution, the interpretation of Civil code rules should accordingly be made with those rules of the Constitution.[20] This is also the reason why in the interpretation of Article 70 of the Civil code, account should be taken of those Fundamental rights. So, even the personality rights that are not explicitly set out in the Civil code can be recognised under Article 70, paragraph 1; for instance, the right to the development of personality is not explicitly established under any Article of the Civil code, but it is legally protected under Article 70, paragraph 1, because this Article must be interpreted according to Articles 1 and 26 of the Constitution, which recognise this right for everyone.[21]

---

[17]See, about this theory, Reis Novais (2006), pp. 72 *et seq.*; Miranda and Medeiros (2010), pp. 335 *et seq.*; Vieira de Andrade (2012), pp. 234 *et seq.*; Miranda (2014), pp. 337 *et seq.*

[18]Miranda and Medeiros (2010), p. 335; Vieira de Andrade (2012), p. 235.

[19]Reis Novais (2006), pp. 73 *et seq.*, 77 *et seq.*; Miranda and Medeiros (2010), p. 335; Vieira de Andrade (2012), pp. 239 *et seq.*

[20]Mota Pinto (2005), p. 43; Mota Pinto (1999), pp. 235 *et seq.*; Dias Oliveira (2012), pp. 591 *et seq.*, 601 *et seq.*

[21]Fundamental rights and personality rights are different from one another; see on this subject Melo Alexandrino (2007), pp. 32 *et seq.*; Miranda (2014), pp. 76 *et seq.*; Gomes Canotilho (2003), p. 396; Castro Mendes (1977), p. 111; Mota Pinto (2000), p. 155.

So Article 70, paragraph 1, of the Civil code is one good example of how the constitutional values can have a significant impact in Civil law. If a personality right is not explicitly established under the Civil code but the Constitutional law demands the protection of it, this can be done under Article 70 of the Civil code.

Still, Article 70 of the Civil code is not the only example of how the Constitutional law can have an impact on Civil law. Other general clauses and rules needing the interpretation of open concepts take a central role here because these concepts should be interpreted according to the Constitutional law. For instance, according to Article 280, paragraph 2, of the Civil code, any act set down in law that is contrary to public policy (*ordem pública*) or to morality (*bons costumes*) is invalid. The interpretation of these legal concepts in accordance with constitutional values assures, as it should, the impact of these values in the relations between private persons.[22]

In exceptional situations, according to authors such as Carlos Mota Pinto,[23] with whom I agree, when from the application of Civil law the legal effect is contrary to the constitutional rights, freedoms and guarantees, the direct application of a constitutional norm, without the mediation of a Civil law rule, may be accepted to regulate situations between private persons.[24] It is necessary, however, that this constitutional rule is able to be immediately applied, *i.e.*, that it is not just a programmatic rule, that it does not need another rule in order to be applicable.

Actually, the applicability of some constitutional rules depends on the initiative of an ordinary legislator. This can be seen, for instance, on the right to privacy. According to Article 26, paragraph 2, of the Constitution, guarantees against the improper procurement and misuse of information regarding persons and families or the use contrary to human dignity shall be set down by the Civil law.[25]

5 Agreements on Personality Rights

5.1 General Considerations

Personality rights, *melius*, some personality rights can be subject to agreements. If one takes as an example the right to one's image, we can see that according to Article 79, paragraph 1, of the Civil code, the exhibition, the reproduction or the commercial exploitation of a person's picture without his or her permission is forbidden. *A contrario sensu*, one can conclude that the commercial or other

[22]Vieira de Andrade (2012), pp. 257 *et seq.*

[23]Mota Pinto (2005), p. 75; Dias Oliveira (2012), pp. 600 *et seq.*

[24]See also Vieira de Andrade (2012), pp. 239 *et seq.*

[25]Mota Pinto (2000), p. 187.

exploitations of the right to one's image is admissible if its holder so authorises.[26,27] So it is possible to make an agreement having as its subject the image of a person.

More generally, also according to Article 81, paragraph 1, of the Civil code, the voluntary limitation of personality rights (right to one's image or other right) is invalid if contrary to public policy principles. This means—in a similar way as analysed about Article 79, paragraph 1, of the Civil code—*a contrario sensu*, that those agreements on personality rights are legally allowed since this is in accordance with public policy principles.[28]

Agreements on personality rights are frequent, for instance, within the exploitation of the image, voice, name of celebrities, such as professional sportsman and women, actors and singers. Usually for a charge, the personality right holder may allow someone else to undertake the exploitation of his right.[29,30] It is important, though, to emphasise that not all the agreements on personality rights are made for a charge; some of them are free of charge. One can easily agree to be a model, for free, to a photographer, to a painter or to a film director who is still learning and needs practice.

Given the nature of personality rights, it is not surprising that, according to Article 81, paragraph 2, of the Civil code, the personality rights limitations can always be revocable. However, if this revocation affects the legitimate expectations of the other part of the agreement and is the cause of damages, the personality right holder must pay compensation for it.[31]

For a better understanding of this situation, it is important to keep in mind that in the Portuguese legal system, the personality right is a complex legal reality. It can be said that all the personality rights have a personal part, but some of them have

[26] Festas (2009), pp. 275 *et seq.*; Menezes Cordeiro (2011), p. 249; Dias Oliveira (2015), p. 221.

[27] According to the Portuguese Supreme Court of Justice, the law permits that the right to one's image may be explored by public exhibition, by recording and by commercial exploitation (Judgment of 25 October 2005, Case No. 05A2577). See also, along the same lines, the Judgment of 7 June 2011, Case No. 1581/07.3TVLSB.L1S1 (Supreme Court of Justice). Available at www.dgsi.pt [Accessed on 30 June 2016].

[28] It is important to stress that the limitation of the exercise of personality rights must be clearly defined. For instance, if someone accepts to have their photo taken for an artistic work, this does not mean that that person accepts the use of those photographs for other goals, such as advertisements. See Judgment of 7th June 2011 (Supreme Court of Justice), note 27.

[29] Capelo de Sousa (1995), p. 246, note 560; Mota Pinto (2001), p. 551; Morais de Carvalho (2003), pp. 52 *et seq.*; Dias Oliveira (2015), p. 221.

[30] According to the 21 March 2012 Lisbon Court of Appeal judgment, the right to one's voice has a patrimonial content, besides the personal one. In this case, what was under litigation was a contract concluded between an actress and a company under which it was stipulated that, during a determined period of time, she should record, for a charge, messages that would be used in the company voicemail. After this period ended and the contract was terminated, the company kept using those records. The Court decided that the company could not do the commercial exploitation of the actress voice, otherwise one would be faced with before an unjustified enrichment. Case No. 1139/09.2YXLSB.L1-2 available at www.dgsi.pt [Accessed on 30 June 2016].

[31] See Dias Oliveira (2012), pp. 121 *et seq.*

also a commercial part.[32] This means that only some personality rights can be subject to agreements on their use for commercial purposes.

According to North American jurisprudence and authors, '(...) the inherent right of every human being to control the commercial use of his or her identity'[33] is called right of publicity. In the Portuguese legal system, I think one cannot talk about an autonomous right of publicity since the possibility to control the use of one's identity in a commercial sense is part of the right of personality.[34]

Besides the question of the commercial exploitation of personality rights, it is also important to stress that not all personality rights can be freely disposed by their holder.

For example, the right to life is a personality right that can and must be used by its holder and defended against anyone who decides to commit injury against it. But when this is a right that cannot be freely used by its own holder, *e.g.*, one cannot commit suicide,[35] one cannot charge for one's life. The commercial exploitation of life would be an act against public policy. In a similar way, personal integrity cannot be commercially exploited, nor can it be freely limited.

However, it is legally allowed for a person to submit himself or herself to medical or drug experimentations that may put life or personal integrity at risk. In the same way, it is also legal for someone to allow his kidney to be taken in order to be used as a transplant for another person. But it would not be legally allowed for a person to charge for a kidney. Actually, under Article 5, paragraph 1, of Law No. 12/93 of 22 April 1993[36]—which rules organ donation and transplantation—the donation of organs, tissues and cells for therapeutic purposes can never be gainful. Its commercialisation is forbidden. But even if this rule did not exist, the selling of a kidney would be invalid because it is contrary to public policy, as set out in Article 81, paragraph 1, of the Civil code.

The voluntary limitation may concern other personality rights apart from life or personal integrity. It may concern rights of personality such as image, voice, name, which may be used both in a personal and in a commercial way. For instance, a person can either object or allow someone to take his or her photograph, and by doing so, one is seizing the right to one's own image in a personal sense. But one may also charge to allow another person to take and publish the photographs. So the

[32]Festas (2009), p. 124; Dias Oliveira (2012), pp. 118 *et seq.*; Mota Pinto (2001), p. 551.

[33]McCarthy (1999–2002), vol. 1, 2002, § 1:3, p. 1-2.1.

[34]Festas (2009), pp. 405 *et seq.*; Menezes Cordeiro (2011), pp. 247 *et seq.*; Dias Oliveira (2012), 118 *et seq.*; Dias Oliveira (2015), pp. 220 *et seq.*

[35]Pessoa Jorge (1968), p. 196; Pais de Vasconcelos (2006), p. 153; Pais de Vasconcelos (2015), pp. 37 and 57; Leite de Campos (1992), p. 59. A different interpretation is given by Brandão Proença (1997), pp. 96 *et seq.*, note 251. According to this, each person has the freedom to use legal drugs, practice self-mutilation, or commit suicide. About this discussion, see Dias Oliveira (2012), pp. 120 and 307.

[36]The Law No. 12/93 of 22 April 1993, Official Gazette, was amended by the Laws No. 22/2007 of 29 June 2007, No. 12/2009 of 26 March 2009, No. 36/2013 of 12 June 2013 and by the Decree-Law No. 168/2015 of 21 August 2015.

right of one's image may be seized both in a personal and in a commercial sense. Also in this case, the voluntary limitation of this right is invalid if contrary to public policy.

Article 81, paragraph 1, of the Civil code is, actually, redundant since under the general clause set out in Article 280, paragraph 2, of the Civil code, the legal acts contrary to public policy are invalid.[37] Also according to Article 280, paragraph 1, of the Civil code, legal acts contrary to the law or morality are invalid as well, and there is no reason not to apply this rule to the voluntary limitation of personality rights.[38]

The reason why there is an explicit reference just to public policy in Article 81, paragraph 1, of the Civil code could be justified by the special nature of personality rights.

Still, public policy is, as said before, an open concept, which is not explicitly consolidated in the Civil code. It must be defined according to the values of the community, reflected in the constitutional rules and principles.[39] The importance of these values is such that it must prevail even in agreements between private persons.[40] Therefore, those agreements in which personality rights are limited in a way that is contrary to the dignity of human[41] or Fundamental rights[42] will be considered invalid because they do not respect public policy.

It is also important to stress that the interpretation and the definition of the concept of public policy may change, and it has changed over the years, in accordance with the modification of society's own values.

Even when the personality rights limitation is valid, according to Article 81, paragraph 2, of the Civil code, as said before, the agreement can always be revocable, notwithstanding the compensation that the personality right holder should pay to those others who had legitimate expectations and were harmed by this revocation.

Still, under the general regime of Contract law, when the personality right holder concludes a contract, he or she can declare, if the other part agrees with it, that he reserves the right to revoke the agreement according to his or her will or if the circumstances specified in the contract are verified.[43] Should this be the case, there will be no obligation to pay damages to other party since the revocation terms were agreed by both parties.

The solution enshrined in Article 81, paragraph 2, of the Civil code, allowing this free revocation, is not a surprise since the dignity of the human person is at

---

[37]Pais de Vasconcelos (2015), p. 53.

[38]Menezes Cordeiro (2011), p. 119; Pais de Vasconcelos (2006), p. 155; Pais de Vasconcelos (2015), pp. 52 *et seq.*; Dias Oliveira (2012), p. 121.

[39]Oliveira Ascensão (2000), pp. 281 *et seq.*; Pais de Vasconcelos (2015), pp. 517 *et seq.*

[40]Mota Pinto (2005), pp. 557 *et seq.*

[41]Article 1 of the Constitution.

[42]Specifically Articles 24 *et seq.* of the Constitution.

[43]Mota Pinto (2001), pp. 555 *et seq.*

stake, along with rights that are important for the development of a person, and these should prevail.

Naturally, even the right to revoke should have limits. For instance, if someone gave a kidney to a person and the transplant has already occurred, the donor cannot revoke her organ donation, asking for the kidney back.

Concerning compensation, it is clear that the harm caused by the revocation and suffered by the ones who had legitimate expectations should be redressed. However, the value of the compensation should not be so high that it, in fact, hinders the right to revoke.[44]

5.2 *Agreements Related to the Commercial Use of the Image of Professional Sportsmen*

In the Portuguese legal system, professional sportsmen's right to use their image commercially is stipulated in Law No. 28/98 of 26 July 1998,[45] under Article 10, according to which professional sportsmen have the right to use their public image, which is associated to their sport, and he or she also has also the right to prevent someone else from using it without authorisation. Accordingly, also under Article 38, paragraph 2, of the Collective Employment Contract signed by the Portuguese Professional Football League and the Professional Football Players Union, the right to use and exploit the image of a player is held by the player himself, though he can assign this right to the football club with which he has a sports contract and while the contract is in force.[46]

In the light of this legal reality, authors such as Oliveira Ascensão[47] argue that the commercial use of professional sportsmen's and sportswomen's image within their sports contract does not have the ethical value demanded by the Portuguese legal system to guarantee the personality rights. So, he concludes, the personality

[44]Pais de Vasconcelos (2006), p. 168.

[45]The Law No. 28/98 of 26 July 1998, Official Gazette, was amended by the Law No. 114/99 of 3 August 1999.

[46]According to the Portuguese Supreme Court of Justice, in the above mentioned judgement of 25 October 2005 (note 27), the agreement, for a charge, on the commercial exploitation of the professional sportsman's image, taken as being in force for a limited period is valid for it is not contrary to the public policy. The Lisbon Court of Appeal, in a judgement dated 18 December 2007, decided that, although the right to one's image is inalienable and cannot be waived, the limitation of the exercise of this right is not forbidden, specifically the cession to others, by football players of their right to use their own image as professional sportsmen. The Court decided that both Article 79, para 1, of the Civil code and Article 10 of Law No. 28/98 were violated by a company owner of a magazine that published stamps with the football players' photographs without their consent nor the consent of those to whom the football players had given the right to exploit their image commercially and exclusively. This company was ordered to compensate the company for material damages and the football players for moral damages.

[47]Oliveira Ascensão (2000), pp. 99 and 79.

rights' legal regime as set out in the Civil code cannot be applied to the commercial use of a professional athlete's image. This author also argues that since the commercial use of such an image benefits from specific regulation, the general legal regime on personality rights protection should not be applied. In this case, advocates Oliveira Ascensão, only the regulation of a patrimonial situation would be at stake, there being no truly ethic substance.

Similarly, Moura Vicente[48] argues that the right to commercial use of the professional sportsmen's and sportswomen's image is not subject to the legal restrictions provided in the Portuguese legal regime on the transmission *inter vivos* of personality rights. According to this author, this right of commercial use would be classified not as a personality right but as an exclusive right *sui generis*, covered by provisions in the law.

In my opinion, one can accept that the commercial use of the right to one's image may have a lesser ethical density than when one talks about its non-commercial use; the values involved are different. However, it is also true that the personality legal interest beneath—the image—cannot be sundered, and so being, the commercial use of the image may affect the non-commercial use of it.

In the specific situation of the commercial use and exploitation of an athlete's image right, it is possible to enter into contracts that authorise its assignment to other persons than the athlete. If one keeps in mind that the image of a person, whether a celebrity or not, is inseparable from the person himself or herself and that the release of it will always have an impact on his or her individuality, and/or identity, it is easier to understand that the commercial and the non-commercial use of the personality right cannot be seen as separate issues. So, even though one can talk about the use of a personality right in a commercial and a non-commercial way, this division is artificial for the right cannot be sundered. It is one and only one.

So, personality rights, like Fundamental rights, are, by nature, undetachable and non-transferable,[49] and any voluntary limitation to the personal use of the personality rights, such as an agreement in which authorisation is given for its commercial use by others than the rightful holder, can affect also the non-commercial use. Therefore, in my opinion, the agreements on the commercial use of personality rights are also subject to the general legal regime of personality rights—with the exception of any and all special rules in force—and according to Article 81, paragraph 1, of the Civil code are always revocable.

If one admits that agreements on the commercial use of personality rights are unilaterally irrevocable, one would also have to admit that the personality right at stake would be transferable,[50] which is not admissible because it would be contrary

[48]Moura Vicente (2008), pp. 277 *et seq*.

[49]According to the 22 September 2005 Lisbon Court of Appeal judgement, Case No 5011/2004-6, personality rights are innate, cannot be waived and inalienable. Available at www.dgsi.pt [Accessed on 30 June 2016].

[50]According to the 21 March 2012 Lisbon Court of Appeal judgement above mentioned (note 30), the contract under which an actress should record voice messages for a company, could not have as an effect the transmission of the actress's right to her voice nor the transmission of the recording

to the dignity of the human person (Article 1 of the Constitution). So, I maintain that the agreements related to the commercial use of the image of professional athletes can, in accordance with Article 81, paragraph 2, of the Civil code, be revoked by them even if damages must be paid to those who had legitimate expectations under the agreement.[51] One can argue that neither Law No. 28/98 of 26 July 1998 nor the Collective Employment Contract signed by the Portuguese Professional Football League and the Professional Football Players Union admits the possibility of revocation and that these are special rules. But it also can be said, as I do, that there is no reason to limit the application of the personality rights general regime, which only completes what is ruled in the special law. Besides, the inapplicability of Article 81, paragraph 2, of the Civil code would, in these cases, be contrary to Articles 1 and 26 of the Constitution,[52] and, as stressed before, the interpretation of Civil law must be done in the light of the Constitutional law.

Furthermore, under Article 26, paragraph 1, of the Constitution, recognition is also made of the Fundamental right to the development of personality. Despite this right not being explicitly set out in a Civil code rule, as said before, the interpretation of Article 70, paragraph 1, of the Civil code must be made in accordance with the constitutional rules and principles.

According to Paulo Mota Pinto,[53] the right to personal development aims both at the protection of personality, since this development is an essential part of everyone's individuality, and also at the general protection of freedom, in the sense that everyone should be able to decide how to act.[54] Therefore, the right to personal development should also be protected within the relations between private persons; in order to guarantee that, the right to personal development is now also recognised as a personality right, which benefits from the protection and remedies stipulated in Civil law.

---

property rights. The voice, which is subject to a personality right and to a fundamental right cannot be transmitted; it only can be limited. If one entered into a contract stipulating the transmission of it, this agreement would be invalid as being contrary to public policy (Article 81, para 1, of the Civil code).

[51]Dias Oliveira (2012), pp. 121 *et seq.*; Palma Ramalho (2012), pp. 796 *et seq.*; Dias Oliveira (2015), p. 224. Differently, see Moura Vicente (2008), pp. 277 *et seq.*; Morais de Carvalho (2003), pp. 56 and 64 *et seq.*, advocates that if someone authorizes the use by others of his or her own personality rights in order to promote goods or services, they cannot, afterwards, unilaterally revoke it. If they do, they will have to pay damages. Festas (2009), pp. 377 *et seq.*, advocates that in order to decide if the revocation is or is not admissible, one must take into account the reason behind this act. One can only admit the unilateral revocation of the agreement if the protection of personal values is at stake and not commercial assets even if related to personality rights.

[52]Mota Pinto (1993), p. 502, stresses that forcing someone to accomplish an obligation that results from a limitation of personality rights would be against the most basic personal rights. According to Leite de Campos (2006), p. 145, any limitation to personality rights is invalid if it does not aim for the free development of personality in respect to the ethical values. See also Pais de Vasconcelos (2015), pp. 53 *et seq.*; Dias Oliveira (2012), pp. 121 *et seq.*

[53]Mota Pinto (2000), p. 160.

[54]Mota Pinto (2000), p. 160; Otero (2010), p. 42.

During their lifetime, people change the direction they have taken for their lives, and it may be important to the personal development of anyone to amend decisions taken before. For instance, one can think of athletes who authorised publication of their naked photographs; years later, the direction their life took—*e.g.*, their religious orientations—may have the result that they do not feel comfortable with the earlier decision. In coherence with their personal development and in order to fulfil themselves as a person, it may be crucial for them to revoke the decision previously given to publish photographs taken years earlier.[55] In this case, I maintain that the athletes, according to Article 81, paragraph 2, of the Civil code, should be able to revoke their authorisation and compensate those with legitimate expectations who were harmed because of this decision. There is no reason, as far as I understand it, to limit the application of Article 81, paragraph 2, of the Civil code in these cases. It is the refusal to apply this rule that may be contrary to the constitutional rules and principles.

However, it is also clear that the exercise of this right to revoke has limits. For instance, one should refuse the exercise of any right in the case of abuse of rights.[56] Under Article 334 of the Civil code, the exercise of a right is illegitimate when its holder manifestly exceeds the limits imposed by good faith (*bona fides*), morality or the social and economic goals of that right.[57]

5.3 Other Agreements Relating to Personality Rights

Besides professional athletes, other people may enter into contracts relating to personality rights, whether they intended to make commercial or non-commercial use of these rights.

The most common examples of these contracts are the ones signed by professional models under which they authorise the use of their image by others or famous actors who do voice-overs in animation films or advertisements and receive a payment in return. Although the right to one's voice is not specifically set out either in the Civil code or in the Constitution, considering that it expresses most clearly the identity of each individual, it has been understood that this right should also be qualified, under Article 70, paragraph 1, of the Civil code, as a right of personality. In the light of this, the right to one's voice benefits from the general legal regime applied to personality rights.

[55]Sousa Ribeiro (1999), p. 433, note 436.

[56]Pais de Vasconcelos (2006), p. 167; Mota Pinto (2001), p. 558.

[57]About abuse of rights, see Ewald Hörster (2003), pp. 280 *et seq.*; Menezes Cordeiro (2015), pp. 269 *et seq.*; Pais de Vasconcelos (2015), pp. 240 *et seq.*; Carvalho Fernandes (2001), pp. 585 *et seq.*; Pires de Lima and Antunes Varela (1988), pp. 555 *et seq.*

In other cases, people may admit limitations to their privacy, by authorising the publication of interviews and reports about their private lives. In return, these persons may receive payments or just public notoriety.

The right to privacy is both a fundamental right (Article 26, paragraph 1, of the Constitution) and a personality right expressly established under Article 80 of the Civil code. According to paragraph 1 of this Article, everyone should be discrete about the private life of others, and in paragraph 2, the extent of this discretion is set out, defined according to the nature of the situation and the status of the persons. This means that the information that can be disclosed about different persons may not be the same. If one thinks about celebrities—politicians, actors, singers, entertainers, athletes, socialites—one may admit a relevant and justifiable public interest in their lives that gives a good reason for disclosure; it even may be relevant because of previous public declarations made by such persons.[58] For instance, if a politician expresses opposition in public to the showing of a film and then goes to the cinema to see it, it is legitimate for this information to be disclosed. Obviously, the information disclosed must always respect the person in question's human dignity, and so the interpretation of this paragraph must also take the Constitution into account.

The right to privacy can also be the subject of agreement, in accordance with Article 81, paragraph 1, of the Civil code, as long as it is not contrary to public policy. Therefore, an agreement stipulating neither an irrevocable renouncement of the right of privacy nor its limitation for far too long a period would be acceptable.[59] In order to be valid, the agreement on the limitation of the right of privacy must be defined both materially and temporally.

In some cases, more controversially, some people agree to their privacy being seriously restricted by authorising their daily life to be recorded, even in the most private situations, 24 hours a day, for several weeks, and broadcasted on television and the Internet. In these TV shows, the participants also accept to be submitted to a vote, in which it will be decided who will continue on the program, effectively acting like elements in a game. Here, one can ask if the agreement related to the limitation of the right of privacy and of the right to image is contrary to the dignity of the human person and, if so, consequently, contrary to the public policy.

According to Pais de Vasconcelos,[60] some broadcasted *reality shows* can call into question the dignity of the human person, and the benefits resulting from it to the participants cannot compensate this injury. Besides, it is clear that the respect of one's right of privacy contributes to guarantee the dignity of the human person.[61]

Vasconcelos de Abreu,[62] on the other hand, considers that the problem should not be faced from a paternalist perspective, in which the person is protected from

---

[58]Mota Pinto (2000), p. 195.

[59]Mota Pinto (2000), p. 191; Mota Pinto (2001), p. 546.

[60]Pais de Vasconcelos (2006), p. 165.

[61]On this question, Mota Pinto (2000), p. 164, quotes the decision No. 263/97 by the Constitutional Court of Portugal.

[62]Vasconcelos Abreu (2005), pp. 116 *et seq.*

himself or herself in order not to injure his or her own dignity. Bearing in mind that the essential core of the dignity of the human person is based on the freedom to choose the guidance of one's life, this author concludes that the intent of the Constitution is to protect freedom of choice and not to limit it, not to force everyone to follow the same course of action.[63]

The truth is that in the Portuguese society, as in other countries, these reality shows have been accepted and usually attract large audiences.

However, it must be stressed that there should always be limits to the freedom of choice, and in some cases the State must protect the person from himself or herself; such is the example of suicide or the irreversible loss of a human organ.

The agreements on personality rights may or may not have a monetary consideration. In both cases, there is always a voluntary limitation of the personality rights and, according to Article 81, paragraph 2, of the Civil code, this limitation is always revocable, even if the agreement stipulates exclusively on the commercial use of personality rights.

6 A Clash of Rights

It may not be possible to reconcile the personality rights of different holders, for instance in cases where personality rights may conflict with other rights or freedoms.

Also the exercise of the right of revocation of personality rights by voluntary limitation may conflict with the other person's rights or freedoms also enshrined in the Constitution, such as the freedom of speech, artistic freedom, private enterprise.

As set out in Article 37, paragraph 1, of the Constitution, everyone has the right to freely express and divulge their thoughts in words, in images or by any other means. Under Article 37, paragraph 4, the notion is enshrined that every natural and legal person shall be equally and effectively ensured the right of reply and to make correction, as well as the right to compensation through damages awarded.

The freedom of cultural creation is set out in Article 42 of the Constitution. In accordance with Article 42, paragraph 1, there shall be freedom of intellectual, artistic and scientific creation, and, as set out in paragraph 2, this freedom comprises the right to invent, produce and divulge scientific and artistic work and includes the protection of copyright law.

In accordance with Article 61, paragraph 1, private economic enterprise shall be undertaken freely within the overall framework defined by the Constitution and the law and with regard for the general interest.

Personality rights,[64] like the Fundamental rights[65] and freedoms, may be limited, for there is no such thing as absolute and total rights in the sense that, according to

---

[63]Reis Novais (2006), p. 31; Mota Pinto (2001), pp. 547 *et seq.*

[64]Menezes Cordeiro (2011), p. 102.

[65]Reis Novais (2006), p. 49.

the specific circumstances, these rights may have to give way before other rights or values. And bearing in mind these rights and freedoms, one can easily think of situations in which the revocation of the voluntary limitation of personality rights may clash with it. For example, a photographer hires a model to take artistic naked photos and shows them in different public exhibitions. Some months later, the model changes her way of life and decides that the exhibition of those photos is against her personal development plan and asks the photographer not to go on using these photos, whether in exhibitions or other places, and to give her the photos and all the corresponding back-ups he has. One can identify here a clear conflict between the right to the development of one's personality and the right to one's image on the one hand and on the other the freedom of expression and the freedom of cultural creation. However, it is important to highlight that these freedoms may also be an expression of the right to personal development. The way to one's own personal development may be through the creation of artistic works and the dissemination of these.[66]

Since the example given is about private relations and not about one private person against the State, the solution to this conflict should be looked for in the Civil law rules, although interpreted according to the constitutional rules and principles. Actually, there is no explicit rule in the Constitution[67] to clarify any situation related to a conflict of rights such as the one under analysis.[68]

According to Article 335, paragraph 1, of the Civil code, in cases of a clash between rights,[69] these being of the same species, the right holders should give way part of their rights in order to allow for each right to produce as many effects as possible without prejudice to the other part. The goal is, then, to permit the restriction of one's rights so that others can benefit from their own rights also. According to Article 335, paragraph 2, of the Civil code, if the rights concerned are not equal or of the same species, the one that should prevail is the one that is considered to be superior.

The best solution, in this case, would be to find a balance between the interests of both parties. If this is not possible, one should keep in mind that the interpretation of legal rules should be made taking into account the global legal system and that also Article 335 of the Civil code must be interpreted and applied within the other rules

[66]Miranda and Medeiros (2010), pp. 923 *et seq.*

[67]Miranda and Medeiros (2010), p. 851.

[68]Although, also under the Constitutional Law, collision of rights can occur. According to Vieira de Andrade (2012), pp. 298 *et seq.*, to solve these problems, one should balance the consequences of the exercise of the specific rights under analyses, and try to find a solution in accordance with Constitutional values.

[69]About the collision of rights in the Portuguese legal system, see Ewald Hörster (2003), pp. 280 *et seq.*; Menezes Cordeiro (2015), pp. 411 *et seq.*; Pais de Vasconcelos (2015), pp. 262 *et seq.*; Carvalho Fernandes (2001), pp. 581 *et seq.*; Pires de Lima and Antunes Varela (1988), pp. 555 *et seq.*

of the Civil code. And, according to Article 81, paragraph 2, of the Civil code, the voluntary limitation of the personality rights is *always* revocable. The right to damages to be received by persons with legitimate expectations regarding the effects of the agreements will be protected only through compensation.[70]

However, in some cases, the holder of the personality right may, according to Article 334 of the Civil code, act as if this was an abuse of rights.[71] As said before, under Article 334 of the Civil code, if the holder of the right manifestly exceeds the limits imposed by good faith, morality or the social and economic goals of that right, its exercise is illegitimate. So, if in the described situation of the model and the photographer the model only wants to revoke her authorisation in order to harm the photographer's career or to negotiate with others the exhibition of the same or other photographs, one would, most probably, be faced with a problem of abuse of rights, for the behaviour of the model is contrary to good faith and does not fill the social goal of the right to revoke as is established in Article 81, paragraph 2, of the Civil code. Actually, this right aims to assure the human person's dignity through the personality rights. If the exercise of the right to revoke does not, in the individual case, have as its aim the guarantee of human dignity but have other goals such as the ones described, the exercise of the right should be considered illegitimate.

7 Conclusion

The rules and principles enshrined in the Portuguese Constitution are real binding rules with which the Civil law, and specifically Contract law, must be in accordance. In order to grant it, the Constitutional Court may undertake evaluation of the constitutionality of the laws before and possibly even after they are enacted. Also, the courts may not apply unconstitutional rules.

According to the Portuguese legal system, agreements on some personality rights are possible. However, the subject matter of these contracts concerns personality rights, and the subject of these rights are legal interests that are also subject to Fundamental rights enshrined in the Constitution. It follows that the Civil law rules governing these agreements must be set out in accordance with the Constitutional law. The interpretation of these rules must also be made according to the Constitution, especially when general clauses and rules with open concepts are applied.

Naturally, only some personality rights can be subject to agreements. And bearing in mind the nature of these rights, it is not surprising that even the agreed limitations of these rights can be revoked by their holder, in accordance with the law.

[70]See, on this question, Mota Pinto (2001), p. 558.

[71]Mota Pinto (2001), p. 558.

Agreements related to the commercial use of the image of professional sportsmen and sportswomen are stipulated in special law. Portuguese authors have discussed whether this is still a question of personality rights limitation or if this right of commercial use should not be classified as a personality right. For the reasons expressed above, these agreements are, in my opinion, also subject to the general legal regime of personality rights.

References

Amaral Cabral R (1989) O Direito à intimidade da vida privada (Breve reflexão acerca do art. 80.° do Código Civil). In: Estudos em memória do Professor Doutor Paulo Cunha, Lisboa, pp 373–406

Antunes Varela J (1982–1984) Alterações legislativas do direito ao nome, Revista de Legislação de Jurisprudência, Year 114: n. 3688, pp 207–212; n. 3689, pp 229–233, n. 3690, pp 260–261, n. 3691, pp 293, 297, n. 3692, pp 323, n. 3693, pp 357–359; Year 115: n. 3694, pp 7–9, n. 3695, pp 37–40, n. 3696, pp 68–72, n. 3700, pp 196–201; Year 116: n. 3710, pp 140–146, n. 3714, pp. 257–258, n. 3715, pp 289–293; Year 117: n. 3721, pp 97–100, n. 3722, pp. 133–136, n. 3723, pp 161–165, n. 3724, pp 196–200, n. 3726, pp 257–262, n. 3729, pp 353–357; Year 118: n 3738, pp 262–267, n. 3739, pp 293–298, n. 3740, pp 321–324; Year 119: n. 3748, pp 197–200

Antunes Varela J (2000) Das Obrigações em geral, vol I, 10th edn. Almedina, Coimbra

Blanco de Morais C (2011) Justiça Constitucional, vol II. Coimbra Editora, Coimbra

Brandão Proença JC (1997) A conduta do lesado como pressuposto e critério de imputação do dano extracontratual. Almedina, Coimbra

Cabral de Moncada L (1995) Lições de Direito Civil, 4th edn. Almedina, Coimbra

Capelo de Sousa R (1995) O direito geral de personalidade. Coimbra Editora, Coimbra

Carvalho Fernandes L (2001) Teoria Geral do Direito Civil, vol I, 3rd edn. Universidade Católica Editora, Lisboa

Carvalho O (1981) Teoria Geral do Direito Civil. Centelha, Coimbra

Castro Mendes J (1977) Direitos, liberdades e garantias – alguns aspectos gerais. In: Estudos sobre a Constituição, vol 1, pp 93–141

Dias Oliveira E (2012) Da responsabilidade civil extracontratual por violação de direitos de personalidade em Direito Internacional Privado. Almedina, Coimbra

Dias Oliveira E (2015) A relevância do right of publicity no âmbito da propriedade intelectual. In: Estudos de Direito Intelectual. Almedina, Coimbra, pp 209–232

Ewald Hörster H (2003) A parte geral do Código Civil português. Almedina, Coimbra

Festas D (2009) Do conteúdo patrimonial do direito à imagem, Contributo para um estudo do seu aproveitamento consentido e *intervivos*. Coimbra Editora, Coimbra

Gomes Canotilho JJ (2003) Direito Constitucional e Teoria da Constituição, 7th edn. Almedina, Coimbra

Gomes Canotilho JJ, Vital Moreira (2007) Constituição da República Portuguesa anotada, vol I, 4th edn. Coimbra Editora, Coimbra

Gomes Canotilho JJ, Vital Moreira (2010) Constituição da República Portuguesa anotada, vol II, 4th edn. Coimbra Editora, Coimbra

Gomes da Silva M (1944) O dever de prestar e o dever de indemnizar, Lisboa

Gomes da Silva M (1965) Esboço de uma concepção personalista do Direito, Revista da Faculdade de Direito da Universidade de Lisboa, XVII, Lisboa

Leite de Campos D (1992) Lições de direitos de personalidade, 2nd edn. Coimbra

Leite de Campos D (2006) A relação da pessoa consigo mesma. In: Comemorações dos 35 anos do Código Civil e dos 25 anos da reforma de 1977, vol II. Coimbra Editora, Coimbra, pp 139–145

McCarthy JT (1999–2002) The rights of publicity and privacy, vol 1 and 2, 2nd edn. West Group, St. Paul
Melo Alexandrino J (2007) Direitos Fundamentais: Introdução geral. Principia, Estoril
Melo Alexandrino J (2015) Lições de Direito Constitucional, vol II. AAFDL, Lisboa
Menezes Cordeiro A (2011) Tratado de Direito Civil, IV, Parte Geral, Pessoas, 3rd edn. Almedina, Coimbra
Menezes Cordeiro A (2015) Tratado de Direito Civil, V, Parte Geral, Exercício Jurídico, 2nd edn. Almedina, Coimbra
Menezes Leitão L (1996) O enriquecimento sem causa no direito civil, Cadernos de Ciência e Técnica Fiscal, 176
Miranda J (2013) Manual de Direito Constitucional, vol VI, 4th edn. Coimbra Editora, Coimbra
Miranda J (2014) Manual de Direito Constitucional, vol II, 5th edn. Coimbra Editora, Coimbra
Miranda J, Medeiros R (2010) Constituição Portuguesa anotada, vol I, 2nd edn. Wolters Kluwer, Coimbra Editora, Coimbra
Morais de Carvalho MM (2003) Merchandising de marcas (A comercialização do valor sugestivo das marcas). Almedina, Coimbra
Mota Pinto CA (2005) In: António Pinto M, Mota Pinto P (eds) Teoria Geral do Direito Civil, 4th edn. Coimbra Editora, Coimbra
Mota Pinto P (1993) O direito à reserva sobre a intimidade da vida privada. Boletim da Faculdade de Direito da Universidade de Coimbra, LXIX, pp 479–585
Mota Pinto P (1999) O direito ao livre desenvolvimento da personalidade. In: Portugal-Brasil Ano 2000. Coimbra Editora, Coimbra, pp 149–246
Mota Pinto P (2000) A protecção da vida privada e a Constituição. Boletim da Faculdade de Direito da Universidade de Coimbra, LXXVI, pp 153–204
Mota Pinto P (2001) A limitação voluntária do direito à reserva sobre a intimidade da vida privada. In: Estudos em Homenagem a Cunha Rodrigues, vol II. Coimbra Editora, Coimbra, pp 527–558
Moura Vicente D (2008) A tutela internacional da propriedade intelectual. Almedina, Coimbra
Oliveira Ascensão J (2000) Direito Civil Teoria Geral, vol I, 2nd edn. Coimbra Editora, Coimbra
Oliveira Ascensão J (2002) A reserva da intimidade da vida privada e familiar. Revista da Faculdade de Direito da Universidade de Lisboa, XLIII, pp 9–25
Otero P (2010) O Direito Constitucional Português, Identidade Constitucional, vol I. Almedina, Coimbra
Pais de Vasconcelos P (2006) Direito de Personalidade. Almedina, Coimbra
Pais de Vasconcelos P (2015) Teoria Geral do Direito Civil, 8th edn. Almedina, Coimbra
Palma Ramalho MR (2012) O direito à imagem dos desportistas. Notas breves. In: Centenário do Nascimento do Professor Doutor Paulo Cunha. Estudos em Homenagem, Almedina, Coimbra, pp 791–801
Pessoa Jorge F (1968) Ensaio sobre os pressupostos da responsabilidade civil, Almedina, Coimbra (reprinted in 1995)
Pires de Lima F, Antunes Varela J (1988) Código Civil anotado, vol I. Coimbra Editora, Coimbra
Ribeiro de Faria J (1990) Direito das Obrigações, vol I. Almedina, Coimbra
Reis Novais J (2006) Direitos Fundamentais, Trunfos contra a maioria. Coimbra Editora, Coimbra
Sinde Monteiro J (2007) Responsabilidade delitual. Da ilicitude. In: Comemorações dos 35 anos do Código Civil e dos 25 anos da reforma de 1977, vol III. Coimbra Editora, Coimbra, pp 453–481
Sousa Ribeiro J (1999) O problema do contrato, As cláusulas contratuais gerais e o princípio da liberdade contratual. Almedina, Coimbra
Trabuco C (2001) Dos contratos relativos ao direito à imagem. O Direito, 133, pp 389–459
Vasconcelos Abreu L (2005) Limitação do direito à reserva sobre a intimidade da vida privada mediante o acordo do seu titular. O caso do *Big Brother*, Revista do Ministério Público, 101, pp 113–118
Vieira de Andrade JC (2012) Os direitos fundamentais na Constituição Portuguesa de 1976, 5th edn. Almedina, Coimbra

The Constitutional Aspect of Canadian Contract Law

Nicolas Lambert

Abstract Constitutions are generally viewed as foundational to other disciplines, especially when they are written and entrenched as in Canada. This 'top-down' perspective provides a partial and arguably fragmented view of Canadian Contract law. The reason is that it does not explain the relationship between the Common law and the Constitution and their reciprocal dynamics. At Common law, the unwritten law is understood as 'foundational' to statute and written law. The problem that arises in Canada is that there does not appear to be a uniform 'general law' that is truly national. Section 92(13) of the Constitution Act, 1867, confers jurisdiction over 'property and civil rights' to provincial legislatures. As a result, Canadian Contract law could be viewed as divided territorially. This view is difficult to sustain in that Canadian unwritten law cannot be a mere transposition of the Common law rules that are otherwise associated with provincial jurisdiction. The alternate question asks to what extent the Canadian Constitution presupposes *ius commune*, i.e. a reservoir of unwritten legal concepts that underlie the Constitution itself. From this perspective, it is not the Constitution that creates Contract law but rather private contractualism that becomes a backbone of the written document. This essay proposes to examine this proposition by providing a reinterpretation of constitutional jurisprudence related to contracts in both of Canada's Constitution Act, 1867, and the Constitution Act, 1982.

1 Introduction

Constitutions are generally viewed as foundational to other disciplines, especially when they are written and entrenched as in Canada. The consequence of this view is that Constitutional law is seen as 'framing' other disciplines, such as contracts. Contract law, from this perspective, becomes a derivative of the Constitution while at the same time marginalising the social and economic role played by the institution of contracts themselves. Contracts could well have a 'constitutional' role depending on how we define the concept of 'Constitution', although this is

N. Lambert (✉)
Faculty of Law, Université de Moncton, Moncton, NB, Canada
e-mail: nicolas.lambert@umoncton.ca

L. Siliquini-Cinelli, A. Hutchison (eds.), *The Constitutional Dimension of Contract Law*, DOI 10.1007/978-3-319-49843-0_10

generally not the view taken by jurists. That being said, Canadian Confederation in 1867 and decolonisation make the traditional view difficult to sustain because English Contract law predates Canadian constitutionalism. The Canadian Constitution thus never truly 'created' Contract law, and we do not doubt that Canada is alone in this position. The traditional view—the 'top-down' constitutional perspective, provides a partial and arguably fragmented view of contractualism. The reason is that it does not explain the relationship between the Common law and the Constitution and their reciprocal dynamics. As Australian jurist Sir Owen Dixon once stated:

> It is easy to treat the written instrument as the paramount consideration, unmindful of the part played by the general law, notwithstanding that it is the source of the legal conceptions that govern us in determining the effect of the written instrument.[1]

In a similar line of thought, the Constitution Act, 1867, states in its Preamble that Canada is to have a 'Constitution similar in Principle to that of the United Kingdom'. As a result, much of the Constitution Act, 1867, presupposes an 'unwritten law' of the land. The key words that we would like to emphasise in this phrase, however, are 'similar in Principle'. The problem that arises in Canada, indeed, is that there does not appear to be a uniform 'general law' that is truly national. Section 92(13) of the Constitution Act, 1867, confers jurisdiction over 'property and civil rights' to provincial legislatures.[2] As a result, Canadian Contract law could be viewed as divided territorially. However, Canadian Common law provinces cannot accurately be described as having different Common law regimes as do American states because the Supreme Court of Canada does not generally treat each province differently when it comes to the Common law.[3] Canada does not have an independent and final system of 'provincial courts' wielding jurisdiction over Private law; even Quebec courts are subject to the supervisory jurisdiction of the Supreme Court of Canada. Common law precedents from Canada's highest court apply throughout Common law Canada, and it is for each individual province to adapt them through statute.[4] On the other hand, even if Canadian Common law provinces are unified through the supervisory jurisdiction of the Supreme Court of Canada, Quebec's Private law remains necessarily written in the Civil code of Quebec.[5]

Thus, the question that arises is whether there can be a national 'unwritten law' that transcends the Constitution itself and that is truly national in that it is not a mere transposition of the Common law. The question that arises is therefore to what extent the Constitution presupposes a *ius commune*. This can be defined as the

---

[1]Dixon (1957), pp. 241–245.

[2]Constitution Act, 1867 (UK), 30 & 31 Vict, c 3 ('Constitution Act, 1867') reprinted in RSC 1985, Appendix II, No. 5.

[3]For purposes of simplification, the term 'Canadian' will be understood as 'common law Canada', in contradistinction to the province of Quebec.

[4]Hogg (2011), para 7.1(a).

[5]Civil code of Québec, CQLR c C-1991.

'reservoir of legal concepts and rules that will implicitly be used to complete the regulatory scheme of any statute'[6] or, more fundamentally, the 'general juristic foundation and conceptual reference point for later substantive legal development, and a compass for the discovery of other, implicit principles of the private law'.[7] Moreover, every legislative act, including civil codes, rests on certain 'primary and fundamental principles which must underlie and sustain all positive legislation'.[8] Indeed, even though provinces retain jurisdiction over property and civil rights, much of Canadian Private law remains federal.[9] In this sense, federal legislation must be based on some underlying principles that transcend both common and civil laws.

It is therefore in this loose sense that we propose to investigate the proposition of a 'general law' of contractualism in so far as it can be found in and around the Canadian Constitution itself. We find this proposition all the more plausible given that, even though they are not mentioned in the Constitution, contracts play an essential role in the Canadian economy. Contracts cross provincial borders, and there is no doubt that this was also the case at Confederation in 1867. More broadly, the Constitution Act, 1982, establishes the Canadian Charter of Rights and Freedoms,[10] and regardless of its applicability to Private law relationships, it does in all cases provide a framework through which contractual freedom, in one form or another, can be exercised. In light of this, we propose to examine constitutional aspect of Canadian Contract law through two different lenses. The first is the Constitution Act, 1867. The second is the Canadian Charter of Rights and Freedoms, which forms part of the Constitution Act, 1982.[11] These two documents were drafted in much different times and could represent different approaches to social and economic regulation, although it is not so clear today to what extent contract rights have received an updated constitutional consideration.

2 Contractualism Under the Constitution Act, 1867

Contractualism and the Constitution Act, 1867, have much more in common than one would think. For one, much of the Constitution Act, 1867, presupposes unwritten tradition. For instance, there is little in the Constitution Act, 1867, that

[6]Macdonald (1997).

[7]Ibid.

[8]Ibid., p. 595.

[9]See the Constitution Act 1867; banking: s 91(15); bills of exchange: s 91(18); promissory notes: s 91(19); interest: s 91(21); bankruptcy and insolvency: s 91(22); copyright: s 91(23); marriage and divorce: s 91(26).

[10]Canadian Charter of Rights and Freedoms, Part I of the Constitution Act, 1982, being Schedule B to the Canada Act 1982 (UK), 1982, c 11 ('Canadian Charter of Rights and Freedoms').

[11]Ibid.

describes the role of the courts. As a result, judicial jurisdiction could be viewed as subsidiary in that it fills the gaps left by the legislature and other branches of government. At the same time, many of these 'gaps' are expected to be left open because they traditionally belong to the judiciary itself.

This idea of subsidiarity also fits well within the Constitution Act, 1867. In spite of not being mentioned in either Constitution Act, subsidiarity can be described as underpinning both the Constitution Acts, 1867 and 1982.[12] This principle of social organisation, drawn from European community law, holds that in matters of joint jurisdiction, decisions should be taken at the closest level of government possible. The principle of subsidiarity, moreover, is of particular relevance to Contract law. Indeed, contractualism can be viewed as the logical end of subsidiarity in so far as it delegates decision-maker not only to the lowest, most local entities, but to the most elemental common denominator: individuals themselves. To this extent, contractualism, with all of its social and economic implications, cannot itself be divorced from the interpretation of the Constitution Act, 1867.

However, subsidiarity is not an end in itself but rather an organising principle that only applies in matters of overlapping jurisdiction. It is thus a means of resolving jurisdictional conflicts because it does recognise the possibility of overlap. However, the position taken by the Canadian courts has been more to deny the existence of conflict and to interpret powers strictly or broadly, to the exclusion of one another. Such simplification is important because it gives us insight, just as a view through a narrowly cracked door, into the underlying principles of the Constitution Act, 1867, that could otherwise be qualified as Canadian *ius commune*.

2.1 Legislative Jurisdiction Over Contracts

Legislative jurisdiction is the starting point to understand jurisdiction over contracts because allocating legislative jurisdiction is one of the main purposes of the Constitution Act, 1867. Generally speaking, the nature and content of Private law is a provincial matter. This is generally based on the fact that jurisdiction over 'property and civil rights' is granted to provincial legislatures through s 92(13) of that Act. This explains why the province of Quebec is one of Civil rather than Common law. Moreover, each provincial legislature is territorially limited such that it may not legislate over a contract that is territorially outside the scope of its jurisdiction; provincial jurisdiction is territorially limited by the phrase 'in each province', contained in the heading of s 92.[13] The result of this view is that federal

[12]Hogg (1993).

[13]The most famous example is *Reference re Upper Churchill Water Rights Reversion Act*, [1984] 1 SCR 297 (Supreme Court of Canada), declaring unconstitutional provincial legislation purporting to expropriate a federally incorporated company located outside the province of Newfoundland and Labrador.

powers have been interpreted restrictively, such that one is under the impression that each Province has its own *ius commune*.

However, the division of powers is tricky because the Constitution Act, 1867, does not grant general jurisdiction to one level of government and specific jurisdiction to others, as in the United States. Rather, each level of government has a list of headings under which it can legislate. Thus, while the Constitution Act, 1867, provides for provincial jurisdiction over 'property and civil rights', the federal Parliament is granted jurisdiction over 'trade and commerce', through s 91(2) of the same act. In *Citizens Insurance Co of Canada v Parsons*,[14] it was argued that a provincial statute regulating insurance was unconstitutional as it pertained to 'trade and commerce', not 'property and civil rights'. However, rather than recognising the potential for jurisdictional overlap, *Parsons* ruled that 'trade and commerce' must be viewed restrictively, while 'property and civil rights', a head of provincial jurisdiction, must be interpreted broadly. Thus, provinces became the principle regulators of contracts in so far as they pertain to 'property and civil rights'. The exception to the rule thus became federal jurisdiction in so far as contract regulation could be viewed as 'trade and commerce'. The Privy Council stated that 'trade and commerce' does not grant federal jurisdiction over a particular trade or commerce such as insurance but only allow general legislation not confined to a particular sector.[15] 'Trade and commerce', on the contrary, did include 'political arrangements in regard to trade in matters of inter-provincial concern, and it may be that they would include general regulation of trade affecting the whole dominion'.[16]

That being said, it would be reductive in our view, even from a strictly constitutional perspective, to view Contract law as exclusively provincial because there are many variations and nuances to s 92(13) that need to be brought to light. To begin, s 94 of the Constitution Act, 1867, provides for the possibility of uniform federal legislation over such matters of Private law, provided, however, that each Common law province adopts the said federal legislation.[17] This provision does not mention Quebec, although nothing would prevent it from adapting such legislation to its own Civil code. Section 92(13) is also subject to specific federal grants of jurisdiction. For instance, the federal Parliament may legislate incidentally in a federal field, such as navigation, banking or labour within the federal sector.[18] Nothing would prevent the federal Parliament from providing, within these particular fields, legislation pertaining to the formation of contracts.[19] Parliament could

[14]*Citizens Insurance Co of Canada v Parsons,* [1881] UKPC 49 (Judicial Committee of the Privy Council).

[15]Ibid, para 113.

[16]Ibid.

[17]Section 94 only mentions the provinces of Ontario, New Brunswick and Nova Scotia, but the academic opinion states that the provision applies *mutatis mutandis* to other confederated provinces. See Scott (1942) and La Forest (1975).

[18]E.g., Canada Labour Code RSC, 1985, c L-2; *Montcalm Construction v Minimum Wage Commission*, [1979] 1 SCR 754 (Supreme Court of Canada).

[19]*Tennant v Union Bank*, [1894] AC 31 (Judicial Committee of the Privy Council).

in such sectors legislate over specific types of contracts, such as navigation, labour and banking, and more generally under the heading of 'trade and commerce'. Some have even suggested that Parliament could enact a federal 'code' pertaining to federal Private law.[20]

However, matters have become increasingly complex. For instance, in order to legislate in a matter that is incidental to federal jurisdiction (property and civil rights), the Supreme Court has stated that it is necessary to weigh the extent of the intrusion against the centrality of the measure against its centrality to the object of the federal head of power. Thus, the more federal legislation encroaches upon 'property and civil rights', the more it will be difficult to justify it under a federal head of power. For example, federal legislation providing for a civil cause of action for breach of federal competition rules was ruled constitutional in so far as it pertained to 'trade and commerce'.[21] In contrast, federal legislation establishing comprehensive securities legislation was invalidated as an overreach in jurisdiction over 'trade and commerce'.[22] To this extent, the *Parsons* ruling still carried much favour, although it is difficult to view the contractual landscape as unchanged. In particular, much of the law of contracts is now legislated in each individual province. It is also open to question to what extent Quebec is more legislated than other provinces in matters pertaining to contract.

In any event, the practical result of the *Parsons* ruling is that much progressive legislation was set aside over the last century because it was enacted by the federal rather than provincial government.[23] Moreover, it must be remembered that unlike the American Supreme Court, the Supreme Court of Canada has final jurisdiction over all matters, including those pertaining to provincial law. This raises the question as to what extent constitutional provisions pertaining to the judiciary recognise a *ius commune* of contracts.

2.2 *Judicial Jurisdiction Over Contract Disputes*

In addition to granting legislative jurisdiction over contracts to the provinces, Canadian courts also tend to view judicial jurisdiction over contracts as principally provincial. While s 92(14) grants jurisdiction over the administration of justice to

[20]Some authors have suggested that Parliament could enact a general contracts act to govern federal law: see Macdonald (1997), pp. 579–622.

[21]*General Motors of Canada Ltd. v City National Leasing Ltd.* [1989] 1 SCR 641 (Supreme Court of Canada).

[22]*Reference re Securities Act*, [2011] 3 SCR 837 (Supreme Court of Canada).

[23]Labour standards legislation: *A.G. Canada v A.G. Ontario (Labour Conventions),* [1937] AC 326 (Judicial Committee of the Privy Council); see also limitation of work hours: *Attorney General of Canada v Attorney General of Ontario and others*, [1937] UKPC 7 (Judicial Committee of the Privy Council); work hours: *Pacific Railway Co. v Attorney-General of British Columbia*, [1948] SCR 373 (Supreme Court of Canada).

the provinces, the federal parliament does have jurisdiction to establish its own courts. That being said, the Constitution Act, 1867, does not provide for a parallel 'federal Court' system as in the United States. Rather, the federal parliament does have the legislative option under s 101 of the Constitution Act, 1867, which it chose to fully exercise in 1971, to establish a court 'for the better administration of the laws of Canada'. The Federal Courts Act thus 'carves out' jurisdiction from the general jurisdiction of provincial superior courts (commonly termed 's 96 courts'), although both are 'superior courts' in that all judges have identical terms of appointment and independence from government,[24] the difference being, however, that federal courts are established under s 101 and are relatively new players trying to find a 'constitutional niche'.

For instance, since their creation, Federal Court jurisdiction over Private law matters such as contract has been contentious. Indeed, the Supreme Court has never viewed 'common law disputes', aside from matters such as Admiralty, which clearly fall within federal territorial jurisdiction, as within the purview of s 101, which qualifies the Court as being 'for the better administration of the laws of Canada'. In other words, 'laws of Canada' must be a dispute based on statute, not Common law rules. The wording of the Constitution, rather than the Federal Courts Act itself, is thus determinant.[25] For example, in *Quebec North Shore Paper v C.P. Ltd.*,[26] a claim for breach of contract was presented before the Federal Court on the basis that legislation granted it jurisdiction to provide a 'remedy under an Act of Parliament or otherwise'. This case could have been viewed as falling within the jurisdiction of the Court because it pertained to the construction of a marine terminal, which for territorial purposes, is normally beyond the legislative jurisdiction of the province. The Supreme Court, however, denied jurisdiction to the Federal Court because in its view, such legislation could not be read as enlarging upon s 101 and the 'administration of laws of Canada'. The Court therefore denied jurisdiction because the bare contention that a contract had been violated, without any relation to federal legislation, was an insufficient basis of jurisdiction.

What is more, even when a suit for breach of contract was brought by the federal government against a private company, the Supreme Court denied jurisdiction to the Federal Court on similar grounds. For example, *McNamara Construction et al. v The Queen* pertained to the breach of construction contracts with the federal government. As a claimant, the Federal government sought to apply the Common

[24]Provincial superior court judges are appointed under s96 of the Constitution Act, 1867, while Federal Court judges are listed in the Federal Courts Act rather than the constitution itself. Both terms of appointment and tenure, are however, substantively identical. See ss 5(2)–5(4) Federal Courts Act, RSC 1985, c F-7 ('FCA').

[25]Sections 17(2)(b)–22(1) of the FCA also grant jurisdiction to the Court in maritime matters, such as (n) 'any claim arising out of a contract relating to the construction, repair or equipping of a ship' and (r) 'any claim arising out of or in connection with a contract of marine insurance'. Relief in favour of the Crown is provided under s 17(5) of the Act, which also grants concurrent jurisdiction to the Federal Courts.

[26]*Québec North Shore Paper Co. v CP*, [1977] 2 SCR 1054 (Supreme Court of Canada).

law rule that the Crown may sue in any court having subject matter jurisdiction. The Supreme Court rejected this contention on the ground that it matters not whether the federal government is a party to the dispute; when a claim is solely based on a contract and not on any enacted statute, there is no basis for Federal Court jurisdiction.[27] Chief Justice Bora Laskin stated:

> I must, with respect, disagree with that reasoning, which adapts to federal Canada a unitary conception, and makes the jurisdiction [sic] of a federal trial Court over a subject of the Crown depend solely on the Crown asserting a claim as plaintiff.[28]

In *R. v Thomas Fuller Construction Co. (1958) Ltd. et al.*,[29] the Supreme Court restricted the jurisdiction of the Federal Court even further. In this instance, the Court stated that in an action by the Crown, the Federal Court did not have jurisdiction over an ancillary claim by one private defendant against another because such a claim arose out of provincial statutes (Negligence Act), which do not qualify as 'laws of Canada' under s 101 of the Constitution Act, 1867. The dissenting opinion of Martland J. stated that there was no contest that the Federal Court did have jurisdiction over the principal claim by the Crown, as granted by federal legislation. Moreover, the success of the ancillary claim was entirely dependent on the principal action. In such a case, it would be proper for the Federal Court to either permit or deny jurisdiction to the whole claim because the fractioning of the dispute could further complicate the resolution of the dispute.

Notwithstanding the criticism of the Federal Courts themselves as constitutionally unnecessary, the issue regarding their jurisdiction is whether Common law qualifies as a 'law of Canada', as per s 101 of the Constitution Act, 1867. The Supreme Court's contention is that only federal legislation, not Common law issues such as breach contract, must be the basis of the contention in order to grant jurisdiction to the Federal Courts. To the Court's credit, s 101 does speak of the 'administration' of 'laws of Canada', which implicitly favours 'legislation' over 'common law' disputes. However, this is a false distinction because all governmental powers have some connection to statute. It is impossible in our view to state that a claim is purely based on contract and there can be no statute involved.

The question of Federal Court jurisdiction, however, is more contentious where 'private' inter-provincial litigation is in issue. There are various statutory bases of jurisdiction,[30] but here again, a mere statutory grant of jurisdiction has never been enough, especially if no 'laws of Canada' are in issue. In these contexts, the dual process of suit and recognition and enforcement can complicate a dispute, complications that do not exist when territorial jurisdiction is treated as a unified whole, as it is in the Federal Courts. Such complications can be heightened when a contract

---

[27] *McNamara Construction et al. v The Queen*, [1977] 2 SCR 654 (Supreme Court of Canada).

[28] Ibid.

[29] *R. v Thomas Fuller Construction Co. (1958) Ltd. et al.*, [1980] 1 SCR 695 (Supreme Court of Canada).

[30] See s 20(1) FCA regarding intellectual property disputes; s 22(1) FCA regarding navigation and shipping.

involves several parties, all residing in different jurisdictions, although all linked in one way or another by federal legislation. In these contexts, the issue is whether there is such thing as a 'federal common law' allowing a claim for damages for breach of contract to be disputed before the Federal Courts.[31] Much of what the Supreme Court stated in *Quebec North Shore* and *MacNamara Construction* answers this question in the negative because it equates Common law jurisdiction with the provinces; only legislation qualifies as a 'law of Canada' under s 101 of the Constitution Act, 1867. Until federal legislation is enacted, there is no federal 'default' Common law serving as a basis for jurisdiction. Thus, there is still much hesitation to grant any substantial jurisdiction to the Federal Courts for matters that have traditionally been viewed as provincial.

2.3 Administrative Jurisdiction Over Contract Disputes

A final problem relating to the Constitution Act, 1867, pertains to administrative jurisdiction over contract disputes. This question is relevant to Contract law because it tells us to what extent contract disputes are 'inherently' judicial in nature or can be delegated to a statutory body such as an administrative tribunal. Thus, while it is not generally viewed from the perspective of the separation of powers, the law relating to the enforcement of contracts is the product of a delicate constitutional balancing act that intersects judicial, legislative and individual responsibilities. Needless to say, this balancing act applies just as much to the Quebec as it does to other provinces.

The problem of delegating 'judicial power' to an administrative body is related to federal power over judicial appointment under s 96 of the Constitution Act, 1867. To recall, s 96 of the Constitution Act, 1867, calls for the federal appointment of superior court judges and under which are detailed their terms of appointment. This apparently innocuous provision, however, has been given a much broader meaning by the courts. As a result, it has not always been easy for provinces to transfer powers that have traditionally been framed as 'judicial' to administrative boards and tribunals.

The problem is that, if a province establishes an institution that acts and looks like a superior court, even though it is called an 'administrative tribunal', it must abide by Section 96 because for all intents and purposes, it is a 'superior court'. This is even more the case when the administrative tribunal in question is protected by a privative clause. In these instances, the creation of an administrative tribunal with superior court powers, albeit protected by any further superior court review or appeal, has been interpreted as contrary to s 96.[32] The test for determining the conflict between the provincial administrative tribunal and s 96 is, however, both

[31]Hogg (2011), para 17.5.

[32]*Attorney General of Quebec et al. v. Farrah*, [1978] 2 SCR 638 (Supreme Court of Canada).

complicated and controversial. To begin, since the provinces had their own institutions prior to confederation, it has been determined that if the power in question was not exclusively within the jurisdiction of superior courts in 1867, it cannot be contrary to s 96. This is the essential question asked by the courts. However, there are two exceptions. First, if the power is not a 'judicial' one, namely one that pertains to the resolution of disputes (i.e., those based on contract), the power will not be held to be contrary to s 96. Second, if the power in question is ancillary to the functions of the tribunal, it will not be contrary to s 96.

These criteria, however, are the combined result of years of case law, and their application has not been consistent. For instance, in *Labour Relations Board of Saskatchewan v John East Iron Works, Limited*,[33] a labour tribunal ordered the reinstatement of six unionised members for discriminatory dismissal, and the Saskatchewan Court of Appeal held that this power was tantamount to that of specific performance and therefore held the *Trade Union Act* unconstitutional. The Privy Council, however, disagreed and stated that the issue was not whether the power in question was unconstitutional but whether the entire scheme made the labour board a 'superior court'. In Lord Simonds's view, the entire scheme was 'administrative' because its purpose was to promote industrial peace, not adjudicate contract rights per se. There could be no conflict between the Act and s 96 of the Constitution Act, 1867.

However, Canadian courts have not followed this approach and have selectively vetoed certain provisions of administrative schemes on the ground that they encroach on superior court powers. Most famously, in *Re Residential Tenancies Act, 1979*,[34] the Supreme Court of Canada invalidated provincial legislation that gave powers to a board to evict tenants and required both tenants and landlords to comply with obligations under the Act. In its decision, the Supreme Court summed up a three-part test in order to determine the compatibility of the tribunal with s 96 of the Constitution and concluded that the enforcement powers given to the tribunal were within the exclusive jurisdiction of superior courts at the time of Confederation. The Court found that the board's enforcement powers were within the jurisdiction of superior courts in 1867, that those powers were 'judicial' and that they were central to the tribunal. As a result, the board's enforcement powers were declared contrary to s 96 of the Constitution Act, 1867.

However, the *Residential Tenancies* case has been controversial. For instance, similar legislation has been upheld in other provinces because it had been established that superior courts did not exercise exclusive but rather concurrent jurisdiction.[35] Thus, the effect of s 96 depends on the province in which it is enforced and the evidence produced. In *Sobeys Stores Ltd. v Yeomans and Labour*

---

[33]*Labour Relations Board of Saskatchewan v John East Iron Works, Limited,* [1949] AC 134 (Supreme Court of Canada).

[34]*Re Residential Tenancies Act, 1979,* [1981] 1 SCR 714 (Supreme Court of Canada).

[35]*Attorney General of Quebec v Grondin*, [1983] 2 SCR 364 (Supreme Court of Canada).

Standards Tribunal (NS),[36] the Supreme Court had to decide whether a labour board's orders of reinstatement for wrongful dismissal were contrary to s 96 in the province of Nova Scotia. This case decided that the impugned power of reinstatement should be characterised broadly as 'labour relations' so as to shift the discussion onto the saving exceptions, namely the nature of the power and its importance in relation to the legislative scheme. However, the most controversial question was which provinces should serve as a benchmark to determine the exclusivity of judicial jurisdiction. The solution in this case was to look at the four founding provinces in 1867 (Ontario, Quebec, New Brunswick, Nova Scotia) and use these as a benchmark for all others. However, here again the Court encountered problems because the impugned power was exclusively judicial only in two provinces, thereby producing a tie. The Court then turned to the situation in the United Kingdom in 1867 and found that unjust dismissal was within the exclusive purview of superior courts, although it was saved because in was incidental to the scheme.

Moreover, later case law brought to light evidentiary problems of the historical inquiry. In *Reference re Amendments to the Residential Tenancies Act (Nova Scotia)*,[37] the Supreme Court acknowledged errors it made in the initial Ontario reference. Since the Ontario reference had been issued in 1981, several provinces continued to allow for administrative enforcement of residential tenancy contracts, although none had been brought to court. Moreover, since the *Sobey's* decision, it was not clear whether the initial Ontario reference would have passed or failed the four-province test. The Supreme Court ruled in the Nova Scotia reference that superior courts did not enjoy exclusive jurisdiction in any province in 1867, especially if the powers were characterised broadly as 'jurisdiction over residential tenancies' rather than narrowly as enforcement powers', as they were in 1981. Therefore, even under the province-by-province approach, the Ontario legislation would have been saved had proper evidence been adduced. The Court defended itself on this point by saying that the government of Ontario conceded the point, so as to move the discussion onto the saving exceptions.[38]

As a result, much of the discussion on judicial powers that had been shifted to the saving exceptions is now returned to the initial hurdle, namely that of judicial exclusivity in 1867. This raises the question as to whether the 'incidental' nature of the power will be of any relevance in future litigation now that the power is characterised broadly. However, regardless of the characterisation question, courts never addressed the problem raised by the Privy Council that courts should not be 'selectively vetoing' legislation but rather looking at it on its whole. All this points to the fact that many legislative schemes that seemed contrary to s 96 in 1981 could well be in conformity therewith, especially if they are characterised more broadly.

---

[36] *Sobeys Stores Ltd. v Yeomans and Labour Standards Tribunal (NS)*, [1989] 1 SCR 238 (Supreme Court of Canada).

[37] *Reference re Amendments to the Residential Tenancies Act (Nova Scotia)*, [1996] 1 SCR 186 (Supreme Court of Canada).

[38] Ibid, para 33.

As a preliminary conclusion, one can state that, in its own way, case law concerning legislative, judicial administrative jurisdiction under the Constitution Act, 1867, provides a 'photo-negative' of Canadian *ius commune*. The portrait that emerges is one where provincial judicial jurisdiction has traditionally been protected while at the same time, rather curiously, allowing for federal oversight through the Supreme Court. Such 'common law constitutionalism' does favour a certain judicial, as opposed to legislative or administrative, aesthetic of legality. Contractualism, individualism and subsidiarity thus reinforce one another through the Constitution Act, 1867.

From this perspective, it is open to question to what extent the Common law of contracts has shaped the Constitution Act, 1867, itself.[39] Common law contractualism could therefore be viewed as the context through which constitutional meaning has been derived. This Common law background of incremental change was solid ground upon which to interpret a Constitution, and this was no doubt a historical necessity given Canada's colonial past. The question that now arises is how the Constitution Act, 1982, changes this by establishing broadly worded Fundamental rights and freedoms, uniformly, throughout Canada.

3 Contractualism and the *Canadian Charter of Rights and Freedoms*

There is no doubt that commerce and trade in the Common law world have traditionally been protected as Fundamental rights.[40] The question that arises in Canada, however, is how contractual rights and freedoms fall within this designation. Traditionally, such rights and freedoms have been conceived as emerging spontaneously from some form of natural economic order. The modern view, however, is that the state must ensure an environment where contract rights can be exercised and maintained. To this extent, the Canadian Charter of Rights and Freedoms is problematic because it presents itself as a form of rational enlightenment but at the same time presupposes that the government distance itself from private relations, especially since conventional thought has promoted its non-application to such relations. The Charter could be seen as providing a new 'baseline' of individual rights,[41] namely by imposing uniform standards across the board, to both federal and provincial institutions. Such a view could thus be antithetical to the idea of 'subsidiarity', as associated with the Constitution Act, 1867. The question that arises is therefore to what extent the Charter continues on

[39] Walters (2001).

[40] The Magna Carta (1215), §41, guarantees merchants 'safe and secure' exit and entry to England 'for buying and selling by the ancient rights and customs, quit from all evil tolls'.

[41] *Continuing Committee of Ministers on the Constitution*, 'Background Notes: Entrenching a *Charter* of Rights', Document No. 830-81/026, 5th July 1980.

with the economic laissez-faire of the Constitution Act, 1867, or whether it can be read as altering this mode of thought without changing Fundamental rights and freedoms associated with private contractualism.

3.1 Application of the Charter to Contractual Relations

There is no doubt that the Constitution places limits on legislation, and this goes just as much for the original Constitution Act, 1867, as it does for the more contemporary Constitution Act, 1982, establishing the Canadian Charter of Rights and Freedoms. However, legislative history of the Charter suggests that Parliament did not want to supplant provincial jurisdiction over Private law, and one of the means of avoiding this was by insisting that the Charter does not apply between private individuals, thereby protecting jurisdiction under s 92(13). During Parliamentary debates on the drafting of the Charter, Justice Minister Jean Chrétien argued that the Charter should not apply to private individuals because this would make every issue constitutional, and thus subject to constitutional amendment.[42] Section 32(1) of the Charter expressly confirms this. Courts have also emulated the American approach by developing what is termed the 'state action doctrine'.

The state action doctrine holds that Fundamental rights do not apply to individuals, only to state actors. One of the most important confirmation of this was the *RWDSU v Dolphin Delivery Ltd.*,[43] a case concerning the practice of 'secondary picketing', i.e. picketing the premises of an employer that is not a party to a labour dispute. In this case, Dolphin Delivery sought a court order restraining the employees' union from picketing on its premises. Lower courts held that secondary picketing constituted inducement to breach of contract and therefore granted the order. Before the Supreme Court, the union defended its actions as freedom of expression (s 2 of the Canadian Charter). This argument, however, was rejected on the ground that the Charter only applies to 'government' and the legislative branches but not to the judiciary and court orders. A Court order does not constitute government action, as *per* s 32(1) of the Charter. In support of this, McIntyre J. stated that s 32(1) explicitly excludes courts from its scope of application and rather limits its scope of application to legislative bodies and 'government' in the executive and administrative senses. At the same time, the Court also stated somewhat confusingly that the Charter applies to the Common law, albeit only when government was a party to the dispute.

The practical consequences of *Dolphin Delivery* has been that the Charter only applies to Common law when the government is a party to the dispute, which in

[42]Testimony of J. Chrétien, Minister of Justice of Canada, in Minutes of Proceedings and Evidence of the Special Joint Committee of the Senate and of the House of Commons on the Constitution of Canada, of 32nd Parl, 1st Sess (29 January 1981) at 48:28.

[43]*RWDSU v Dolphin Delivery Ltd.*, [1986] 2 SCR 573 (Supreme Court of Canada).

itself is contrary to the very notion of 'common law'. It also goes against American jurisprudence, which found that discriminatory restrictive covenants are not enforceable in so far as they are unconstitutional.[44] The US Supreme Court did not go as far as to declare the covenants unconstitutional but stated that courts could not lend themselves to their enforcement since that in itself would constitute unconstitutional state action. In contrast, in Canada, when a private dispute is purely based on Common law rules, Fundamental rights and freedoms spelled out in the Constitution will not form part of the 'applicable law' of the dispute. It is not clear, however, what practical consequences will flow from this. For one, provincial legislation under s 92(13) has allowed for statutes prohibiting certain behaviours such as those described in American case law. Contracts that are contrary to these statutes can be held unlawful, just as the legislation itself can be held unconstitutional if it excludes certain categories of persons from its scope of protection.[45]

For instance, in *Godbout v Longueuil (City)*, a municipal by-law requiring municipal employees to reside within the municipality has been held contrary to the right to privacy under s 5 of the Quebec Charter.[46] In this case, the municipal resolution required all new employees to reside within the municipality. As an employer, the municipality required all new employees to sign a declaration stating that if they moved out, they could be terminated without notice. The court was unanimous in declaring the residence requirement as contrary to Quebec legislation. However, a minority of judges went further and stated that the residence requirement was contrary to s 7 of the Canadian Charter. The controversy on this last point derives from the fact that municipalities are provincial legislative emanations and therefore not strictly 'governmental' as per s 32(1) of the Canadian Charter. The minority addressed this and stated that they fall within that provision even if they cannot be described as strictly 'governmental'. Thus, in addition to its contrariety to s 5 of the Quebec Charter, the minority went on to describe the requirement as contrary to the liberty interest contained in s 7 of the Canadian Charter. The waiver in this respect was both unlawful and unconstitutional.

The controversy raised by *Godbout*, however, hinges not on the application of the Charter to statutory entities such as municipalities[47] but rather on the applicable law to governmental entities, whatever their shape and how it might differ from that to be applied between private actors *per se*. For one, since *Godbout*, courts have held that damages are available under s 24(1) of the Charter, thereby developing what has been termed a doctrine of 'constitutional torts'. The key decision on this point is *Vancouver (City) v Ward*, a case concerning an unconstitutional search and

[44] *Shelley v Kraemer*, 334 US 1 [1948] (United States Supreme Court).

[45] *Vriend v Alberta*, [1998] 1 SCR 493 (Supreme Court of Canada): teacher terminated for his homosexuality, successfully contested the exclusion of 'sexual orientation' from provincial legislation as being contrary to s 15 of the Canadian Charter of Rights and Freedoms.

[46] *Godbout v Longueuil (City)*, [1997] 3 SCR 844 (Supreme Court of Canada).

[47] The application of the Charter to municipalities was confirmed in *Greater Vancouver Transportation Authority v Canadian Federation of Students—British Columbia Component*, [2009] SCC 31 (Supreme Court of Canada).

seizure that otherwise did not give way to liability in tort.[48] At the same time, and what makes this decision controversial, is that courts have traditionally refused to develop distinct regimes of liability on the sole grounds that government is a party to the dispute.[49] In this respect, the role of the Constitution as an exclusive element of the 'applicable law' of government contracts is not entirely on clear and stable ground.

The converse trend, thereby limiting the likelihood of a distinct Public law regime of liability, is the recognition that rights and freedoms are not solely antagonistic to government but requiring reconciliation between individuals. Indeed, much of the thinking in relation to Fundamental rights is predicated on the notion that government is both the problem and the solution to a rights violation *via* a court order. The converse position is that fundamental individual rights and freedoms need to be balanced with one another, regardless of whether they are claimed in a judicial forum. Thus, the mere proposition that the Charter applies in no way recognises that a claim of rights is valid, nor does it assume that a formal 'judicial' claim has been made. This is indeed how courts have increasingly been addressing claims involving different private actors.[50] Such an approach recognises the concurrency of fundamental values and Common law principles and could well give rise to richer jurisprudence than what is available today, without, however, necessarily reversing any of the outcomes.

3.2 *Contractual Freedom as a Fundamental Right*

The legal continuity of s 96 jurisprudence can be found in Charter litigation through what is conventionally termed the 'right to contract'. As is well known, the Canadian Charter is not one of social and economic rights,[51] but this does not prevent it from protecting certain contracting interests. In this respect, and to give more concrete significance to the expression, the 'right to contract' pertains to any government that interferes with a protected right or freedom and whose main incidence is to prevent or prohibit the exercise of private contracting. The ambit of this right is thus dependent on the nature of the interference by government action, statute in particular. That being said, there is no distinct limit for this right since any breach of the Constitution that involves the exercise of contract rights could be viewed as a breach of a right to contract.

For instance, in *R. v Big M Drug Mart Ltd.*,[52] a case pertaining to the constitutionality of 'Lord's Day' legislation preventing Sunday shopping, the Supreme

[48] *Vancouver (City) v Ward*, [2010] SCC 27 (Supreme Court of Canada).

[49] *Lapierre v A.G. (Que.)*, [1985] 1 SCR 241 (Supreme Court of Canada).

[50] *Multani v Commission scolaire Marguerite-Bourgeoys*, [2006] SCC 6 (Supreme Court of Canada) at para 30.

[51] Jackman and Porter (2007).

[52] *R. v Big M Drug Mart Ltd.*, [1985] 1 SCR 295 (Supreme Court of Canada).

Court stated that any law that prevents non-Christians the right to work on Sunday infringes upon freedom of religion. Another example is *Irwin Toy Ltd. v Quebec (Attorney General)*,[53] a case pertaining to the regulation of commercial advertising directed at children. The claims in that case were not allowed, although one of the arguments was set aside on the technical grounds, namely that s 7 of the Charter (right to liberty and 'fundamental justice') does not apply to a private corporation. As to freedom of expression, the court found no unconstitutionality in the province's legislation and rather found that it conformed with general principles of Contract law, namely the law relating to contracts with minors.

Section 7 of the *Charter*, however, remains one of the most invoked rights in the context of freedom of contract and at the same time one of the Charter's most elusive provisions. One of the first attempts to circumscribe its scope was *Re B.C. Motor Vehicle Act*,[54] where the province of British Columbia defended its legislation imposing absolute liability and imprisonment for certain motor vehicle offences on the ground that s 7 only provided procedural and not substantive protections. The Supreme Court, however, rejected the argument stating that even if direct evidence of such a reading had been given—which it had—it could not, however authoritative the evidence is, freeze the meaning of the Charter. As a result, Section 7 has since been invoked in various ways so as to protect various forms of economic 'liberty'.

In *Chaoulli v Quebec (Attorney General)*,[55] the Supreme Court of Canada recognised that wait times for certain medical interventions and the correlative prohibition on private insurance schemes was contrary to s 1 of Quebec's Charter of Human Rights and Freedoms (freedom and security of the person) and s 7 of the Canadian Charter. At the time of the ruling, Quebec legislation prohibited the use of private insurance for certain treatments, and this in order to favour a single tier insurance scheme. Moreover, the scheme did not prohibit private practice, only private insurance. However, evidence showed that individuals had died while waiting for medical treatment. Thus, the prohibition of private health insurance had, in the majority's view, the effect of favouring the very rich, who did not require health insurance in order to receive prompter treatment. For three dissenting judges, the question transgressed constitutional justiciability because it challenged a legislative choice. The challenge also asserted a right (treatment in a reasonable time) that could not be qualified as a principle of 'fundamental justice'. The ruling has not been, however, the death knell of Canada's public health care system.

However, a much more aggressive interpretation of s 7 of the Charter can be found in *Wilson v Medical Services Commission of British Columbia*.[56] In this case,

[53]*Irwin Toy Ltd. v Quebec (Attorney General)*, [1989] 1 SCR 927 (Supreme Court of Canada).

[54]*Re B.C. Motor Vehicle Act*, [1985] 2 SCR 486 (Supreme Court of Canada).

[55]*Chaoulli v Quebec (Attorney General)*, [2005] 1 SCR 791 (Supreme Court of Canada).

[56]*Wilson v Medical Services Commission of British Columbia*, [1988] BCJ No 1566 (British Columbia Court of Appeal), leave to appeal to Supreme Court of Canada refused, [1988] 2 SCR viii.

the Supreme Court of British Columbia ruled that legislation and its regulations placing geographic restrictions for the issuance of billing numbers to new doctors and those coming from outside the province violated principles of fundamental justice guaranteed by s 7 of the Charter. The Court found that by restricting the practice of medicine, the Act violated the Charter because it did not specify applicants' procedural rights. The province took the position that procedural deficiencies could be rectified by Common law principles of natural justice and in any event that applicants could apply for judicial review. However, the court held that the *Act* provided 'areas of uncontrolled discretion, left substantial scope for arbitrary conduct'. Accordingly, it was held to be 'so procedurally flawed' that it could not stand. In support, the Court listed many provisions that the Act did not provide, *inter alia*, a 'duty to decide', means for applicants of knowing where their services might be required and whether their application was being considered. These considerations seem superficial, and it is difficult to understand why they should offend principles of fundamental justice, especially when these details can be determined by regulation. Indeed, this decision combines two weak arguments—vagueness and restrictions on economic liberty—as bases for holding a law unconstitutional. These cases aside, few precedents have used s. 7 in order to challenge government action in order to assert contractual freedom.

3.3 Enforcement of Contracts as a Fundamental Right

Beyond the exact meaning of s 7 of the Charter, the residual debate is arguably much larger and complicated because it pertains to the enforcement of contracts. This raises two problems. The first is the position of the courts when faced with their 'fundamental breach' of a contract term. The second relates to the enforcement of contracts across provincial borders.

Of course, 'Fundamental Rights' and 'fundamental breach' are only terminologically related. The latter doctrine pertains to the problem of enforcing a contractual exclusion of liability when a violation goes to the heart of what was contracted. In response to this doctrine, the Supreme Court of Canada stated in *Tercon Contractors Ltd. v British Columbia (Transportation and Highways)* that it does not belong to courts to judge the reasonableness of freely contracted individual choices. As a result, a contract could conceivably exclude all liability arising between the parties.[57] The argument in this case could well be a constitutional one in so far as the courts do not see it as their role to make choices for individuals. The doctrine of fundamental breach, in this regard, is ultimately about individuals' 'fundamental right to contract' and the responsibility that goes along with freedom

[57]*Tercon Contractors Ltd. v British Columbia (Transportation and Highways)*. [2010] SCC 4 (Supreme Court of Canada).

to consent. A contract, in this regard, could (rightly or wrongly) be qualified as a relationship where only one party is obligated to the other.

This solution raises questions as to how individuals can exclude judicial jurisdiction when the legislature itself cannot do so.[58] Moreover, it is also important to remember the context that led the courts to accept this proposition. The Canadian conception of what is a contract is, in this regard, particular. With all their insistence of bilateral consideration and reciprocal benefit, Canadian courts have incrementally recognised that bid submissions to government are susceptible of creating contractual obligations prior to the actual award of the construction contract. Thus, calls for tender can be viewed as contractual, especially when they are made by government and establish a formalised submission process.[59] At the same time, contractual liability was all the more necessary, given that courts did not view contracting awards as judicially reviewable.[60] That being said, courts also decided that each submission entails the formation of a distinct contract (contract A) from the actual contract that is to be awarded (contract B). A violation of the terms of the process can give rise to 'breach of contract' and thus to damages for the would-be winner. The basis for such damages is entirely contractual, and the victim of the breach is not required to demonstrate any tort such as public misfeasance. The measure of damages is therefore the profits expected from the award of the contract.[61]

In these instances, the application of a constitutional 'liberty interest' referred to in *Godbout* could well have its relevance because it is specifically to protect government from specious claims of lost profits that total exclusions of liability have become necessary. Such exclusions of liability, however, do not disincentivise bidders from working with government given its economic pre-eminence. The result, however, is that public procurement contract litigation established the contractual benchmark not only in Construction law but more broadly in the general law of Contracts. Total exclusions of liability are thus possible in consumer contracts, regardless of the harm inflicted, be it bodily harm or death. Granted, individuals should be responsible for what they sign. However, we question whether a liberty interest, as framed in *Tercon*, can be generalised from a context where the greatest risk for one party is lost profits and the other is too big to fail.

This brings us to the second problem of enforcing contracts, namely whether there is any difference between enforcing a judgment from one province to another, as opposed to the enforcement of foreign, non-Canadian judgments. Naturally, the fact that the Charter establishes uniform 'baseline' standards of justice throughout the country supposes that there is some mutual recognition between Canadian

[58]See para 2.3 above, 'Administrative jurisdiction over Contract Disputes'.

[59]*R. (Ontario) v Ron Engineering*, [1981] 1 SCR 111 (Supreme Court of Canada).

[60]*Shell Canada Products Ltd. v Vancouver (City)*, [1994] 1 SCR 231 (Supreme Court of Canada).

[61]*Envoy Relocation Services Inc. v Canada* (Attorney General), 2013 ONSC 2034 (Ontario Superior Court of Justice), has been described as the 'mother of all tender cases'—the award for damages against government was $29 million for breach of the 'bidding contract'.

provinces. Yet it was not until 1990 that the Supreme Court of Canada recognised that by stating in *Morguard Investments Ltd. v De Savoye* that the conventional territorial view of judicial jurisdiction 'fl[ies] in the face of the obvious intention of the Constitution to create a single country'.[62] The Court added that mobility rights in the Canadian Charter of Rights and Freedoms make it difficult to view the provinces completely isolated from one another, as different countries.[63] *Morguard* was not about binding extra-provincial courts to one another's precedents but whether Canadian judgments should be provided with greater recognition in Canada than those of foreign countries. The answer, in this regard, was firmly 'yes'.

The facts in *Morguard* could seem particular, yet they are all too common. The dispute related to the enforcement of a default judgement against a non-resident of the province of Alberta. The defendant mortgagee owned property in Alberta but resided in the neighbouring province of British Columbia. Having defaulted in his payments, action was successfully taken against him in Alberta, following which the judgments were enforced against him in his province of residence. The problem that arose in this case was whether the law to be applied in the recognition and enforcement of judgments was the same as between all jurisdictions, Canadian and foreign, or whether the recognition and enforcement of such judgments within Canada was constitutionally unified and therefore operated under a different regime, to which the Supreme Court answered with a clear 'no'. The standards of justice in Canada are unified, and therefore courts cannot treat judgments from sister provinces as they would any foreign judgment.

4 Conclusion

Traditionally, constitutions are studies for what they say, whether explicitly or implicitly. One does not instinctively look for what is not there. This approach, however, may be misleading. Indeed, fundamental points are often those that are unsaid because they already garner social agreement. This may well be the case of contracts. Even though contracts are not specifically mentioned in the Canadian Constitution, it does set out their 'outer shell', and this constitutional 'outer shell' tells us much about contracts, even though it is not as precise as the law of contracts itself. This essay began by questioning the proposition that Canadian Contract law is derived from the Constitution. It ended with an examination of the idea of contractual freedom, as exemplified in case law pertaining to the Canadian Charter. Both these views describe the outer shell of Contract law, which could otherwise be qualified as Canada's *ius commune* of contracts. Thus, while the Canadian Constitution says little about the institution of contracts, the law of Contracts could just as

[62] *Morguard Investments Ltd. v De Savoye*. [1990] 3 SCR 1077 (Supreme Court of Canada), para 36.

[63] Canadian Charter of Rights and Freedoms.

well be described as a bedrock of the Constitution rather than a mere derivative thereof.

Moreover, the introduction of the Charter and the Constitution Act, 1982, is an opportunity to reconsider this view. Rather than re-ascribing Private law to constitutional shadows, the Constitution Act, 1982, could be an opportunity for reaffirming the role of the state in the development of contractual freedom. That being said, many of the ideas underlying the Constitution Act, 1867 and 1982, may not be easy to discuss, although that does not mean they should be ignored. It would be all too easy to set aside the discussion of *ius commune* on the pretence that it does not exist or that in cannot exist in a federal state such as Canada. The supremacy of the Canadian Constitution does not mean that all discussions should end with its wording.

Acknowledgements Thank you to Micheline Gleixner and Jules César Katagurutse for reviewing this chapter. Any residual errors remain my own.

References

Dixon O (1957) The common law as an ultimate constitutional foundation. ALJ 21:240–254

Hogg PW (1993) Subsidiarity and the division of powers in Canada. NJCL 3:341–355

Hogg PW (ed) (2011) Constitutional law of Canada. Carswell, Toronto

Jackman M, Porter B (2007) Socio-economic rights under the Canadian charter. In: Langford M (ed) Social rights jurisprudence: emerging trends in international and comparative law. CUP, New York, pp 209–229

La Forest GV (1975) Delegation of legislative power in Canada. McGill Law J 21(1):131–147

Macdonald RA (1997) Encoding Canadian civil law. In: Brierley JEC et al (eds) Mélanges Paul André Crépeau. Yvon Blais, Cowansville, pp 579–640

Scott FR (1942) Section 94 of the British North America Act. CBR 20:525–544

Walters MD (2001) The common law constitution in Canada: return of *lex non scripta* as fundamental law. UTLJ 51(2):91–141

Reflections on the *Pactum* in the Public and Private Spheres

Luca Siliquini-Cinelli

Abstract This chapter delves into the nature of the *pactum* as both substantial and functional bond, as well as mythical canon of any contractual-constituting initiative in the public and private spheres. The aim is to show that the movement toward the conceptualisation of good faith as an organising principle and implied term in the Common law tradition is due to the need to counterbalance our inhuman condition as made manifest by the humanitarian façade of the modern constitutional project. This claim is supported by an unconventional method of investigation that will promote the comparison between the role of political action at the public level and the increasing utilisation of the doctrine of good faith in Contract law theory and practice.

1 Introduction

The idea to embark upon the editing of this book was born from the writing of a paper whose aim was to address the reasons and extent to which, within the area of specific performance, the development of the law of contract is currently influenced by constitutional values and Fundamental rights issues in South Africa, the UK and Australia.[1] On that occasion, particular attention was dedicated to the analysis of how and why the common trend towards good faith and contractual fairness in these jurisdictions is characterised by a clear divergence of positivistic methodologies. In light of that study and its outcomes, other chapters deal with the interplay of Fundamental rights and Constitutional/Contract law on a comparative basis to

This chapter is based on a paper presented at the Annual Conference of the UK Branch of the International Association for Philosophy of Law and Social Philosophy (IVR), held at the School of Law, Queen's University Belfast, on 23 October 2015. The theme of the conference was *Public/ Private: Unlocking the Boundaries of Legal Thought*. I wish to thank all those who provided me with valuable suggestions. I am particularly grateful to Oscar Roos for constructive comments on an earlier draft. Errors are mine only.

[1]Siliquini-Cinelli and Hutchison (2016).

L. Siliquini-Cinelli (✉)
Department of Law, Liverpool Hope University, Liverpool, UK
e-mail: siliqul@hope.ac.uk

L. Siliquini-Cinelli, A. Hutchison (eds.), *The Constitutional Dimension of Contract Law*, DOI 10.1007/978-3-319-49843-0_11

provide the reader with other compelling accounts of several core components of the contractarian dimension.

The appearance of the present contribution at the end of this collection of essays is due not only to its length but also to its essence, which is far less positivistic and more philosophical[2] than that of the pieces that precede it. The intent is indeed to offer a general theoretical framework to contextualise further the constitutionalisation of Contract law from a broader perspective of inquiry. This will be done by addressing what the *pactum*, as both substantial and functional bond and mythical canon of any contractual-constituting initiative, is currently experiencing in the West at the private and public levels.

Supiot is of the opinion that the Westernisation of living standards is informed by the liberal ideology of 'contractualism', that is, by 'the idea that the contractual bond is the ultimate form of social bond and is destined to replace the unilateral imperatives of the law everywhere'.[3] Rather than being something to favour, Supiot maintains that the West's belief in contractualism ought to be challenged as it drains the law's anthropological function by 'conceiv[ing] of society as a sum of individuals motivated by self-interested calculation'.[4] The reason for this is, Supiot notes, the instrumentalist role assumed by 'the law of contract . . . [in] market operations'.[5]

Importantly, Supiot further distinguishes the ideology of contractualism from its material counterpart, which he defines as the 'process of contractualisation' and which is aimed at extending all those 'contractual techniques' that are in line with the liberal conception of societal relations and the West's aspiration for global, systematic unity. The role that Supiot assigns to contractualism in the 'blurring of the distinction between public and private'[6] appears to be consistent with Cotterrell's notion of 'legal ideology of contract'. According to Cotterrell, the ideology of contract is indeed made up of two different elements: one referring to the humanising fiction perpetrated through contracts, the other to the pervasiveness of contractual relationships and the relevance of their repercussions for society at large. More specifically, with respect to the former component, Cotterrell specifies that '[t]he ideological significance of legal contract form lies in the idea of legal *equivalence*, the exact legal balancing of reciprocal rights and obligations of formally equal contracting parties assumed to be acting freely'.[7] However, Cotterrell notes, '[i]n this way the law systematically interprets actual relations and conditions of inequality and substantial unfreedom as relations of equality and free choice, and attaches legal consequences accordingly'.[8] The second element is,

---

[2]On the importance of having a philosophical approach to comparative law, see Ewald (1995). See also Samuel (1998).

[3]Supiot (2007), p. 83.

[4]Ibid., p. 84. See also Collins (1999), pp. 128–147.

[5]Supiot (2007), p. 85.

[6]Supiot (2007), p. 106.

[7]Cotterrell (2008), p. 175. (Emphasis in original).

[8]Ibid.

instead, that of universality in the sense that this ideology performs its instances in everyday life because it is capable 'of being applied [also] to ... relations not directly concerned with economic production'.[9] Through this double-featured structure and force, '[t]he pervasive legal ideology of contract ... promotes the breakdown of all major status differentials unconnected with the needs of an economy based on market exchanges and confirms and defines the particular form of individualism in them of which capitalist social relations are conceptualised'.[10]

What is of significance for our purposes is that, once combined, Supiot's and Cotterrell's accounts of what contractualism and the contractualisation of human existence entail are in line with the well-known notion of *homo oeconomicus*, that is, of a subject who does not act freely in determining who she is as a person but merely behaves according to reason-oriented inputs.[11] The paradigm of *homo oeconomicus* is in this sense the protagonist of a form of society underpinned by inter-subjectivity without subjects. This self-dissolving essence of *homo oeconomicus* is due to the fact that reason is common to of all us, and thus, as Kahn has pointed out, 'is not self-defining'.[12] When we pursue our own *interest*, that is, when we let our attitude be determined by the outcome of a *rational* calculation (Heidegger would call it the 'calculating self-adjustment of *ratio*'[13]), we do not *actively* decide for and against something or someone but merely dwell in what we should perhaps define as a procedural—as opposed to absolute—truth. Consequently, to speak of 'rational action' is nothing but an oxymoron: action is never as rational, or predictable, as behaviour is. This explains why the civilising mission of contract[14] has played a pivotal role in the formation of our post-historical and post-political condition by displacing the self-affirming properties of action. As such, it has also revealed the illusory character of social contract theories and the modern constitutional ideal as we are accustomed to consider them.

To understand this fully, attention should be paid to the opposed condition that the humanising (that is, self-defining, historical, and political) *deditio in fidem* expressed in and performed through the pact is assuming in the constitutional (public) and contract (private) spheres in Western jurisdictions. The need to conduct such an analysis is related to (1) the move of Western civilisation towards a global model of society underpinned by the notions of 'civilised economy' and

[9]Ibid., p. 176.

[10]Ibid.

[11]My approach to *homo oeconomicus* is purely philosophical. Given how often the term 'self-determination' is used to describe this form of conduct, it is expected that some commentators would not share this view. See Schütte, in this book.

[12]Kahn (2008), p. 175. See also Stein (1980), p. 3.

[13]Heidegger (1998a), p. 50.

[14]Supiot (2007), pp. 79–86.

'good economic governance'[15]; (2) the increased reference to the doctrine of good faith in Common[16] law jurisdictions, which notwithstanding their emphasis on the pursuit of self-interest has reached an unprecedented extension, as is made evident with the recent Canadian and Irish cases of *Bhasin v. Hrynew* and *Flynn v. Breccia.*[17]

This chapter is structured as follows. Section 2 will engage with the former trend in light of the modern constitutional project as epitomised by Hobbes' social contract theory. Section 3 will prepare the ground for the neo-realist contextualisation of the latter phenomenon by reflecting on Comparative law's

[15]Both terms refer to the belief that governments should educate consumers and build or reform institutions to regulate economic activities according to rational global standards determined by outsiders.

[16]I use capital 'C' to refer to the Common law as a legal tradition. Common (with an uppercase c) law and common law are two different things: while the former is a legal tradition marked by a number of particular characteristics, the latter refers to only a part of the Common law (and includes elements of both case law and Customary law).

[17][2014] SCC 71 (Supreme Court of Canada) and [2015] IEHC 547 (Irish High Court) respectively. The growing relevance of good faith in the Common law tradition may also be witnessed in the (not linear and at time inconsistent) developments of the subject in England, Australia, New Zealand, and Scotland (a mixed legal jurisdiction). Cf. *Lymington Marina Ltd v MacNamara* [2007] Bus LR Digest D29 (England and Wales Court of Appeal (Civil)); *Socimer International Bank Ltd v Standard Bank London Ltd,* [2008] 1 Lloyd's Rep 558 (England and Wales Court of Appeal (Civil)); *Yam Seng Pte Ltd v International Trade Corporation Ltd,* [2013] EWHC 111 QB (England and Wales High Court (Queen's Bench)); *North East Solutions Pty Ltd v Masters Home Improvement Australia Pty Ltd* [2016] VSC 1 (Supreme Court of Victoria); *Pacioccio v Australia and New Zealand Banking Group Limited,* [2015] FCAFC 50 (Federal Court of Australia); *Mineralogy Pty Ltd v Sino Iron Pty Ltd,* (No 6) [2015] FCA 825 (Federal Court of Australia); *Commonwealth Bank of Australia v Barker* [2014] HCA 32 (High Court of Australia); *Bobux Marketing Ltd v Raynor Marketing Ltd,* [2002] 1 NZLR 506 (Court of Appeal of New Zealand); *Smith v Bank of Scotland,* [1997] SC (HL) 111 (House of Lords).

It seems that the courts shared Martijn W. Hesselink's conviction that 'common law lawyers should not fear the concept of good faith.' See Hesselink (2010), p. 648. *Contra*, arguing that good faith in the performance of contracts 'is not a concept foreign to the common law', see Allsop JC's remarks in *United Group Rail Services Ltd v Rail Corporation New South Wales,* [2009] NSWCA 177, para 634 [58] (New South Wales Court of Appeal), and in *Paciocco v Australia and New Zealand Banking Group Limited,* cited above, para 287. To be compared to Bingham LJ's statements in *Interfoto Picture Library Ltd v StilettoVisual Programmes Ltd* [1989] QB 433, paras 439 and 445. See also Lowly and Rawlings (2005), p. 83. See also Carter (2012), p. 22.

Given the scope of this contribution, in the following pages I will not deal with the content of these judgements, nor with their analytical repercussions. Suffice to say that in *Bashin*, before awarding to good faith the status of an *organising principle* 'in order to make the common law less unsettled and piecemeal, more coherent and more just' (at [33]), Cromwell J discussed the US scenario and endeavoured in a comparative enterprise among Common law jurisdictions to point out how, from the UK to the Australia, the doctrine of good faith has become increasingly important in recent years. Yet it would be prudent to set the US apart from comparable cases because of its well-known 'exceptionalism', which in Contract law assumes the form of the peculiar relationship between the Anglo component of its legal system as a whole and a code (the Uniform Commercial Code) in which, along with the doctrine of fair dealing, the duty to act in good faith is normativised. For a compelling account on the role that good faith and bad faith play in American Public law, see Pozen (2016).

status and methodologies of inquiry at the time of writing. Section 4 will then move on to comparing the humanising, active role that good faith plays in Contract law theory and practice with Hobbes' juridical-institutional model of society. Concluding remarks will follow.

2 The *Pactum* at the Public Level

Authority and sovereignty disappeared in the West long ago, when power absorbed them both. As I have been claiming for some time now, the substitution of authority and sovereignty with power has occurred alongside the absorption of the (self-defining, historical and political) negativity of action and experience by the (self-dissolving, post-historical and post-political) positivity of reason-oriented behaviour and knowledge. The effects of this artifice have become particularly noticeable since the fall of the 'bipolar' system. Several data suggest indeed that what the Western paradigm of global civilisation has been undergoing since the end of the 'bipolar' age is a two-pronged trend. At the public level, the authoritarian and sovereign character of the *pacta sunt servanda* doctrine appears to have been increasingly weakened by the force through which soft-networked mechanisms of managerial post-national governance displace the irreducibility of foundation that characterises both political action[18] and any constituting initiative. The shift from 'input' (negative) to 'output' (positive) forms of legitimation and accountability in which post-national governance's liquid working logic is rooted may be used to support this argument. The same may be said with respect to the fact that constitutionalism is said to have become conceptually transnational,[19] or that public autonomy has ceased to be relevant,[20] and that the basic conceptual configurations of the kino-political paradigm of our time (i.e., movement) have no origin.[21] If we are all 'migrants' rather than 'citizens', it might be noted, it is because the functioning of flows, junctions, circulations, circuits and re-circulations drains the constitutive properties of political action by giving priority to the dynamism that keeps our post-historical and post-political condition alive.

[18]It should be clarified at this early stage that, contrary to Arendt, I conceive of the 'will' as a vital component of political action.

[19]Zumbansen (2012) and Goderis and Versteeg (2015). See Sects. 3 and 4, below.

Arendt's insight into the vanishing of (legal and political) authority may be of assistance here. In her words, the loss of authority 'is tantamount to the loss of the groundwork of the world, which indeed . . . has begun to shift, to change and transform itself with ever-increasing rapidity from one shape into another . . . '. See Arendt (2006a), p. 95. See also ibid. p. 91, and (2006b), pp. 171–206. Yet some commentators might contend that this depends on how the transposition of constitutions to external arenas is historically interpreted. See Frankenberg (2012).

[20]Somek (2012), p. 58.

[21]Nail (2015), pp. 21–38.

Similarly, the fast-developing spread of fluid schemes of global governance seems to indicate that our current inhuman condition is due to what Agamben has defined as the 'complete confusion' between 'juridification and commodification of human relations'.[22] Therefore, it seems difficult to dispute that, as Negri has summarised, '[t]he passage from government to governance infringes [upon] the unitary regulation of the systems of public law'.[23]

On the contrary, I submit, the notion of contractual good faith as an organising principle or implied duty is increasingly (and perhaps unconsciously) used within the Private law dimension as a tool to counterbalance this dehumanising phenomenon.[24] An inquiry into the intensification of the use of the doctrine of good faith in Common law countries—that is, in jurisdictions whose Contract law is underpinned by the reason-oriented, behavioural logic of consideration—from a post-humanist[25] perspective would prove that, at least to a certain extent, contracts are being used as an instrument of government rather than governance.[26]

The contract's paradoxical development may not only serve either to confirm or question the above suggestions on the status of the public sphere but also shed new light on what unites the demise of law's anthropological and socio-political functions—which I have addressed in my previous works—with the essence of our dehumanised condition, as well as with the use of bio-politics as its signature. This in turn depends on our ability and willingness to interpret correctly what the *pactum* has been experiencing in both public and private dimensions. For my own part, I believe that the starting point of such an intellectual endeavour should be Arendt's account of the Hobbesian strategy to preserve the bourgeois' economic interests and imperialist expansion . In particular, according to Arendt, the artificial birth of the Leviathan was based 'not on some kind of constituting law . . . which determines the rights and wrongs of the individual's interest with respect to public affairs, but on the individual interests themselves.'[27] This is so because '[p]ower, according to Hobbes, is the accumulated control that permits the individual to fix prices and regulate supply and demand in such a way that they contribute to his own advantage'.[28]

Arendt's claim lent considerable support from Weiss and Hobson's exemplary study on the symbiosis between modern state formation and economics,[29] Gellner's historical reconstruction of the rise of economic nationalism between the sixteenth

---

[22]Agamben (2012a), p. 40. To be compared to the notion of 'mercatocracy' used by Cutler (2003).

[23]Negri (2010), p. 217.

[24]Supiot (2007), pp. 83 and 103, correctly links the 'weakening of the State' brought about by the processes of '(re-)territorialization' to the ideology of 'contractualism'.

[25]The label 'post-humanist' refers to the need to protect and promote human values and Fundamental rights through politics and justice whilst at the same time neutralising humanism's secular *exclusions*. The increase in inequality brought about by the (allegedly civilising) globalisation of trade is testament to this. See Rosanvallon (2013).

[26]Zumbansen (2007).

[27]Arendt (1973), p. 139. See also Arendt (2005), pp. 98–99.

[28]Ibid.

[29]Weiss and Hobson (1995).

and eighteen centuries,[30] Thornhill's contention that in many cases statehood depends on transnationalism,[31] and O'Donoghue's description of constitutionalism as an instrument of 'governance' rather than 'government'.[32] The revolutionary lucidity of Arendt's argument may therefore help us uncover the limits of classic approaches to the modern constitutional process and thus uncover the relationship between the double-featured condition undergone by the contract at the time of writing.

Martin Loughlin's scholarship on Hobbes and sovereignty may serve as an example. In one of his major works, *The Idea of Public Law*, Loughlin has defined sovereignty not only as 'the foundational concept underpinning public law [which] stands as a representation of the autonomy of the political' but also as 'a function of the institutional arrangements established as a consequence of the formation of the modern state'.[33] The conceptualisation of 'the people' as a collective political actor is then rooted in the foundation of the sovereign state and idea that public power acquires an ontologically autonomous status.[34] Thus, to Loughlin, sovereignty is a never-ending politico-relational enterprise between constituted and constituent powers. In promoting this regulatory view, Loughlin also explained why, being autonomous, political power cannot be encapsulated within a specific place once and for all but must be let free to circulate and express itself in every political relationship.[35]

I agree with Tierney that Loughlin's account 'helps us to bypass two caricatures prominent within public law scholarship' in the UK, namely the 'law as politics' and the 'pure theory of positive law'.[36] More precisely, I share Loughlin's belief in the importance of distinguishing between the *political conception* of sovereignty from its *institutional configuration*—a view that recalls the politico-theological distinction between *creatio* and *conservatio*, and in particular Erich Peterson's 1935 separation between *kingdom* and *government*.[37] However, Loughlin's contention that as long as 'novel institutional arrangements' do not affect 'the question of "ultimate" authority', sovereignty is preserved[38] does not help us appreciate that the substitution of political government with administrative governance occurred along the path initiated by power's absorption of authority and sovereignty.

---

[30]Gellner (1983).

[31]Thornhill (2012).

[32]O'Donoghue (2014).

[33]Loughlin (2003), pp. 93 and 80, respectively.

[34]Ibid., p. 78. From this it inevitably follows that the concept of constitutional pluralism is an oxymoron. See Loughlin (2014).

[35]Ibid., p. 83.

[36]Tierney (2008), p. 15.

[37]Agamben (2011a).

[38]Loughlin (2003), p. 95; Loughlin (2008), pp. 56–59. Similar suggestions are made by many. Others argue instead for the possibility of relativising the concept of legitimacy/authority itself. See van der Vossen (2011); Roughan (2011). See also the (2013) 4(3) Issue of *Transnational Legal Theory*.

Similarly, Loughlin's account of the Hobbesian contractarian model of sovereignty falls short of offering us the tools that we need to understand the unofficial essence of the nation state's building process in its entirety. I refer particularly here to Loughlin's suggestion that Hobbes' social contract theory is 'a purely juristic account of the state'.[39] This is a view that is entirely different from Arendt's argument that 'Hobbes' picture of man defeats his purpose of providing the basis of a Commonwealth and gives instead a consistent pattern of attitudes through which every genuine community can easily be destroyed'.[40]

Hence, I would rather suggest that we commence our attempt to ascertain the condition of the *pactum* at the public level with Arendt's and Agamben's shared interest in what the constitution and development of the nation state has revealed about the subjects of bio-politics. Notwithstanding the different trajectories of their thoughts,[41] the common denominator in Arendt's and Agamben's scholarship is indeed that no rights can be guaranteed to those who are deprived of membership in a political community.

Agamben famously argued that the politico-juridical figure of the Western tradition is that of *homo sacer*, that is, of a man who cannot be officially killed and yet should such a killing occur, no one would be held responsible. This figure has emerged through the formation of a zone of indistinction between bare life (*zoē*) and political existence (*bios*), mentioned earlier. Hence, *contra* Foucault, Agamben showed that the bio-political violence that humans experience daily, and that reached its culmination with the Nazi death camp, had its inception long before modernity, at the point when the regulative apparatus of the *oikonomia* first emerged[42]; rather, the modern nation state has merely placed bio-politics 'at the centre' of its own 'calculations' by using the declaration of rights as a way to blur the distinction between bare life and its political counterpart. More particularly, '[d] eclarations of rights represent the originary figure of the inscription of [the] natural into the juridico-political order of the nation-state'.[43]

What matters for the scope of our discussion is that Agamben assigned to the formation of bourgeois democracy and the voiding of the distinction between public and private a key role in this process. Similarly, Arendt referred to the intrusion of the bourgeois' emancipation into the realm of the political to point out that Hobbes' cruel artifice stands in clear opposition to the notions of political freedom and political community out of which, we are told, the modern

[39]Loughlin (2015), p. 6. See also Loughlin (2012), p. 282: 'The modern constitution is … conceived by Hobbes to be a contract entered into by the people to establish a comprehensive framework through which the institutions of government are established and the exercise of their powers regulated'.

[40]Arendt (1973), p. 140. On this point, see also Franz Borkenau's scholarship on Hobbes.

[41]Agamben (2016), p. 23. For an introduction, see Liska (2013).

[42]Agamben (2011b); see also Agamben (2007a, 2012a, 2013a, 2015).

[43]Agamben (1998), pp. 6 and 127. See also ibid. p. 121; Agamben (2016), p. 263, where Agamben seems to contradict himself on the use of the terms 'natural' and 'bare' life.

constitutional initiative arose.[44] The reason for this is that both concepts depend on 'the company of other men who [are] in the same state, and ... [need] a common public space to meet them—a politically organised world ... into which each of the free men could insert himself by word and deed'.[45] Conversely, '[w]here men live together but do not form a body politic', this peculiar form of freedom does not manifest itself: '[w]ithout a politically guaranteed public realm, freedom lacks the worldly space to make its appearance'.[46] For the constitution of a body politic to occur, the subjects must have the capacity to enjoy political freedom through deed and action; that is, they must have the political 'capacity to act', as Barbour has rightly noted.[47] This definition of the body politic is clearly related to what Arendt argued about the disappearance of the 'private/public' sphere divide as brought about by the socialisation of humankind's existence.[48] In particular, Arendt's conceptualisation of political freedom and the role that the spontaneity of political action plays in its formation and protection can be overlapped with her metaphorical description of the public realm as a 'table' that prevents the 'people gathered around' from 'falling over each other'.[49]

If Agamben's bio-political reconstruction and Arendt's contentions about the rise of society, nature of the body politic and Hobbes' instrumentalist strategy are correct, it would mean that, in his fight against the fear of death (*homo homini lupus*), Hobbes aimed at more than simply securing the stability and peace that humans need for self-preservation. More particularly, Arendt's claims lead one to think that the nation state is perhaps the West's greatest paradox of the last three centuries: the same (exceptional, as Schmitt would say) sovereign contractual-constitutionalising process of pure, immediate and simultaneous 'potentiality' and 'actuality'[50] that led to the formation of the modern form of polity, and whose humanitarian façade was aimed at guaranteeing our existential political freedom through the safety of the newly formed community (*homo homini deus*), is best understood as a politico-juridical fiction put forward for speculative reasons.

The influence that Stoic universalism and structuralisation of human existence has had on the development of Western tradition and formation of the modern nation state[51] further confirms that what we are dealing with is but a process that commenced long ago. From this it follows that Hobbes' illusory device leaves us

---

[44] Arendt (1998), p. 68.

[45] Arendt (2006a), p. 147.

[46] Ibid. See also ibid. p. 153.

[47] Barbour (2013), p. 307. (Emphasis added).

[48] Arendt (1998), pp. 28 and 46.

[49] Arendt (1998), p. 53. See also Agamben (2005), pp. 95 and 106.

The table metaphor recalls Heidegger's (otherwise very different) scholarship on the role of 'nearness' in every *act* of 'ek-sistence'. In Heidegger's words, 'the human being, existing as a transcendence that exceeds in the direction of possibilities, is a *creature of distance*'. See Heidegger (1998b), p. 135.

[50] Agamben (1998), pp. 44–48.

[51] Cassirer (1946), pp. 163–75.

with an interrogative of the first order regarding our inhuman condition: whether the modern form of politico-national community into which we think we were born—and whose signification, we argue, has been transcended by its 'post-' variant[52]—ever actually existed. More than 50 years ago, MacPherson insisted that it did not. More precisely, while explaining why 'the seventeenth-century concepts of freedom, rights, obligation, and justice are all [shaped] by [the] concept of possession', MacPherson argued that Hobbes wanted to establish a 'possessive market society' and demonstrated that for Hobbes, the state of nature is already a community of 'civilised' people. From a sociological perspective, '[Hobbes'] state of nature is a statement of the behaviour to which men as they now are, men who live in civilized societies and have the desires of civilized men, would be led if all law and contract enforcement ... were removed'. Thus, '[t]he state of nature is a deduction from the appetites and other faculties not of man as such but of civilized men'.[53]

Yet it could be objected that MacPherson's argument is not of great assistance to us as it is well known that the Hobbesian state of nature has never been a real epoch in historical terms but merely represents 'a principle internal to the City'.[54] The point, however, is that Hobbes fictionally referred to an ahistorical, and thus inhuman, model of society to elaborate on a concept of sovereign power and body politic that equally rejected what makes us human. Thus, Arendt claimed that Hobbes' political roadmap 'exclu[ded] in principle ... the idea of humanity'.[55] For different reasons and through different patterns of inquiry, Agamben too uncovered the illusory humanitarian character of the nation state by identifying a link between its secular functioning and the administrative apparatus of the Church: considering that 'theology [has] resolv[ed] itself into atheism' because of the administrative regulative model prompted by the Church, '[m]odernity, removing God from the world, has not only failed to leave theology behind, but in some ways has done nothing other than to lead the project of the providential *oikonomia* to completion'.[56] If that is the case, then the fact that 'popular sovereignty [is] by now an expression drained of all meaning'[57] comes as no surprise: it is the inevitable

[52]The founding of dedicated law journals and book series, as well as the launch of new undergraduate and postgraduate courses in transnational and global law worldwide, are testament to this subject's increasing relevance within legal discourse. For present purposes, in addition to Teubner's scholarship on post-national societal constitutionalism, see Twining (2009), Kuo (2010), Handl et al. (2012), Dobner and Loughlin (2010), Walker (2012), Krisch (2010), Amhlaigh et al. (2013), Zumbansen (2013) and Helfand (2015). See also the (2008) 6(3)–(4) Special Issues of the International Journal of Constitutional Law on the symposium 'Constitutionalism in an Era of Globalization and Privatization', and the interview with Canada's Prime Minister Justin Trudeau in the *New York Times*, in which Canada is defined as the 'first post-national state', Available at: http://www.nytimes.come/2015/12/13/magazine/trudeaus-canada-again.html?_r=0. Accessed 15 February 2016.

[53]MacPherson (1962), pp. 3, 22, 29, and 46.

[54]Agamben (1998), p. 105.

[55]Arendt (1973), p. 157.

[56]Agamben (2011b), pp. 286–287. See also Agamben (2015), pp. 42–69.

[57]Agamben (2012b), p. 4.

outcome prompted by the working logic of the Western politico-juridical conception according to which human existence and interaction ought to be *managerially administered* rather than *politically governed.*

A neorealist[58] comparison between the contractarian and allegedly humanitarian narrative of the rise of the Leviathan and the bio-political essence of the nation state shows then that the proposed distinction between modernity and what came after it—namely our global, transnational age—is misleading.

3 On Comparative Law and Its Method(s): Knowledge *vs* Experience

Before going any farther with our inquiry, a methodological clarification is in order. Some commentators would indeed deem the aim of this contribution to be pretentious, or at least inappropriate, from a purely Comparative law perspective. This would be a conservative reaction to the fact that, over the last two decades, Comparative law has branched out in new directions, galvanising legal theorists and practitioners; sparking novel sociopolitical, legal and business models; and attracting worldwide attention. Despite arguments to the contrary, Comparative law has thus become a key instrument of thought. The need that has emerged in recent years to introduce the reader to Comparative law discourse,[59] as well as the multitude of studies that have appeared on its method(s) and culture(s),[60] are indicative of the fact that 'comparative law is constantly evolving, in imperfect parallel with the development of law, and society, at large'.[61]

This attitude has had an inevitable impact on the boundaries, and thus identity, of Comparative law itself, as is demonstrated by the way in which scholars from different disciplines have contributed to what was once seen as an exclusively internal debate. This was primarily caused by the attraction that the concept of (legal) 'culture' (and thus, I would add, 'consciousness' in Gadamerian terms) began to develop for comparatists and by the subsequent need to clarify what it could reveal and eventually lead to.[62] Fletcher's belief that the value of applying the comparative inquiry to the legal domain lies in the fact that 'it expands the agenda of available possibilities'[63] is a clear testament to this in that it poses the basis for cultural criticism. It cannot be doubted that while trying to understand the political

[58]D'Agostini (2014).

[59]Husa (2015), Tushnet (2014), Samuel (2014b), Smits (2014), Örücü and Nelken (2007) and Gordley (2006).

[60]Adams and Heirbaut (2014), Adams and Bomhoff (2012), Van Hoecke (2011), Van Hoecke (2004), Siems (2014), Monateri (2012) and Clark (2012).

[61]Michaels (2015), p. 1.

[62]Legrand and Munday (2003), Nelken and Feest (2001) and Nelken (1997).

[63]Fletcher (1998), p. 695.

relationship between law's regulative instances and those it tries to protect by imposing respect for itself and/or stimulating that respect, comparatists, legal sociologists and, in part, legal anthropologists and historians have entered each other's areas of specialisation; they have 'borrowed' notions, doctrines, methodologies and strategies in adopting the same constructivist logic of 'transplant' that the majority of them criticised when arguing for the need to respect what identifies the 'other'.

This doctrinal trend deserves an extended treatment, certainly more than can be provided here. It must thus suffice to highlight that the uniqueness that characterises the comparative method and its aims has certainly been influenced by it—positively or negatively, depending on the perspective of inquiry. The issue then arises as to whether this scholarly approach to Comparative law poses a threat to law's existential special domain[64]—that is, to the essence of the authoritarian and sovereign institutionalising processes that render law properly legal within normative discourse and power theory. Perhaps the answer to this interrogative may be found in the extent to which the crucial distinction between *social rules* and *legal norms* has been mistakenly displaced from view within legal discourse. And indeed, it is indicative of the confusion that affects the debate that we have reached a stage at which it is thought that the comparative assessment of legal phenomena may be done through the analysis of 'empirically substantiated *behavioural* patterns',[65] thus obscuring how and why law's mythical essence and anthropological and socio-political existential function depend on the subject's free action.

Yet it could be conceded that this may be an inevitable outcome in an age of numberless processes of diversification or fragmentation—i.e., of pluralisation of regulative sources and norm-setting bodies at the macro, meso and micro levels, as well as of 'regime shifting'[66] mechanisms. Hence, Séan Patrick Donlan rightly pointed out that Comparative law's 'methodological pluralism' has become the 'norm' in Comparative law.[67] Having a multidisciplinary approach to (comparative) law and legal reasoning is indeed indispensable to overcoming the limits of reductionist approaches.[68] Pihlajämaki's belief that '[w]e should not become obsessive about defining disciplinary boundaries now that we have finally managed to start removing them'[69] is therefore more than welcome. Yet every interdisciplinary method may also prove to be unsatisfactory.[70] The time seems therefore ripe to admit that the confusion that this process has generated constitutes not the consequence but rather the cause, of why, in Örücü's words, 'the basic problems

[64]In addition to Cotterrell's (2013), p. 23, scholarship on law 'as a flexible, but distinctive and unifying, value structure' with 'a specific effectivity', see Bertea (2009) and Croce (2014).

[65]de Coninck (2010), p. 348; de Coninck (2012). See also Parisi and Luppi (2012).

[66]Benvenisti and Downs (2007) and Zürn and Faude (2013).

[67]Donlan (2014).

[68]Redgwell (2012) and Siliquini-Cinelli (2014).

[69]Pihlajämaki (2014), p. 121.

[70]Husa (2014).

[of comparative law] have remained the same' and why '[t]here is no one definition of what comparative law and comparative method are'.[71] Millns' consideration that 'the methodology of legal comparison remains relatively unadvanced' should thus be investigated from this critical perspective.[72]

From a purely methodological point of view, this means that the two main questions upon which the comparative enterprise within the legal discourse is based, namely 'what is law' and 'what is comparison',[73] are still to be answered. Thus, if one seeks a better understanding of what Comparative law is about, he or she would have to make sense of a series of arguments according to which various things should be compared. These things include cases (Markesinis); legal systems or their rules (Watson); the relationship among system theories (or assumptions and idea) as forces capable of 'structuring' legal rules (Luhmann, Valcke); legal systems and their institutions (Bell and, in part, Örücü); the evolutionary stages of legal concepts and legal institutions (Gutteridge); legal rules in context (Siems, and Örücü, who includes in this notion 'the mysteries of the interaction of social norms and legal rules'[74]); (legal) attitudes (and, thus, commitments) and (concepts of) laws intended neither as 'real/objective facts' nor as (positivistic) 'rules' as 'acts of communication' (Van Hoecke, Samuel); legal institutions and the 'prevailing styles of legal thought' (Ewald); legal arguments or the language used in them (Bomhoff, Fletcher respectively); institutions and the intellectual structures that express them (Sunde); sets of legal rules, legal domains, forms of legal reasoning (Valcke and Grellette); legal-cultural developments and their adaptation (Nelken); the 'cognitive structure' of a legal culture (Legrand, whose quotation usually leads to that of Watson in light of the debate that opposing approaches to legal transplants has generated); concepts of law (Donlan, Heckendorn, Van Hoecke, Husa, Nelken, Melissaris and other legal pluralists); historical developments in the law (Donlan); legal traditions as 'sets of information' (Glenn); legal ideologies (Cotterrell); the economic efficiency of a norm (Parisi, Luppi); EU policies and their implementation (Knill); and legal anthropologies (Mertz, Goodale) and physiologies (Horry, Plamer, Brewer, Cutler). Stemming from the broad field of Public/Constitutional and Administrative Comparative law, we could also include in the list judicial politics (Chavez, Ginsburg, Vanberg, Hirschl, Halberstam, Sheppele); the development of constitutional scholarship (von Bogdandy); and counter-terrorism laws (Kent, Roach).

William Twining is therefore right when he writes that 'comparative law has not defined subject-matter'.[75] In addition, if Comparative law has witnessed an

[71]Örücü (2007), p. 43. A suggestion that seems to be supported by Cotterrell's (at times ambiguous) belief that Comparative law's and legal sociology's 'most general and most scientific projects—to understand law in its development and its variety as an aspect of social life—are identical' see Cotterrell (2003), p. 134.

[72]Millns (2014), p. 285.

[73]Samuel (1998, 2011, 2014a, b).

[74]Örücü (2007), p. 58.

[75]Twining (2000), p. 45. On comparative law's limits in overcoming the challenges that globalisation poses to legal scholarship, see Goodwin (2013), pp. 692–694.

explosion,[76] this has surely been responsible for methodological confusion. It thus cannot surprise anyone that it was the comparatists themselves who blurred one of the most important distinctions behind what makes us human—namely that between 'knowledge' and 'experience'—a distinction that, I believe, should be rediscovered and vehemently promoted in the challenge to our behavioural 'form-of-(non-)living' .

Indeed, Comparative law is either—and simultaneously and/or indirectly—understood as a *discipline/technique/intellectual activity* (Frankenberg, Muir Watt, Van Hoecke, Glenn, Fletcher, Hage, Örücü, Michaels, Samuel, Bell, Adams, Jansen, Löhnig, Monateri, Andenas, Fairgrieve, Rosenfeld, Sajó, Clark, Stapleton, von Bogdandy), as a *science* (Rabel, Sacco, Gutteridge, Örücü, Van Hoecke, Millns, Husa, Hage, Cotterrell, Samuel, Bell, Grossfeld, Valcke, Grellette) or as an act of (local and cultural) *experience* (Curran, Millns, Nelken, Örücü, Grossfeld, Sunde, Adams, Cotterrell, Brownsword, Legrand, Bell, Lasser, Husa, King, Dupret—a vision that has been endorsed by those who understand the legal phenomenon in terms of a 'shared normative experience'[77]). Finally, there are commentators who, in addressing Comparative law's functional attitude as put forward by Zweigert and Kötz (and further pursued by Husa; Michaels; de Coninck and, in part, Valcke; and Grellette), make a claim for the impossibility of reducing its aims to a single methodology of inquiry (Gutteridge, Örücü, Glenn, Brownsword, Adams, Griffiths, Donlan, von Bar, Karhu); others, however, argue for the importance of recognising the possible 'subversive' attitude of Comparative law (Fletcher, Muir Watt) or of having a legal-hermeneutical (Legrand), legal-cultural (Van Hoecke and Warrington), cultural-epistemological (Samuel), heuristic (Husa) or descriptive or purposive approach to it (McEvoy, Valcke).

The variety of these approaches is clearly rooted in the multiple substrata that characterise law's '*norm*-alising' enterprise. In addition, their pluralistic essence is informed by the roadmap pursued by contemporary legal scholarship broadly understood, which is to use the 'multiple shifting boundaries of law—as discipline, as practice, as focus of study, as form of knowledge'[78] to try to explain *the* law's detachment from the state. More importantly for our purposes, from a purely Comparative law perspective, these accounts seem to find a unifying sentiment in the belief that the comparative method is an 'empirical, descriptive research design using "comparison" as a technique to cognise',[79] as well as in those accounts that define Comparative law in terms of a multi-featured 'disciplined practice'.[80] Considering, on the one hand, Pascal's suggestion that there is nothing in the real world that can escape the explanatory temptation of scientific reason and, on the other hand, the wave of disciplinary borrowing described above, it is anything but a coincidence that these claims seem to be in line with the school of thought

[76]Smits (2006), p. xvii.

[77]Melissaris (2009) and Melissaris (2014).

[78]Dedek and Van Praagh (2015), p. xv.

[79]Örücü (2007), p. 48.

[80]Adams and Bomhoff (2012), p. 4.

according to which culture is a 'moral and *cognitive experience*' and that '[a]ny juristic study is . . . a social practice, an intervention in the social world and a way of interpreting that world'[81].

In this respect, what is surprising about the dynamics that these accounts express is the extent of the displacement of the anthropological and philosophical difference between 'knowledge' (*cognitum*) and 'experience' (*nōtum*) or between objective scientific reason that opens a space that remains empty[82] and subjective being-in-*there* that fills that space. Among other factors, this dichotomy has informed the very essence and development of the Western tradition since Pythagoras. It would be beyond the scope of our analysis to describe its emergence and trajectory to date. It must suffice to spend a few words on those thinkers whose reflections may help explain what will be claimed in the next section of this contribution, namely Heidegger, Cassirer and Agamben.

Heidegger thought it necessary to reconsider completely the problem of knowledge in order to demonstrate that it cannot be solved by distinguishing between subject and object. Through a reasoning that will take him close to Parmenides' insights,[83] Heidegger challenged the metaphysical assumptions of scientific knowledge by reaffirming the primacy of man's phenomenological 'ek-sistence' against the illusion brought about by the Western 'onto-theo-logical' tradition as initiated by Plato and Aristotle. This also led him to challenge both the functionalisation of the spirit and modern subjectivism as prompted by Descartes, according to whom knowing is the primary mode of interaction between the subject and an object. To the contrary, Heidegger pointed at what precedes the *cogito*. By delving into the original and modern meanings of (scientific) method, *technē* and *ēpisēme*, Heidegger insisted on *Dasein*'s phenomenological encounter with what constitutes its 'ek-sistence'.[84] Yet, as will be discussed towards the end of the chapter, the 'unfolding' of this phenomenon depends, in turn, on our *willingness* 'to stand in the openness of beings'.[85]

In a no-less-revolutionary and yet completely different way, Cassirer united several opposing claims when inquiring into the cultural debacle of modern times, which in his view is related to science's focus on the cause of phenomena and its aim to simplify the accidental particularity of reality and our experience of it. In particular, Cassirer was of the opinion that human experience had always been 'an organized and articulated experience'.[86] 'What is commonly called the sensory

[81]Cotterrell (2008), pp. 308 and 43 respectively (emphases added). See also Cotterrell (2012).

[82]Kahn (2010), p. 175, according to whom '[r]eason is not self-defining'. See also Kahn (2008).

[83]Although in a different way, Heidegger put forward this argument throughout his scholarship. See paragraphs 12–13 of *Being and Time*, as well as *On the Essence of Truth*, *Letter on Humanism*, *The Thing*, *The Age of World Picture*, *Introduction to Metaphysics*, *What is Called Thinking?*, *Identity and Difference*, *Discourse on Thinking*, *The Nature of Language*, *The Question Concerning Technology*, and *Modern Science, Metaphysics, and Mathematics*.

[84]Heidegger (2008), p. 88. See also ibid., p. 237.

[85]Heidegger (2014), p. 24. See also ibid., pp. 15, 23–24, 33, 49, and 189.

[86]Cassirer (1944), p. 208. See also ibid., pp. 29, 34, 60, and 73.

consciousness, the content of the "world perception"', he wrote in the second volume of *The Philosophy of Symbolic Forms*, '... this is itself a product of abstraction, a *theoretical* elaboration of the "given"'.[87] This theoretical process is nothing but 'perceptive knowledge': '[a]ll conceptual knowledge is necessarily based on intuitive knowledge, and all intuitive knowledge on perceptive knowledge'.[88] This explains why 'symbolic expression is the common denominator in all [man's] activities'.[89] From this it flows that the problem of human knowledge cannot be understood without delving into the relationship between man and the symbolic forms that reality (and, thus, the experience we make of it) may assume.[90] As was pointed out in the essay known in English as *The Logic of the Cultural Sciences*, this is so because neither (scientific) thought nor experience 'is able to determinate the "initself" of man except by pointing it out in the phenomena'.[91] Thus, 'instead of saying that the human intellect is in need of "images" we should rather say that it is in need of symbols' as 'refracting media'.[92] In contrast with Heidegger, Cassirer thus found in the phenomenology of the symbol(s) the way to explain why the problem of representation (and, thus, perception, conception and expression) is itself 'the central problem of knowledge'.[93]

According to Cassirer, there is a clear zone of indistinction, or intersection, between pure immediacy and epistemological thought. This zone is represented by the *symbol*, that is, by the instrument with which we mediate reality and make a synthesis of it ('all cultural activities ... fulfil one and he same task: the task of objectification'.[94] The symbol thus mediates between reality and subjectivity because, instead of having independent 'existence as part of the physical world[,] it has "meaning"'.[95] This is why, in the history of humankind, the symbol has assumed different *forms*: myth, language, religion, art, history and science. In this sense, what matters for our purposes here is that (1) as the structure of perceptive knowledge demonstrates, the symbol operates even in the first and entirely non-scientific category of apprehension and self-consciousness, that of the myth (which is why Cassirer could argue that the 'relations which [myth] postulates are not logical relations' and at the same time speak of 'mythical thinking'); (2) while myth, language, religion, history and art are influenced by human experience, the essence of all perceptive-organisational form(s) of representation has been nullified

[87]Cassirer (1955b), p. xvi (emphasis added). See also Cassirer (1955a), pp. 89, 107, 111, and 114; Cassirer (1957), p. xiii.

[88]Cassirer (1957), p. 47. Cotterrell's notion of 'cognitive experience' is in line with this form of perceptive knowledge.

[89]Cassirer (1946), p. 45.

[90]See, in particular, Cassirer (1996), pp. 194–200.

[91]Cassirer (2000), p. 102.

[92]Cassirer (1944), p. 57 and Cassirer (1957), p. 1.

[93]Cassirer (1996), p. 193.

[94]Cassirer (1946), p. 45.

[95]Cassirer (1944), p. 57.

by scientific-rational thought. More precisely, the *modality* through which sense-experience produces self-consciousness has become entirely systematic and turned out to be knowledge once a totalising *intellectual symbol* (science) entered the scene. Moved by the 'arrogance' of providing reality with an organising and indifferent unity, this new 'form of objectification' 'has no actual existence as a part of the physical world; it has a "meaning"'.[96] Moved by the 'arrogance' of providing reality with an organising and indifferent unity of phenomenological understanding, science is a 'stage of theoretical knowledge [that] creates a new form of objectification'.[97] Thus, to Cassirer, '[t]o "know" is to advance from the immediacy of sensation and perception to the purely cogitated and mediated "cause," to dissect the simple matter of sensory impressions into strata of "grounds" and "consequences"'.[98]

Agamben too discussed the dichotomy between knowledge and experience, clarifying that while science (whose subject 'is the *noūs* ... which is separate from experience, "impassive" and "divine"'[99]) is aimed at achieving verifiable knowledge, experience (whose subject is 'common sense, something existing in every individual') 'is incompatible with certainty [because] once an experience has become measurable and certain, it immediately loses its authority'.[100] To understand this fully, we must first internalise that 'for Antiquity the central problem of knowledge is not the relationship between a subject and an object, but the relationship between the one and the many'. This is so because 'what is posed for us as the question of experience arose in Antiquity as the question of the relation ... between the separate intellect and particular individuals, between the one and the many, between the intelligible and the sensory, between the human and the divine'. This is why, Agamben notes, by remaining 'faithful to the separation of experience and science, human knowledge and divine knowledge', '[t]raditional experience ... is in fact the experience of the boundary between these two spheres[, namely] death'.[101]

The distinction between intellectual knowledge and *praxis* constitutes the pillar of Agamben's inquiry into the illusion that characterises the Western notion civilisation.[102] What is worth noticing for the scope of this contribution is that, through a distortive anthropological shift, modern science has abolished the distinction between knowledge and experience by making the latter 'the locus—the

[96]Cassirer (1996), p. 217; Cassirer (1944), p. 57.

[97]Cassirer (1996), p. 217.

[98]Cassirer (1955a), p. 73.

[99]Agamben (2007b), p. 18.

[100]Ibid. p. 20. Cassirer also writes that '[i]n the objective content of science individual features are forgotten and effaced, for one of the principal aims of scientific thought is the elimination of all personal and anthropomorphic elements. See Cassirer (1944), pp. 1–22, 207–221, and 228.

[101]Ibid., p. 121.

[102]Agamben (2011b), pp. 122 and 141. Similarly, Marramao (2005, 2007, 2013) places the voiding of experience at the centre of modern secularisation.

"method"; that is, the pathway—of knowledge'.[103] Cassirer offered a similar historical reconstruction; in explaining why the 'modern theory of man lost its intellectual centre [through] a complete anarchy of thought', he maintained that in modern times 'the quest is ... for a general theory of man based on empirical observations and on general logical principles [through] the [scientific] removal of all the artificial barriers that had hitherto separated the human world from the rest of the nature'.[104] Unfortunately, for scientific behaviour to absorb the boundlessness, unpredictability and fallibility of any *act* of experience, its promoters had to 'recast experience and rethink intelligence, first of all expropriating their different subjects and replacing them with a single new subject ... which is none other than their conjunction at an abstract Archimedean point: the Cartesian *cogito*, consciousness'.[105]

In this sense, the total penetration of this mechanical form-of-(non-)living into the deliberative and fallible formation and performance of our volitions, and thus into the *active* determination and *experience* of our uniqueness, should lead us to admit that 'the question of experience can be approached nowadays only with an acknowledgement that it is no longer accessible to us'. This is so because of the role assumed by the 'experiment', which is the enactment of the 'scientific verification of experience ... permitting sensory impression to be deduced with the exactitude of quantitative determinations and, therefore, the prediction of future impressions'. This anthropological shift, Agamben further maintains, has displaced experience 'as far as possible outside the individual: on to instruments and numbers'.[106]

Cassirer had assigned to the scientific experiment the same anthropological role 50 years before Agamben.[107] Later on in his research, he held that '[h]uman culture taken as a whole may be described as the process of man's progressive self-liberation' from the conflicting oscillation between 'stabilisation' and 'evolution', 'objectivity' and 'subjectivity', 'universality' and 'individuality' that has afflicted humans ever since.[108] By offering us the 'assurance of a constant world',[109] and thus perfect harmony through which to control the chaotic movement of what makes us human, science has become the main tool in the quest for this self-liberating order from the 'reason'/'imagination' dichotomy.

The re-discovery of the distinction between self-dissolving knowledge and behaviour and self-defining experience and action may therefore shed new light on the paradoxical condition of the *pactum* in the Public and Private law dimensions that lies at the centre of the chapter. For the very same reason, it can also help us uncover what unites the fictional nature of nation state and the roadmap pursued by

[103] Agamben (2007b), p. 22.
[104] Cassirer (1944), pp. 21 and 13 respectively.
[105] Agamben (2007b), p. 21.
[106] Ibid., p. 20.
[107] Cassirer (1955b), p. 44.
[108] Cassirer (1944), pp. 222–228, at 228; see also Cassirer (2000).
[109] Cassirer (1944), p. 207.

the promoters of the global model of society underpinned by notions of 'civilised economy' and 'good economic governance'. If we agree with Cassirer that the alleged objectiveness of reality is always tested by the critical character of our sensory consciousness,[110] we may soon realise that what we (think) we know about these facts is actually very different from the daily experience we have of them.

4 *Pactum*, Oath and (Good) Faith

4.1 Why Hobbes

The necessity of saying a few words on the need to re-discover the importance of the distinction between knowledge and experience in Constitutional and Contract law discourse is not only related to the role that the latter has in theoretical inquiry. What is of significance for present purposes is rather that, according to Arendt, it was experience (and in particular, the experience of freedom) that rendered the American Revolution successful, unlike its French counterpart,[111] and that Hobbes himself put this dichotomy at the centre of his reflections on the formation and functioning of the body politic.[112] Indeed, it is through the systematic and mechanic conceptualisation of reality that, as Pocock has carefully discussed, Hobbes 'historicis[ed] faith in a new way, one of the highest relevance to politics'.[113] This was done by 'declaring God to be non-existent or irrelevant [because] the whole body of our faith is reducible to the construction of a system of authors and of authority, existing through time and resting on the statements they transmit, our opinion of the authority they have as transmitters, and the authority of the previous speakers, back to God himself, whom we accept as author in the act of accepting any one of them'.[114]

This also suggests that the constitution of the Leviathan may be considered as one of Heidegger's 'inceptions' through which, since Plato, Western metaphysical thought has displaced the self-conscious human subject and thus the radically finite meaning of human existence. It is indeed anything but a coincidence that, while listing the elements of which the *statum civitatis* as common-*wealth* is made, Hobbes adds the particle 'good' before 'will'.[115] Hobbes' aim is to captivate human conduct[116] by setting a limit for something that, being irreducible, cannot,

[110]Cassirer (1955b), pp. 30–33.

[111]Arendt (2006b), pp. 156–170. To Arendt, political action can *only* be such through collective experience. See also Arendt (2005), p. 127.

[112]For two recent accounts, see Galimberti (2016), p. 442; Wootton (2016), pp. 286–299.

[113]Pocock (1989), p. 165. The 'knowledge-experience' antithesis is particularly emphasised in *Behemoth* as well (1990), pp. xvi–xviii.

[114]Pocock (1989), p. 165. See also ibid., pp. 165–66.

[115]Hobbes (1998), p. 116. See also Hobbes (1990), pp. 42 and 58; Hobbes (2009), ch. 17 and 29.

[116]See what Holmes argues in his Introduction to Hobbes' *Behemoth* (1990), p. xi.

per se, be imprisoned. More precisely, believing that man's sinful nature is what causes death among men, Hobbes captivated human action by setting a limit on its essence and performativity so that it could be transformed into behaviour, that is, into a form of conduct that can be controlled. As a result, the ambiguity of experience is replaced with the objectifying and structuralising properties of knowledge. The artificial (i.e., based on geometry and physics) constitution of the Leviathan demands the nullification of the self-asserting 'I-*will*' and its compliance with what Kant, the philosophical father of capitalist reason and distribution of property rights,[117] will define as the universal 'categorical imperative' ('I-will-and-can*not*', to be discussed below).

Hence Hobbes' post-historical and post-political project falls within the broad purview of foundational constitutionalism, that is, the 'idea of a political and social order not based on history and tradition but shaped by humankind along rational lines'.[118] From this it follows that Hobbes is the key to understanding the 'form-of-(non-)living' that underpins our global age. Some commentators may propose that this could be contended for all the political philosophers of the seventeenth century, particularly Locke. However, it was with Hobbes that the modern administrative *ufficium* of mechanical *governance* was inaugurated, in which, to use Pocock's words, 'the whole content of revealed religion is potentially of concern to the civil magistrate'.[119] By 'religion', we should mean the juridico-political *deditio in fidem* that in Greek and Roman times linked the city and the people together.[120] The term 'concern' indicates instead the theoretical premise for the practical voiding that the Hobbesian sovereign, as mere civil magistrate, makes of the public-religious bond with the intent to let civil society's capitalist (and, thus, scientific) interests dissolve the *act* of political *government*. In this way, through what Legendre has rightly defined as the 'logic of assembling', the socio-political and economic order is continuously created, destroyed and re-created for instrumentalist economic purposes as needed.[121] If 'the established tradition of bourgeois society [is] to consider political institutions exclusively as an instrument for the protection of private property',[122] it becomes evident why 'Hobbes … is the only great philosopher to whom the bourgeoisie can rightly and exclusively lay claim'.[123] Arendt has noted that the first step in this roadmap was taken when the bourgeois as 'ruling class in capitalist production … turned to politics out of economic necessity'.[124] Our duty is to point out that this is, in truth, a never-ending process because such emancipation can only be protected as long as 'wealth' is used as 'capital' through reification.[125]

[117]On this point, see Kant's *Metaphysics of Morals* and Benjamin's *Capitalism as Religion*.

[118]Krisch (2010), p. 18.

[119]Pocock (1989), p. 166.

[120]In different terms, see Schiavone (2012), pp. 123–125.

[121]Legenre (2009), p. 41. See also Supiot (2007), p. 31.

[122]Arendt (1973), p. 149.

[123]Ibid., p. 139.

[124]Ibid., p. 126.

[125]Arendt (1998), pp. 139 and 299–300.

Once we acknowledge this, it becomes clear why the intrusion of the administrative *technē oikonomikē* within the domain of the political has not only caused the erosion of the democratic conception of substantial equality but has also determined the birth of the modern state as a mere bureaucratic administrative apparatus in the Weberian sense. To link Weber's notion of 'rational bourgeois economic life' and Agamben's above-quoted conviction that 'the planetary petty bourgeoisie is probably the form in which humanity is moving toward its own destruction' is thus inevitable. If, indeed, 'the concept of the state presupposes the concept of the political',[126] what remains in front of us is nothing but a value-free and post-political *homo animalis* who administers the reason and interest-oriented behavioural interaction of (non-)humans as contracting units.

4.2 Why Good Faith?

Civil law jurisdictions have always had a strong approach to good faith. The fact that the Italian 1942 Civil code was the first in Europe to contain a specific provision on pre-contractual good faith is just an example.[127] Others may be Rudolph von Jhering's and Gabriele Fagella's 1860 and 1906 accounts of the importance of *culpa in contrahendo* and *bona fides*,[128] or Emilio Betti's insistence on an integrative approach to good faith according to which each party has the implied duty to take into account the other's rights and interests.[129]

The Common law courts' recent interest in contractual faithfulness, however, stands in clear opposition to the self-interested logic that underpins both the bargain theory of consideration at the private level and Hobbes' project at the public one. This innovative trend should not be taken for granted, as the neoclassical 'consideration-offer-acceptance' trinity[130] of the civilising mission of contract has not only played a pivotal role in the development of the Common law tradition to date but, among other factors, has determined the World Trade Organisation's preference for Common law systems. From this it follows that when analysing the Common law's contemporary approach to good faith, attention has to paid to (1) humankind's animalisation as brought about by the displacement of traditional politico-juridical

[126] Schmitt (2007), p. 19.

[127] Cf. Art. 1337 Civil code.

[128] See, respectively, *Culpa in Contrahendo der Schadensersatz bei nichtigen oder nicht zur Perfection gelangten Verträgen, in Jahrbücher für die Dogmatik des heutigen röminschen und deutschen Privatrechts*, IV.1; *Dei Periodi Precontrattuali e della loro vera ed esatta costruzione scientifica*, in *Studi Giuridici in Onore di Carlo Fadda*, III, 271. In particular, Fagella showed the importance of distinguishing three different periods of good faith (the period before any offer has been drafted; the period during which an offer is drafted; the period when the offer has been made). Cf. Saleilles (1907).

[129] Betti (1953), p. 90.

[130] Hamson (1938), p. 234.

categories; and (2) to the imperativeness of the post-humanist challenge brought about by the global governance model of the *lex mercatoria*.

The political use of contractual good faith at the centre of this contribution, I contend, suggests that the solution to this delicate double-featured issue is (also) coming from the Private law sphere. While describing the ideology of contractualism, mentioned earlier, Supiot has acutely noted that 'questions that were previously the remit of the State are now referred to the contract and negotiation'.[131] The movement toward the conceptualisation of good faith as an implied term and organising principle, I submit, ought to be inscribed within this phenomenon. More precisely, it is due to the need to counterbalance our inhuman condition.[132]

Once analysed from this perspective of inquiry, it emerges that what we are witnessing through the emphasis on good faith in Contract law theory and practice is the use of Private law's symbolic normative forms to counterbalance our inhuman condition as made manifest by the humanitarian façade of the modern constitutional project. Yet the technical paradox cannot go unnoticed: contractual good faith is becoming the medicine used to heal the wounds caused by the fallacies of the constitutional ideal, that is, of an ideal which is the expression of a contractarian approach to social phenomena. Or we may say that contract is simultaneously employed for sterile regulative reasons at large, as well as a humanising, political principle at the private level.

That this contradictory phenomenon cannot be understood without inquiring into the illusionist scheme that led to the creation of the Hobbesian common-*wealth* is proved by the way in which Australian courts have been using the doctrine of good faith over the last two decades. Australia lacks a comprehensive protection of Human rights and fundamental freedoms at the federal level. This is because its Constitution has neither a Bill of Rights nor strong and effective equal treatment provisions. As a result, the Australian judge is, so to speak, 'forced' to prioritise a contextual rather than formalist approach to ensure respect for fundamental values.[133] As the development of the role of good faith in contracting suggests, Australian courts use the law of contract at times to establish at the private level what the public one cannot provide. This is so notwithstanding the changes in judicial trajectories with respect to the source, content and extent of a general contractual duty of good faith, which should be inscribed in the understandable

[131]Supiot (2007), p. 103.

[132]Cf. Schiavone (2012), pp. 145–153 and 221–224.

[133]On this point, see George Williams' scholarship on Human Rights protection.

need for caution.[134] Similarly, the transplant of the Human rights and unfair contract terms of supra-national regimes into the UK through the Human Rights Act 1998 and the Unfair Terms in Consumer Contracts Regulations 1999 makes the interpreter wonder why, in the land of *Walford v. Miles* in which good faith has long been considered a 'legal irritant',[135] the theoretical accomplishment of the transition 'from liberties to rights'[136] could not have been obtained independently from within.

The combination of these facts with the pre-juridical, mythical origins of faith and action[137] and the importance that good faith is assuming within the Common law tradition should make us wonder whether we are in fact capable of internalising what the mythical, faithful bond that lies at the core of the *pactum* really entails. At first glance, the answer appears to be that we can comprehend and describe it in light of our existential need to make sense of the phenomena that shape our lives. And indeed, Cassirer was of the opinion that, particularly in the sphere of myth, 'we sense . . . the feeling that human culture is not something given and self-evident, but rather that it is a kind of miracle that requires explanation'.[138]

Unfortunately, our intellectual enterprise to discern the humanising force that, through action, good faith plays in Contract law can be immediately challenged from the outset by the very supra-logical essence of any faithful act. If there is one clear message to be taken from Kierkegaard's *Fear and Trembling*, it is that the realm of faith is inaccessible to human discourse and logic. Yet it might be noted that this is, in truth, not even a matter of concern in our post-historical and post-political age—the reason being, as mentioned earlier, that what constitutes human uniqueness is to be found in our faculty to decide both 'for' and 'against' something or someone and then *act*-ively perform our volition in deciding who we are as persons. And if we bear in mind that the law's regulative function depends on the interference of the jurist over the (actively decisive) unpredictability of what makes us human,[139] it follows that the behavioural modes of human existence and

---

[134]In *Pacioccio v Australia and New Zealand Banking Group Limited,* quoted above, Allsop CJ described good faith as a 'normative standard' and further maintained that 'it is a good example of the presence of values in the common law', at paras 290 and 287 respectively. His Honour also described good faith 'as an implication or feature of Australian contract law attending the performance of the bargain and its construction and implied content', at para 287. The lead on this issue was taken in the early 1990s by the New South Wales Court of Appeal, followed by the Victorian Court of Appeal and the Federal Court. The debate about the existence of an implied contractual obligation of good faith tends to be accompanied by that about the effective purview of its content (i.e., reasonableness, fair dealing, etc.) and the existence of fiduciary obligations. Recently, cf. *Mineralogy Pty Ltd v Sino Iron Pty Ltd* (No 6), [2015] FCA 825 (Federal Court of Australia), paras 998–1019.

[135]Teubner (1998), p. 11. To be compared with the more recent developments quoted at the beginning of this chapter.

[136]Costigan and Thomas (2005), p. 51. But see also du Bois' contribution to this book, arguing the Human Rights Act has had very little impact thus far on the law of contract.

[137]Agamben (2005); Agamben (2011b), pp. 15–29; Agamben (2016), p. 23.

[138]Cassirer (2000), p. 3.

[139]Heidegger (2012), p. 31; Heidegger (2008), pp. 283–284.

socialisation prompted at the centre of this contribution displace the need for political and juridical subjectivitisation and representation.

In other words, if what makes us human is unable to perform itself through the constitutive essence of (political) action, we no longer have any existential experience of ourselves. This also explains why the shift from 'input' to 'output' forms of legitimation and accountability in which the experimentalist architecture of inter-connected channels of post-national governance is rooted is one of the main aspects of the current dissolution of what makes us human: in an age in which authority and its foundation have disappeared, there have emerged liquid, soft-networked schemes of post-national governance—that is, value-free mechanisms that transcend state-based patterns of government and regulation—that work according to 'output' forms of legitimation and accountability.

For the very same reason, however, the Common law judge's interest in the faithful, and thus mythical, component of the contractual bond, may be interpreted as an attempt to put the self-defining (i.e., humanising) properties of action back on stage through contracts. Yet it could be argued that by imposing the duty to act in good faith upon the parties to a contract, the Common law judge is in fact reproducing within the Private law dimension Hobbes' behavioural mechanisms of societal interaction and, thus, limiting private autonomy. However sound, this argument would not consider what is required for the mythical component of an *act* of (good) faith to perform its humanising instances and constitute both individual and collective forms of experience.

Mythical thinking, human experience and indeed action are all related. Cassirer demonstrated this clearly. While explaining that 'myth ... expresses an original direction of the human spirit, an independent configuration of man's *consciousness*',[140] Cassirer held that 'mythical consciousness ... "explains" the individual event by postulating individual *acts of the will*'.[141] It is in this sense that we should overlap Hobbes' intention to neutralise human action with Cassirer's explanation of why mythical consciousness depends 'on man's self-limitation in his immediate relation to reality, as a *willing and acting subject*'.[142]

The same applies to the mythical essence of (good) faith. As set out by Agamben, '*fides* is ... a verbal *act*, as a rule accompanied by an oath, with which one abandons oneself completely to the "trust" of someone and obtains, in exchange, that one's protection. The object of the fides is, in every case, as in the oath, conformity between the parties' words and actions.'[143] From this passage, it emerges that in an age such as ours, in which financial and free-market-capitalist *praxis* feed on depoliticisation and dejuridification[144] by making (non-)humans mechanically behave rather than spontaneously act, the mythical and sacred (p)*act*

[140]Cassirer (1955b), p. 3.

[141]Ibid., p. 48. (Emphasis added).

[142]Ibid., p. 85. (Emphasis added).

[143]Agamben (2011b), p. 27. (Emphasis added).

[144]Straume and Humphrey (2011).

of (good) faith that should hold humankind together at the public level becomes irrelevant. That is why, at the time of writing, politics has 'assume[d] the form of an *oikonomia*, that is, of a governance of empty speech over bare life'.[145] Conversely, the performative essence of the faithful bond that characterises the contract within the Private law dimension leads to the rediscovery of action and language through the deactivation of *homo oeconomicus*' behavioural schemes of interaction.

That said, the last element that we need in order to understand fully what is happening to the (p)*act* of *deditio in fidem* on the public and private scales in the West is Kant's categorical imperative to 'act according to that maxim whose universality as law you can at the same time will'.[146] The reason for addressing Kant's maxim is threefold: first, because of Agamben's argument on the dehumanising function played by modern Human rights charters; second, because, as pointed out earlier, the formation of Hobbes' dehumanising common-*wealth* required the nullification of the self-asserting 'I-*will*' and its compliance with Kant's categorical 'I-will-and-can*not*'; finally, because while Kant conceived of the categorical imperative as a way to protect capital interests and property rights, legal scholars have, perhaps unconsciously, obscured his dehumanising and post-political approach to life by transplanting it into Human rights discourse.

By way of example, Besson described Human rights as 'a sub-set of universal moral rights (*i*) that protect fundamental and general interests (*ii*) against the intervention, or in some cases non-intervention, of (national, regional or international) public institutions (*iii*)'.[147] Later on, Besson enlarged the extent of the relationship between morality and law and, building on Raz, claimed that legal rights 'are moral interests recognised by the law as sufficiently important to generate moral duties'.[148] Legal Human rights serve the same function as they 'are fundamental and general moral interests recognised by the law as sufficiently important to generate moral duties'. Yet these two categories are autonomous: 'moral rights can exist independently from legal rights', and some legal rights 'may not actually protect pre-existing moral rights or create moral rights'. In this case, they are 'legal duties at the most'.[149] Besson's taxonomical approach is, however, merely notional because 'respect for universal moral [i.e., not just human] rights *ought to be voluntary* in priority ... independently from any institutional involvement'.[150]

While Besson's use of the term 'voluntary' seems to suggest that what is at stake here is the subject's self-defining (i.e., active) comportment, the Kantian (i.e., behavioural) principle that informs her normative rationalism is evident. Notably, Kant promoted an idea of moral conduct that 'tells the agent to subordinate the will

---

[145]Ibid., p. 72.

[146]Kant (1997), p. 54.

[147]Besson (2013), p. 341.

[148]Ibid., p. 345.

[149]Ibid.

[150]Ibid., p. 346. (Emphasis added).

to the universal perspective of reason itself'.[151] As acutely noted by Arendt, not only is morality excluded from Kant's precept[152] (as it is in Besson's narrow notion of 'legal duties'), but Kant's strategy targets what constitutes our uniqueness: the humanising conflict that takes place within the will between *velle* and *nolle*.[153] Hence, Kant used his categorical imperative to dream of a contractarian, totalising, perpetual common-*wealth* of peace and contemplation in which economic security is provided by the fact that '[t]he subject is now to give to himself the principle of his own being: reason'.[154] Yet, as Arendt taught us, the ultimate basis of human (civil) rights is political action, and political action cannot be built on contemplation.This is why the regulative belief that underpins Kantian ethics has turned out to be one of the main components of the notions of 'civilised economy', 'good economic governance' and, through them, our behavioural animalisation. The post-historical and post-political essence of the civilising mission of contract and modern constitutional project are indeed in line with neo-Kantian forms of social analysis, such as that of von Kempski, according to whom all social sciences, including jurisprudence, can be explained through the dehumanised behavioural schemes offered by mathematical economics.

This is also demonstrated by the way in which the Kantian metaphysical principle that defines what is 'right' is structurally related to a peculiar universalist conception of one of (contract) law's key elements, that of 'legal duty', which also figures in Besson's reflections. Building on Schopenhauer and Heidegger, Agamben has shown that 'Kant represents the moment when the [Western] ontology of command and having-to-be reaches its most extreme elaboration and, by penetrating into the ontology of substance and being, seeks to transform it from within'.[155] This is so because in describing 'the nature of the command and duty stemming from the law in terms of an external constraint[, Kant] transfers this definition to morality in the form of autoconstraint (*Selbstzwang*)'.[156] Thus, Kant developed an 'ontology of operativity' in which 'being and acting are indeterminated and contracted onto one another, and being becomes something that does not simply *exist*, but *has to be* brought about'.[157] Agamben concedes that 'the command ... presupposes a will'.[158] However, from the perspective of the ruled, the humanising properties of action are replaced by Kant's practical

[151]Kahn (2012), p. 127.

[152]Arendt (2003), pp. 68 and 70–72.

[153]Arendt (1978), p. 63.

[154]Kahn (2010), p. 59.

[155]Agamben (2013b), p. 121. See also Agamben (2013b) and Agamben (2011b).

[156]Agamben (2013b), p. 114.

[157]Ibid., p. 118.

[158]Ibid., p. 129.

reason.[159] The paradox of Kantian auto-constraint is thus clear: it is 'an objective command which assumes the form of a subjective impulse (*Triebfeder*)'.[160]

5 Conclusion

We can now attempt to overlap the Kantian ontology of duty with good faith's self-defining component discussed earlier that, by placing the parties on a moral-political, and thus equally humanising, platform of interaction, tries to counter the modern constitutional ideal as well as the global paradigms of 'civilised economy' and 'good economic governance'.

As the influence of constitutional values and Fundamental rights policies on Contract law's mechanisms and settings that this book has addressed indicates, the contract is gradually becoming the 'political community of equals'[161] to which Besson refers when explaining how the law makes universal moral rights 'Human Rights *strictu sensu*'.[162] In light of the foregoing discussion, it seems difficult to dispute that the intensification in the use of contractual good faith is a pivotal component of this phenomenon and, in particular, of the constitutionalisation of Contract law.

Some commentators would probably deem this suggestion to be misleading and/or mystifying. In particular, they might point to the illusory essence of consensualism because '[a]lthough contract purports to replace or supplement the obligations of public law with "private law", every such attempt is subject to judicial review'.[163] The same might be said regarding the *ex-post* requirements with which the parties may be required to comply to secure, say, the passage of property rights. Both contentions would certainly be appropriate. However,

159 See Caputo (2001), pp. 42–43: what we are standing before here is the '"thinking thing" fully in charge of its potencies and possibilities, surveying the contents of its mind to sort out which among them represents something *objective* out there in the external world and which should be written off as merely internal and *subjective*' (emphases added). Cf. Arendt (1978), p. 86.

160 Agamben (2013b), p. 114.

161 The inequality of bargaining power and the fact that commercial interests do not necessarily need to be sacrificed on the altar of good faith are of course different issues from those discussed here. As Consumer law and unconscionable conduct regimes, broadly understood, make clear, what is relevant in the courtroom is the modality through which this power is exercised and the reasons why it is exercised that way.

162 Besson (2013), p. 346.

163 Joo (2013), p. 64.

paraphrasing Heidegger with the due caution,[164] we may say that the 'temporal determinateness'[165] of the contr-*act* is expressed by the parties' 'anticipatory resoluteness'.[166] Consequently, what happens after the parties finalise the agreement through action and deed does not alter the fact that, while at the public level the Kantian imperative has a self-dissolving, captivating effect,[167] the performative essence of the parties' faithful relationship transforms the contract into a political space of appearance for each of them. In other words, the contr-*act* 'deactivates the very excess of signification' of the Kantian subjectless categorical imperative. If the 'only foundation of man is ... his own action, his own giving himself grounds',[168] the p-*act*-um becomes a 'mark of factical experience', that is, the uncovering signature of the parties' self-conscious projection and re-*flexion*.

To comprehend the legal dimension of this process fully, we should bear in mind why Agamben is also of the opinion that Kant's ontology of operativity and command found its greatest expression in Kelsen's pure theory of (Public) law and notion of sovereignty—that is, in the positivist conception that sees '[t]he relationship between norm and behaviour ... not [as] a relation of being but a

[164]The use of Heidegger at this stage of our inquiry requires prudence because of his commitment to fighting the metaphysical tradition of subjectivity which, as set out in *Besinnung*, he believed culminated in the 'modern historical animal'. Yet in *The Fundamental Concepts of Metaphysics*, Heidegger clearly distinguished between human comportment as acting and doing, and animal behaviour as a disinhibited, captivated form of conduct, which confirms the appropriateness of his scholarship for the purposes of our discussion. Attention should also be paid to Heidegger's peculiar use of the 'will' in the lectures on Nietzsche that he gave between 1936 and 1940, that is, in the years of his much-discussed 'reversal'. I particularly refer to the first and second Volumes of *Nietzsche*, in which Heidegger's decisionism is prominent, as it is in his lectures and writings of the 1940s such as *Basic Concepts*. More specifically, to Heidegger, decision (*Entscheidung*) is the fundamental act of self-appropriation (*Selbstbehauptung*). Thinking, which becomes the central topic of Heidegger's later works, is the most powerful expression of this event (*Ereignis*) as he himself describes it. Finally, the role that Heidegger gives to the 'decisive essence of willing' towards our 'open resoluteness' in his *Introduction to Metaphysics*, published in 1953, is in line with that which he expounded in *Being and Time*, published in 1927. His admiration for Paul, the founder of the faculty of the will, is therefore less surprising than it might first appear.

[165]Heidegger (2008), pp. 163, 175, 232 and 238–39. See also ibid. pp. 40, 237, 386, and 470. Agamben has recently contended that '[t]o the primacy [that Heidegger confers on] care over use corresponds, in the second division of [Being and Time], the primacy of temporality over spatiality'. If that is the case, it would prove worthwhile to ascertain whether the contractual notion of good faith shares some elements—and if so, which ones, why, and to what extent—with Heidegger's conception of care as 'the fundamental structure of Dasein'. See Agamben (2016), pp. 43 and 38 respectively.

[166]Heidegger (2008), pp. 372, 236, and 386.

[167]'Kant's blindness', Agamben writes, 'is not to have seen that, in the society that was arising with the industrial revolution, in which human beings had been subjected to forces that they could not in any way control, the morality of duty would habituate them to consider obedience to a command ... an act of freedom'. See Agamben (2013b), p. 123.

[168]Agamben (1999), p. 135.

relation of having-to-be'.[169] The term 'behaviour', I contend, is obviously not casual because what takes place in Kelsen's juridification of the Kantian regulative paradigm is the displacement of the subject's free 'action' as informed by the internal conflict from which the sovereign choice between *velle* and *nolle* arises. What is neglected by Kelsen is thus the sovereignty of the will to perform the self-understanding of humans' uniqueness through the affirmation or negation of a future project, as it is in Hobbes.[170] This is why Caputo writes that 'Kant is the Chief of Police' who 'always tell[s] us what is possible and what is not [by] laying down the conditions of the possibility of this or that'.[171] That Kantian philosophy is ahistorical and apolitical[172] is thus proved by the fact that this sort of coercion does not require the personality of those who are subject to it.[173] Consequently, while Kelsen's Kantian-oriented 'legal ought' is the expression of a 'depsychologized will'[174] similar to that which Hobbes places at the centre of his post-historical and post-political construct, the emphasis on contractual good faith that has recently emerged in Common law countries replaces the self-defining properties of action back on stage.

References

Adams M, Bomhoff J (eds) (2012) Practice and theory in comparative law. CUP, Cambridge

Adams M, Heirbaut D (eds) (2014) The method and culture of comparative law. Hart Publishing, Oxford

Agamben G ([1995] 1998) Homo sacer. Sovereign power and bare life. Heller-Roazen D trans. SUP, Stanford

Agamben G (1999) *Se*: Hegel's absolute and Heidegger's *Ereignis*. In: Potentialities. Hellen-Roazen D trans. SUP, Stanford, pp 116–137

Agamben G ([2002] 2004) The open. Man and animal. Attell K trans. SUP, Stanford

Agamben G ([2000] 2005) The time that remains. A comment on the Letter to the Romans. Daily P trans. SUP, Stanford

Agamben G ([1978] 2007a) Infancy and history. Heron L trans. Verso, New York

Agamben G ([2005] 2007b) Profanations. Fort J trans. Zone Books, New York

[169]Agamben (2013b), p. 124. Agamben clarifies that even though Kant 'believed himself to have secured . . . the possibility of metaphysics and to have founded, at the same time, an ethics that was neither juridical nor religious[, his] ontology is in truth an ontology of command [in which] the guarantee of the effectiveness of duty is . . . the law'. See Agamben (2013b), pp. 122, 123, and 112 respectively. See also Agamben (2004), pp. 49–92.

[170]Agamben's quotation of Arendt's evaluation of Kant's influence over Eichmann's behaviour is fundamental. See Agamben (2013b), p. 123. Cf. also Heidegger (1995), pp. 232 and 240, where human comportment is defined as 'acting and doing', and animal behaviour as 'being driven forward' by stimuli that captivate the subject's existence.

[171]Caputo (2001), p. 49.

[172]Cf. Kymlicka (2002), p. 209; Arendt (2003), pp. 70–72.

[173]Bernd (2015).

[174]Kelsen (1957), p. 215.

Agamben G ([2007] 2011a) The kingdom and the glory. For a theological genealogy of economy and government. Chiesa L, Mandarini M trans. SUP, Stanford
Agamben G ([2008] 2011b) The sacrament of language. An archaeology of the oath. Kotso A trans. SUP, Stanford
Agamben G ([2009] 2012a) Introductory note on the concept of democracy. In: Democracy in what state? Columbia University Press, New York, pp 1–5
Agamben G ([2010] 2012b) The church and the kingdom. de la Durantaye L trans. Seagull, New York
Agamben G ([2011] 2013a) The highest poverty. Monastic rules and form-of-life. Kotso A trans. SUP, Stanford
Agamben G ([2012] 2013b) Opus dei. An archaeology of duty. Kotso A trans. SUP, Stanford
Agamben G (2015) Stasis. Civil war as a political paradigm. Heron N trans. SUP, Stanford
Agamben G ([2014] 2016) The use of bodies. Kotso A trans. SUP, Stanford
Amhlaigh CM, Michelon C, Walker N (eds) (2013) After public law. OUP, Oxford
Arendt H (1973) The origins of totalitarianism. Harvest Book, New York
Arendt H (1978) The life of the Mind, vol II. Harvest Book, New York
Arendt H (1998) The human condition. University of Chicago Press, Chicago
Arendt H (2003) Some questions of moral philosophy. In: Kohn J (ed) Responsibility and judgement. Shocken Books, New York, pp 49–146
Arendt H (2005) Introduction into politics. In: Kohn J (ed) The promise of politics. Shocken Books, New York, pp 93–100
Arendt H (2006a) Between past and future. Penguin Classic, London
Arendt H (2006b) On revolution. Penguin Classic, London
Betti E (1953) Teoria generale delle obbligazioni I. Giuffrè, Milano
Benvenisti E, Downs GW (2007) The empire's new clothes: political economy and the fragmentation of international law. SLR 60:595–631
Barbour C (2013) Between politics and law: Hannah Arendt and the subjects of rights. In: Goldoni M, McCorkindale C (eds) Hannah Arendt and the law. Hart Publishing, Oxford, pp 307–319
Bernd L (2015) Sympathy for the devil(s)? Personality and legal coercion in Kant's *Doctrine of Law*. Jurisprudence 6(1):25–46
Bertea S (2009) The normative claim of law. Hart Publishing, Oxford
Besson S (2013) The right to have rights: from human rights to citizens' rights and back. In: Goldoni M, McCorkindale C (eds) Hannah Arendt and the law. Hart Publishing, Oxford, pp 335–355
Caputo JD (2001) On religion. Routledge, London
Carter JW (2012) Contract law in Australia, 6th edn. LexisNexis, Chatswood
Cassirer E (1944) An essay on man. YUP, New Haven
Cassirer E (1946) The myth of the state. YUP, New Haven
Cassirer E ([1923] 1955a) The philosophy of symbolic forms, vol I. Manheim R trans. YUP, New Haven
Cassirer E ([1925] 1955b) The philosophy of symbolic forms, vol II. Manheim R trans. YUP, New Haven
Cassirer E ([1929] 1957) The philosophy of symbolic forms, vol III. Manheim R trans. YUP, New Haven
Cassirer E ([1928] 1996) The philosophy of symbolic forms, vol. IV. Kros JM trans. YUP, New Haven
Cassirer E ([1942] 2000) The logic of the cultural sciences. Lofts SG trans. YUP, New Haven
Claire Cutler A (2003) Private power and global authority. CUP, Cambridge
Clark DS (ed) (2012) Comparative law and society. Edward Elgar Publishing, Cheltenham
Collins H (1999) Regulating contracts. OUP, Oxford
Coninck J (2010) The functional method of comparative law. *Quo vadis*? RabelsZ 74:318–350

Coninck J (2012) Comparisons in private patrimonial law: towards a bottom-up approach using (cross-cultural) behavioural economics. In: Adams M, Bomhoff J (eds) Practice and theory in comparative law. CUP, Cambridge, pp 258–278
Costigan R, Thomas PA (2005) The human rights act: a view from below. J Law Soc 32(1):51–67
Cotterrell R (2003) Comparatists and sociology. In: Legrand P, Munday R (eds) Comparative legal studies. Traditions and Transitions. CUP, Cambridge, pp 131–153
Cotterrell R (2008) Living law. Ashgate, Aldershot
Cotterrell R (2012) Comparative sociology of law. In: Clark DS (ed) Comparative law and society. Edward Elgar Publishing, Cheltenham, pp 39–60
Cotterrell R (2013) The jurist's conscience: reflections around Radbruch. In: Del Mar M, Michelon C (eds) The anxiety of the jurist. Ashgate, Aldershot, pp 13–26
Croce M (2014) Is law a special domain? In: Donlan SP, Heckendorn Urscheler L (eds) Concepts of law. Ashgate, Aldershot, pp 153–168
D'Agostini F (2014) Realismo? Una questione non controversa. Bollati Boringhieri, Turin
Dedek H, Praagh S (eds) (2015) Stateless law. Evolving boundaries of a discipline. Ashgate, Aldershot
Dobner P, Loughlin M (eds) (2010) The twilight of constitutionalism? OUP, Oxford
Donlan SP (2014) World is crazier and more of it than we think: reflections on legal-comparative methodologies. University of Limerick. Available at https://media.heanet.ie/page/4471ea6688e5121d813dcf4be700c021The
Ewald W (1995) Comparative jurisprudence (I): what is like to try a rat? Univ Penn Law Rev 143:1889–2149
Fletcher GP (1998) Comparative law as a subversive discipline. AJCL 49:683–700
Frankenberg G (2012) Constitutions in transfer–territoriality and extra-territoriality. In: Handl G, Zekoll J, Zumbansen P (eds) Beyond territoriality: transnational legal authority in an age of globalization. Brill, Leiden, pp 261–294
Galimberti U ([1999] 2016) Psiche e techne. L'uomo nell'età della tecnica. Feltrinelli, Milan
Gellner E (1983) Nations and nationalism. Basil Blackwell, Oxford
Goderis B, Versteeg M (2015) Transnational constitutionalism: a conceptual framework. In: Galligan DJ, Vertseeg M (eds) Social and political foundations of constitutions. CUP, Cambridge, pp 103–133
Goodwin M (2013) Embracing the challenge: legal scholarship in a global era. TLT 4(4):686–699
Gordley J (2006) An introduction to the comparative study of private law. CUP, Cambridge
Hamson CJ (1938) The reform consideration. LQR 54:233–257
Handl G, Zekoll J and Zumbansen P (eds) (2012) Beyond territoriality: transnational legal authority in an age of globalization. Brill, Leiden
Heidegger M ([1983] 1995) The fundamental concepts of metaphysics: world, finitude, solitude. McNeill W, Walker N trans. IU Press, Indianapolis
Heidegger M (1998a) On the essence of ground. In: McNeill W (ed) Pathmarks. CUP, Cambridge
Heidegger M ([1982] 1998b) Parmenides. Schuwer A, Rojcewiz R trans. IU Press, Indianapolis
Heidegger M ([1927] 2008) Being and time. MacQuarrie J, Robinson E trans. Harper, New York
Heidegger M ([1977] 2012) Four seminars. Mitchell A, Raffoul F trans. IU Press, Indianapolis
Heidegger M ([1953] 2014) Introduction to metaphysics. Fried G, Polt R trans. (eds) YUP, New Haven
Helfand MA (ed) (2015) Negotiating state and non-state law. The challenge of global and local legal pluralism. CUP, Cambridge
Hesselink MW (2010) The concept of good faith. In: Hartkamp AS et al (eds) Towards a European civil code. Kluwer Law International, Alphaen aan den Rijn, pp 619–649
Hobbes T ([1642] 1998) In: Thuck R, Silverthorne M (eds) On the citizen. Cambridge University Press, Cambridge
Hobbes T ([1651] 2009) In: Gaskin JCA (ed) Leviathan. Oxford University Press, Oxford
Hobbes T ([1681] 1990) Behemoth or the long parliament. Tönnies F ed. University of Chicago Press, Chicago

Husa J (2014) Interdisciplinary comparative law – between Scylla and Charybdis? J Comp Law 9 (1):28–42
Husa J (2015) A new introduction to comparative law. Hart Publishing, Oxford
Joo TW (2013) Contracts, courts, and the construction of consent. In: DiMatteo LA et al (eds) Commercial contract law. CUP, Cambridge, pp 41–66
Kahn PW (2008) Putting liberalism in its place. Princeton, PUP
Kahn PW ([2007] 2010) Out of Eden. Adam and Eve and the problem of evil. PUP, Princeton
Kahn PW (2012) Political theology. Four new chapters on the concept of sovereignty. Columbia University Press, New York
Kant I ([1785] 1997) Foundations of the metaphysics of morals. Beck LW trans. Library of Liberal Arts
Kelsen H (1957) Value judgements in the science of law. In: Kelsen H (ed) What is justice? Justice, law and politics in the mirror of science. UC Press, Los Angeles/London, pp 209–230
Krisch N (2010) Beyond constitutionalism. The pluralist structure of postnational law. OUP, Oxford
Kuo M-S (2010) The end of constitutionalism as we know it? Boundaries and the state of global constitutional (dis)ordering. TLT 1(3):329–369
Kymlicka W (2002) Contemporary political philosophy: an introduction. OUP, Oxford
Legenre, P ([2004] 2009) L'Occidente Invisible. Paolo Heritier trans. Medusa Edizioni, Milan
Legrand P, Munday R (eds) (2003) Comparative legal studies. Traditions and transitions. CUP, Cambridge
Liska V (2013) A lawless legacy: Hannah Arendt and Giorgio Agamben. In: Goldoni M, McCorkindale C (eds) Hannah Arendt and the law. Hart Publishing, Oxford, pp 89–97
Loughlin M (2003) The idea of public law. CUP, Cambridge
Loughlin M (2008) Reflections on the idea of public law. In: Christodoulidis E, Tierney S (eds) Public law and politics. Ashgate, Aldershot, pp 47–65
Loughlin M (2012) The foundations of public law. CUP, Cambridge
Loughlin M (2014) Constitutional pluralism: an oxymoron? GC 3(1):9–30
Loughlin M (2015) The constitutional imagination. MLR 78(1):1–25
Lowry J, Rawlings P (2005) Insurers, claims and the boundaries of good faith. MLR 68(1):82–110
MacPherson CB (1962) The political theory of possessive individualism. OUP, Oxford
Marramao G (2005) Potere e secolarizzazione. Le categorie del tempo. Bollati Boringhieri, Turin
Marramao G ([1992] 2007) *Kairós*. Towards and ontology of "Due Time". Trans. Larrey P., Cattaneo, S. trans. The Davis Group, Aurora
Marramao G (2013) Dopo il Leviatano. Individuo e comunità. Bollati Boringhieri, Turin
Melissaris E (2009) Ubiquitous law. Legal theory and the space for legal pluralism. Ashgate, Aldershot
Melissaris E (2014) A sense of law: on shared normative experiences. In: Donlan SP, Heckendorn Urscheler L (eds) Concepts of law. Ashgate, Aldershot, pp 109–122
Michaels R (2015) Transnationalizing comparative law. MJECL 12(2)
Millns S (2014) Making the case for European comparative legal studies in public law. In: Adams M, Heirbaut D (eds) The method and culture of comparative law. Hart Publishing, Oxford, pp 283–300
Monateri PG (ed) (2012) Methods of comparative law. Edward Elgar Publishing, Cheltenham
Nail T (2015) The figure of the migrant. SUP, Stanford
Negri A (2010) Sovereignty between government, exception and governance. In: Kalmo H, Skinner Q (eds) Sovereignty in fragments. The past, present and future of a contested concept. CUP, Cambridge, pp 205–221
Nelken D (ed) (1997) Comparing legal cultures. Dartmouth, Aldershot
Nelken D, Feest J (eds) (2001) Adapting legal cultures. Hart Publishing, Oxford
O'Donoghue A (2014) Constitutionalism in global constitutionalisation. CUP, Cambridge
Örücü S (2007) Developing comparative law. In: Örücü E, Nelken D (eds) Comparative law. Hart Publishing, Oxford, pp 43–65

Örücü E, Nelken D (eds) (2007) Comparative law. A handbook. Hart Publishing, Oxford
Parisi F, Luppi B (2012) Comparative law and economics: accounting for social norms. In: Clark DS (ed) Comparative law and society. Edward Elgar Publishing, Cheltenham, pp 92–104
Pihlajämaki H (2014) Comparative context in legal history: are we all comparatists now? In: Adams M, Heirbaut D (eds) The method and culture of comparative law. Hart Publishing, Oxford, pp 121–132
Pocock JGA ([1971] 1989) Politics, language and time. University of Chicago Press, Chicago
Pozen D (2016) Constitutional bad faith. HLR 129(4):886–955
Redgwell C (2012) 60 years of comparative law scholarship in the International and Comparative Law Quarterly. Int Comput Law Quart 61(1):1–26
Rosanvallon P (2013) The society of equals. Harvard University Press, Cambridge
Roughan N (2011) The relative authority of law: a contribution to "pluralist jurisprudence". In: Del Mar M (ed) New waves in philosophy of law. Palgrave Macmillan, New York, pp 254–277
Saleilles R (1907) De la responsabilité précontractuelle; à propos d'une etude nouvelle sur la matière, RTD civ. 697
Samuel G (1998) Comparative law and jurisprudence. Int Comp Law Quart 47(4):817–836
Samuel G (2011) Does one need an understanding of methodology in law before one can understand methodology in comparative law? In: Van Hoecke M (ed) Methodologies of legal research. Hart Publishing, Oxford, pp 177–207
Samuel G (2014a) An introduction to comparative law method and theory. Hart Publishing, Oxford
Samuel G (2014b) What is legal epistemology? In: Adams M, Heirbaut D (eds) The method and culture of comparative law. Hart Publishing, Oxford
Schiavone A ([2005] 2012) The invention of law in the west. Carden J, Shugaar A trans. Harvard University Press, Cambridge
Schmitt C ([1932] 2007) The concept of the political. George Swab trans. University of Chicago Press, Chicago
Siems M (2014) Comparative law. CUP, Cambridge
Siliquini-Cinelli L (2014) *Imago veritas falsa*: for a (post-) Schmittian decisionist theory of law, legal reasoning and judging. Aust J Leg Philos 39:118–139
Siliquini-Cinelli L, Hutchison A (2016) Constitutionalism, good faith and the doctrine of specific performance: rights, duties and equitable discretion. SALJ 133(1):73–101
Smits J (2006) Preface. In: Elgar encyclopedia of comparative law. Edward Elgar Publishing, Cheltenham
Smits J (2014) Contract law. A comparative introduction. Edward Elgar Publishing, Cheltenham
Somek A (2012) Constituent power in national and transnational contexts. TLT 3(1):31–60
Stein P (1980) Legal evolution. The story of an idea. Cambridge University Press, Cambridge
Straume IS, Humphrey JF (eds) (2011) Depoliticization. The political imaginary of global capitalism. NSU Press, Malmo
Supiot A ([2005] 2007) *Homo juridicus*. On the anthropological function of the law. Brown S trans. Verso, New York
Teubner G (1998) Legal irritants: good faith in British law or how unifying law ends up in new divergences. MLR 61(1):11–32
Thornhill C (2012) National sovereignty and the constitution of transnational law: a sociological approach. TLT 3(4):393–460
Tierney S (2008) Sovereignty and the idea of public law. In: Christodoulidis E, Tierney S (eds) Public law and politics. Ashgate, Aldershot, pp 15–25
Tushnet M (2014) Advanced introduction to comparative constitutional law. Edward Elgar Publishing, Cheltenham
Twining W (2000) Globalization and legal theory. Butterworths, London
Twining W (2009) General jurisprudence. Understanding law from a global perspective. CUP, Cambridge

van Der Vossen B (2011) Legitimacy and multi-level governance. In: Del Mar M (ed) New waves in philosophy of law. Palgrave Macmillan, New York, pp 233–253
Van Hoecke M (ed) (2004) Epistemology and methodology in comparative law. Hart Publishing, Oxford
Van Hoecke M (ed) (2011) Methodologies of legal research. Hart Publishing, Oxford
Walker N (2012) Postnational constitutionalism and postnational public law: a tale of two neologisms. TLT 3(1):61–85
Weiss L, Hobson JH (1995) States and economic development. Polity Press, Cambridge
Wootton D (2016) The invention of science. A new history of the scientific revolution. Penguin, London
Zumbansen P (2007) The law of society: governance through contract. Indiana J Glob Leg Stud 14 (2):191–233
Zumbansen P (2012) Carving out typologies and accounting for differences across systems: towards a methodology of transnational constitutionalism. In: Rosenfeld M, Sajó A (eds) The Oxford handbook of comparative constitutional law. OUP, Oxford, pp 75–97
Zumbansen P (2013) Why global law is transnational. TLT 4(4):463–475
Zürn M, Faude B (2013) On fragmentation, differentiation and coordination. GEP 13:119–130

MIX
Papier aus verantwortungsvollen Quellen
Paper from responsible sources
FSC® C105338

FSC
www.fsc.org

If you have any concerns about our products,
you can contact us on
ProductSafety@springernature.com

In case Publisher is established outside the EU,
the EU authorized representative is:
Springer Nature Customer Service Center GmbH
Europaplatz 3, 69115 Heidelberg, Germany

Printed by Libri Plureos GmbH
in Hamburg, Germany